Odd Is on Our Side

CREATED BY

DEAN KOONTZ

WRITTEN BY **FRED VAN LENTE** AND **DEAN KOONTZ**

ILLUSTRATIONS BY **QUEENIE CHAN**

BALLANTINE BOOKS

NEW YORK

Odd Is on Our Side is a work of fiction. Names, characters, places, and incidents are the products of the author's imagination or are used fictitiously. Any resemblance to actual events, locales, or persons, living or dead, is entirely coincidental.

A Del Rey Trade Paperback Original

Published in the United States by Del Rey Books, an imprint of The Random House Publishing Group, a division of Random House, Inc., New York.

Del Rey is a registered trademark and the Del Rey colophon is a trademark of Random House, Inc.

Grateful acknowledgment is made to Hal Leonard corporation for permission to reprint an excerpt from "You're the Devil in Disguise"
Words and Music by Bill Grant, Bernie Baum and Florence Kaye
Copyright © 1963; Renewed 1991 Elvis Presley Music (BMI)
Worldrights Rights for Elvis Presley Music Administered by Cherry River Music Co.
International Copyright Secured All Rights Reserved
Reprinted by permission.

ISBN 978-0-345-51560-5

Printed in the United States of America

www.delreybooks.com

4 6 8 9 7 5

Cover Design—David Stevenson

Toning Assistant—Dee DuPuy

CONTENTS

By Dean Koontz

The City • Innocence • 77 Shadow Street
What the Night Knows • Breathless • Relentless
Your Heart Belongs to Me • The Darkest Evening of the Year
The Good Guy • The Husband • Velocity • Life Expectancy
The Taking • The Face • By the Light of the Moon
One Door Away from Heaven • From the Corner of His Eye
False Memory • Seize the Night • Fear Nothing • Mr. Murder
Dragon Tears • Hideaway • Cold Fire • The Bad Place
Midnight • Lightning • Watchers • Strangers • Twilight Eyes
Darkfall • Phantoms • Whispers • The Mask • The Vision
The Face of Fear • Night Chills • Shattered
The Voice of the Night • The Servants of Twilight
The House of Thunder • The Key to Midnight
The Eyes of Darkness • Shadowfires • Winter Moon
The Door to December • Dark Rivers of the Heart • Icebound
Strange Highways • Intensity • Sole Survivor
Ticktock • The Funhouse • Demon Seed

ODD THOMAS

Odd Thomas • Forever Odd • Brother Odd • Odd Hours
Odd Interlude • Odd Apocalypse • Deeply Odd • Saint Odd

ODD THOMAS GRAPHIC NOVELS
(with Queenie Chan)

In Odd We Trust • Odd Is On Our Side • House of Odd

FRANKENSTEIN

Prodigal Son • City of Night • Dead and Alive
Lost Souls • The Dead Town

A Big Little Life: A Memoir of a Joyful Dog Named Trixie

Odd
Is on
Our
Side

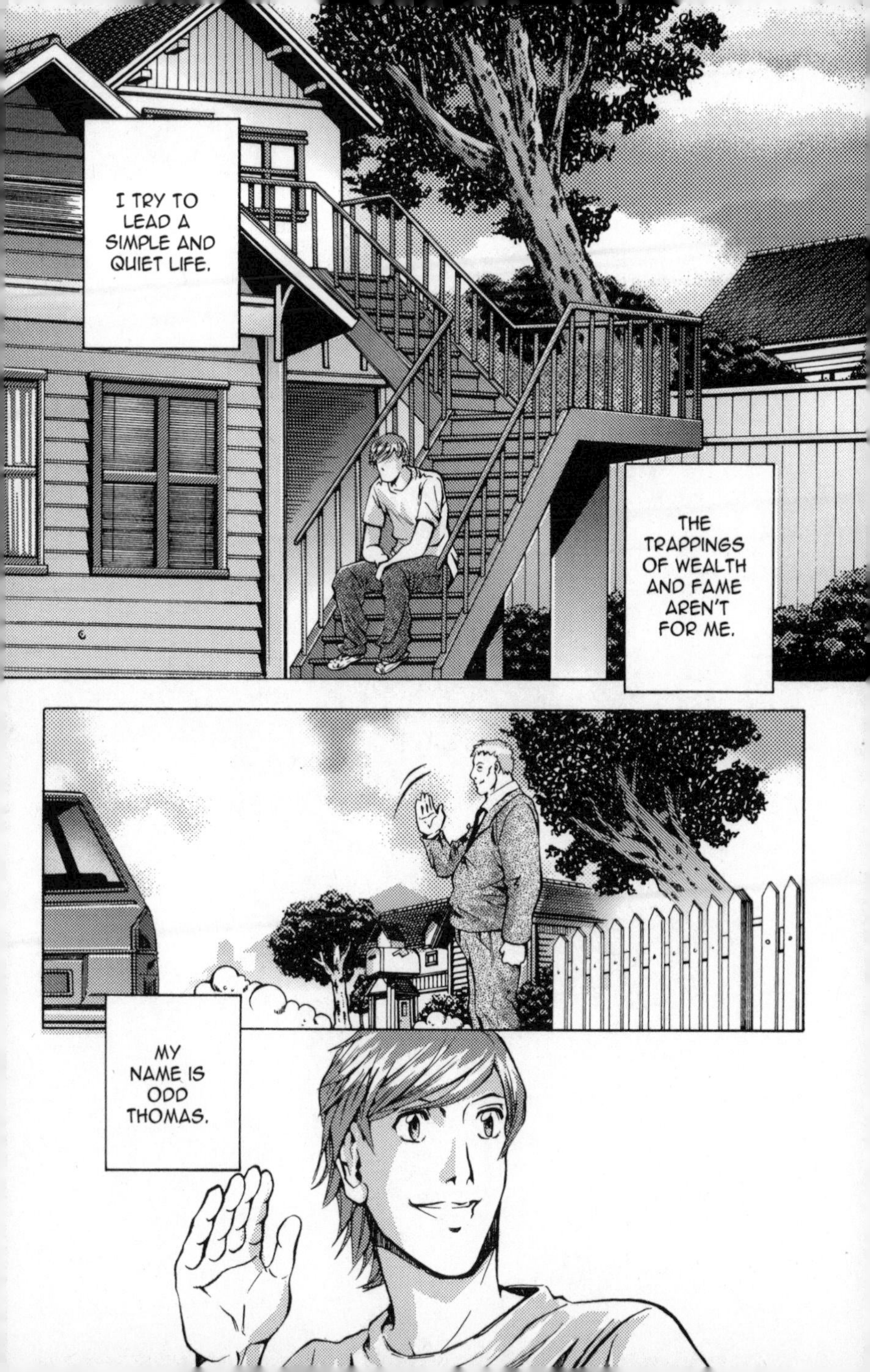

I TRY TO LEAD A SIMPLE AND QUIET LIFE.
THE TRAPPINGS OF WEALTH AND FAME AREN'T FOR ME.
MY NAME IS ODD THOMAS.

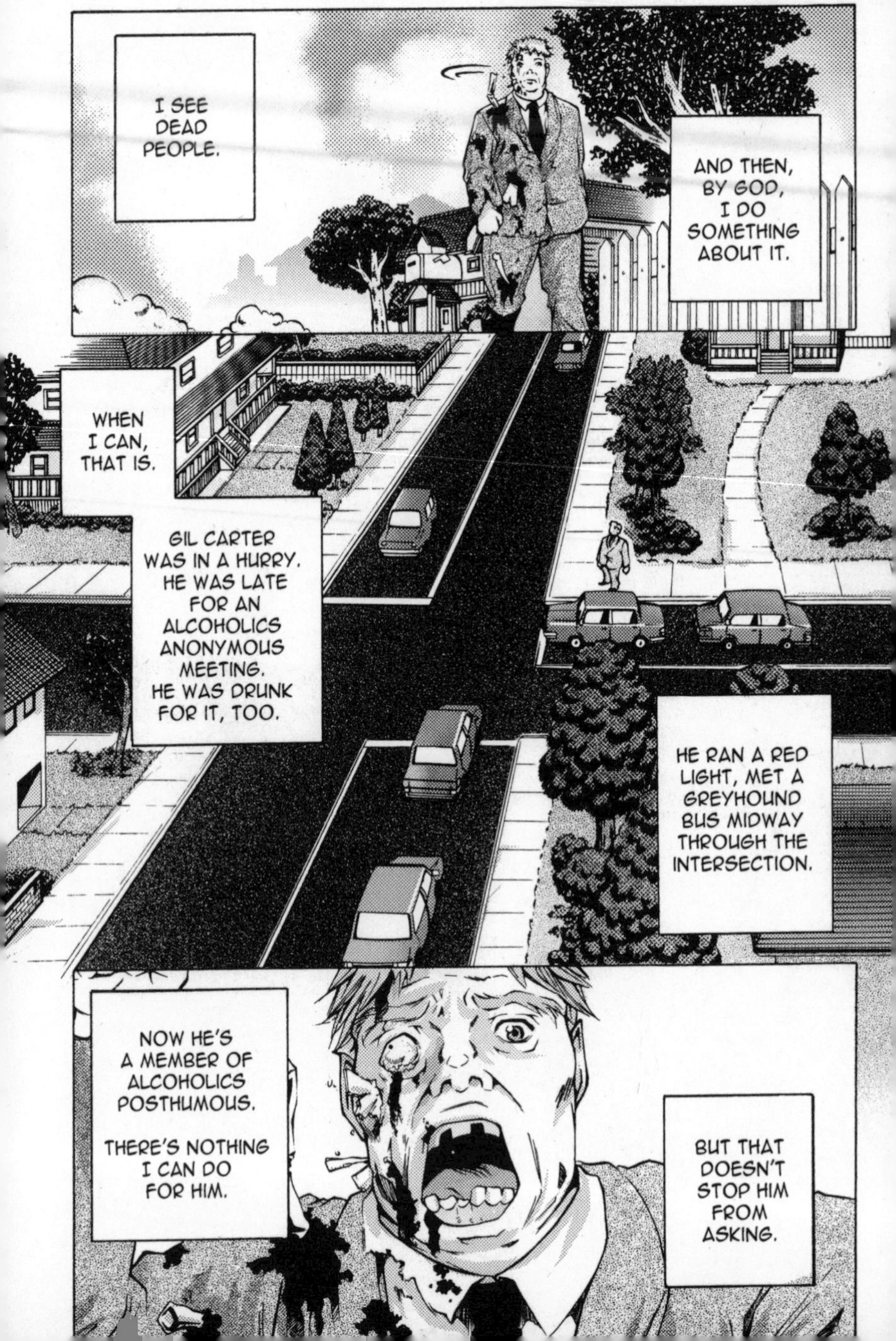
I SEE DEAD PEOPLE.
AND THEN, BY GOD, I DO SOMETHING ABOUT IT.
WHEN I CAN, THAT IS.
GIL CARTER WAS IN A HURRY. HE WAS LATE FOR AN ALCOHOLICS ANONYMOUS MEETING. HE WAS DRUNK FOR IT, TOO.
HE RAN A RED LIGHT, MET A GREYHOUND BUS MIDWAY THROUGH THE INTERSECTION.
NOW HE'S A MEMBER OF ALCOHOLICS POSTHUMOUS.
THERE'S NOTHING I CAN DO FOR HIM.
BUT THAT DOESN'T STOP HIM FROM ASKING.

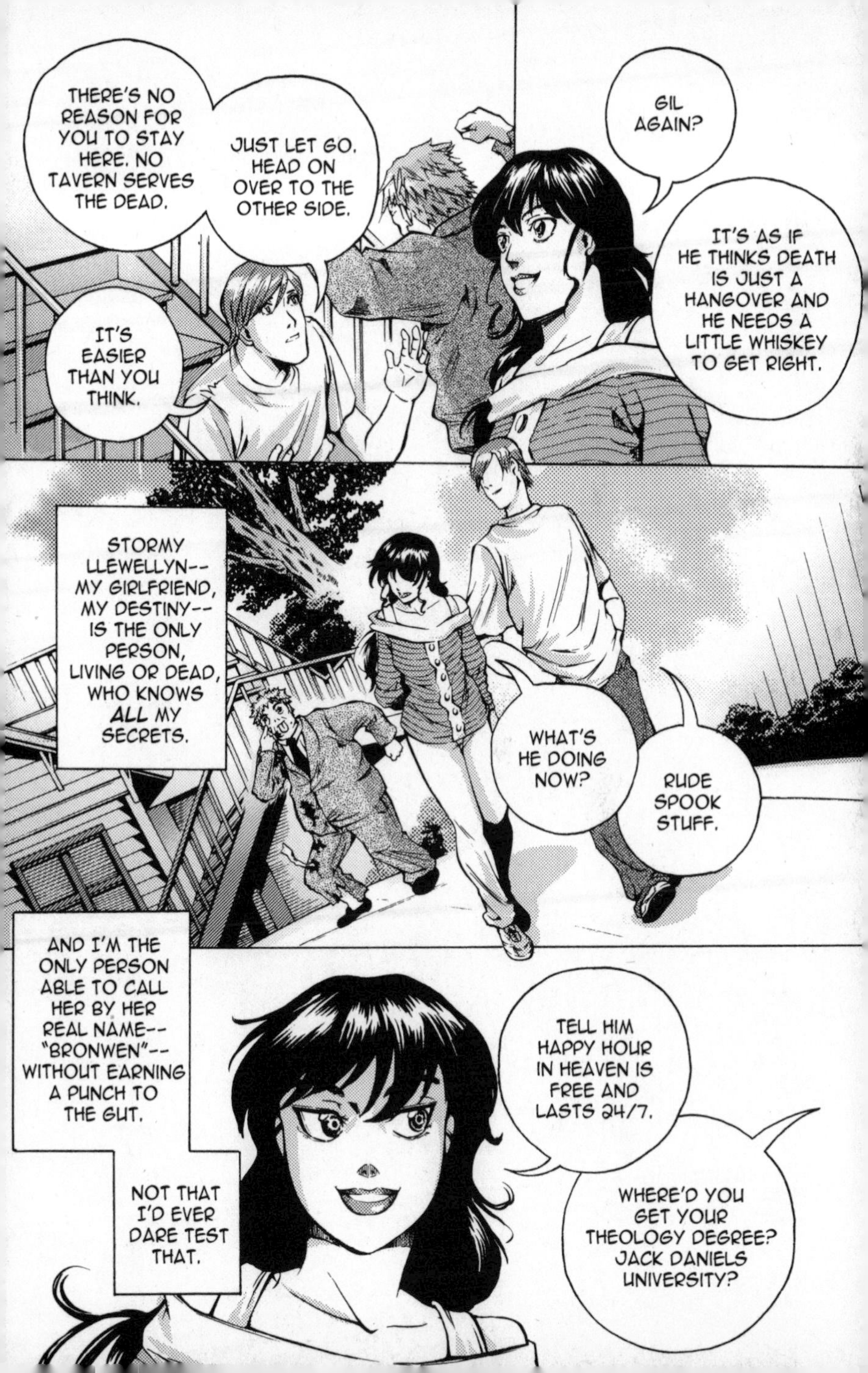
THERE'S NO REASON FOR YOU TO STAY HERE. NO TAVERN SERVES THE DEAD.
JUST LET GO. HEAD ON OVER TO THE OTHER SIDE.
IT'S EASIER THAN YOU THINK.
GIL AGAIN?
IT'S AS IF HE THINKS DEATH IS JUST A HANGOVER AND HE NEEDS A LITTLE WHISKEY TO GET RIGHT.
STORMY LLEWELLYN-- MY GIRLFRIEND, MY DESTINY-- IS THE ONLY PERSON, LIVING OR DEAD, WHO KNOWS ALL MY SECRETS.
WHAT'S HE DOING NOW?
RUDE SPOOK STUFF.
AND I'M THE ONLY PERSON ABLE TO CALL HER BY HER REAL NAME-- "BRONWEN"-- WITHOUT EARNING A PUNCH TO THE GUT.
NOT THAT I'D EVER DARE TEST THAT.
TELL HIM HAPPY HOUR IN HEAVEN IS FREE AND LASTS 24/7.
WHERE'D YOU GET YOUR THEOLOGY DEGREE? JACK DANIELS UNIVERSITY?

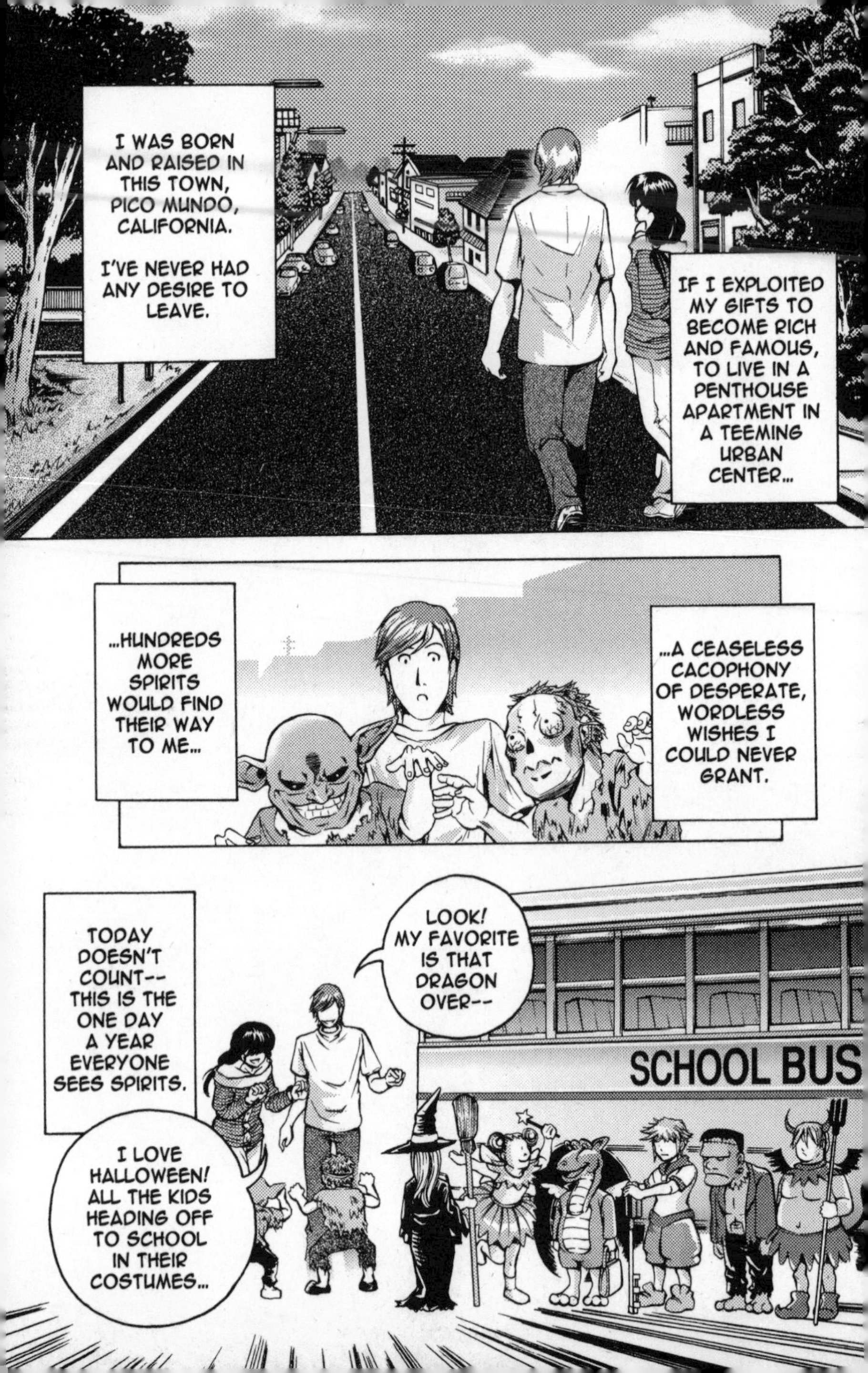
I WAS BORN AND RAISED IN THIS TOWN, PICO MUNDO, CALIFORNIA.
I'VE NEVER HAD ANY DESIRE TO LEAVE.
IF I EXPLOITED MY GIFTS TO BECOME RICH AND FAMOUS, TO LIVE IN A PENTHOUSE APARTMENT IN A TEEMING URBAN CENTER...
...HUNDREDS MORE SPIRITS WOULD FIND THEIR WAY TO ME...
...A CEASELESS CACOPHONY OF DESPERATE, WORDLESS WISHES I COULD NEVER GRANT.
TODAY DOESN'T COUNT-- THIS IS THE ONE DAY A YEAR EVERYONE SEES SPIRITS.
I LOVE HALLOWEEN! ALL THE KIDS HEADING OFF TO SCHOOL IN THEIR COSTUMES...
LOOK! MY FAVORITE IS THAT DRAGON OVER--
SCHOOL BUS

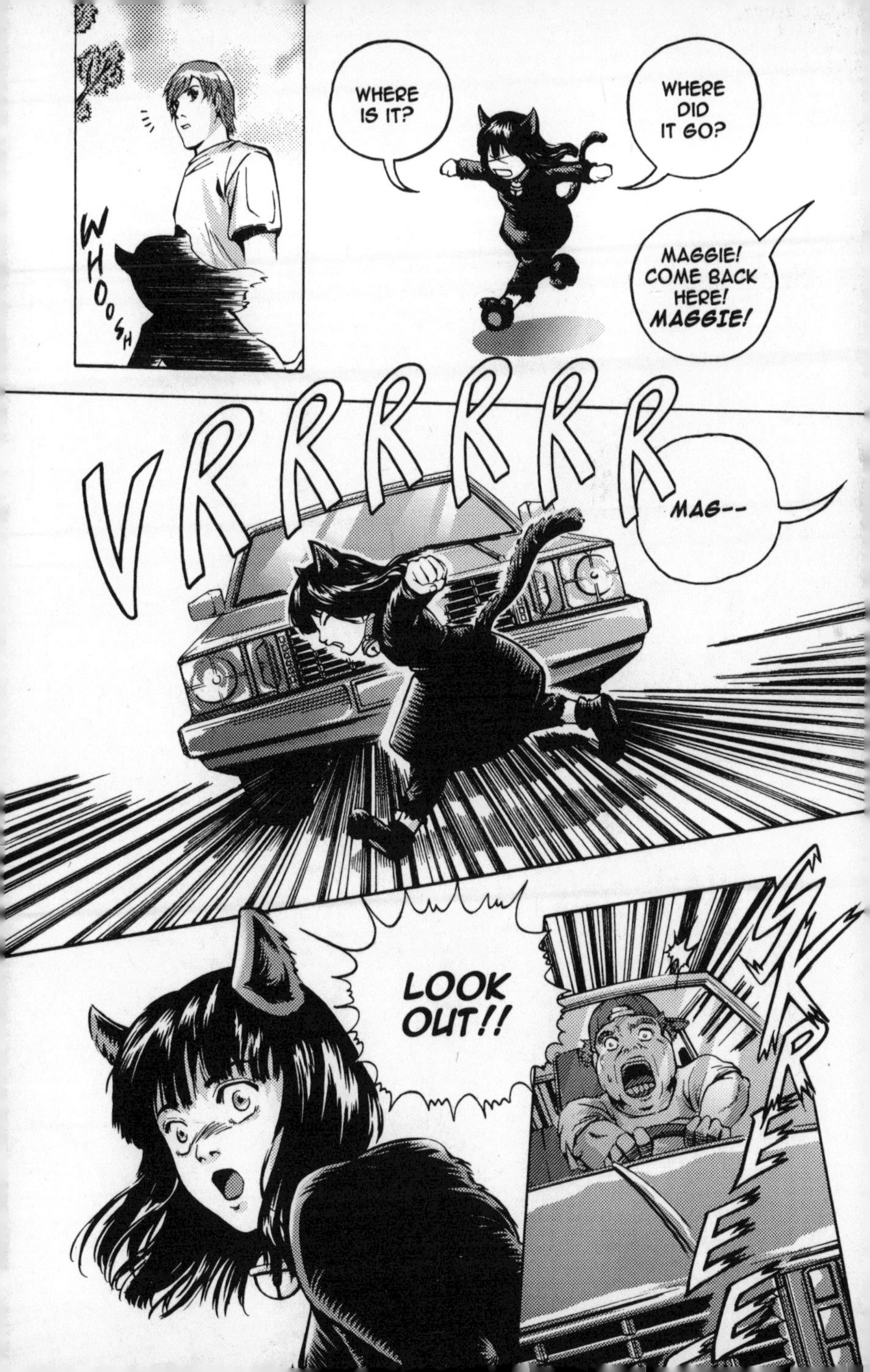
WHOOSH
WHERE IS IT?
WHERE DID IT GO?
MAGGIE! COME BACK HERE! MAGGIE!
VRRRRRR
MAG--
LOOK OUT!!
SKREEEE

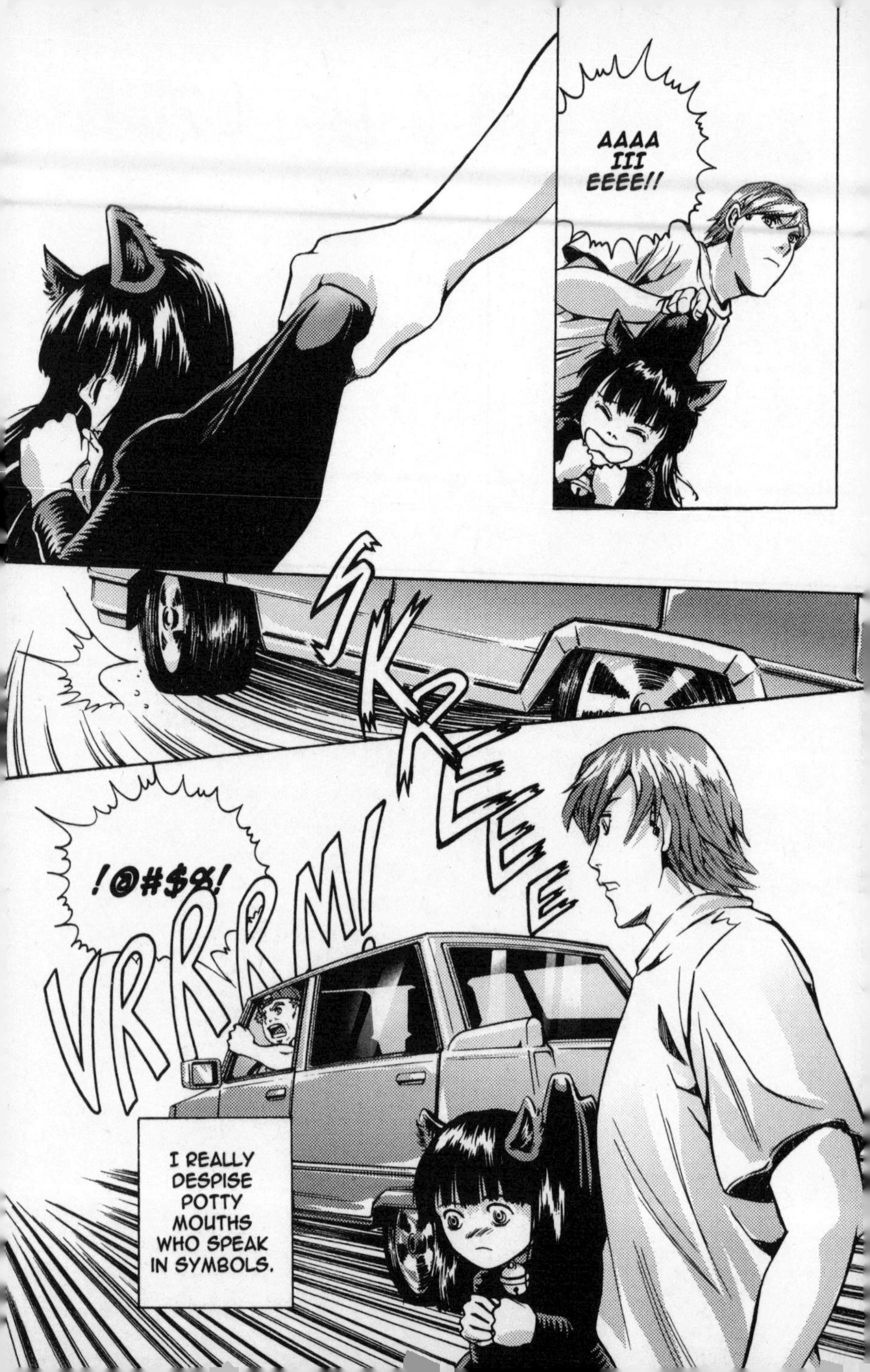
AAAA III EEEE!!
SKREEEE
VRRRM!
!@#$%!
I REALLY DESPISE POTTY MOUTHS WHO SPEAK IN SYMBOLS.

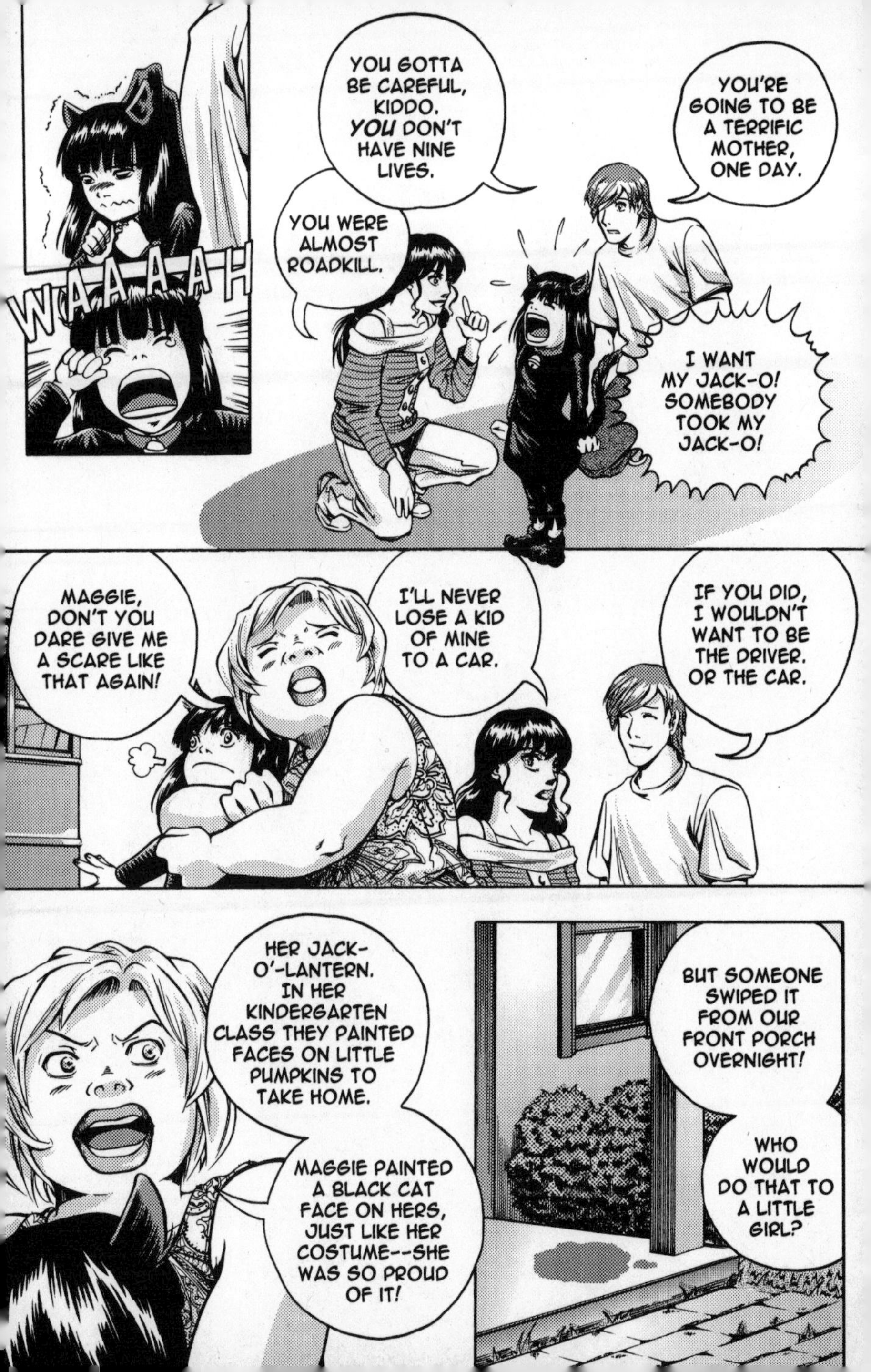
WAAAAH
YOU GOTTA BE CAREFUL, KIDDO. *YOU* DON'T HAVE NINE LIVES.
YOU WERE ALMOST ROADKILL.
YOU'RE GOING TO BE A TERRIFIC MOTHER, ONE DAY.
I WANT MY JACK-O! SOMEBODY TOOK MY JACK-O!
MAGGIE, DON'T YOU DARE GIVE ME A SCARE LIKE THAT AGAIN!
I'LL NEVER LOSE A KID OF MINE TO A CAR.
IF YOU DID, I WOULDN'T WANT TO BE THE DRIVER. OR THE CAR.
HER JACK-O'-LANTERN. IN HER KINDERGARTEN CLASS THEY PAINTED FACES ON LITTLE PUMPKINS TO TAKE HOME.
MAGGIE PAINTED A BLACK CAT FACE ON HERS, JUST LIKE HER COSTUME--SHE WAS SO PROUD OF IT!
BUT SOMEONE SWIPED IT FROM OUR FRONT PORCH OVERNIGHT!
WHO WOULD DO THAT TO A LITTLE GIRL?

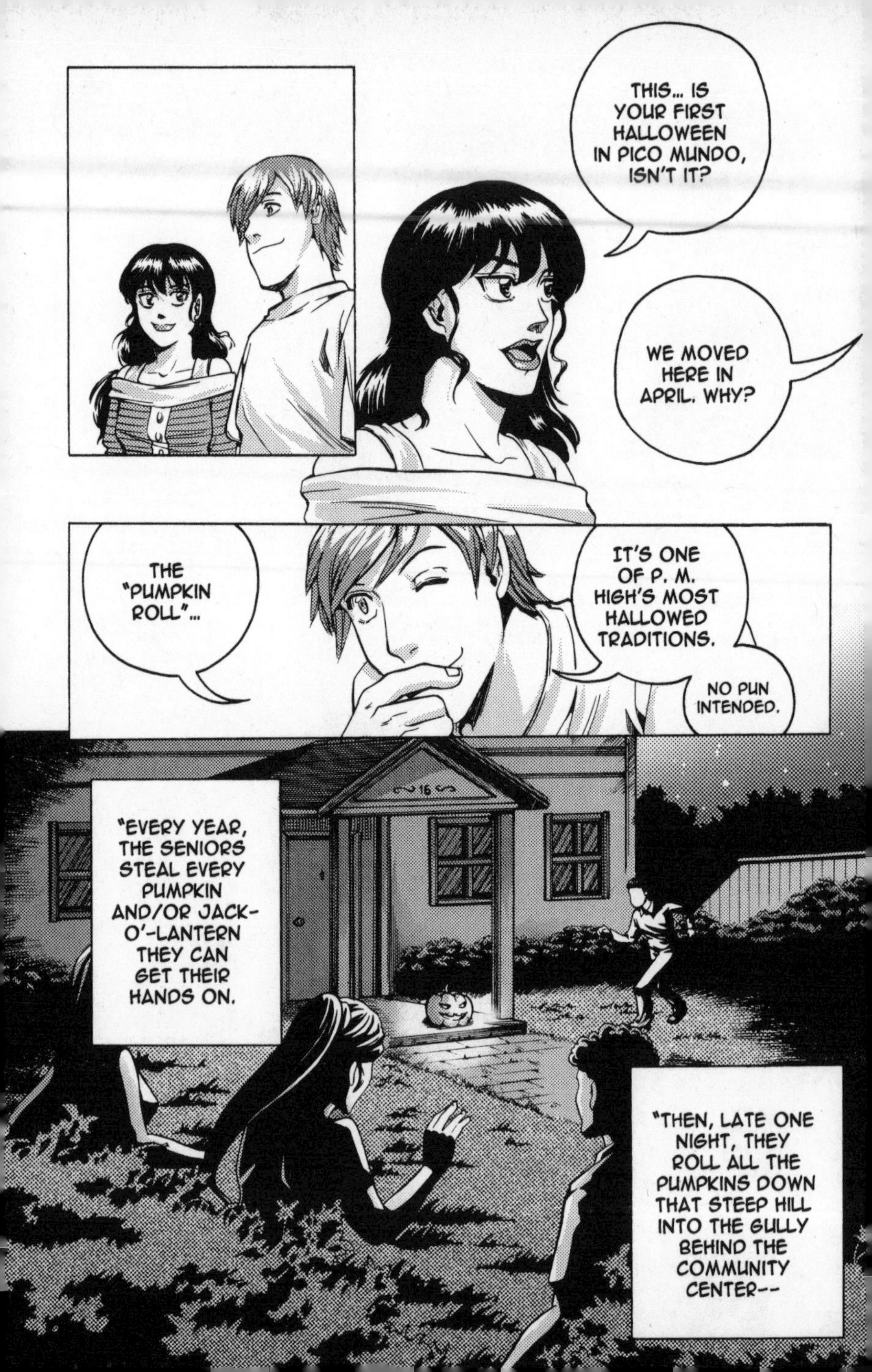

THIS... IS YOUR FIRST HALLOWEEN IN PICO MUNDO, ISN'T IT?
WE MOVED HERE IN APRIL. WHY?
THE "PUMPKIN ROLL"...
IT'S ONE OF P. M. HIGH'S MOST HALLOWED TRADITIONS.
NO PUN INTENDED.
"EVERY YEAR, THE SENIORS STEAL EVERY PUMPKIN AND/OR JACK-O'-LANTERN THEY CAN GET THEIR HANDS ON.
"THEN, LATE ONE NIGHT, THEY ROLL ALL THE PUMPKINS DOWN THAT STEEP HILL INTO THE GULLY BEHIND THE COMMUNITY CENTER--

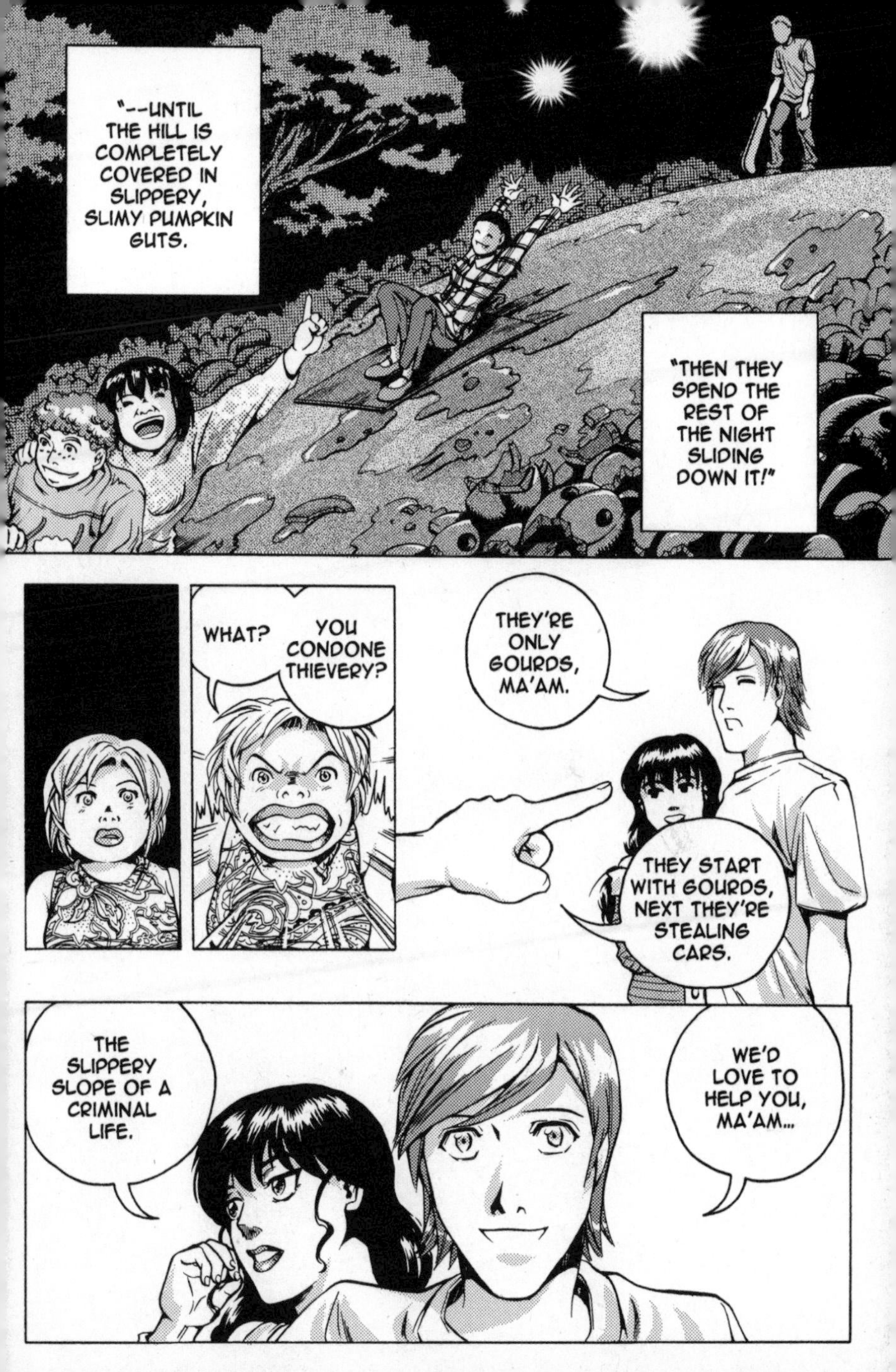
"--UNTIL THE HILL IS COMPLETELY COVERED IN SLIPPERY, SLIMY PUMPKIN GUTS.
"THEN THEY SPEND THE REST OF THE NIGHT SLIDING DOWN IT!"
WHAT?
YOU CONDONE THIEVERY?
THEY'RE ONLY GOURDS, MA'AM.
THEY START WITH GOURDS, NEXT THEY'RE STEALING CARS.
THE SLIPPERY SLOPE OF A CRIMINAL LIFE.
WE'D LOVE TO HELP YOU, MA'AM...

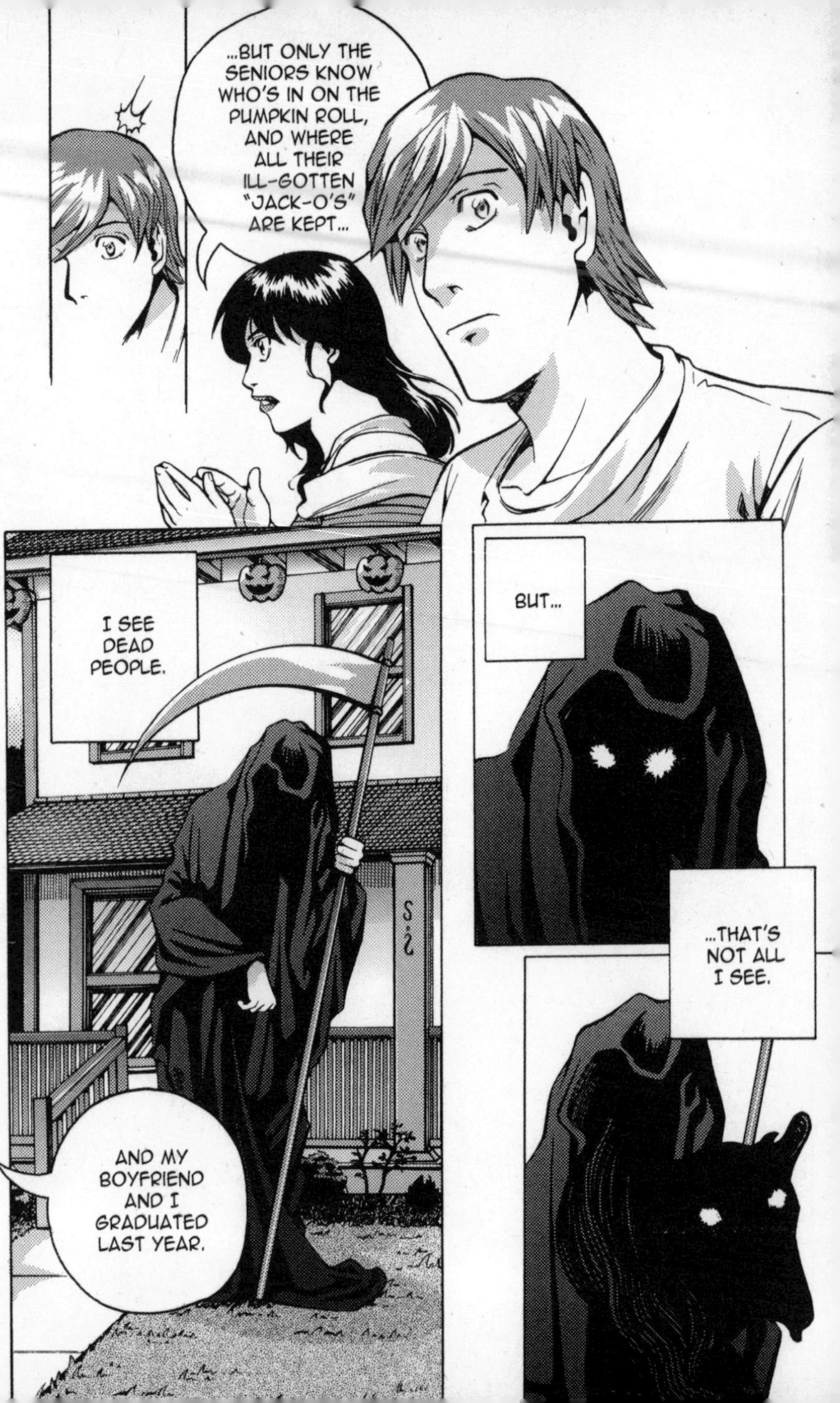
...BUT ONLY THE SENIORS KNOW WHO'S IN ON THE PUMPKIN ROLL, AND WHERE ALL THEIR ILL-GOTTEN "JACK-O'S" ARE KEPT...
I SEE DEAD PEOPLE.
AND MY BOYFRIEND AND I GRADUATED LAST YEAR.
BUT...
...THAT'S NOT ALL I SEE.

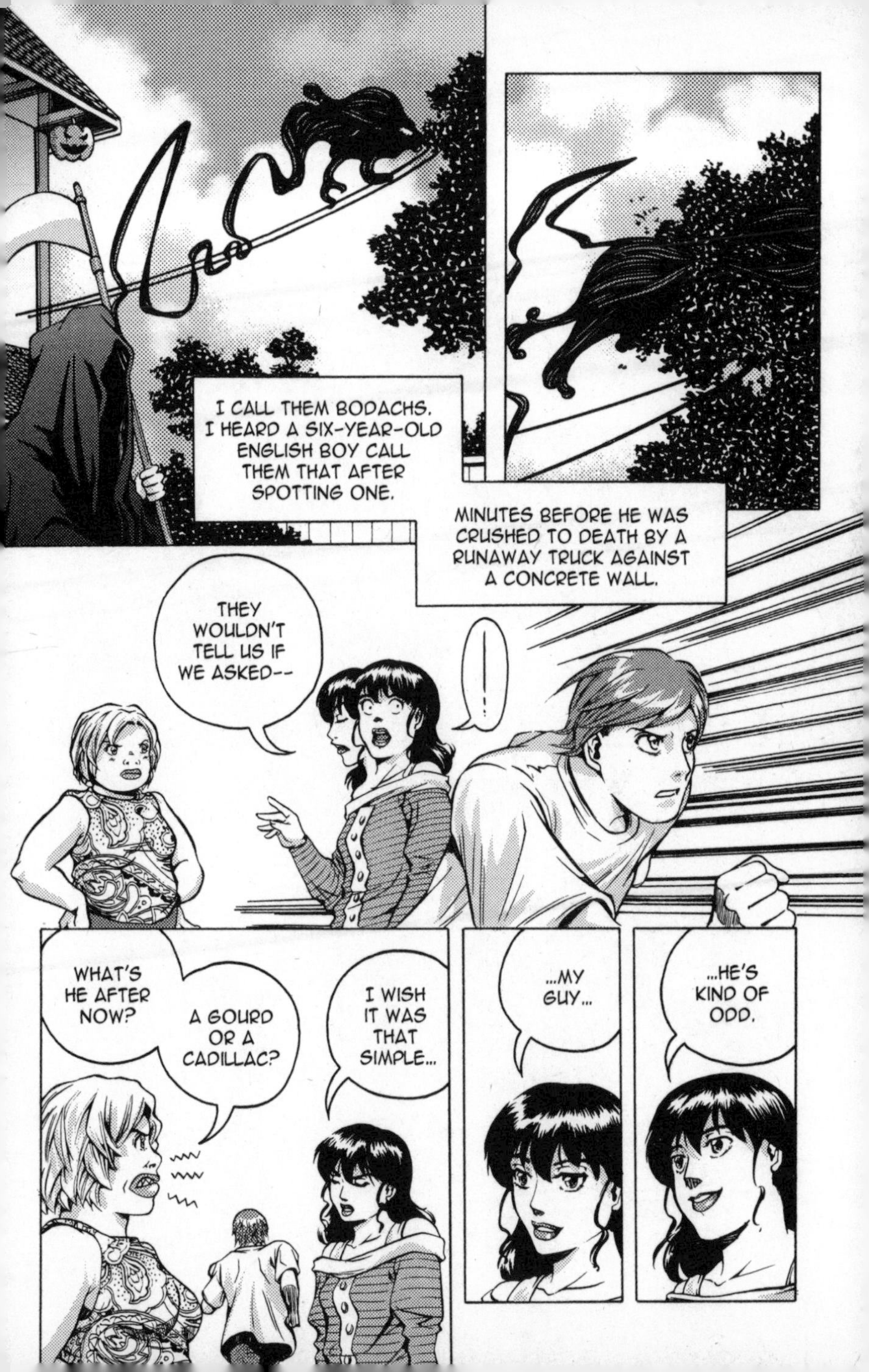

I CALL THEM BODACHS. I HEARD A SIX-YEAR-OLD ENGLISH BOY CALL THEM THAT AFTER SPOTTING ONE.
MINUTES BEFORE HE WAS CRUSHED TO DEATH BY A RUNAWAY TRUCK AGAINST A CONCRETE WALL.
THEY WOULDN'T TELL US IF WE ASKED--
!
WHAT'S HE AFTER NOW?
A GOURD OR A CADILLAC?
I WISH IT WAS THAT SIMPLE...
...MY GUY...
...HE'S KIND OF ODD.

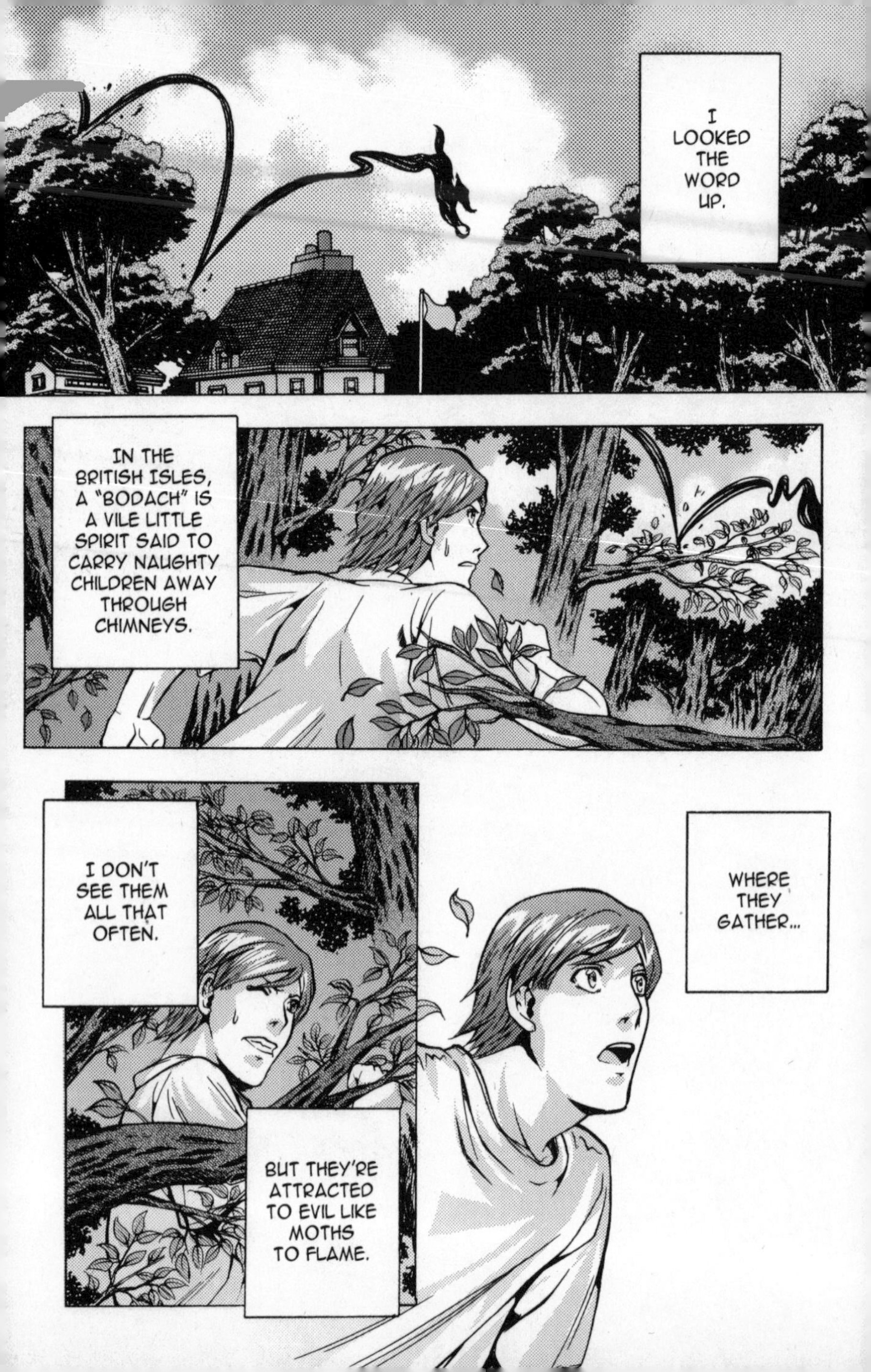
I LOOKED THE WORD UP.
IN THE BRITISH ISLES, A "BODACH" IS A VILE LITTLE SPIRIT SAID TO CARRY NAUGHTY CHILDREN AWAY THROUGH CHIMNEYS.
I DON'T SEE THEM ALL THAT OFTEN.
WHERE THEY GATHER...
BUT THEY'RE ATTRACTED TO EVIL LIKE MOTHS TO FLAME.

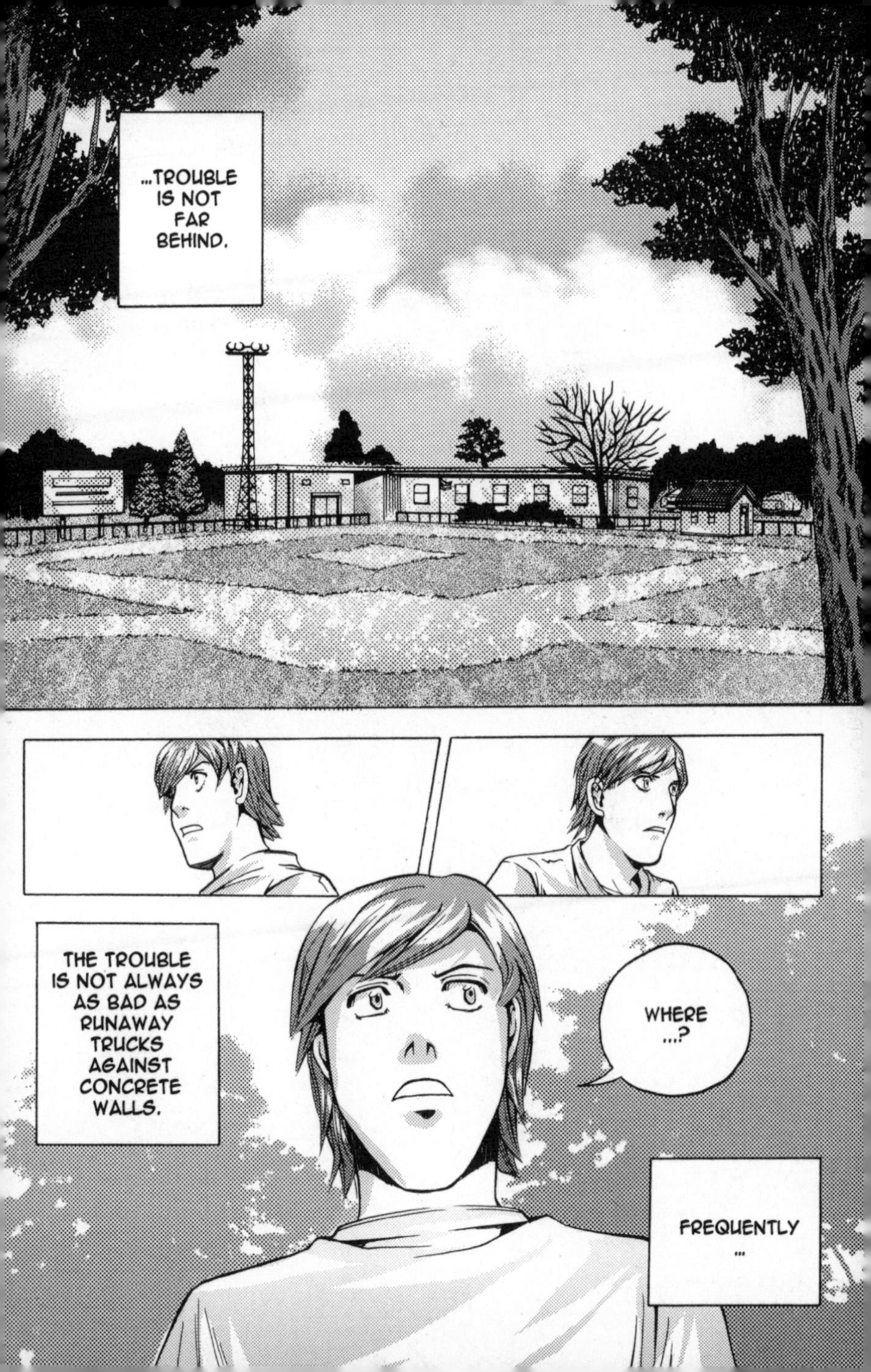
...TROUBLE IS NOT FAR BEHIND.
THE TROUBLE IS NOT ALWAYS AS BAD AS RUNAWAY TRUCKS AGAINST CONCRETE WALLS.
WHERE ...?
FREQUENTLY ...

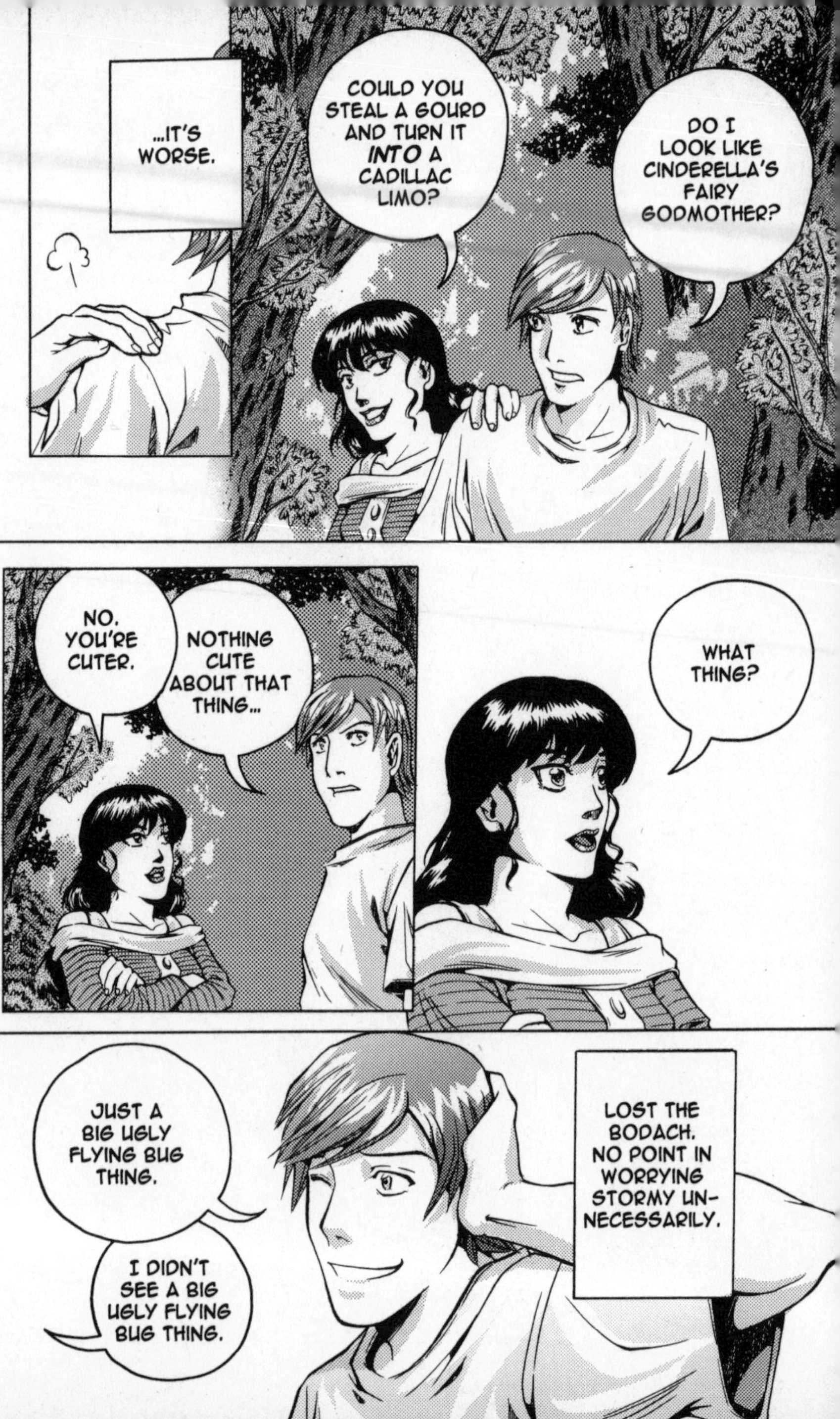
...IT'S WORSE.
COULD YOU STEAL A GOURD AND TURN IT *INTO* A CADILLAC LIMO?
DO I LOOK LIKE CINDERELLA'S FAIRY GODMOTHER?
NO. YOU'RE CUTER.
NOTHING CUTE ABOUT THAT THING...
WHAT THING?
JUST A BIG UGLY FLYING BUG THING.
I DIDN'T SEE A BIG UGLY FLYING BUG THING.
LOST THE BODACH. NO POINT IN WORRYING STORMY UN-NECESSARILY.

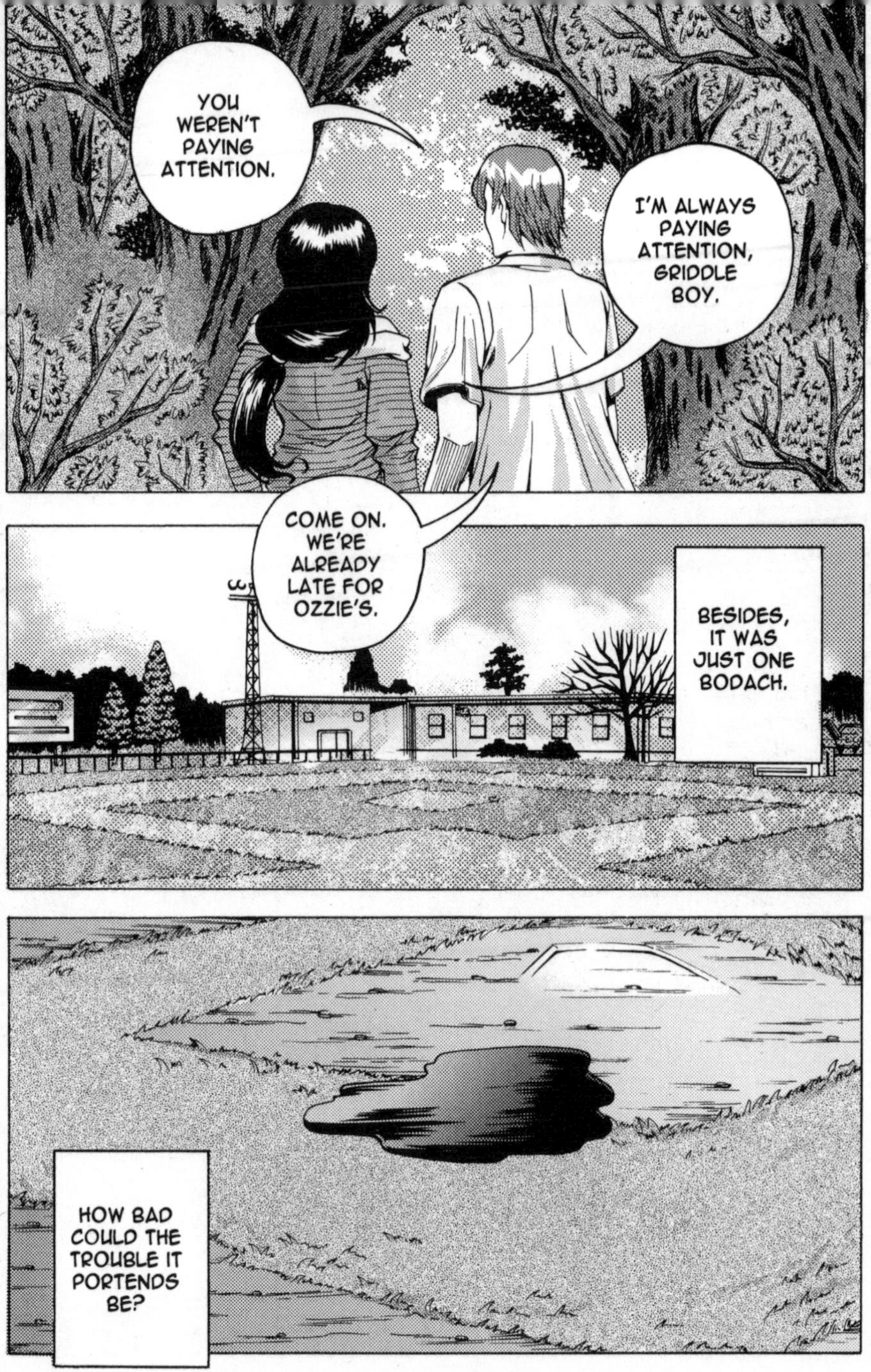
YOU WEREN'T PAYING ATTENTION.
I'M ALWAYS PAYING ATTENTION, GRIDDLE BOY.
COME ON. WE'RE ALREADY LATE FOR OZZIE'S.
BESIDES, IT WAS JUST ONE BODACH.
HOW BAD COULD THE TROUBLE IT PORTENDS BE?

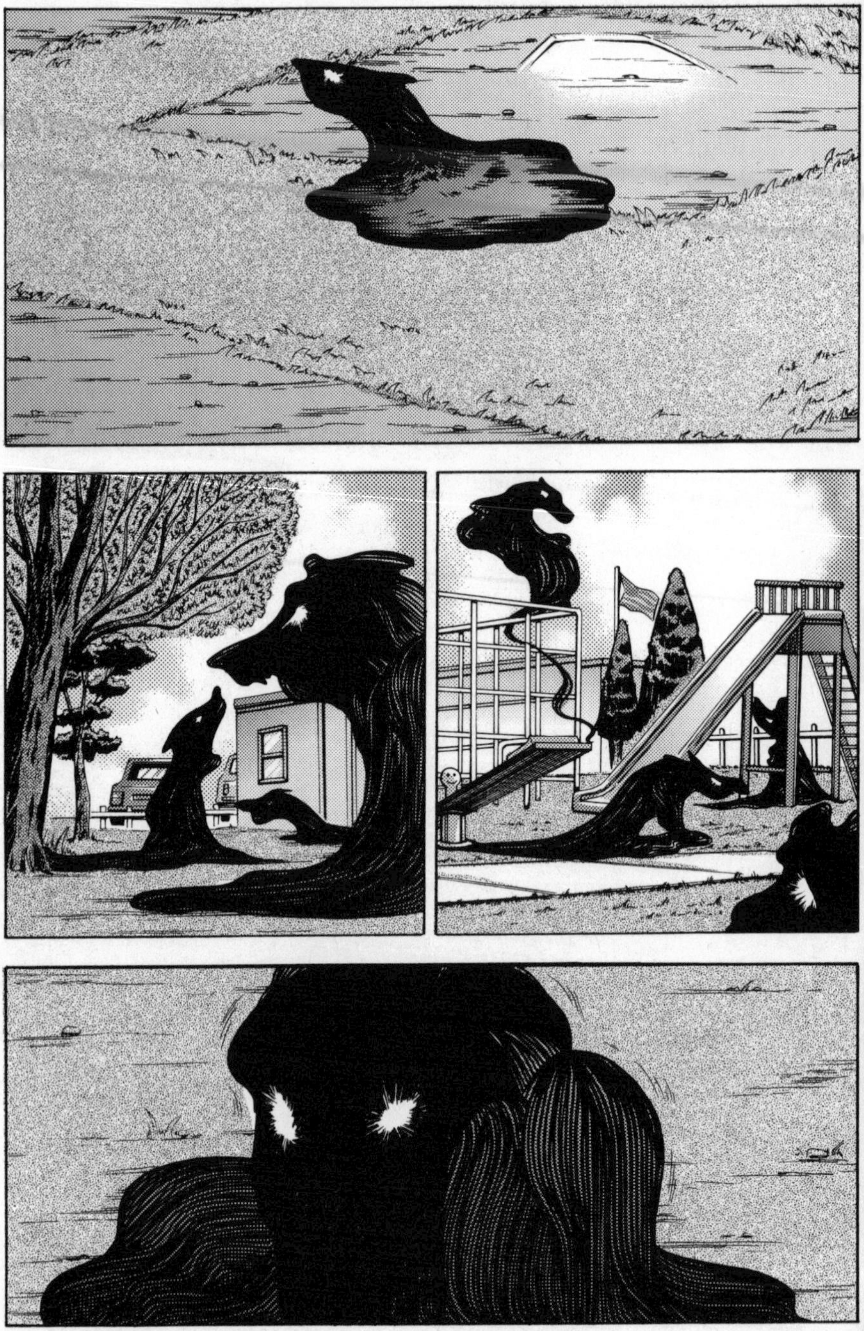

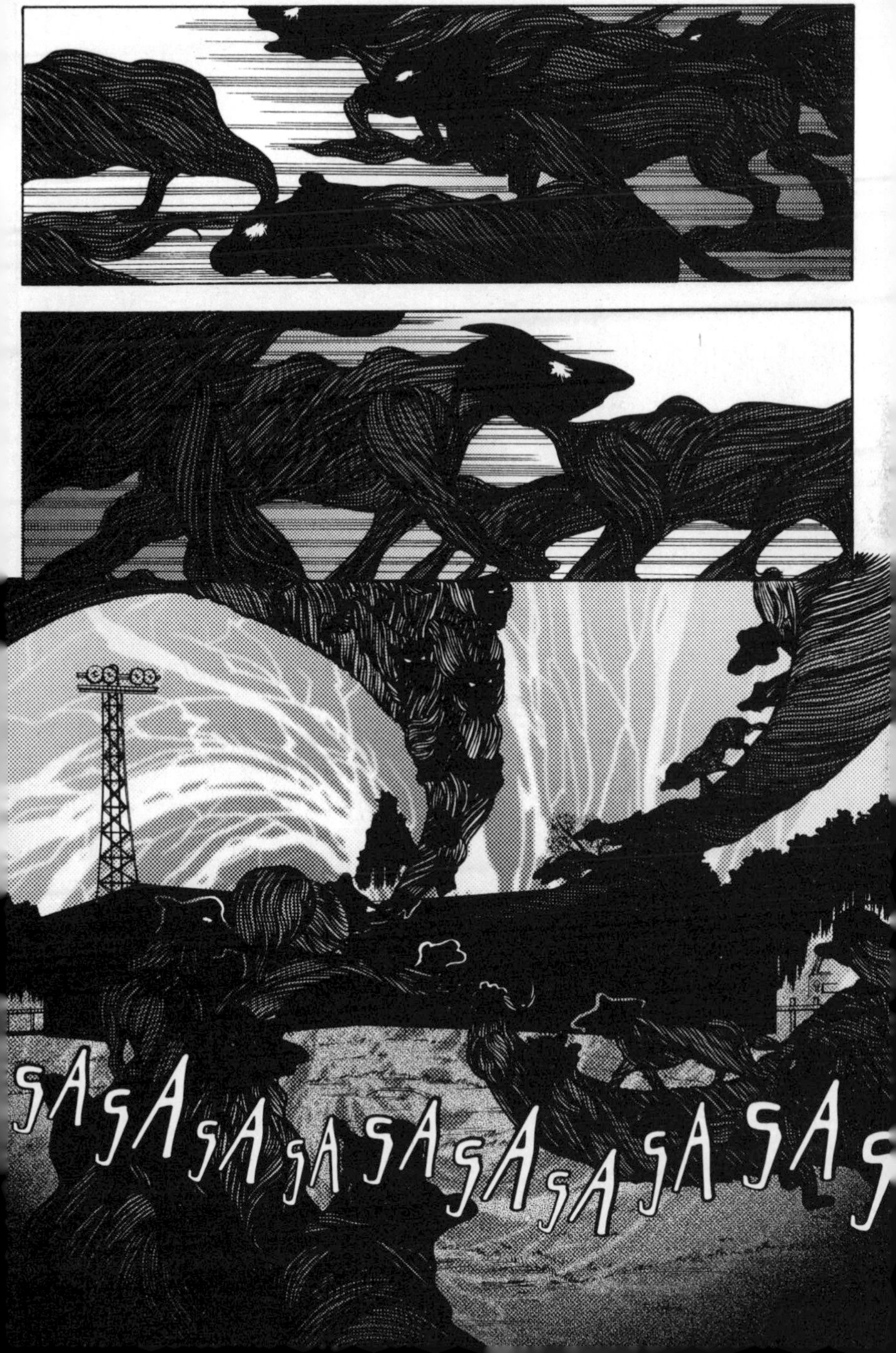
SASASASASASASASASAS

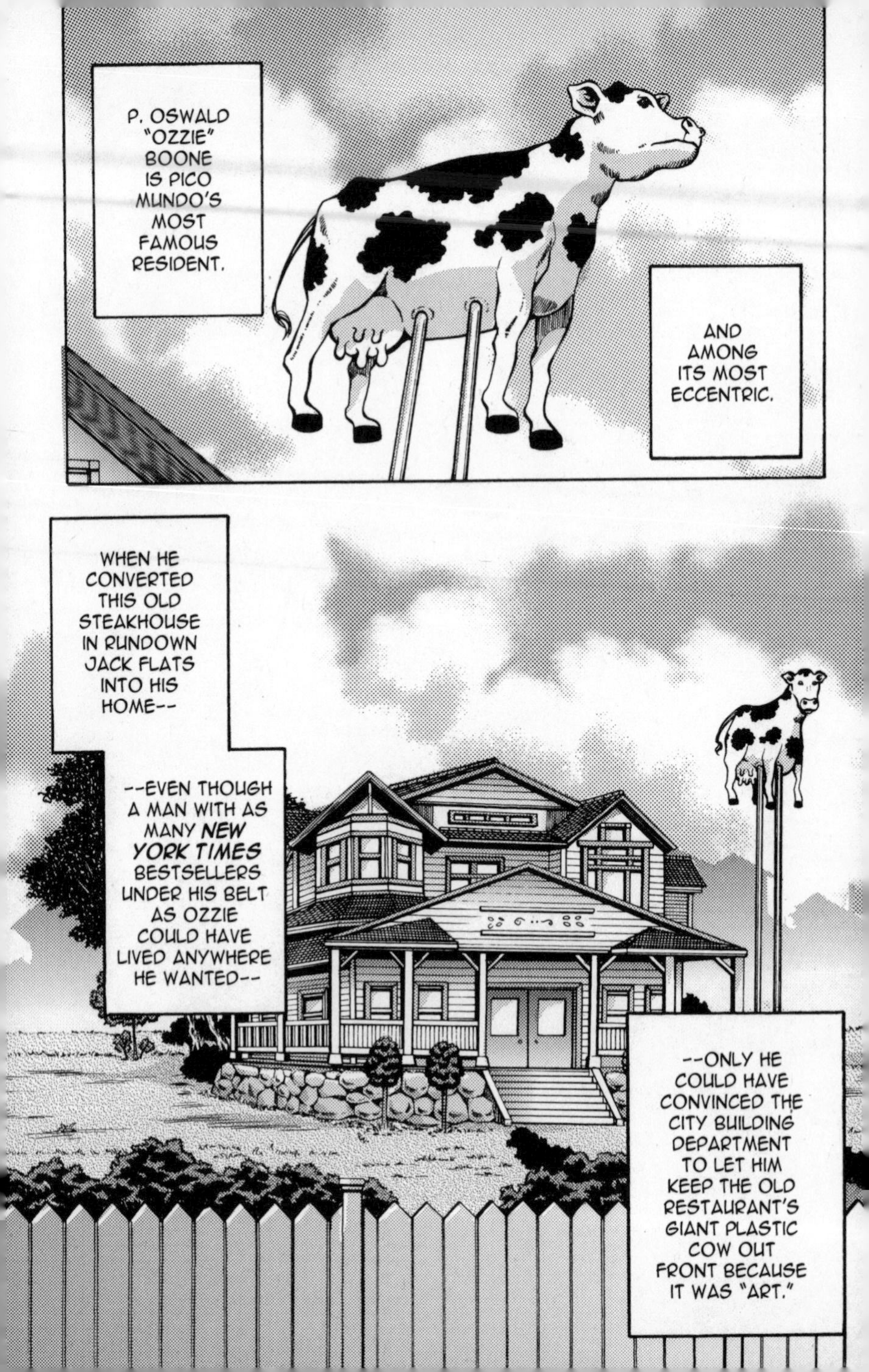
P. OSWALD "OZZIE" BOONE IS PICO MUNDO'S MOST FAMOUS RESIDENT.
AND AMONG ITS MOST ECCENTRIC.
WHEN HE CONVERTED THIS OLD STEAKHOUSE IN RUNDOWN JACK FLATS INTO HIS HOME--
--EVEN THOUGH A MAN WITH AS MANY *NEW YORK TIMES* BESTSELLERS UNDER HIS BELT AS OZZIE COULD HAVE LIVED ANYWHERE HE WANTED--
--ONLY HE COULD HAVE CONVINCED THE CITY BUILDING DEPARTMENT TO LET HIM KEEP THE OLD RESTAURANT'S GIANT PLASTIC COW OUT FRONT BECAUSE IT WAS "ART."

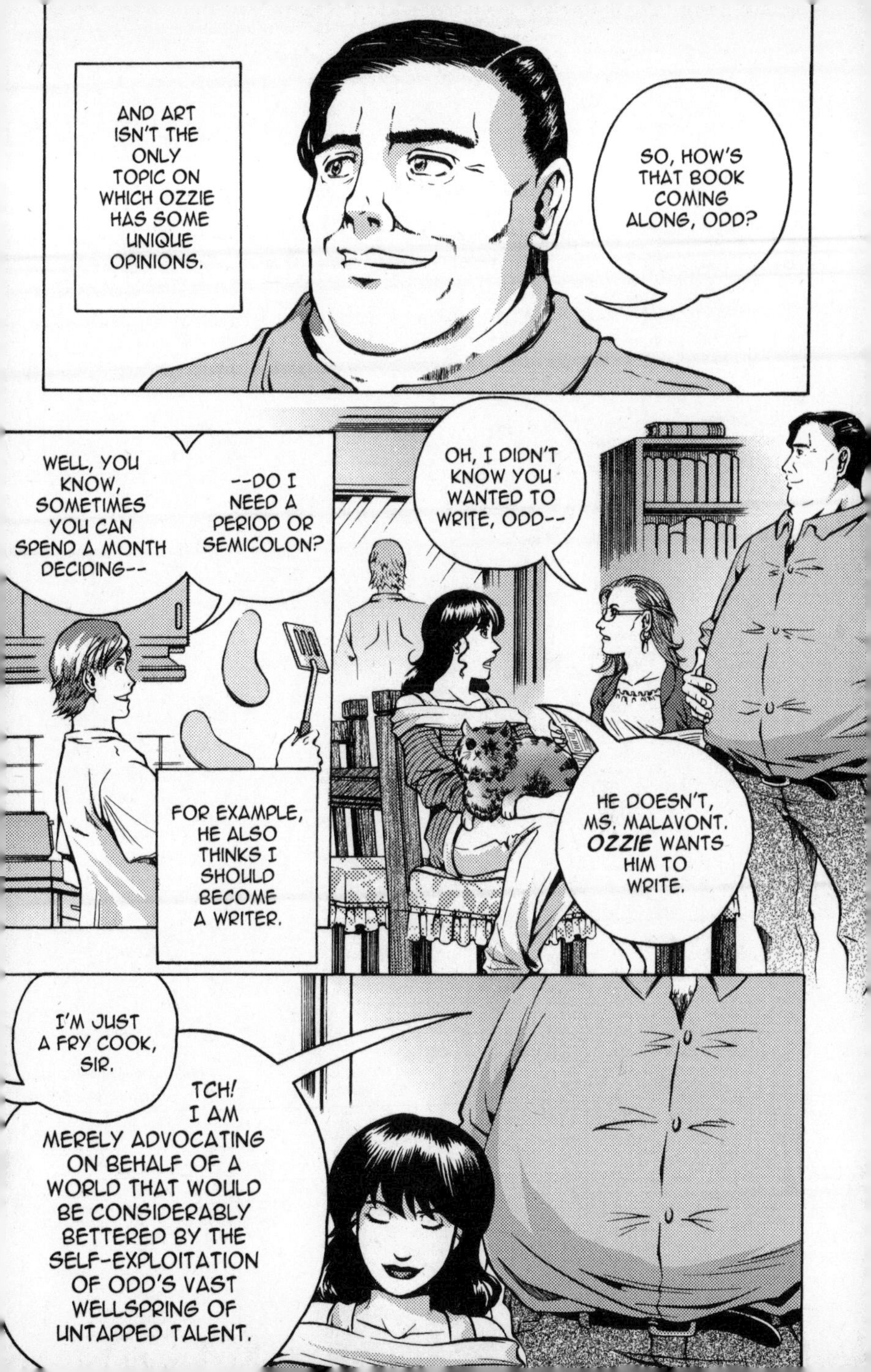
AND ART ISN'T THE ONLY TOPIC ON WHICH OZZIE HAS SOME UNIQUE OPINIONS.
SO, HOW'S THAT BOOK COMING ALONG, ODD?
WELL, YOU KNOW, SOMETIMES YOU CAN SPEND A MONTH DECIDING--
--DO I NEED A PERIOD OR SEMICOLON?
OH, I DIDN'T KNOW YOU WANTED TO WRITE, ODD--
FOR EXAMPLE, HE ALSO THINKS I SHOULD BECOME A WRITER.
HE DOESN'T, MS. MALAVONT. OZZIE WANTS HIM TO WRITE.
I'M JUST A FRY COOK, SIR.
TCH! I AM MERELY ADVOCATING ON BEHALF OF A WORLD THAT WOULD BE CONSIDERABLY BETTERED BY THE SELF-EXPLOITATION OF ODD'S VAST WELLSPRING OF UNTAPPED TALENT.

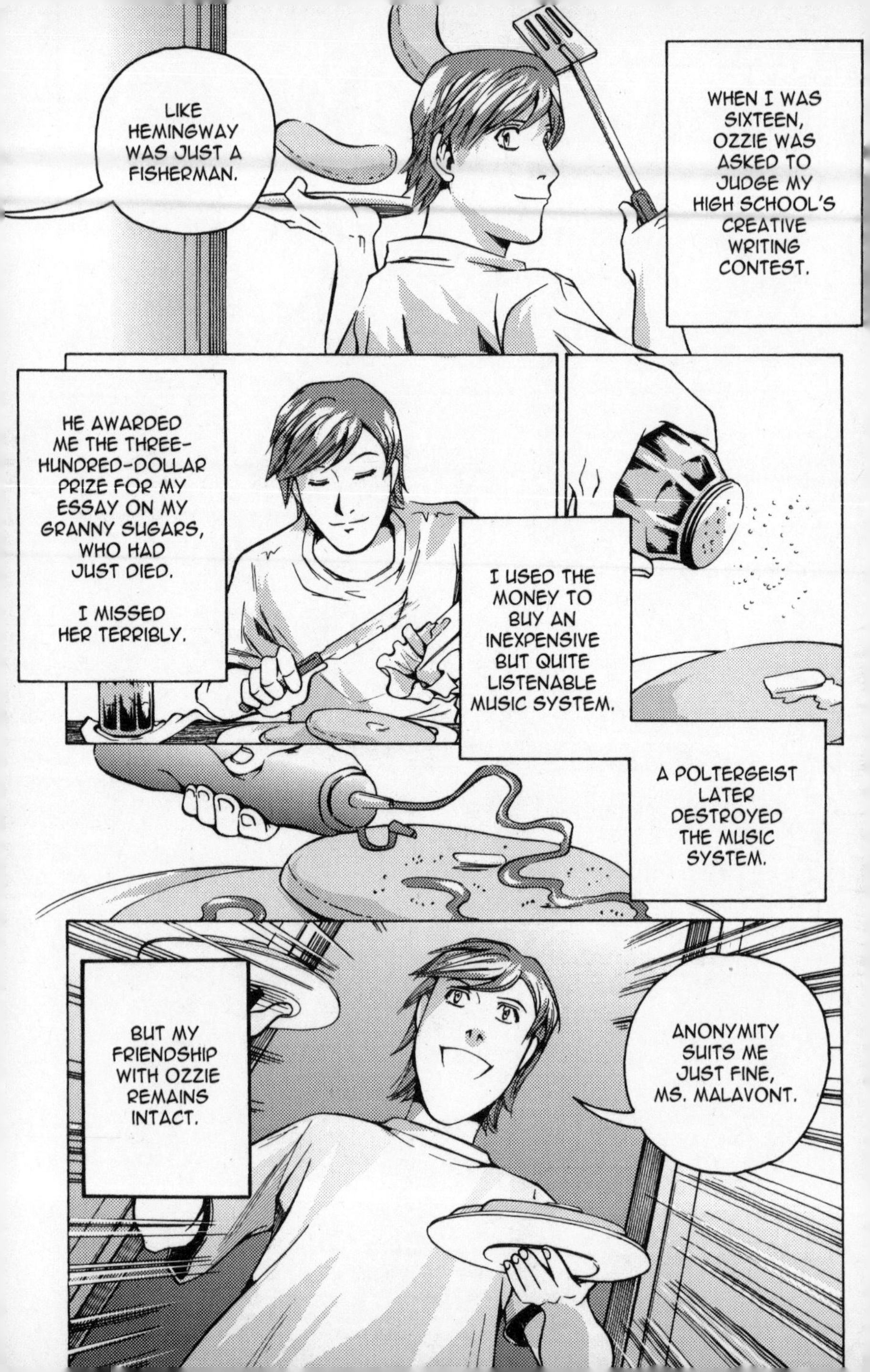
LIKE HEMINGWAY WAS JUST A FISHERMAN.
WHEN I WAS SIXTEEN, OZZIE WAS ASKED TO JUDGE MY HIGH SCHOOL'S CREATIVE WRITING CONTEST.
HE AWARDED ME THE THREE-HUNDRED-DOLLAR PRIZE FOR MY ESSAY ON MY GRANNY SUGARS, WHO HAD JUST DIED.
I MISSED HER TERRIBLY.
I USED THE MONEY TO BUY AN INEXPENSIVE BUT QUITE LISTENABLE MUSIC SYSTEM.
A POLTERGEIST LATER DESTROYED THE MUSIC SYSTEM.
BUT MY FRIENDSHIP WITH OZZIE REMAINS INTACT.
ANONYMITY SUITS ME JUST FINE, MS. MALAVONT.

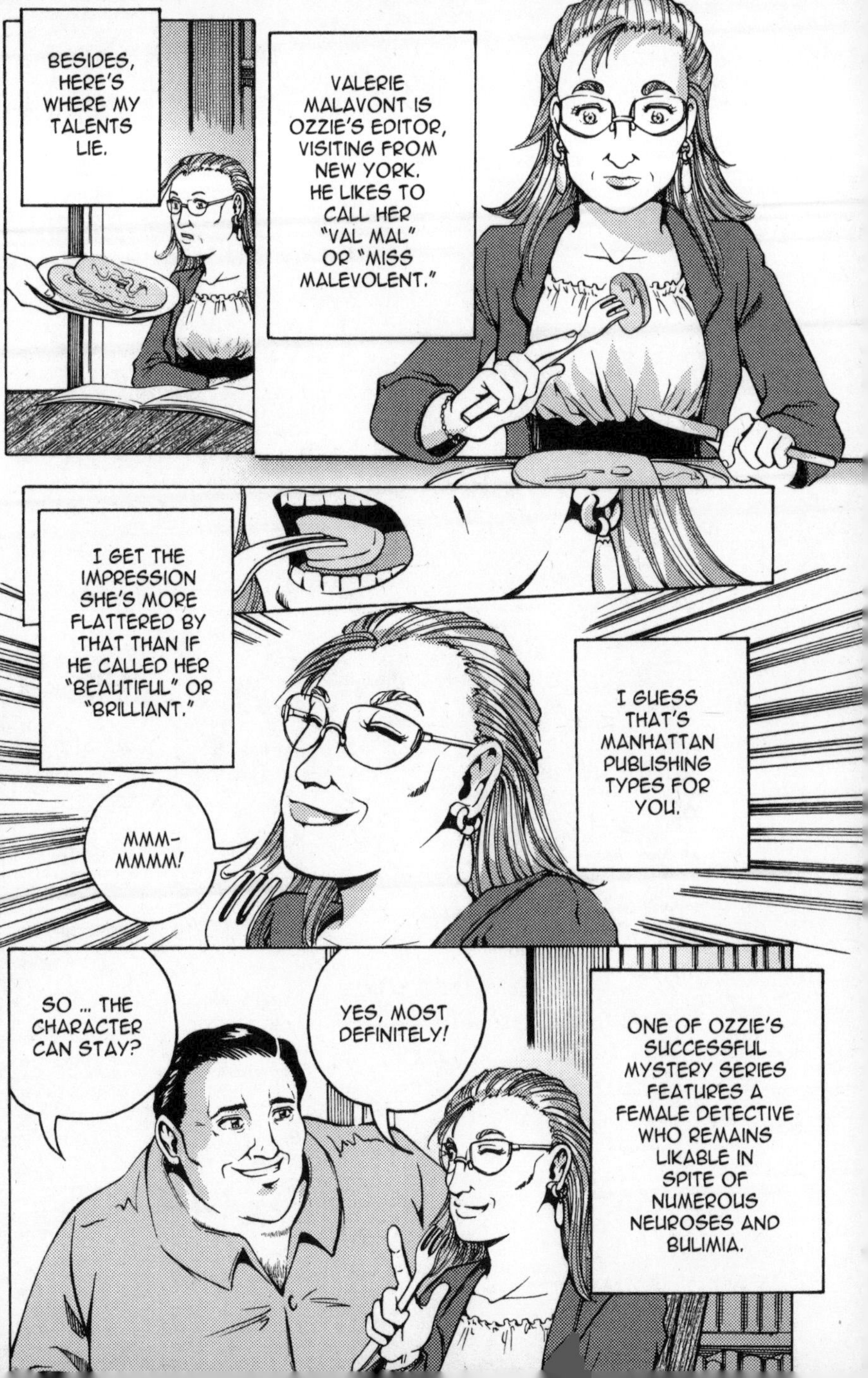
BESIDES, HERE'S WHERE MY TALENTS LIE.
VALERIE MALAVONT IS OZZIE'S EDITOR, VISITING FROM NEW YORK. HE LIKES TO CALL HER "VAL MAL" OR "MISS MALEVOLENT."
I GET THE IMPRESSION SHE'S MORE FLATTERED BY THAT THAN IF HE CALLED HER "BEAUTIFUL" OR "BRILLIANT."
I GUESS THAT'S MANHATTAN PUBLISHING TYPES FOR YOU.
MMM-MMMM!
SO ... THE CHARACTER CAN STAY?
YES, MOST DEFINITELY!
ONE OF OZZIE'S SUCCESSFUL MYSTERY SERIES FEATURES A FEMALE DETECTIVE WHO REMAINS LIKABLE IN SPITE OF NUMEROUS NEUROSES AND BULIMIA.

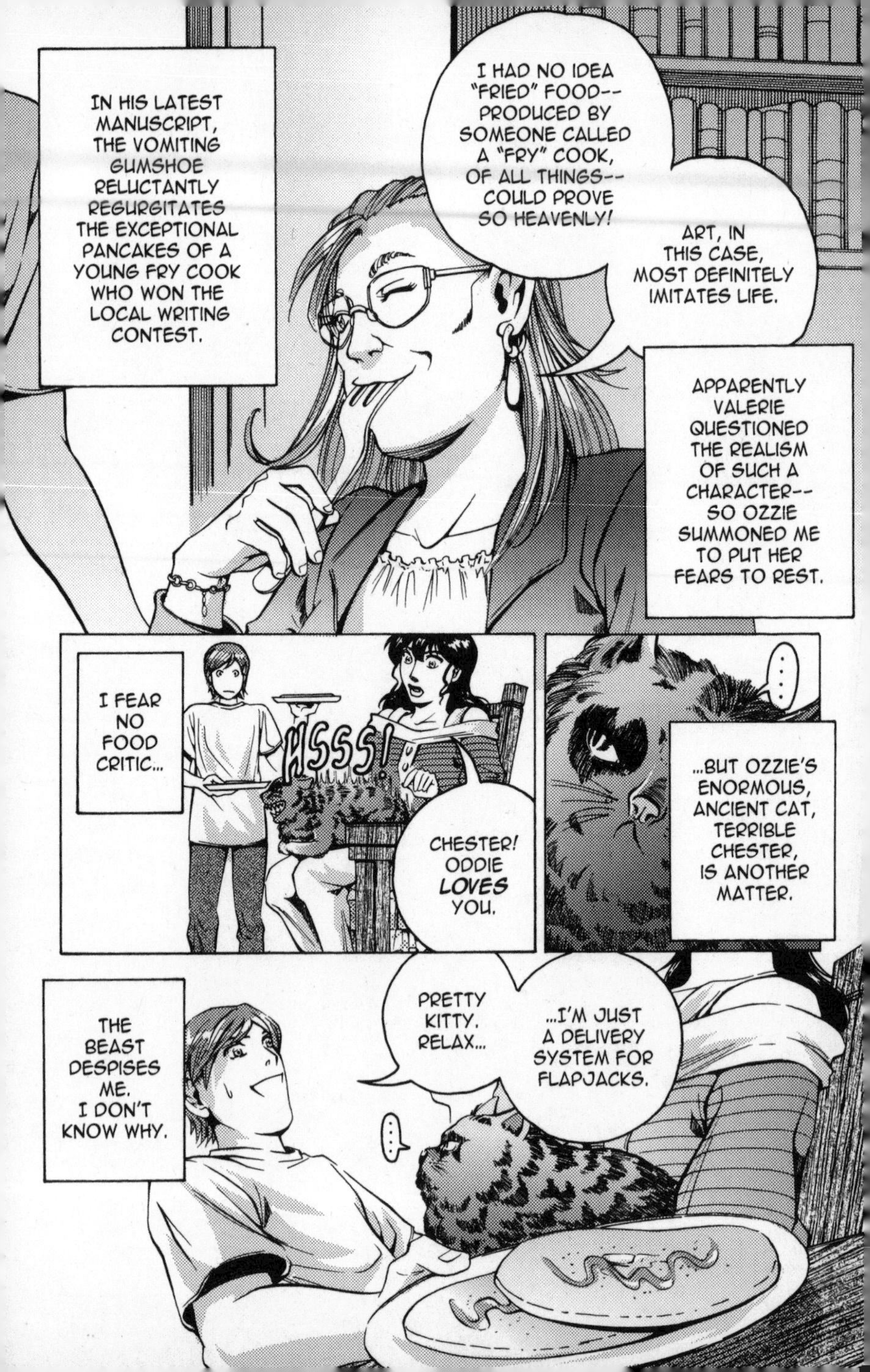

IN HIS LATEST MANUSCRIPT, THE VOMITING GUMSHOE RELUCTANTLY REGURGITATES THE EXCEPTIONAL PANCAKES OF A YOUNG FRY COOK WHO WON THE LOCAL WRITING CONTEST.
I HAD NO IDEA "FRIED" FOOD-- PRODUCED BY SOMEONE CALLED A "FRY" COOK, OF ALL THINGS-- COULD PROVE SO HEAVENLY!
ART, IN THIS CASE, MOST DEFINITELY IMITATES LIFE.
APPARENTLY VALERIE QUESTIONED THE REALISM OF SUCH A CHARACTER-- SO OZZIE SUMMONED ME TO PUT HER FEARS TO REST.
I FEAR NO FOOD CRITIC...
HSSS!
CHESTER! ODDIE *LOVES* YOU.
...
...BUT OZZIE'S ENORMOUS, ANCIENT CAT, TERRIBLE CHESTER, IS ANOTHER MATTER.
THE BEAST DESPISES ME. I DON'T KNOW WHY.
PRETTY KITTY. RELAX...
...I'M JUST A DELIVERY SYSTEM FOR FLAPJACKS.
...

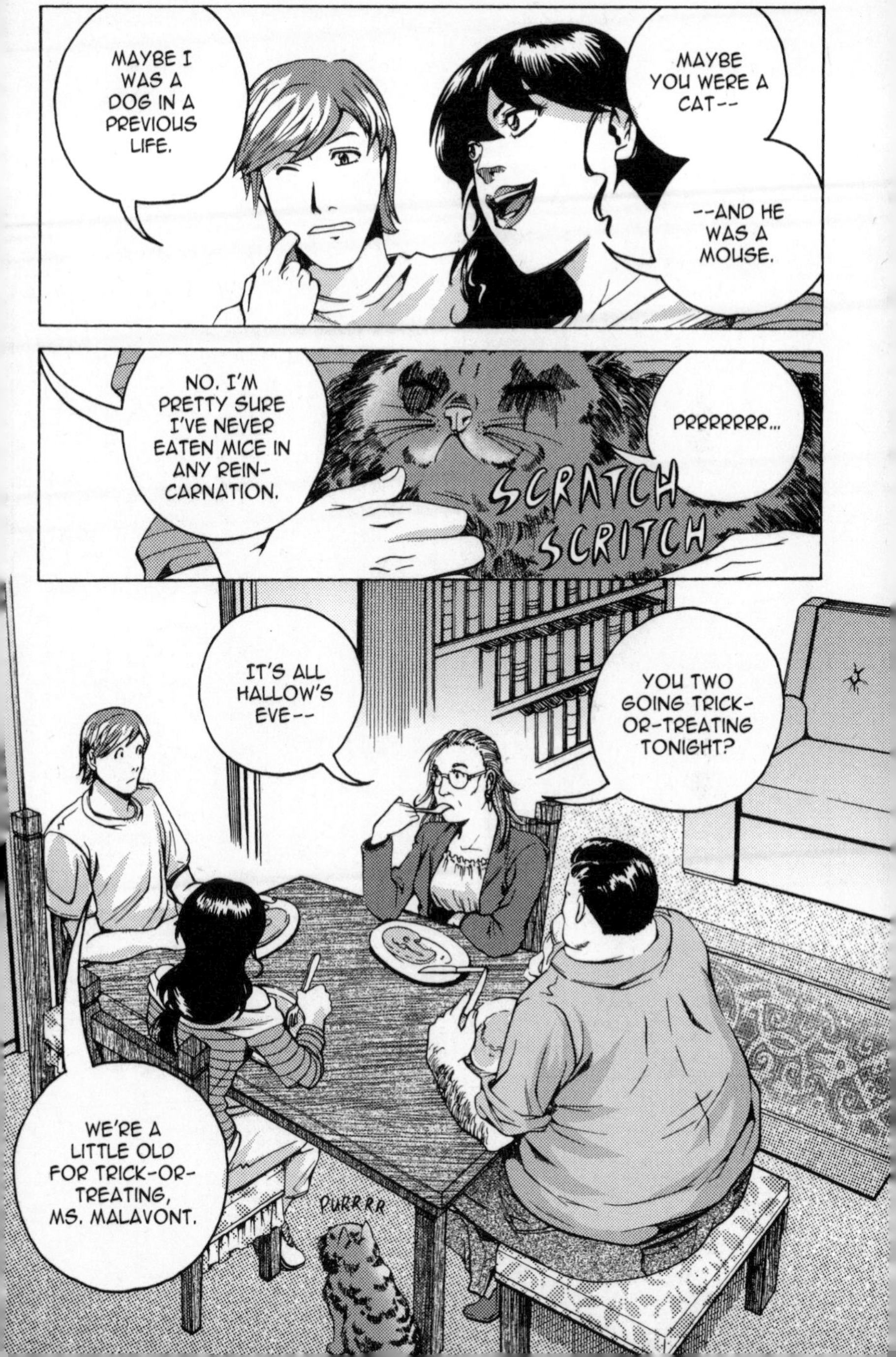
MAYBE I WAS A DOG IN A PREVIOUS LIFE.
MAYBE YOU WERE A CAT--
--AND HE WAS A MOUSE.
NO. I'M PRETTY SURE I'VE NEVER EATEN MICE IN ANY REIN-CARNATION.
PRRRRRRR...
SCRATCH SCRITCH
IT'S ALL HALLOW'S EVE--
YOU TWO GOING TRICK-OR-TREATING TONIGHT?
WE'RE A LITTLE OLD FOR TRICK-OR-TREATING, MS. MALAVONT.
PURRRR

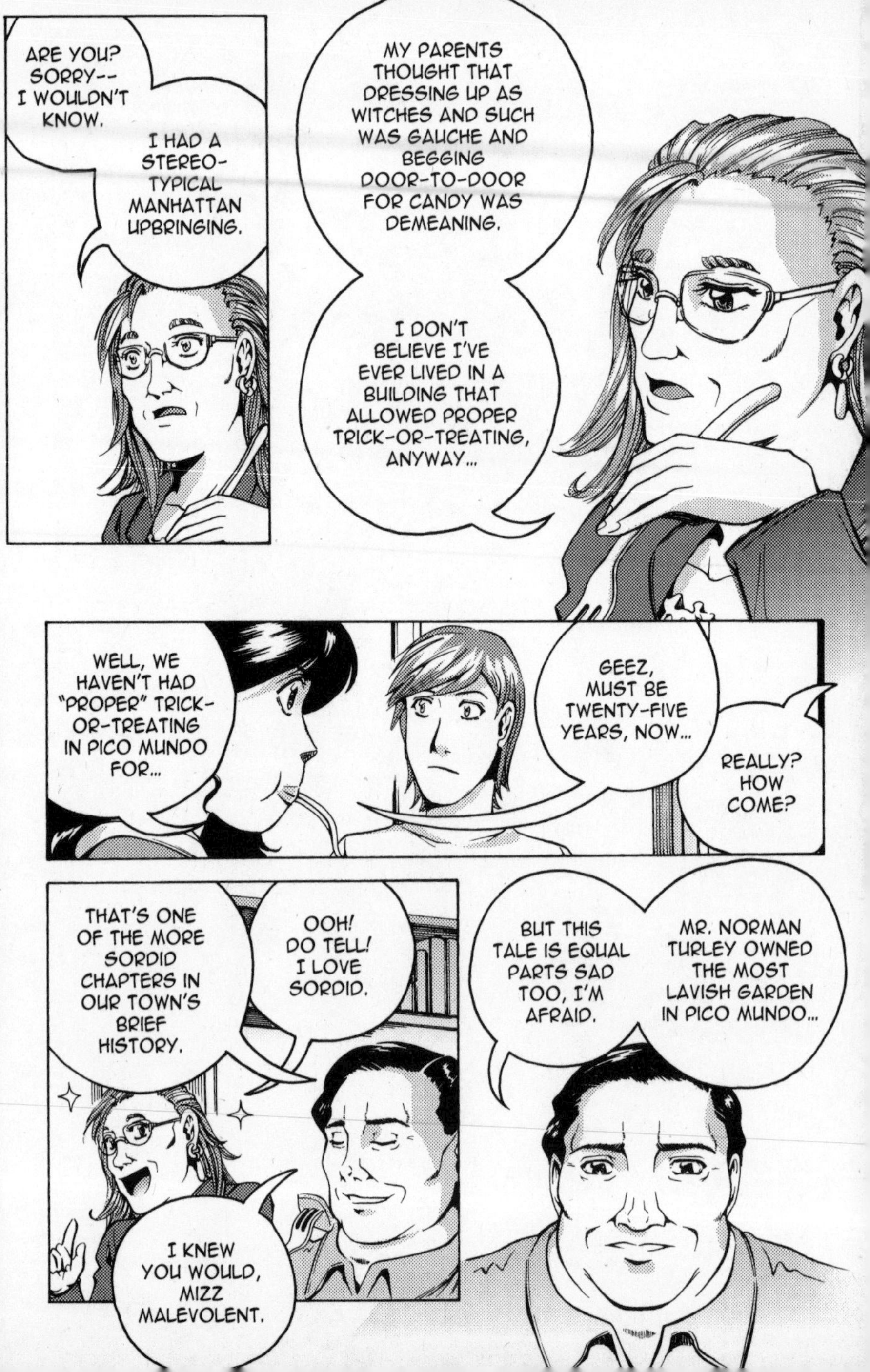
ARE YOU? SORRY-- I WOULDN'T KNOW.
I HAD A STEREO-TYPICAL MANHATTAN UPBRINGING.
MY PARENTS THOUGHT THAT DRESSING UP AS WITCHES AND SUCH WAS GAUCHE AND BEGGING DOOR-TO-DOOR FOR CANDY WAS DEMEANING.
I DON'T BELIEVE I'VE EVER LIVED IN A BUILDING THAT ALLOWED PROPER TRICK-OR-TREATING, ANYWAY...
WELL, WE HAVEN'T HAD "PROPER" TRICK-OR-TREATING IN PICO MUNDO FOR...
GEEZ, MUST BE TWENTY-FIVE YEARS, NOW...
REALLY? HOW COME?
THAT'S ONE OF THE MORE SORDID CHAPTERS IN OUR TOWN'S BRIEF HISTORY.
OOH! DO TELL! I LOVE SORDID.
I KNEW YOU WOULD, MIZZ MALEVOLENT.
BUT THIS TALE IS EQUAL PARTS SAD TOO, I'M AFRAID.
MR. NORMAN TURLEY OWNED THE MOST LAVISH GARDEN IN PICO MUNDO...

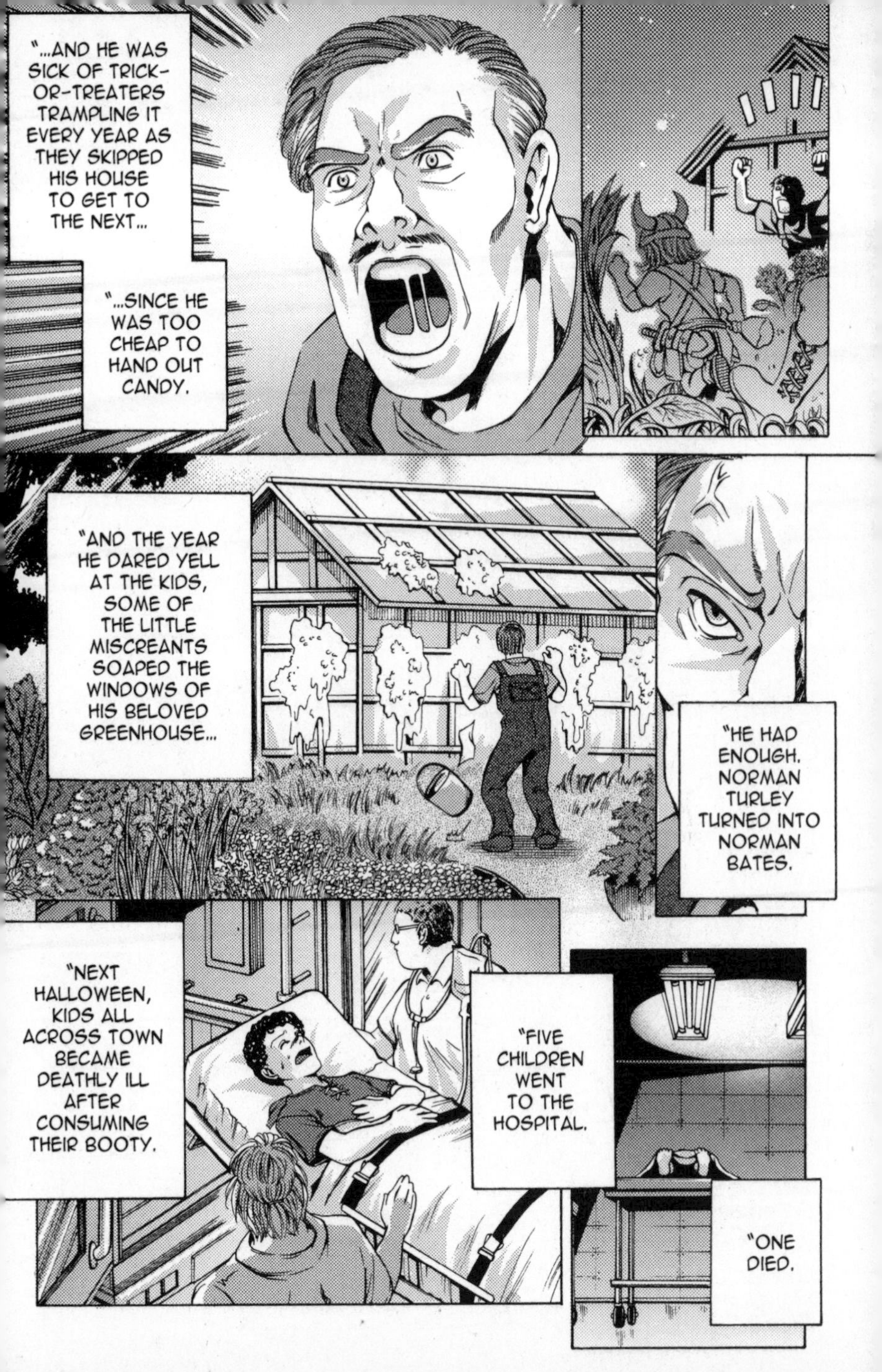
"...AND HE WAS SICK OF TRICK-OR-TREATERS TRAMPLING IT EVERY YEAR AS THEY SKIPPED HIS HOUSE TO GET TO THE NEXT...
"...SINCE HE WAS TOO CHEAP TO HAND OUT CANDY.
"AND THE YEAR HE DARED YELL AT THE KIDS, SOME OF THE LITTLE MISCREANTS SOAPED THE WINDOWS OF HIS BELOVED GREENHOUSE...
"HE HAD ENOUGH. NORMAN TURLEY TURNED INTO NORMAN BATES.
"NEXT HALLOWEEN, KIDS ALL ACROSS TOWN BECAME DEATHLY ILL AFTER CONSUMING THEIR BOOTY.
"FIVE CHILDREN WENT TO THE HOSPITAL.
"ONE DIED.

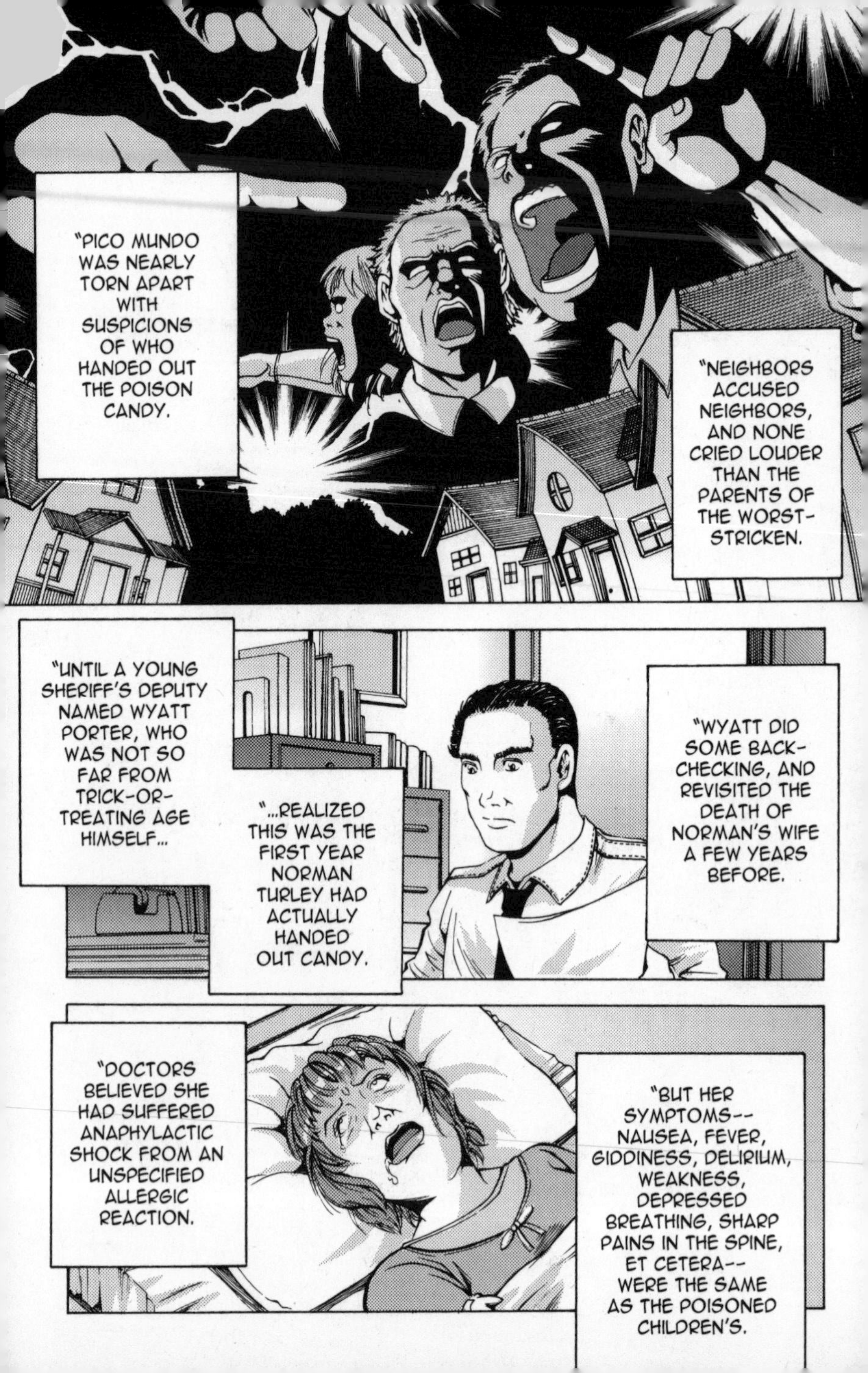
"PICO MUNDO WAS NEARLY TORN APART WITH SUSPICIONS OF WHO HANDED OUT THE POISON CANDY.
"NEIGHBORS ACCUSED NEIGHBORS, AND NONE CRIED LOUDER THAN THE PARENTS OF THE WORST-STRICKEN.
"UNTIL A YOUNG SHERIFF'S DEPUTY NAMED WYATT PORTER, WHO WAS NOT SO FAR FROM TRICK-OR-TREATING AGE HIMSELF...
"...REALIZED THIS WAS THE FIRST YEAR NORMAN TURLEY HAD ACTUALLY HANDED OUT CANDY.
"WYATT DID SOME BACK-CHECKING, AND REVISITED THE DEATH OF NORMAN'S WIFE A FEW YEARS BEFORE.
"DOCTORS BELIEVED SHE HAD SUFFERED ANAPHYLACTIC SHOCK FROM AN UNSPECIFIED ALLERGIC REACTION.
"BUT HER SYMPTOMS--NAUSEA, FEVER, GIDDINESS, DELIRIUM, WEAKNESS, DEPRESSED BREATHING, SHARP PAINS IN THE SPINE, ET CETERA--WERE THE SAME AS THE POISONED CHILDREN'S.

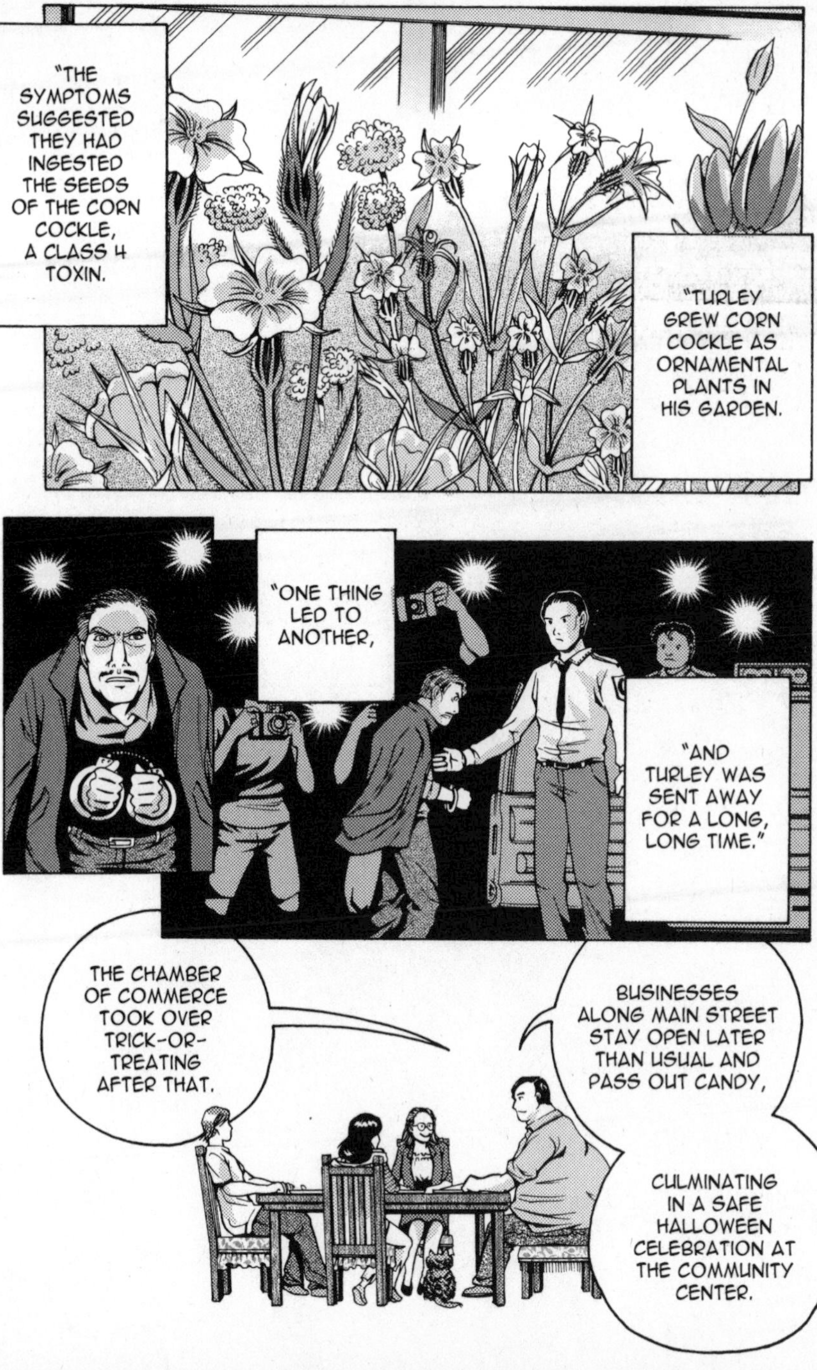
"THE SYMPTOMS SUGGESTED THEY HAD INGESTED THE SEEDS OF THE CORN COCKLE, A CLASS 4 TOXIN.
"TURLEY GREW CORN COCKLE AS ORNAMENTAL PLANTS IN HIS GARDEN.
"ONE THING LED TO ANOTHER,
"AND TURLEY WAS SENT AWAY FOR A LONG, LONG TIME."
THE CHAMBER OF COMMERCE TOOK OVER TRICK-OR-TREATING AFTER THAT.
BUSINESSES ALONG MAIN STREET STAY OPEN LATER THAN USUAL AND PASS OUT CANDY,
CULMINATING IN A SAFE HALLOWEEN CELEBRATION AT THE COMMUNITY CENTER.

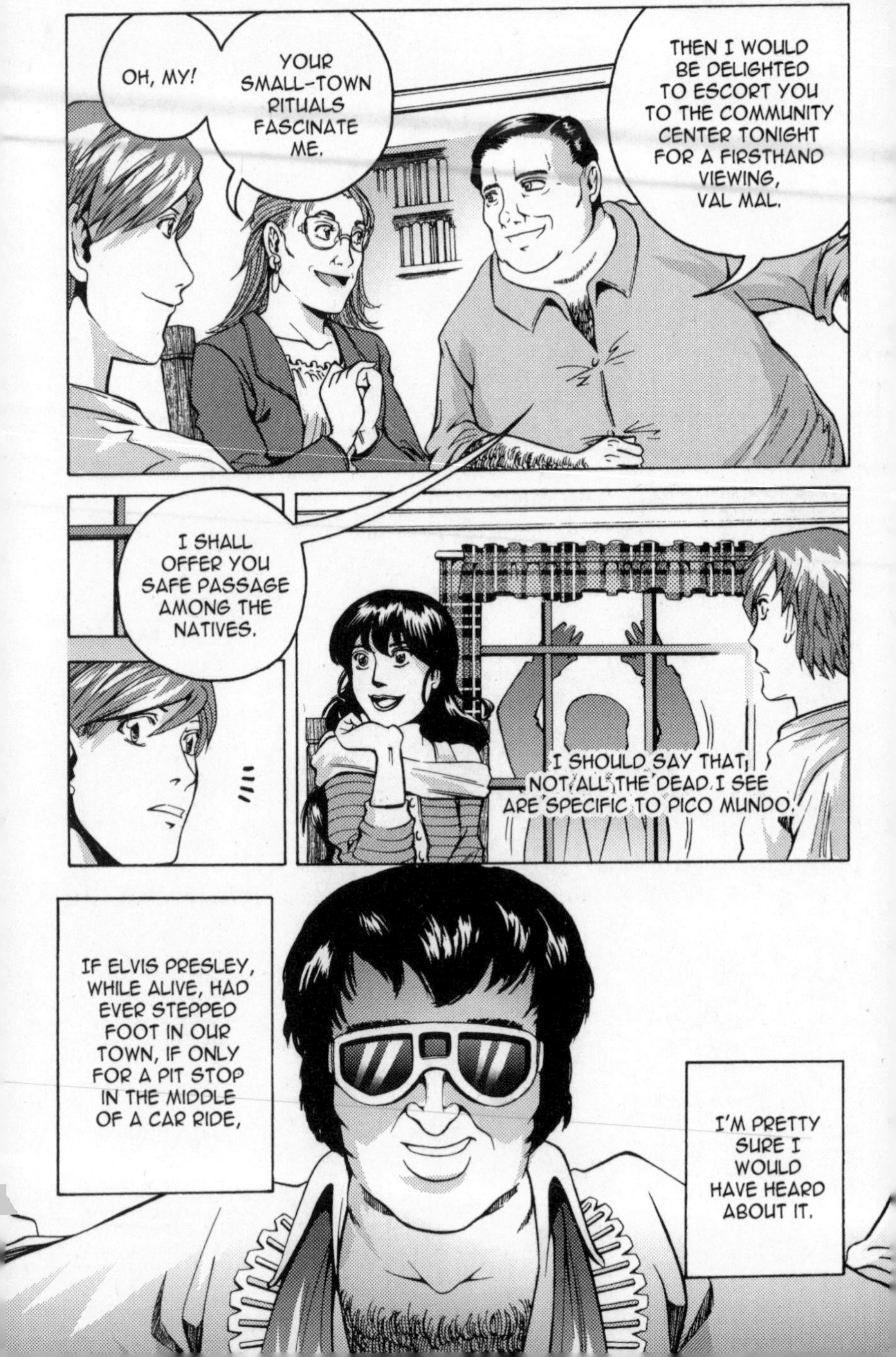
OH, MY!
YOUR SMALL-TOWN RITUALS FASCINATE ME.
THEN I WOULD BE DELIGHTED TO ESCORT YOU TO THE COMMUNITY CENTER TONIGHT FOR A FIRSTHAND VIEWING, VAL MAL.
I SHALL OFFER YOU SAFE PASSAGE AMONG THE NATIVES.
I SHOULD SAY THAT NOT ALL THE DEAD I SEE ARE SPECIFIC TO PICO MUNDO.
IF ELVIS PRESLEY, WHILE ALIVE, HAD EVER STEPPED FOOT IN OUR TOWN, IF ONLY FOR A PIT STOP IN THE MIDDLE OF A CAR RIDE,
I'M PRETTY SURE I WOULD HAVE HEARD ABOUT IT.

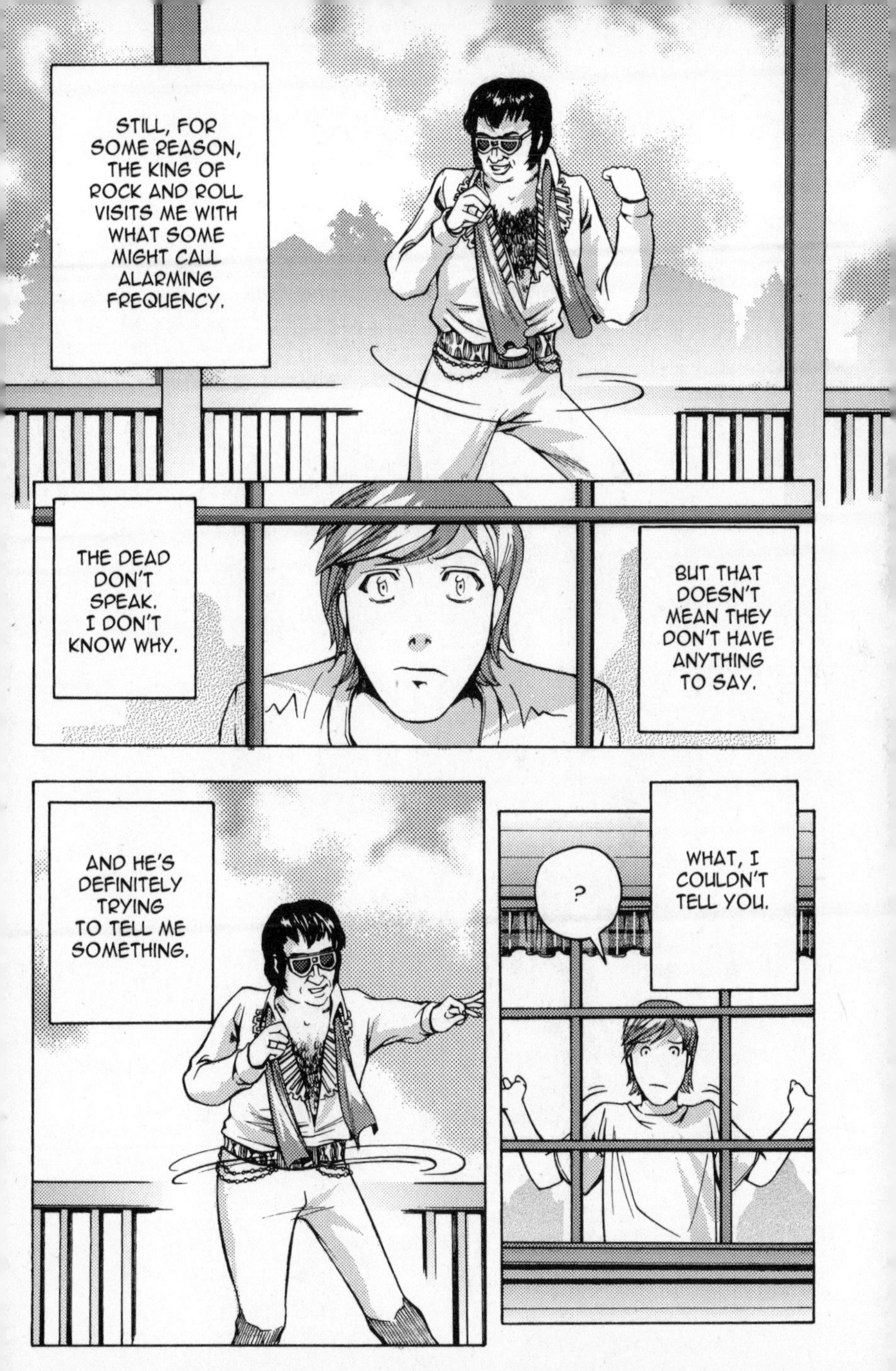
STILL, FOR SOME REASON, THE KING OF ROCK AND ROLL VISITS ME WITH WHAT SOME MIGHT CALL ALARMING FREQUENCY.
THE DEAD DON'T SPEAK. I DON'T KNOW WHY.
BUT THAT DOESN'T MEAN THEY DON'T HAVE ANYTHING TO SAY.
AND HE'S DEFINITELY TRYING TO TELL ME SOMETHING.
WHAT, I COULDN'T TELL YOU.
?

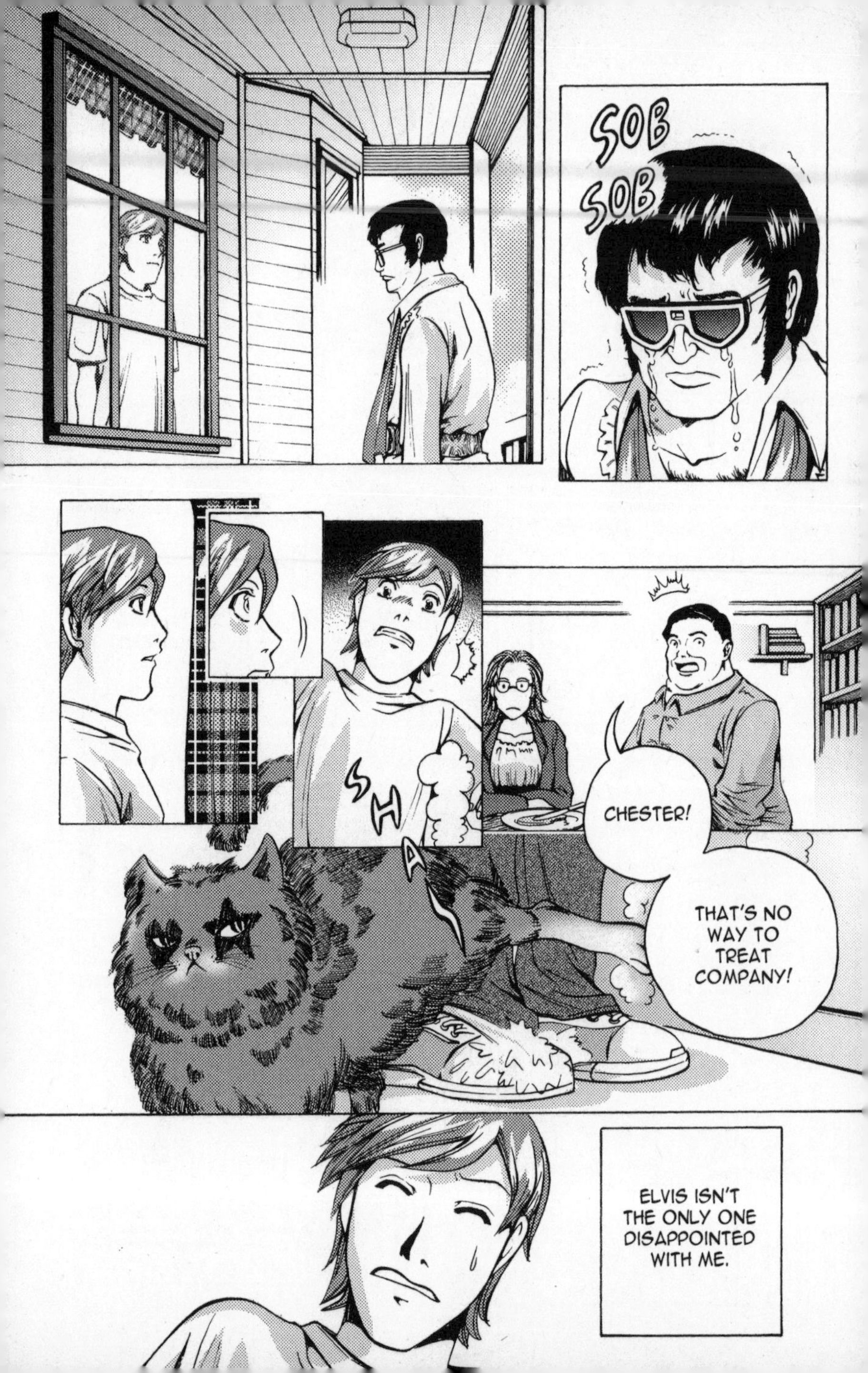
SOB
SOB
SHA
CHESTER!
THAT'S NO WAY TO TREAT COMPANY!
ELVIS ISN'T THE ONLY ONE DISAPPOINTED WITH ME.

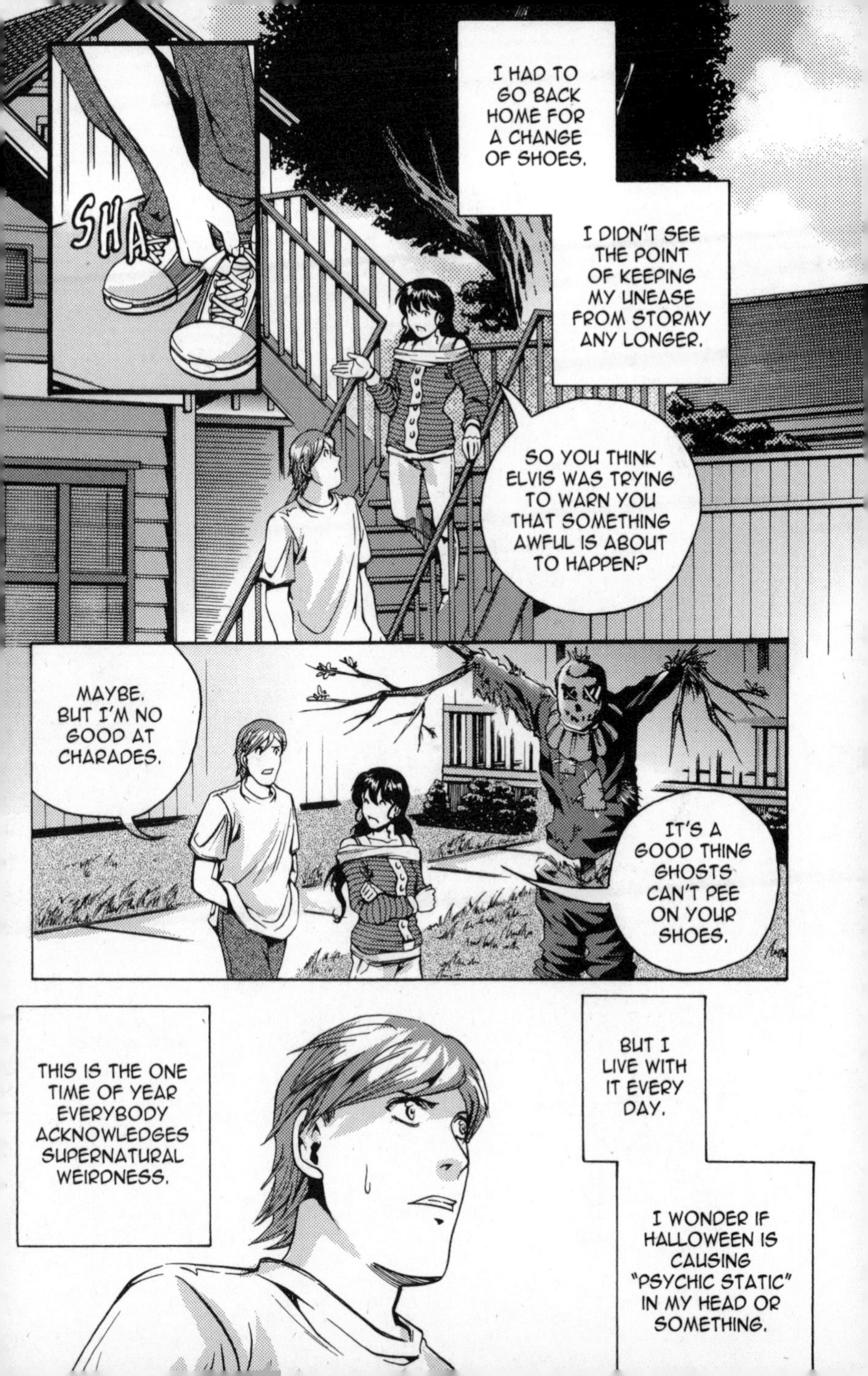
I HAD TO GO BACK HOME FOR A CHANGE OF SHOES.
SHA
I DIDN'T SEE THE POINT OF KEEPING MY UNEASE FROM STORMY ANY LONGER.
SO YOU THINK ELVIS WAS TRYING TO WARN YOU THAT SOMETHING AWFUL IS ABOUT TO HAPPEN?
MAYBE. BUT I'M NO GOOD AT CHARADES.
IT'S A GOOD THING GHOSTS CAN'T PEE ON YOUR SHOES.
THIS IS THE ONE TIME OF YEAR EVERYBODY ACKNOWLEDGES SUPERNATURAL WEIRDNESS.
BUT I LIVE WITH IT EVERY DAY.
I WONDER IF HALLOWEEN IS CAUSING "PSYCHIC STATIC" IN MY HEAD OR SOMETHING.

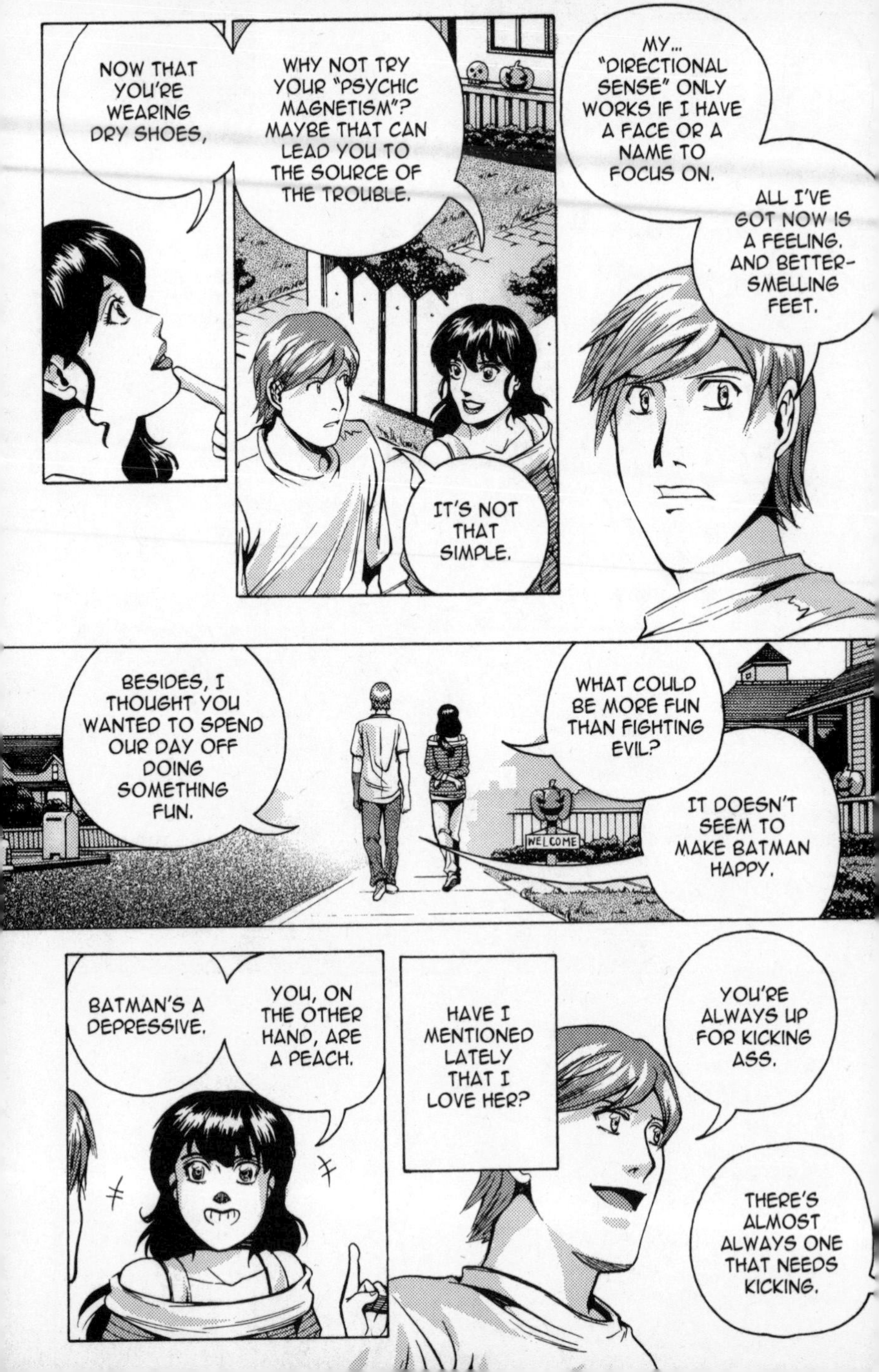
NOW THAT YOU'RE WEARING DRY SHOES,
WHY NOT TRY YOUR "PSYCHIC MAGNETISM"? MAYBE THAT CAN LEAD YOU TO THE SOURCE OF THE TROUBLE.
IT'S NOT THAT SIMPLE.
MY... "DIRECTIONAL SENSE" ONLY WORKS IF I HAVE A FACE OR A NAME TO FOCUS ON.
ALL I'VE GOT NOW IS A FEELING. AND BETTER-SMELLING FEET.
BESIDES, I THOUGHT YOU WANTED TO SPEND OUR DAY OFF DOING SOMETHING FUN.
WELCOME
WHAT COULD BE MORE FUN THAN FIGHTING EVIL?
IT DOESN'T SEEM TO MAKE BATMAN HAPPY.
BATMAN'S A DEPRESSIVE.
YOU, ON THE OTHER HAND, ARE A PEACH.
HAVE I MENTIONED LATELY THAT I LOVE HER?
YOU'RE ALWAYS UP FOR KICKING ASS.
THERE'S ALMOST ALWAYS ONE THAT NEEDS KICKING.

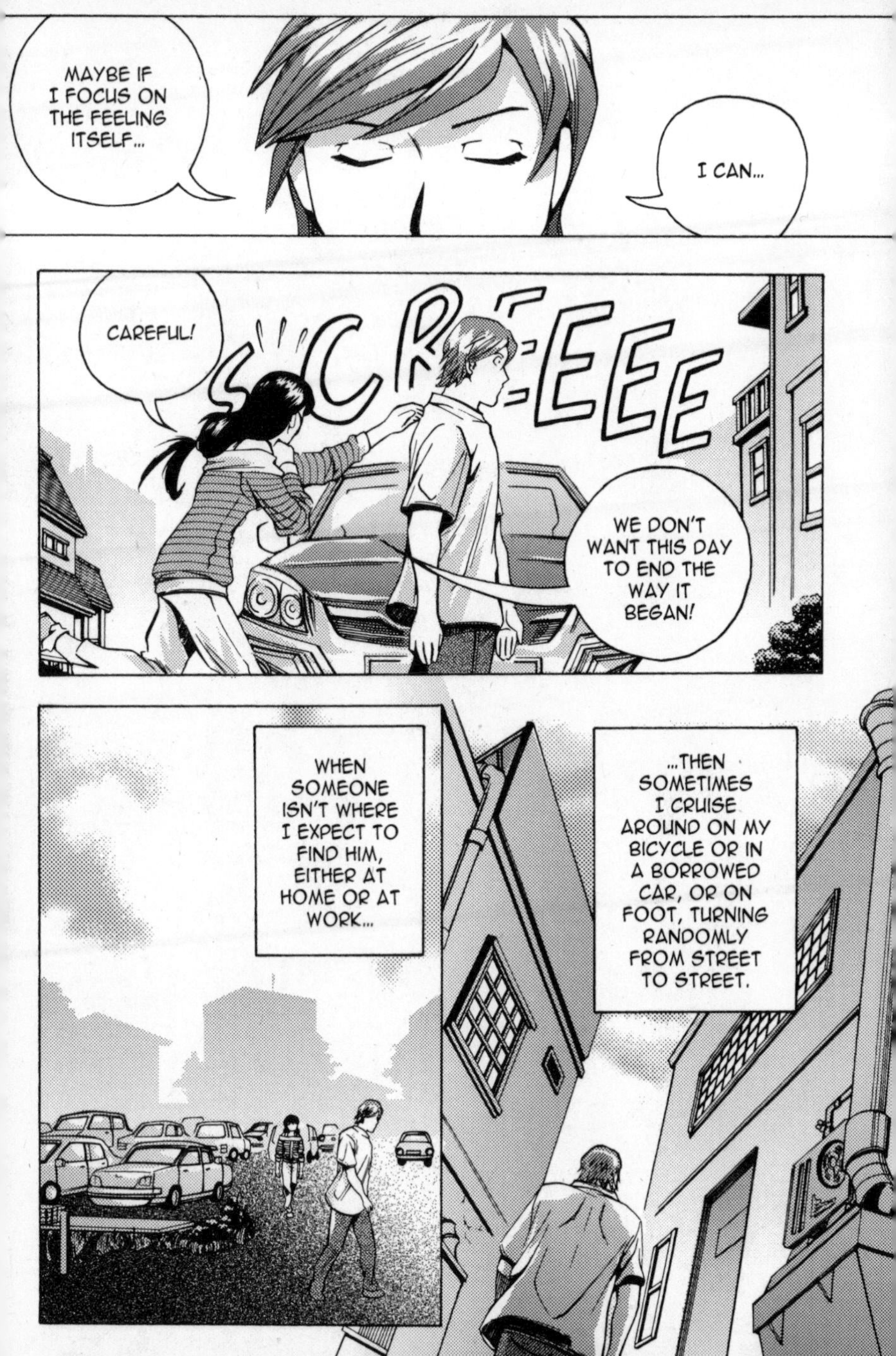
MAYBE IF I FOCUS ON THE FEELING ITSELF...
I CAN...
CAREFUL!
SCREEEE
WE DON'T WANT THIS DAY TO END THE WAY IT BEGAN!
WHEN SOMEONE ISN'T WHERE I EXPECT TO FIND HIM, EITHER AT HOME OR AT WORK...
...THEN SOMETIMES I CRUISE AROUND ON MY BICYCLE OR IN A BORROWED CAR, OR ON FOOT, TURNING RANDOMLY FROM STREET TO STREET.

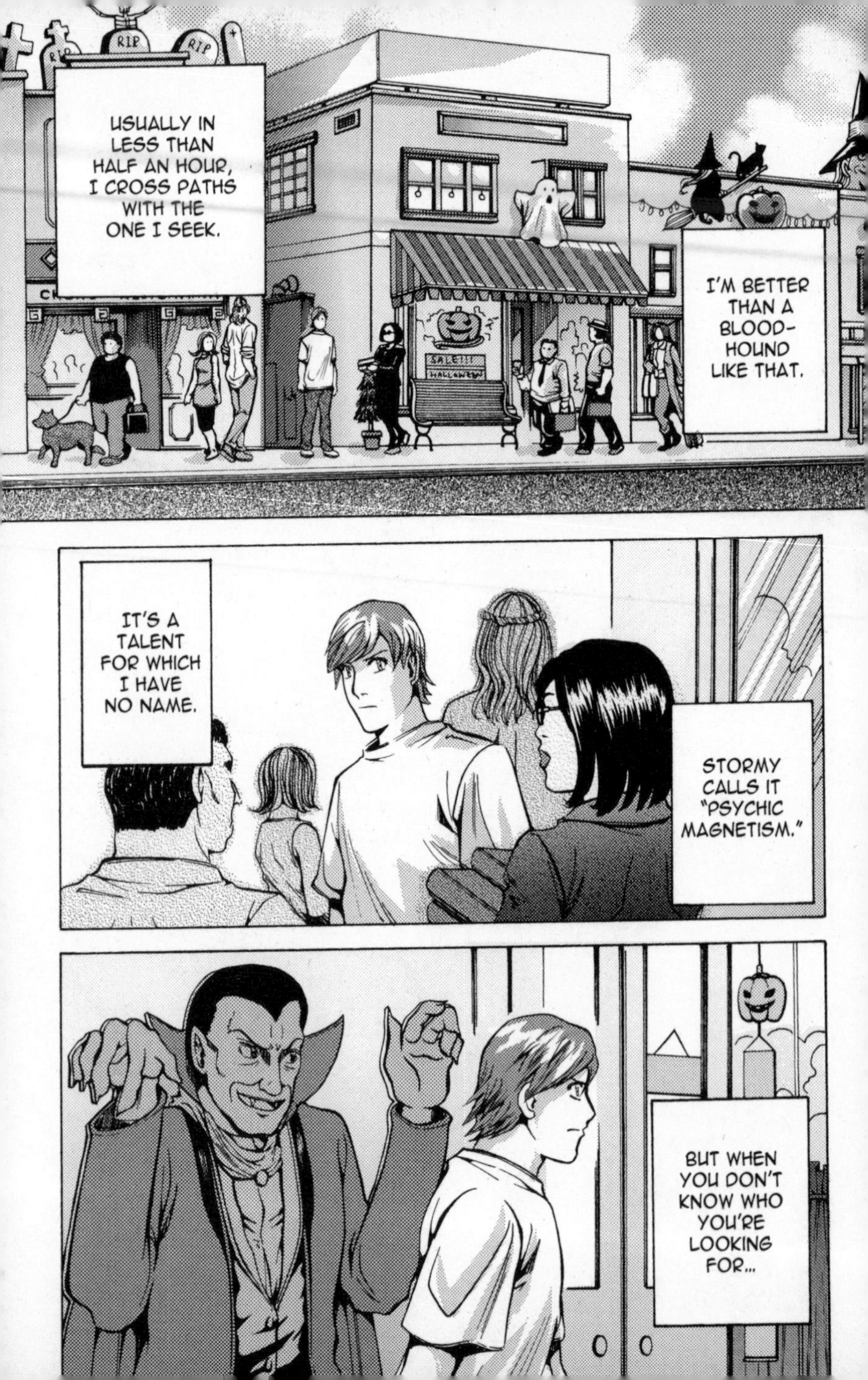
USUALLY IN LESS THAN HALF AN HOUR, I CROSS PATHS WITH THE ONE I SEEK.
I'M BETTER THAN A BLOOD-HOUND LIKE THAT.
IT'S A TALENT FOR WHICH I HAVE NO NAME.
STORMY CALLS IT "PSYCHIC MAGNETISM."
BUT WHEN YOU DON'T KNOW WHO YOU'RE LOOKING FOR...

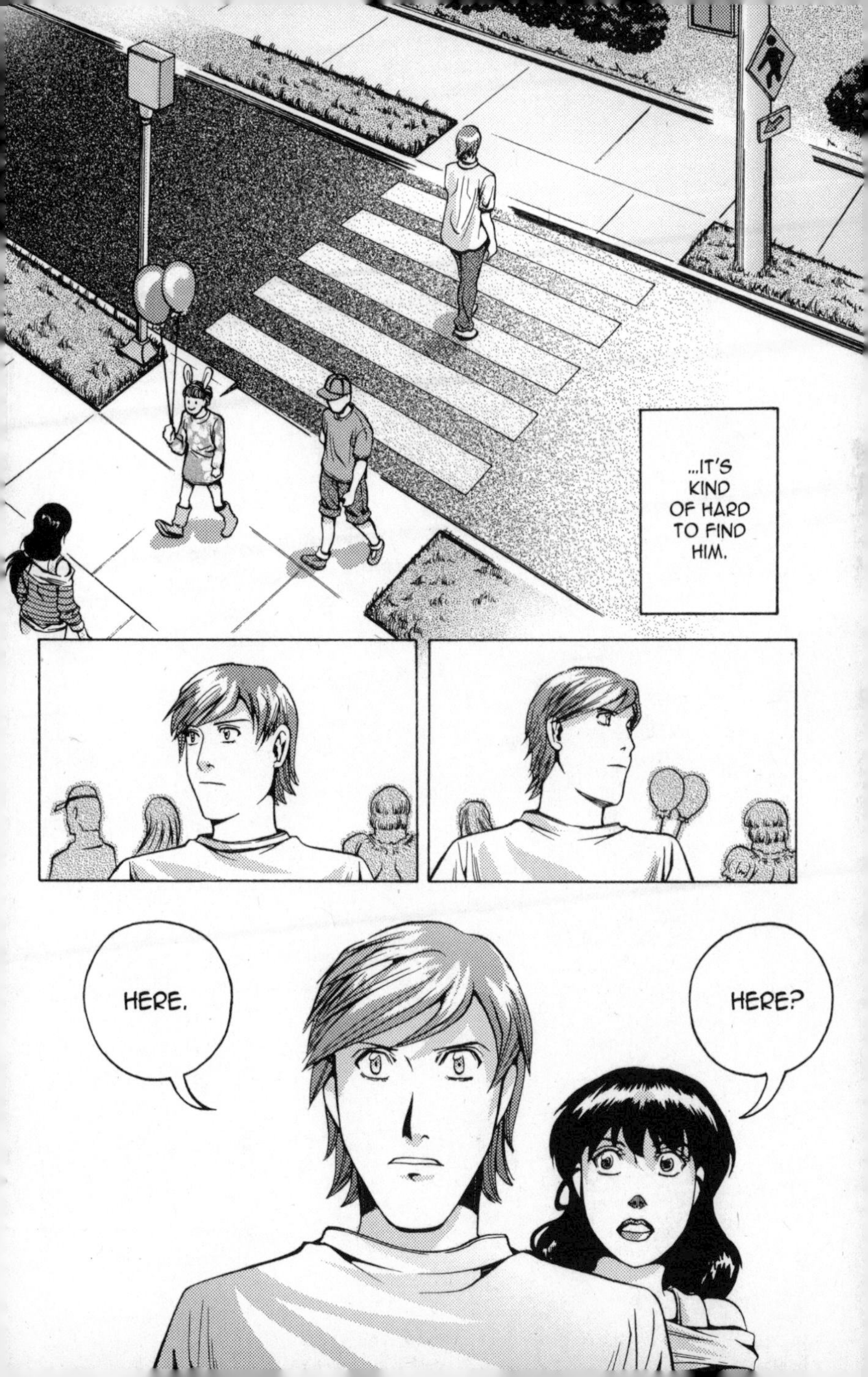
...IT'S KIND OF HARD TO FIND HIM.
HERE.
HERE?

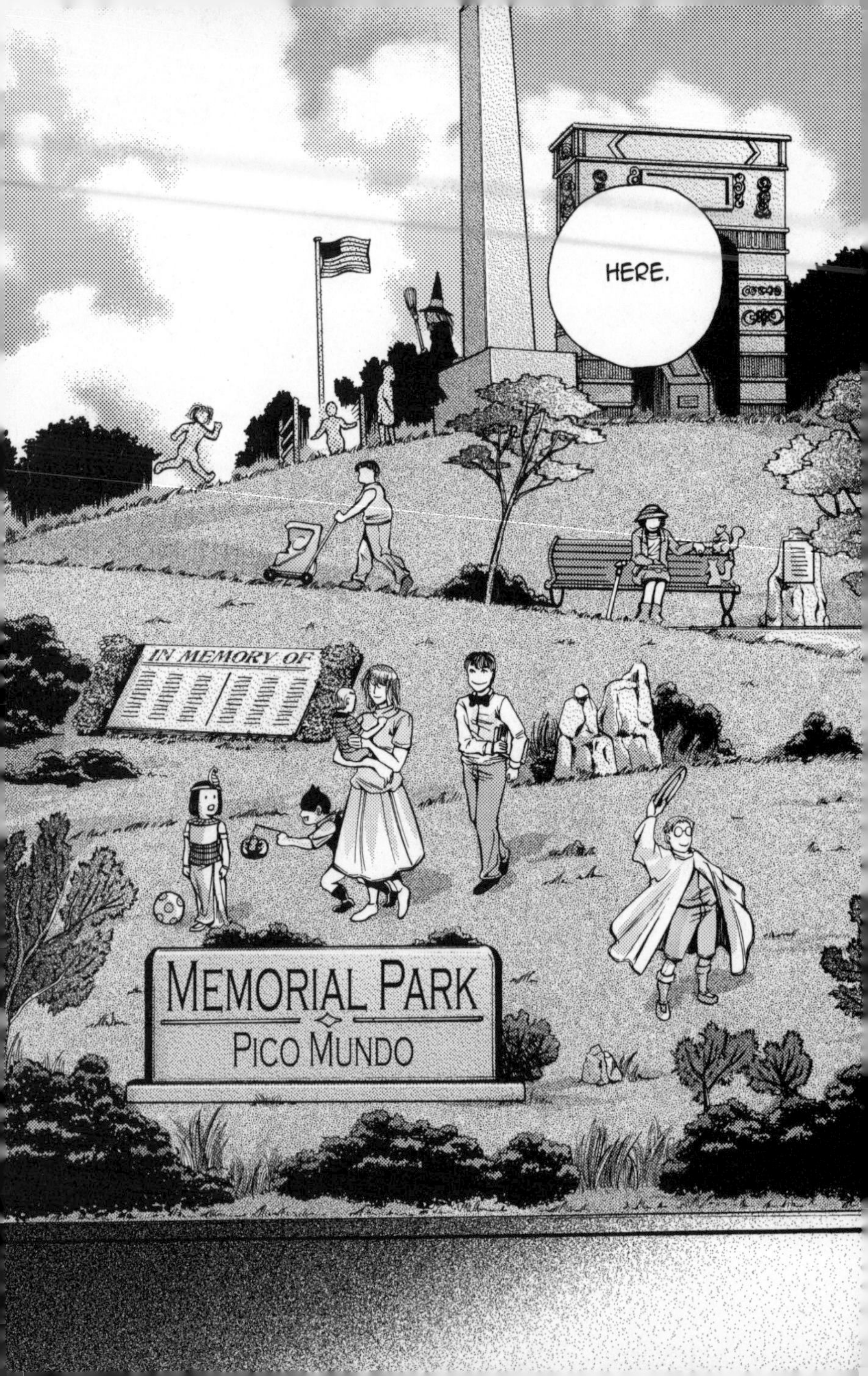
HERE.
IN MEMORY OF
MEMORIAL PARK
PICO MUNDO

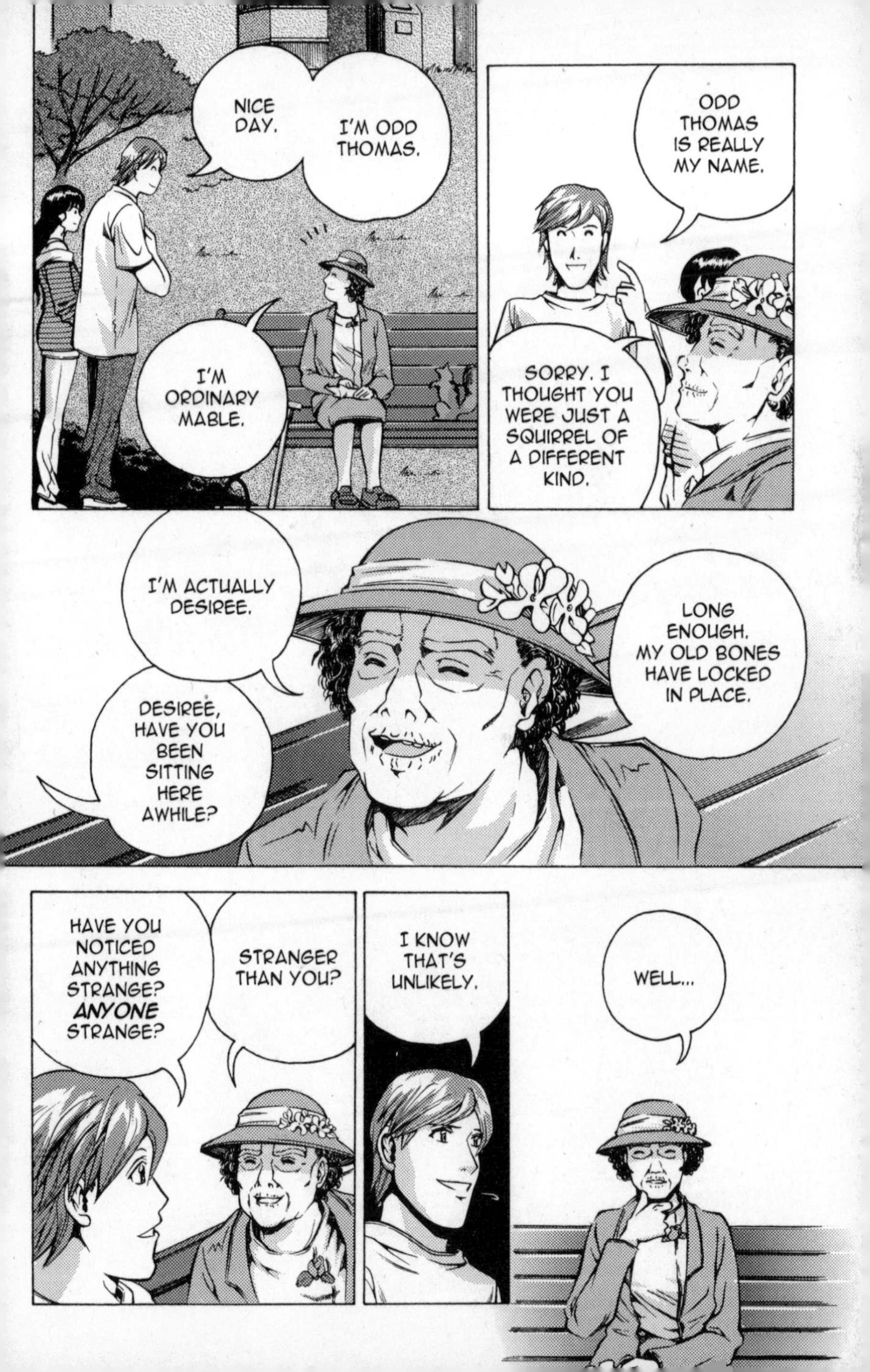
NICE DAY.
I'M ODD THOMAS.
I'M ORDINARY MABLE.
ODD THOMAS IS REALLY MY NAME.
SORRY. I THOUGHT YOU WERE JUST A SQUIRREL OF A DIFFERENT KIND.
I'M ACTUALLY DESIREE.
DESIREE, HAVE YOU BEEN SITTING HERE AWHILE?
LONG ENOUGH. MY OLD BONES HAVE LOCKED IN PLACE.
HAVE YOU NOTICED ANYTHING STRANGE? *ANYONE* STRANGE?
STRANGER THAN YOU?
I KNOW THAT'S UNLIKELY.
WELL...

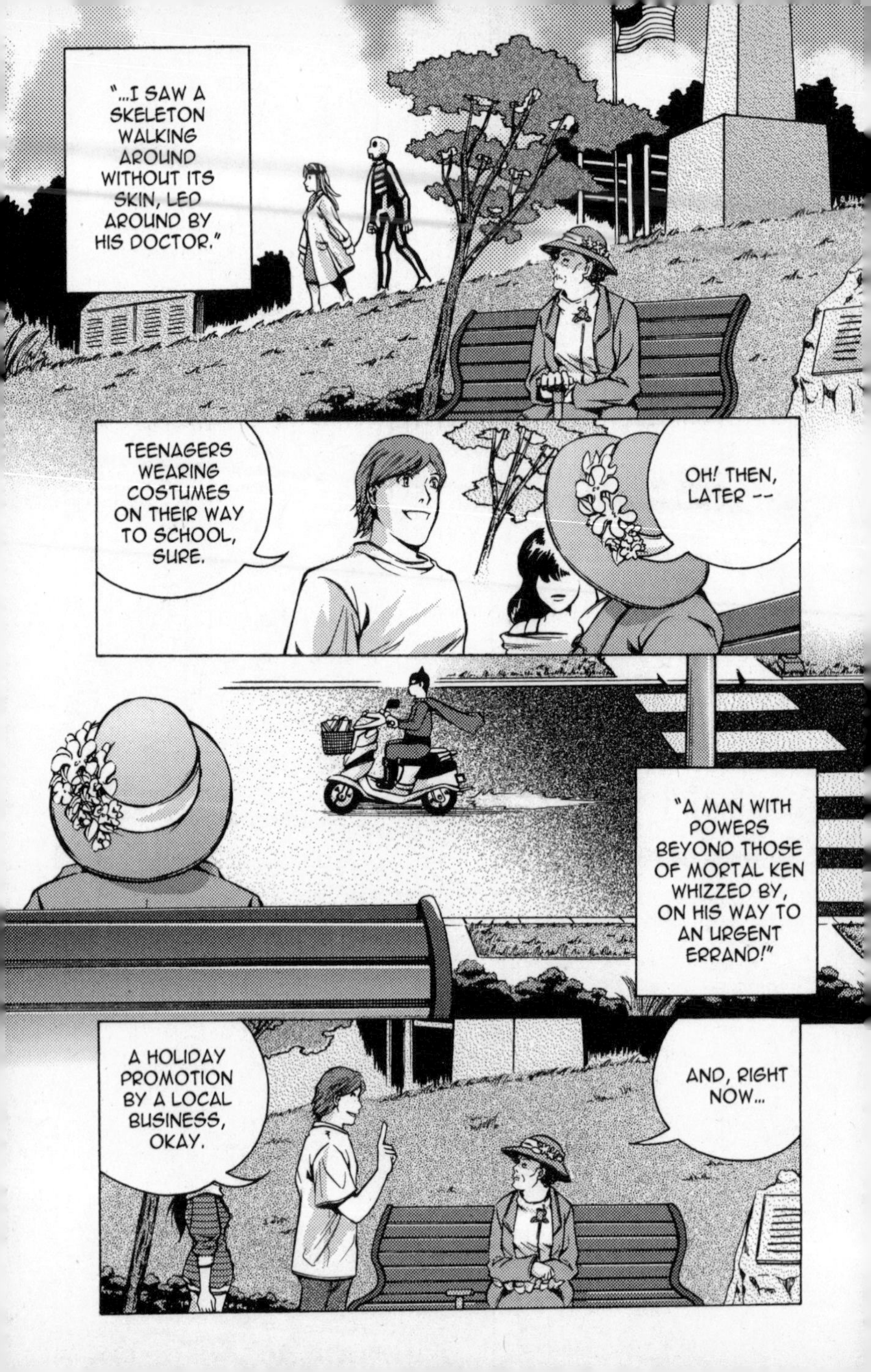
"...I SAW A SKELETON WALKING AROUND WITHOUT ITS SKIN, LED AROUND BY HIS DOCTOR."
TEENAGERS WEARING COSTUMES ON THEIR WAY TO SCHOOL, SURE.
OH! THEN, LATER --
"A MAN WITH POWERS BEYOND THOSE OF MORTAL KEN WHIZZED BY, ON HIS WAY TO AN URGENT ERRAND!"
A HOLIDAY PROMOTION BY A LOCAL BUSINESS, OKAY.
AND, RIGHT NOW...

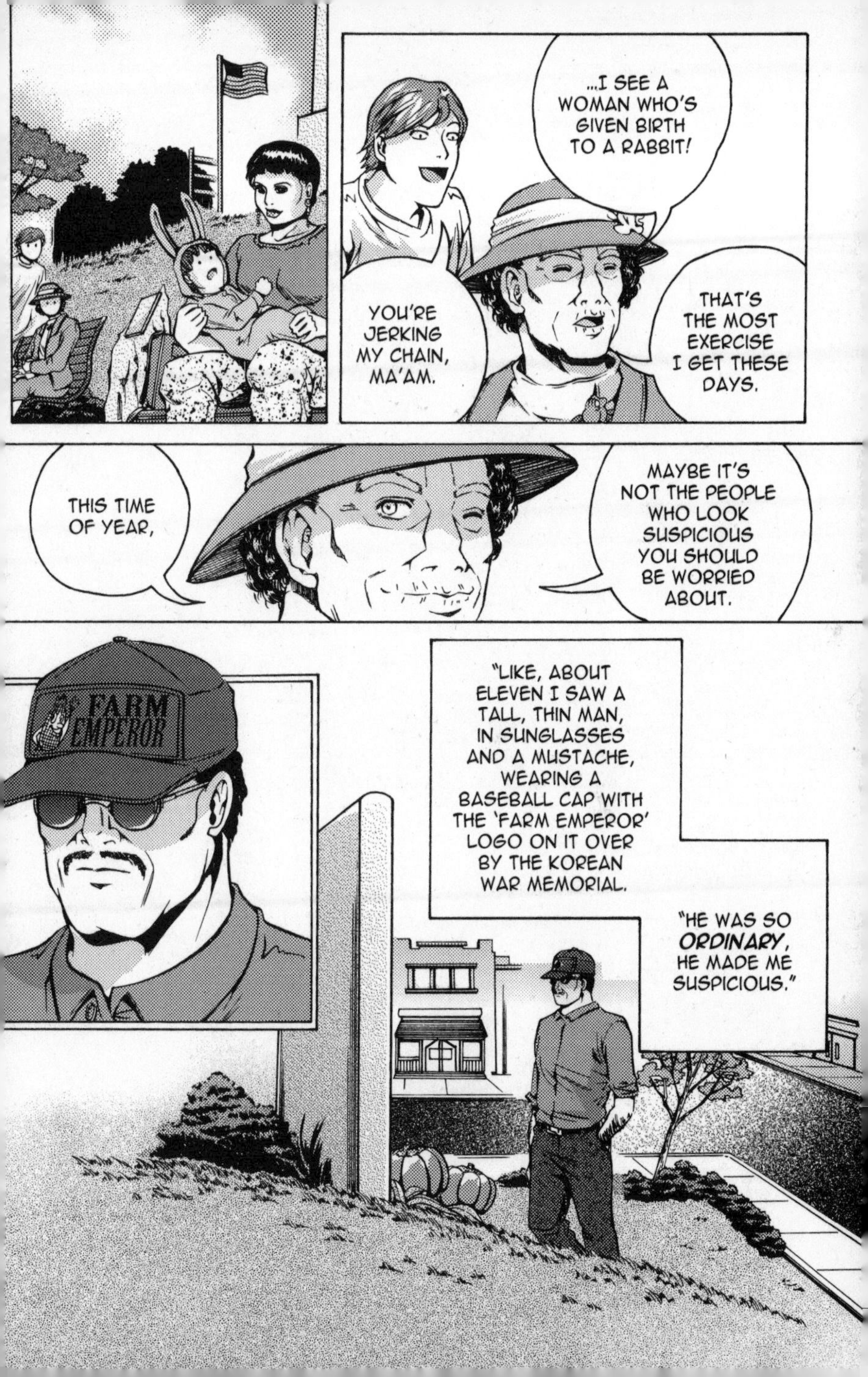
...I SEE A WOMAN WHO'S GIVEN BIRTH TO A RABBIT!
YOU'RE JERKING MY CHAIN, MA'AM.
THAT'S THE MOST EXERCISE I GET THESE DAYS.
THIS TIME OF YEAR,
MAYBE IT'S NOT THE PEOPLE WHO LOOK SUSPICIOUS YOU SHOULD BE WORRIED ABOUT.
FARM EMPEROR
"LIKE, ABOUT ELEVEN I SAW A TALL, THIN MAN, IN SUNGLASSES AND A MUSTACHE, WEARING A BASEBALL CAP WITH THE 'FARM EMPEROR' LOGO ON IT OVER BY THE KOREAN WAR MEMORIAL.
"HE WAS SO ORDINARY, HE MADE ME SUSPICIOUS."

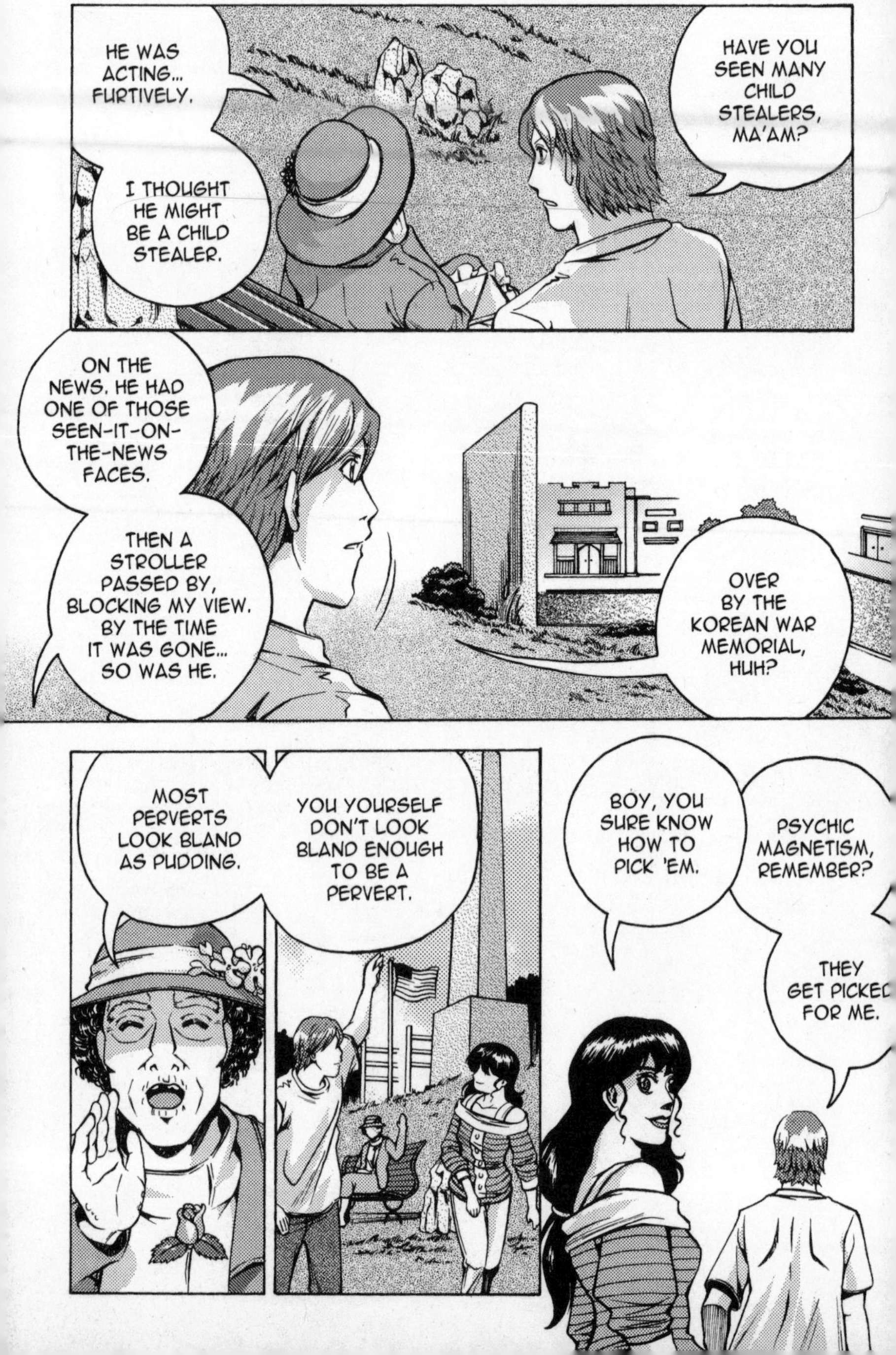
HE WAS ACTING... FURTIVELY.
I THOUGHT HE MIGHT BE A CHILD STEALER.
HAVE YOU SEEN MANY CHILD STEALERS, MA'AM?
ON THE NEWS. HE HAD ONE OF THOSE SEEN-IT-ON-THE-NEWS FACES.
THEN A STROLLER PASSED BY, BLOCKING MY VIEW. BY THE TIME IT WAS GONE... SO WAS HE.
OVER BY THE KOREAN WAR MEMORIAL, HUH?
MOST PERVERTS LOOK BLAND AS PUDDING.
YOU YOURSELF DON'T LOOK BLAND ENOUGH TO BE A PERVERT.
BOY, YOU SURE KNOW HOW TO PICK 'EM.
PSYCHIC MAGNETISM, REMEMBER?
THEY GET PICKED FOR ME.

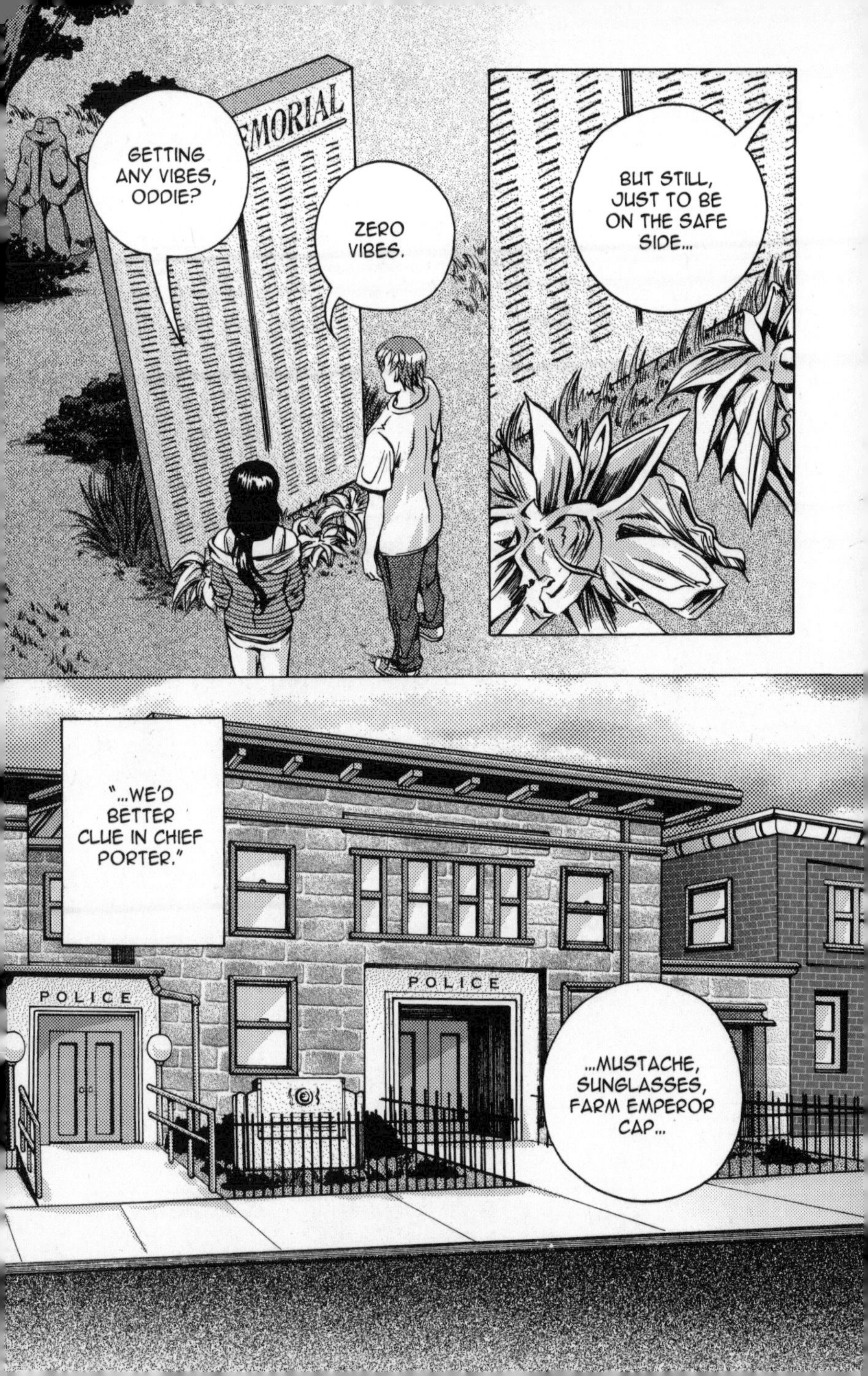

EMORIAL
GETTING ANY VIBES, ODDIE?
ZERO VIBES.
BUT STILL, JUST TO BE ON THE SAFE SIDE...
"...WE'D BETTER CLUE IN CHIEF PORTER."
POLICE
POLICE
...MUSTACHE, SUNGLASSES, FARM EMPEROR CAP...

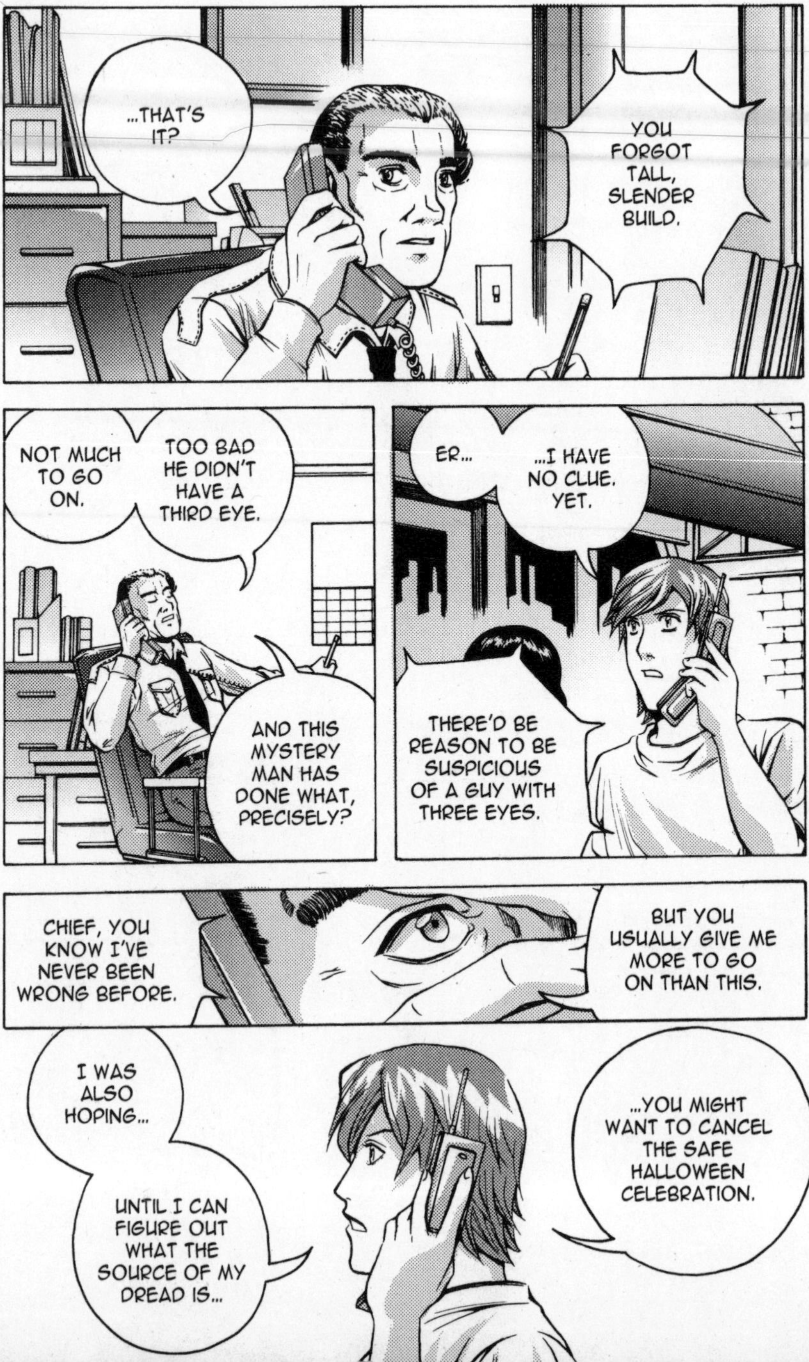
...THAT'S IT?
YOU FORGOT TALL, SLENDER BUILD.
NOT MUCH TO GO ON.
TOO BAD HE DIDN'T HAVE A THIRD EYE.
AND THIS MYSTERY MAN HAS DONE WHAT, PRECISELY?
ER...
...I HAVE NO CLUE. YET.
THERE'D BE REASON TO BE SUSPICIOUS OF A GUY WITH THREE EYES.
CHIEF, YOU KNOW I'VE NEVER BEEN WRONG BEFORE.
BUT YOU USUALLY GIVE ME MORE TO GO ON THAN THIS.
I WAS ALSO HOPING...
UNTIL I CAN FIGURE OUT WHAT THE SOURCE OF MY DREAD IS...
...YOU MIGHT WANT TO CANCEL THE SAFE HALLOWEEN CELEBRATION.

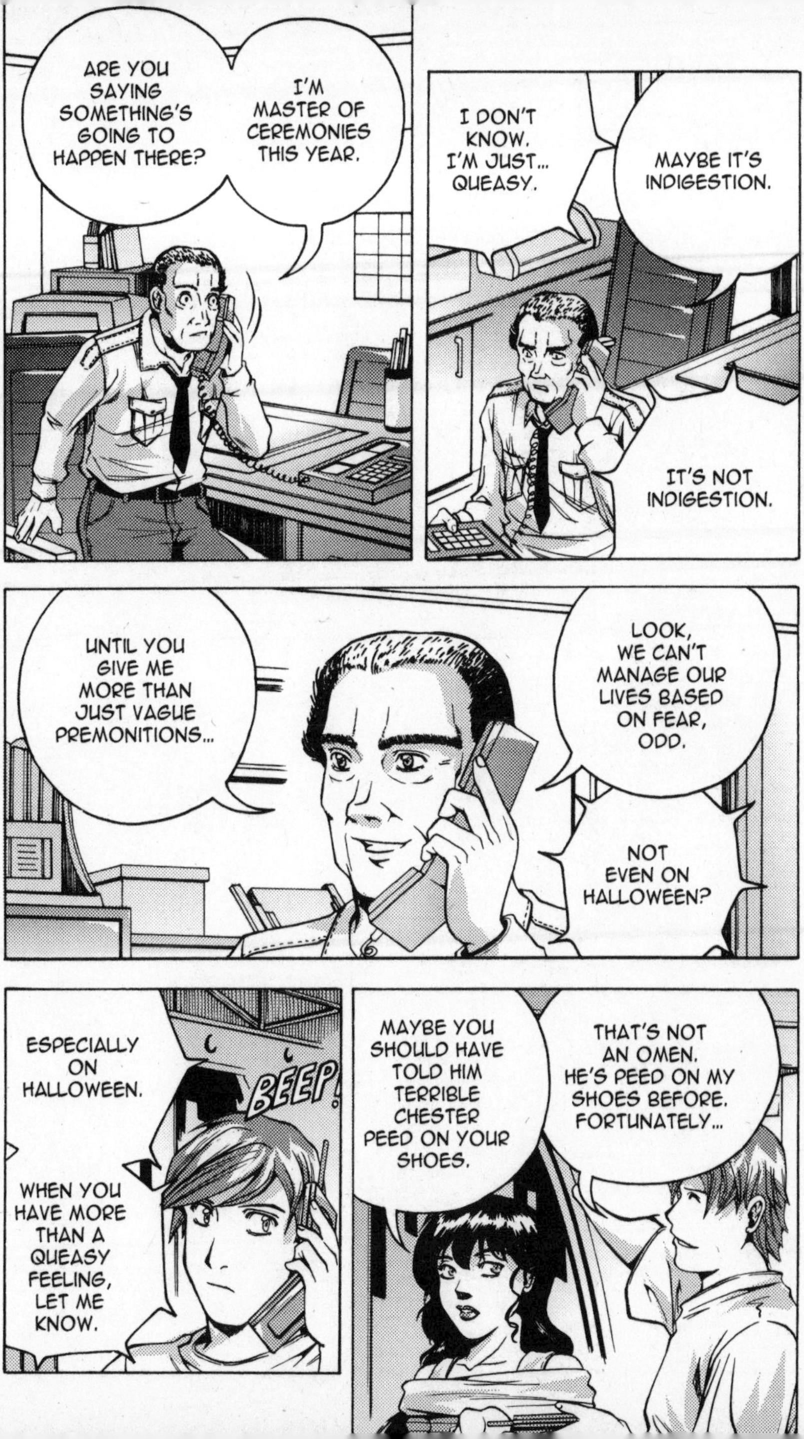
ARE YOU SAYING SOMETHING'S GOING TO HAPPEN THERE?
I'M MASTER OF CEREMONIES THIS YEAR.
I DON'T KNOW. I'M JUST... QUEASY.
MAYBE IT'S INDIGESTION.
IT'S NOT INDIGESTION.
UNTIL YOU GIVE ME MORE THAN JUST VAGUE PREMONITIONS...
LOOK, WE CAN'T MANAGE OUR LIVES BASED ON FEAR, ODD.
NOT EVEN ON HALLOWEEN?
ESPECIALLY ON HALLOWEEN.
BEEP!
WHEN YOU HAVE MORE THAN A QUEASY FEELING, LET ME KNOW.
MAYBE YOU SHOULD HAVE TOLD HIM TERRIBLE CHESTER PEED ON YOUR SHOES.
THAT'S NOT AN OMEN. HE'S PEED ON MY SHOES BEFORE. FORTUNATELY...

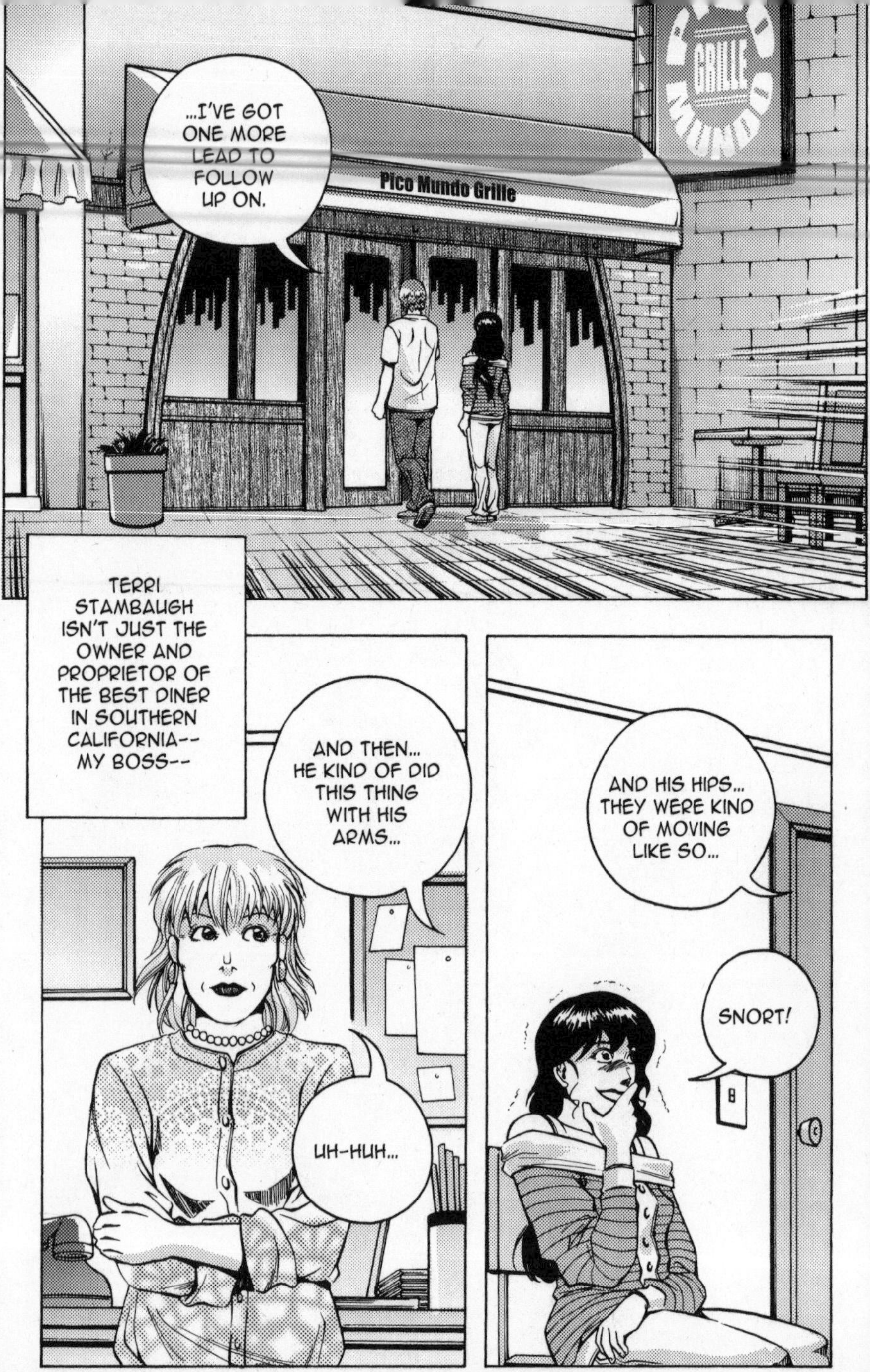
GRILLE
PICO MUNDO
...I'VE GOT ONE MORE LEAD TO FOLLOW UP ON.
Pico Mundo Grille
TERRI STAMBAUGH ISN'T JUST THE OWNER AND PROPRIETOR OF THE BEST DINER IN SOUTHERN CALIFORNIA-- MY BOSS--
AND THEN... HE KIND OF DID THIS THING WITH HIS ARMS...
UH-HUH...
AND HIS HIPS... THEY WERE KIND OF MOVING LIKE SO...
SNORT!

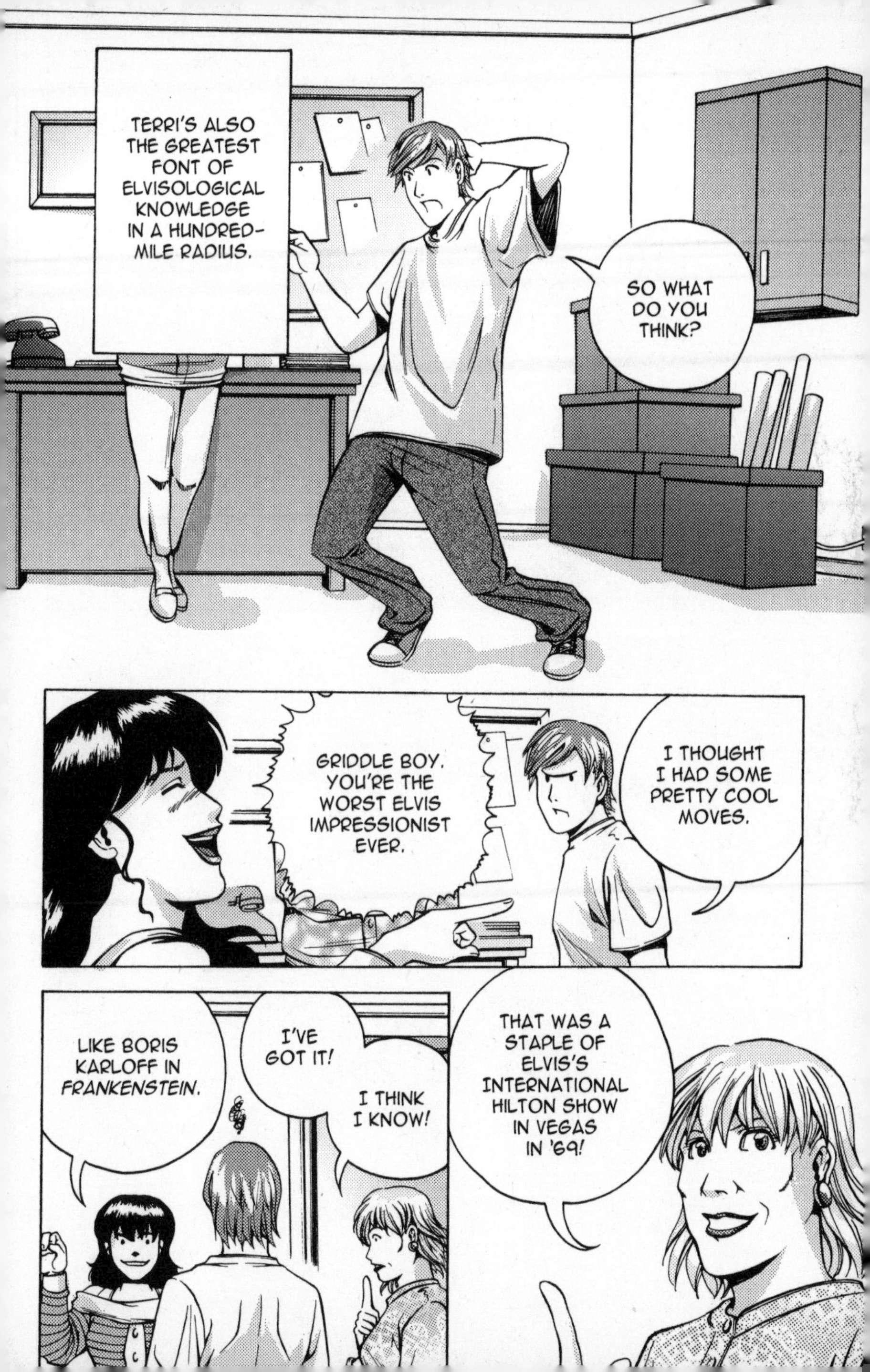
TERRI'S ALSO THE GREATEST FONT OF ELVISOLOGICAL KNOWLEDGE IN A HUNDRED-MILE RADIUS.
SO WHAT DO YOU THINK?
GRIDDLE BOY. YOU'RE THE WORST ELVIS IMPRESSIONIST EVER.
I THOUGHT I HAD SOME PRETTY COOL MOVES.
LIKE BORIS KARLOFF IN FRANKENSTEIN.
I'VE GOT IT!
I THINK I KNOW!
THAT WAS A STAPLE OF ELVIS'S INTERNATIONAL HILTON SHOW IN VEGAS IN '69!

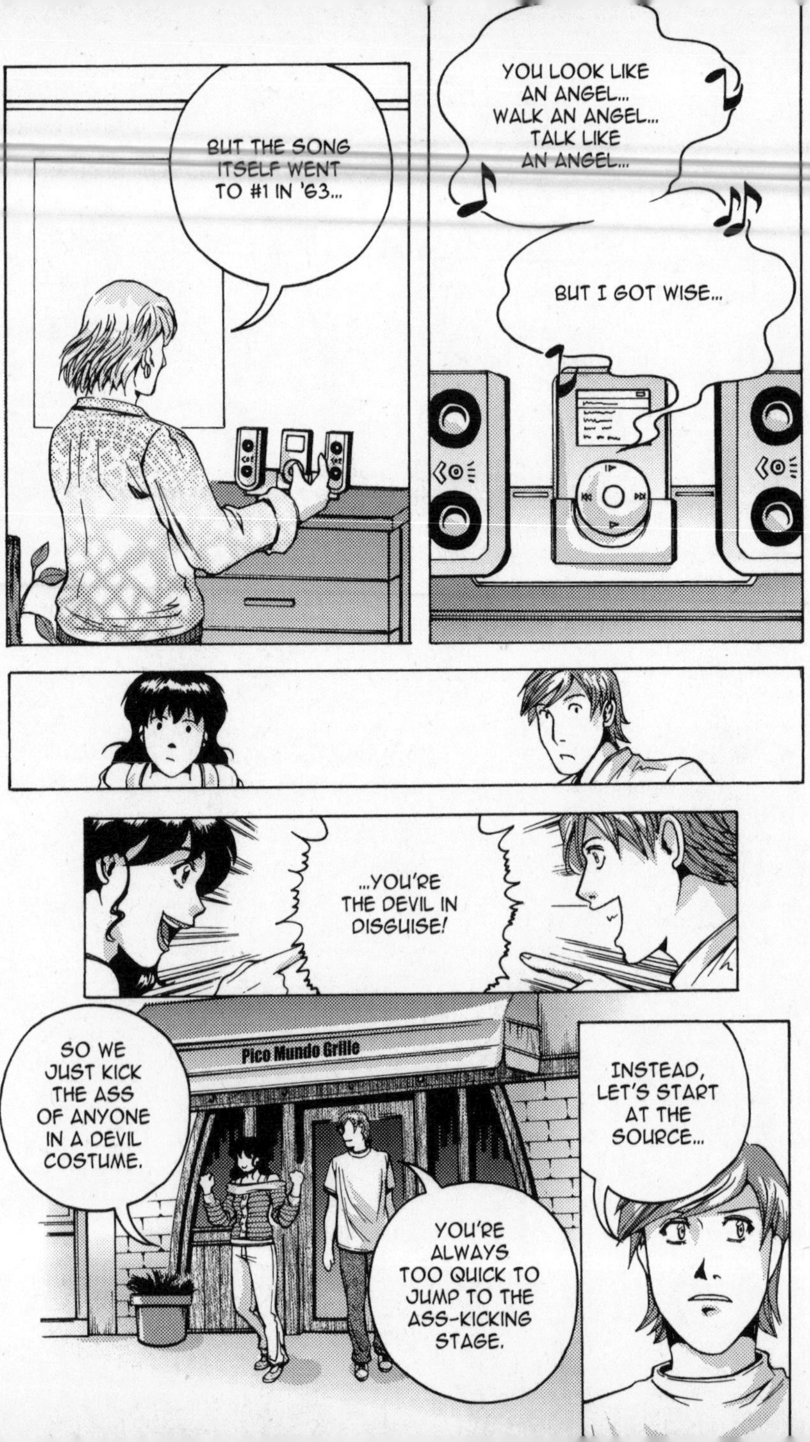
BUT THE SONG ITSELF WENT TO #1 IN '63...
YOU LOOK LIKE AN ANGEL... WALK AN ANGEL... TALK LIKE AN ANGEL...
BUT I GOT WISE...
...YOU'RE THE DEVIL IN DISGUISE!
Pico Mundo Grille
SO WE JUST KICK THE ASS OF ANYONE IN A DEVIL COSTUME.
YOU'RE ALWAYS TOO QUICK TO JUMP TO THE ASS-KICKING STAGE.
INSTEAD, LET'S START AT THE SOURCE...

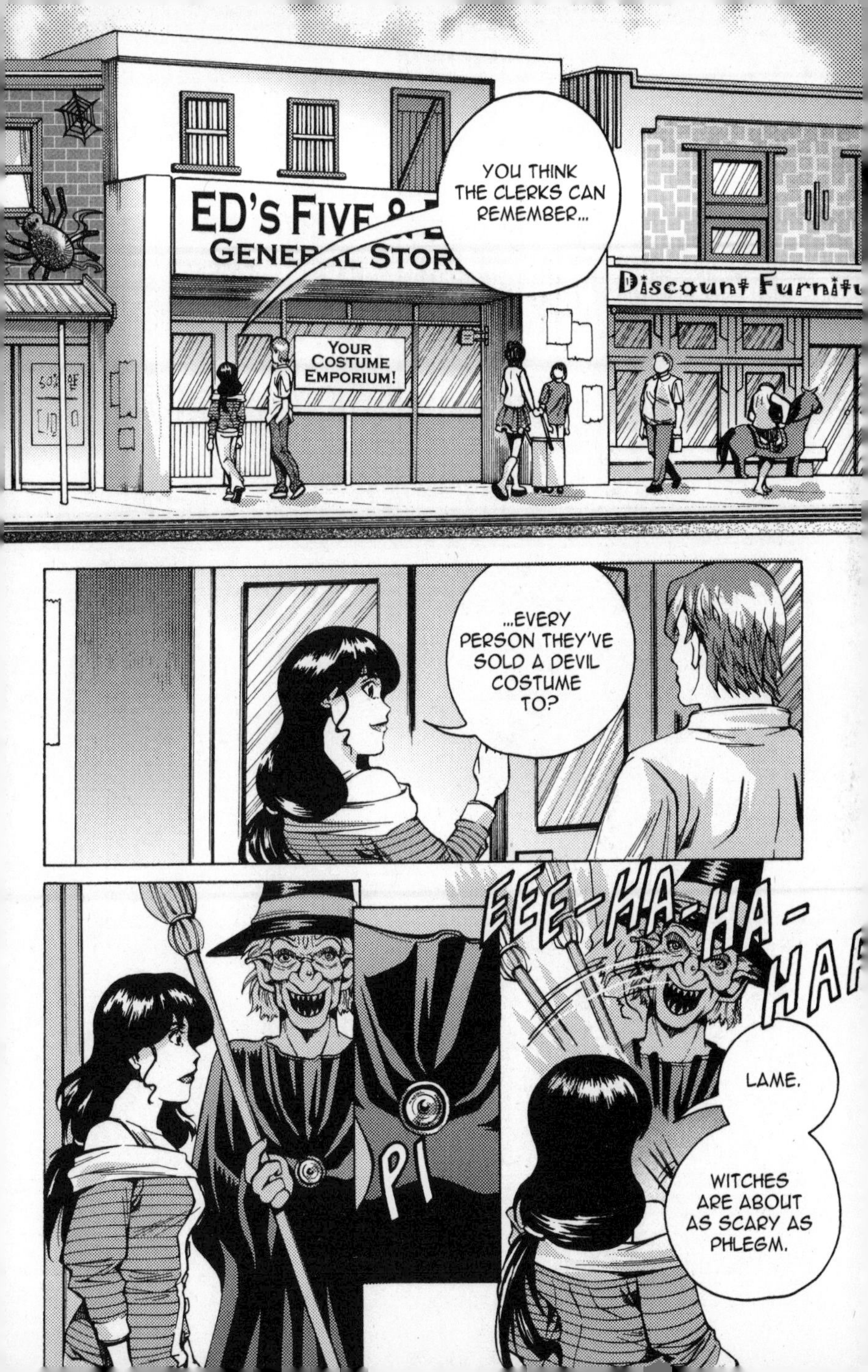

ED's FIVE &
GENERAL STORE
Discount Furnitu
YOUR COSTUME EMPORIUM!
YOU THINK THE CLERKS CAN REMEMBER...
...EVERY PERSON THEY'VE SOLD A DEVIL COSTUME TO?
PI
EEE-HA-HA-HA
LAME.
WITCHES ARE ABOUT AS SCARY AS PHLEGM.

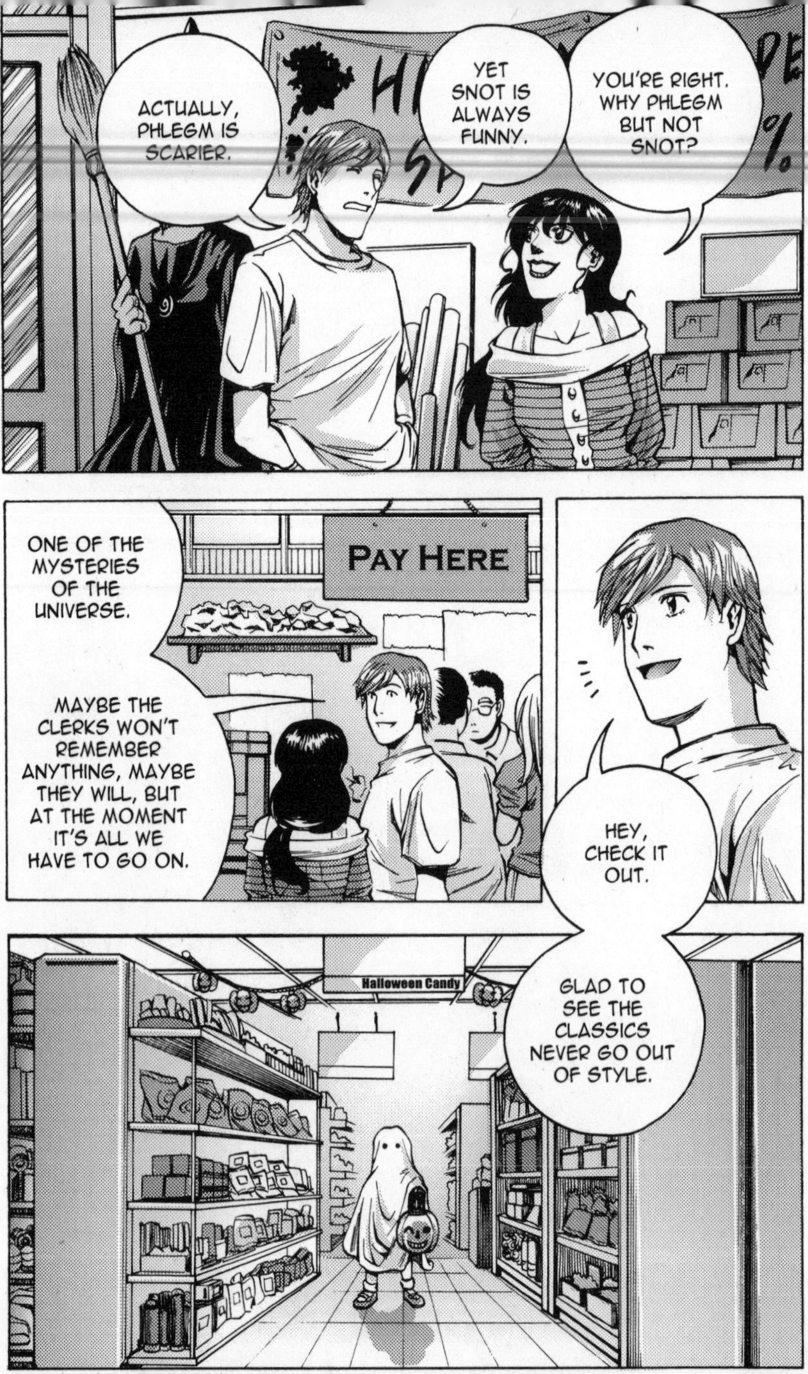
ACTUALLY, PHLEGM IS SCARIER.
YET SNOT IS ALWAYS FUNNY.
YOU'RE RIGHT. WHY PHLEGM BUT NOT SNOT?
PAY HERE
ONE OF THE MYSTERIES OF THE UNIVERSE.
MAYBE THE CLERKS WON'T REMEMBER ANYTHING, MAYBE THEY WILL, BUT AT THE MOMENT IT'S ALL WE HAVE TO GO ON.
HEY, CHECK IT OUT.
GLAD TO SEE THE CLASSICS NEVER GO OUT OF STYLE.
Halloween Candy

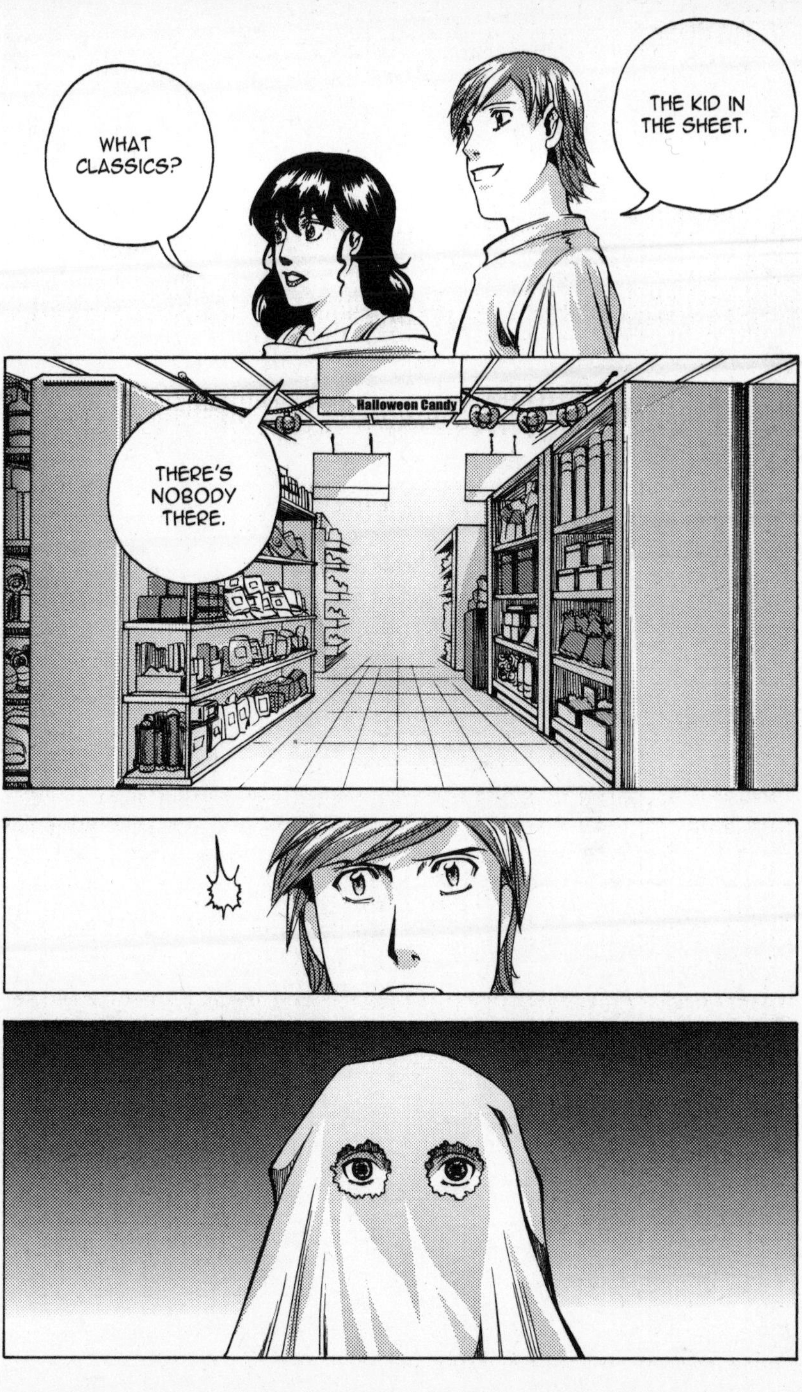
WHAT CLASSICS?
THE KID IN THE SHEET.
Halloween Candy
THERE'S NOBODY THERE.

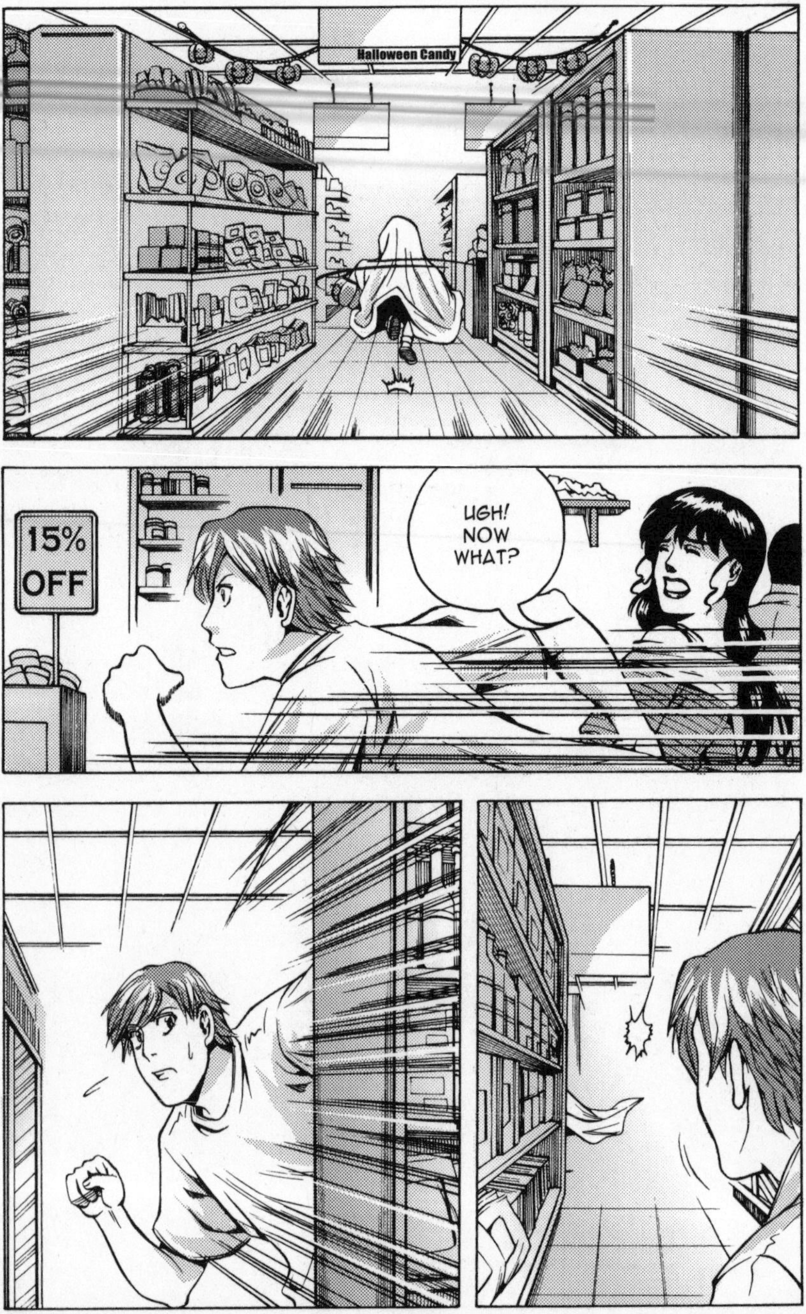
Halloween Candy
15% OFF
UGH! NOW WHAT?

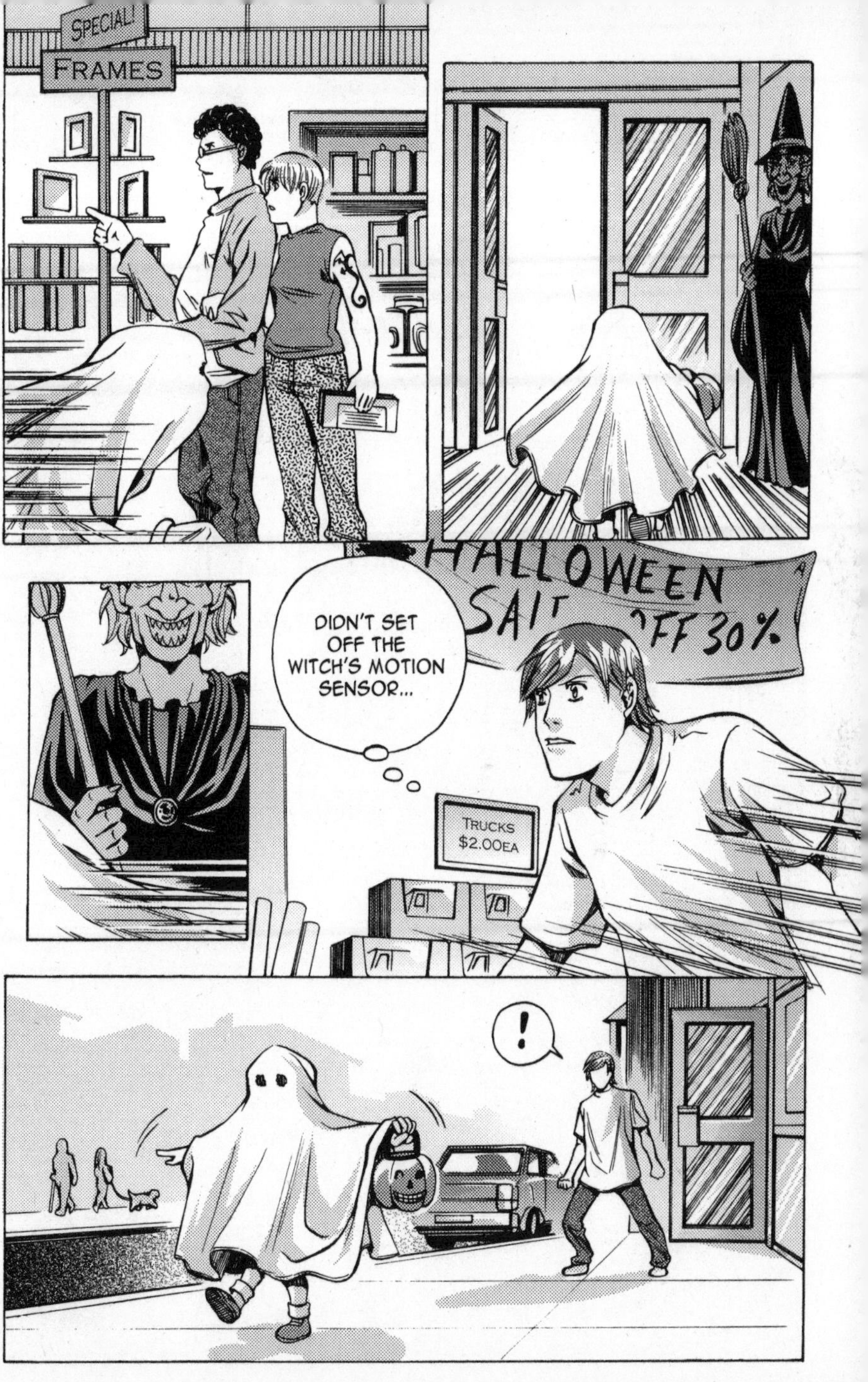
SPECIAL!
FRAMES
HALLOWEEN
SAL
FF 30%
DIDN'T SET OFF THE WITCH'S MOTION SENSOR...
TRUCKS
$2.00EA
!

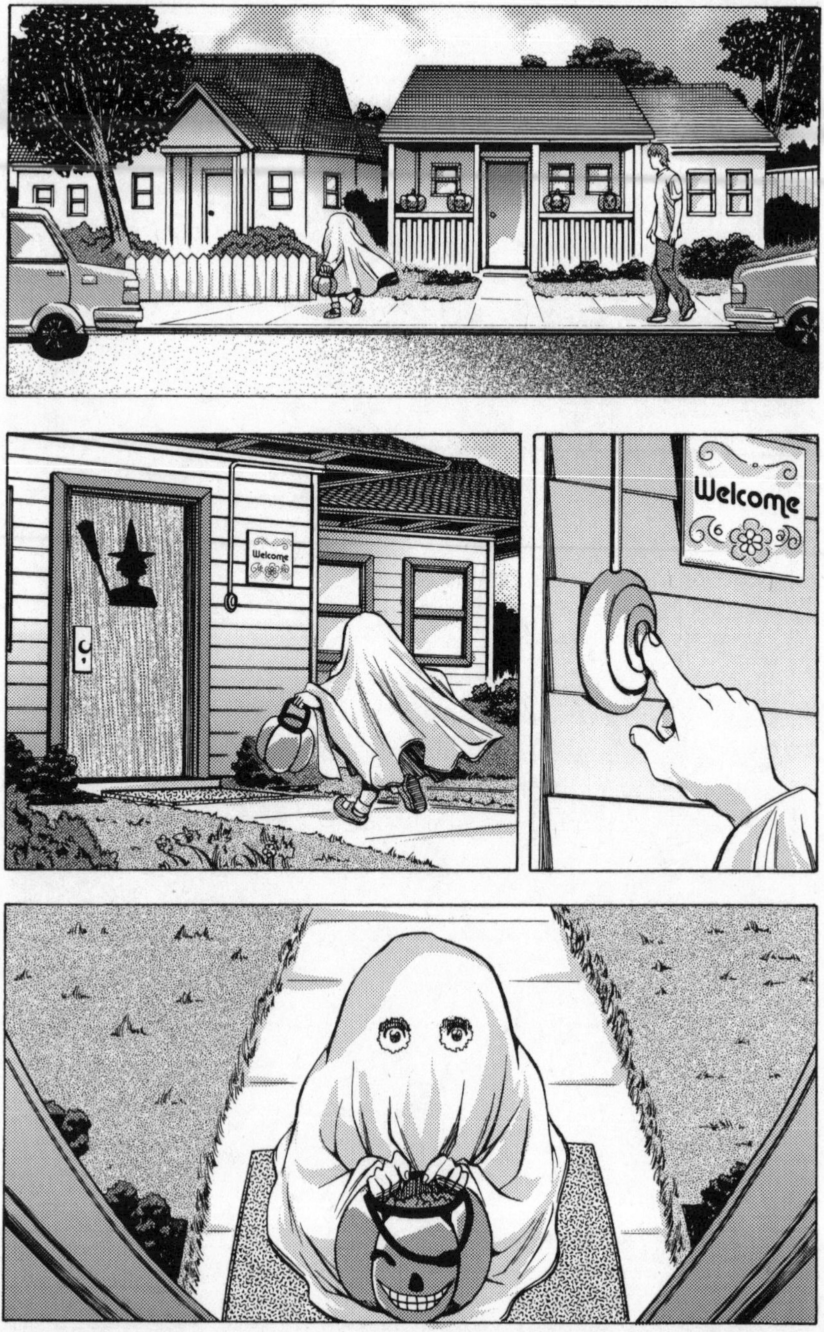
Welcome
Welcome

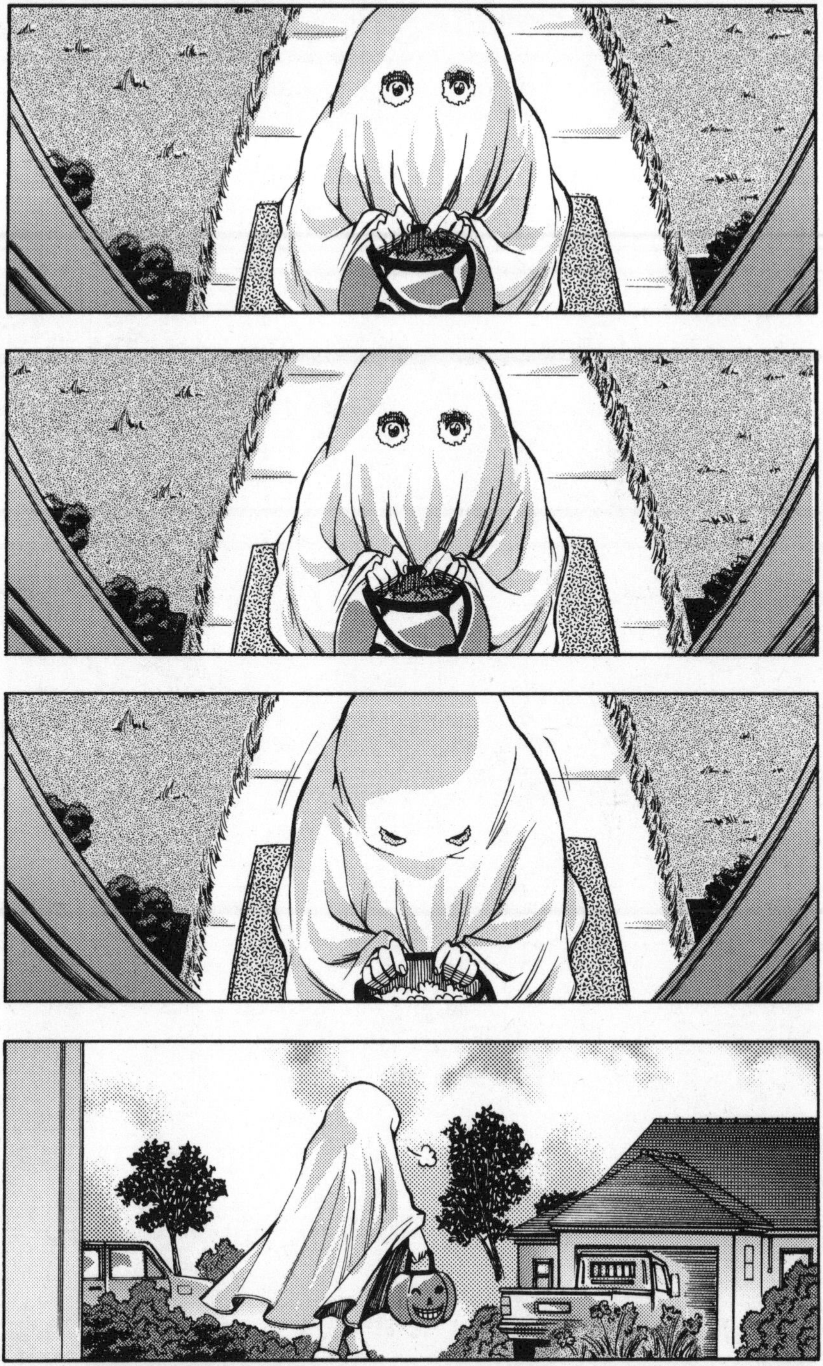

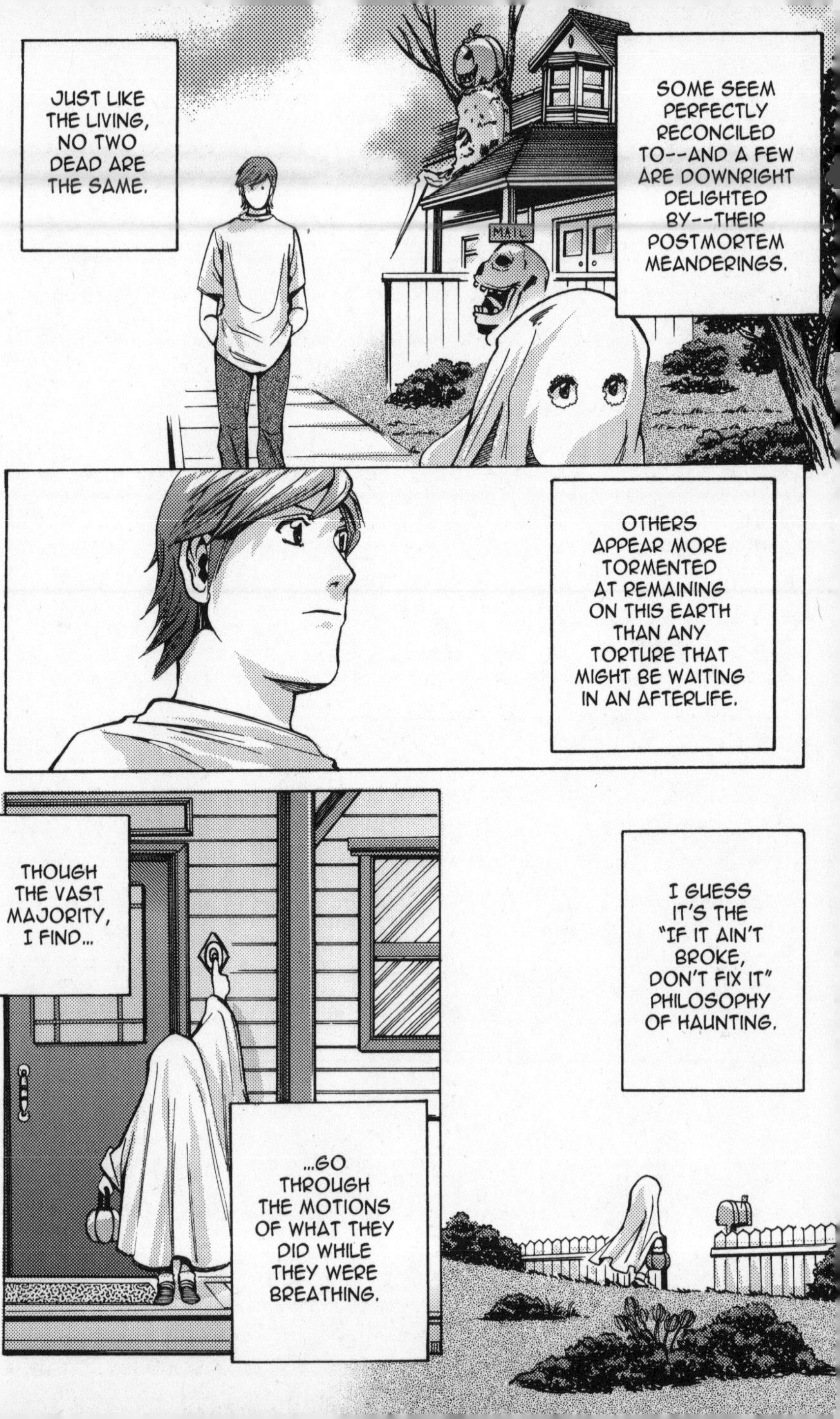
JUST LIKE THE LIVING, NO TWO DEAD ARE THE SAME.
SOME SEEM PERFECTLY RECONCILED TO--AND A FEW ARE DOWNRIGHT DELIGHTED BY--THEIR POSTMORTEM MEANDERINGS.
MAIL
OTHERS APPEAR MORE TORMENTED AT REMAINING ON THIS EARTH THAN ANY TORTURE THAT MIGHT BE WAITING IN AN AFTERLIFE.
THOUGH THE VAST MAJORITY, I FIND...
...GO THROUGH THE MOTIONS OF WHAT THEY DID WHILE THEY WERE BREATHING.
I GUESS IT'S THE "IF IT AIN'T BROKE, DON'T FIX IT" PHILOSOPHY OF HAUNTING.

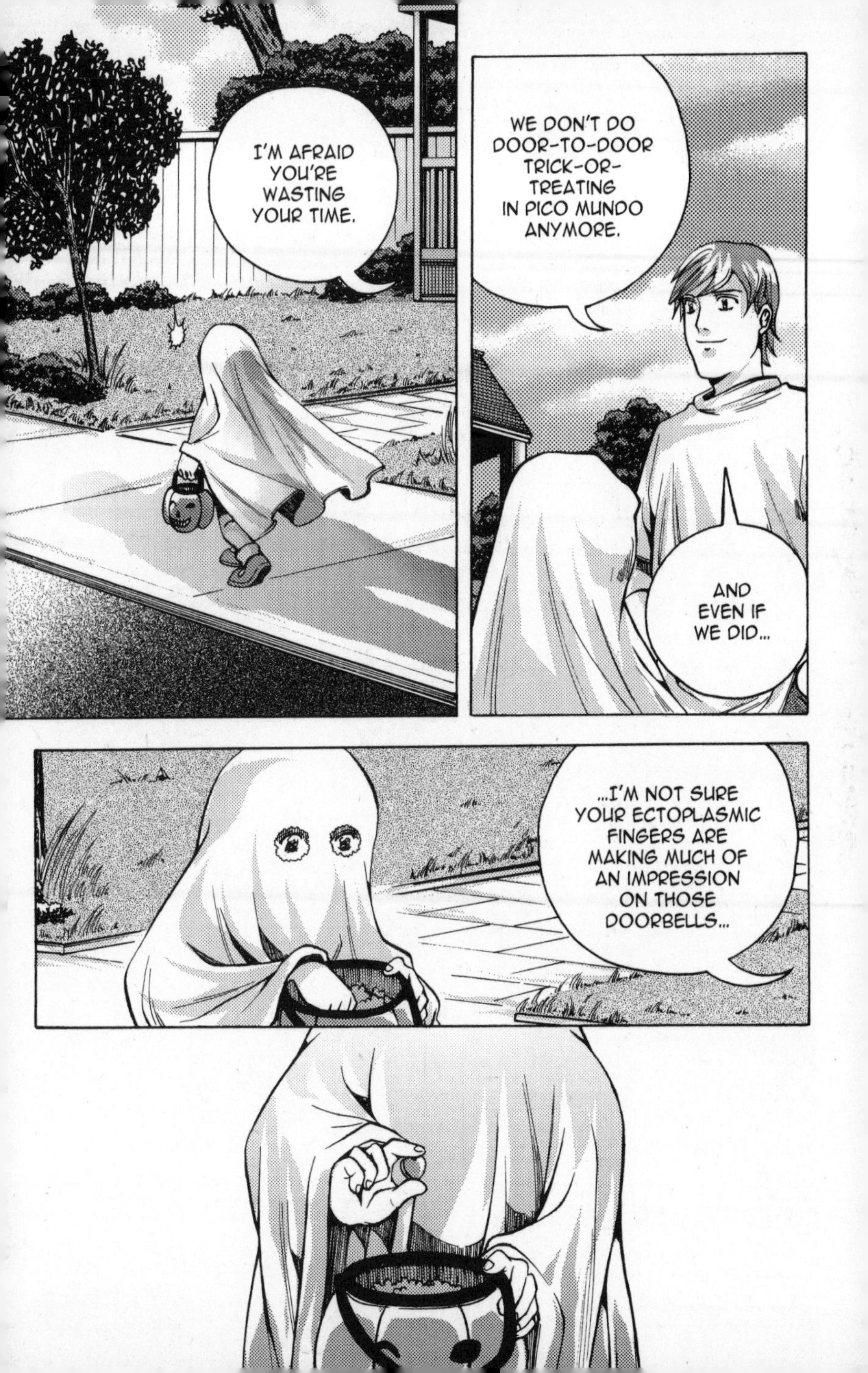
I'M AFRAID YOU'RE WASTING YOUR TIME.
WE DON'T DO DOOR-TO-DOOR TRICK-OR-TREATING IN PICO MUNDO ANYMORE.
AND EVEN IF WE DID...
...I'M NOT SURE YOUR ECTOPLASMIC FINGERS ARE MAKING MUCH OF AN IMPRESSION ON THOSE DOORBELLS...

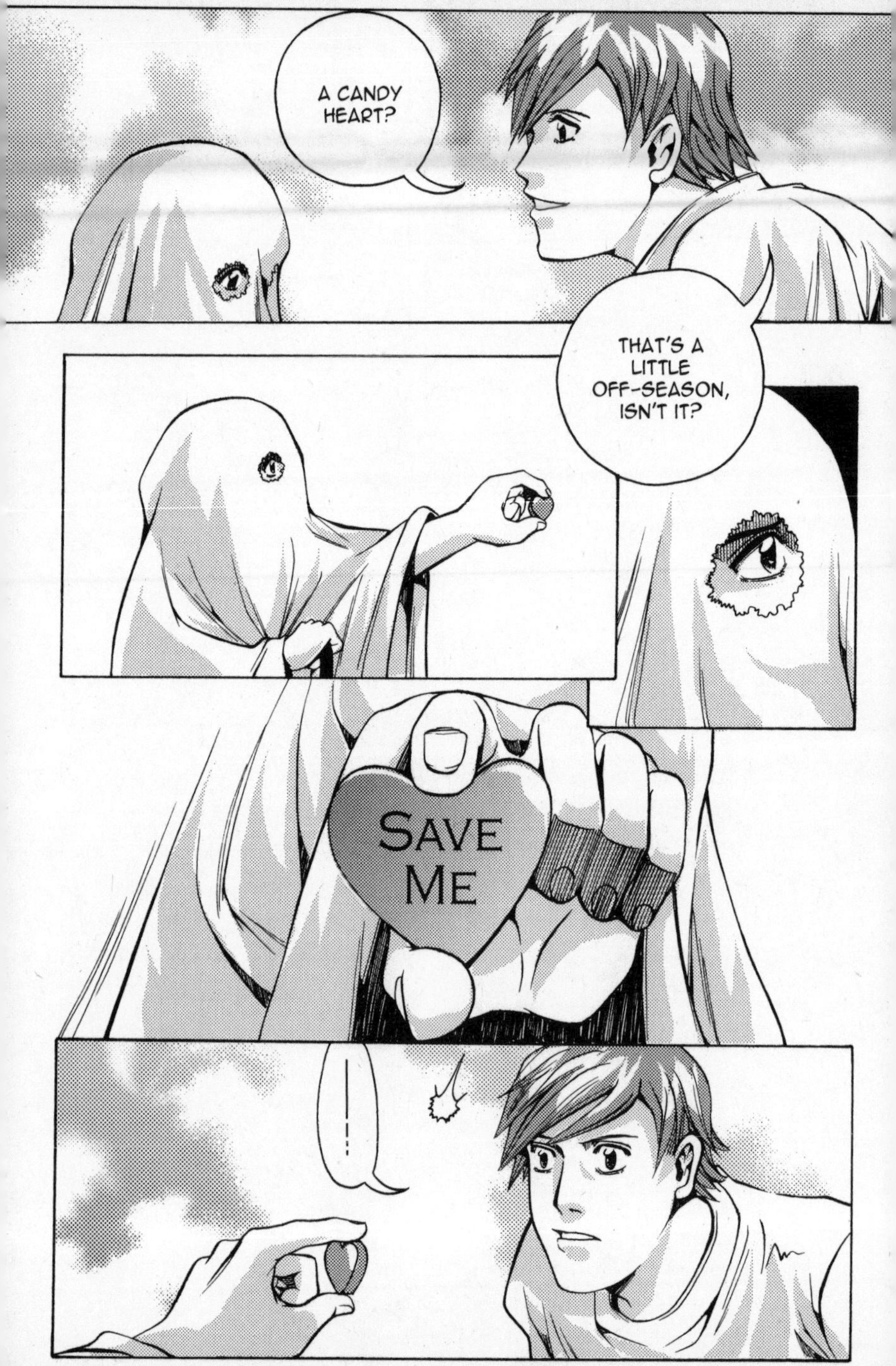
A CANDY HEART?
THAT'S A LITTLE OFF-SEASON, ISN'T IT?
SAVE ME
--!!

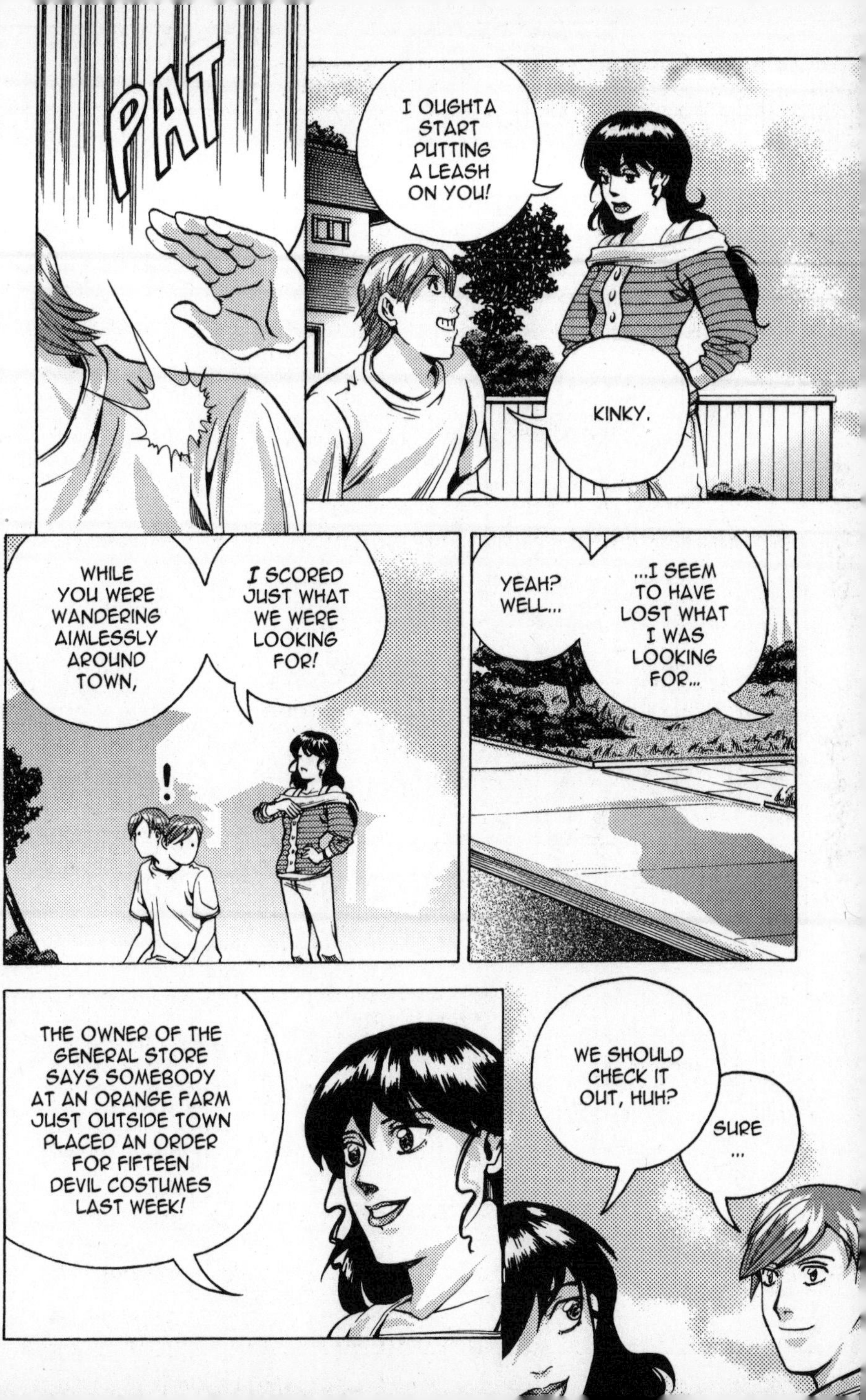
PAT
I OUGHTA START PUTTING A LEASH ON YOU!
KINKY.
WHILE YOU WERE WANDERING AIMLESSLY AROUND TOWN,
I SCORED JUST WHAT WE WERE LOOKING FOR!
!
YEAH? WELL...
...I SEEM TO HAVE LOST WHAT I WAS LOOKING FOR...
THE OWNER OF THE GENERAL STORE SAYS SOMEBODY AT AN ORANGE FARM JUST OUTSIDE TOWN PLACED AN ORDER FOR FIFTEEN DEVIL COSTUMES LAST WEEK!
WE SHOULD CHECK IT OUT, HUH?
SURE ...

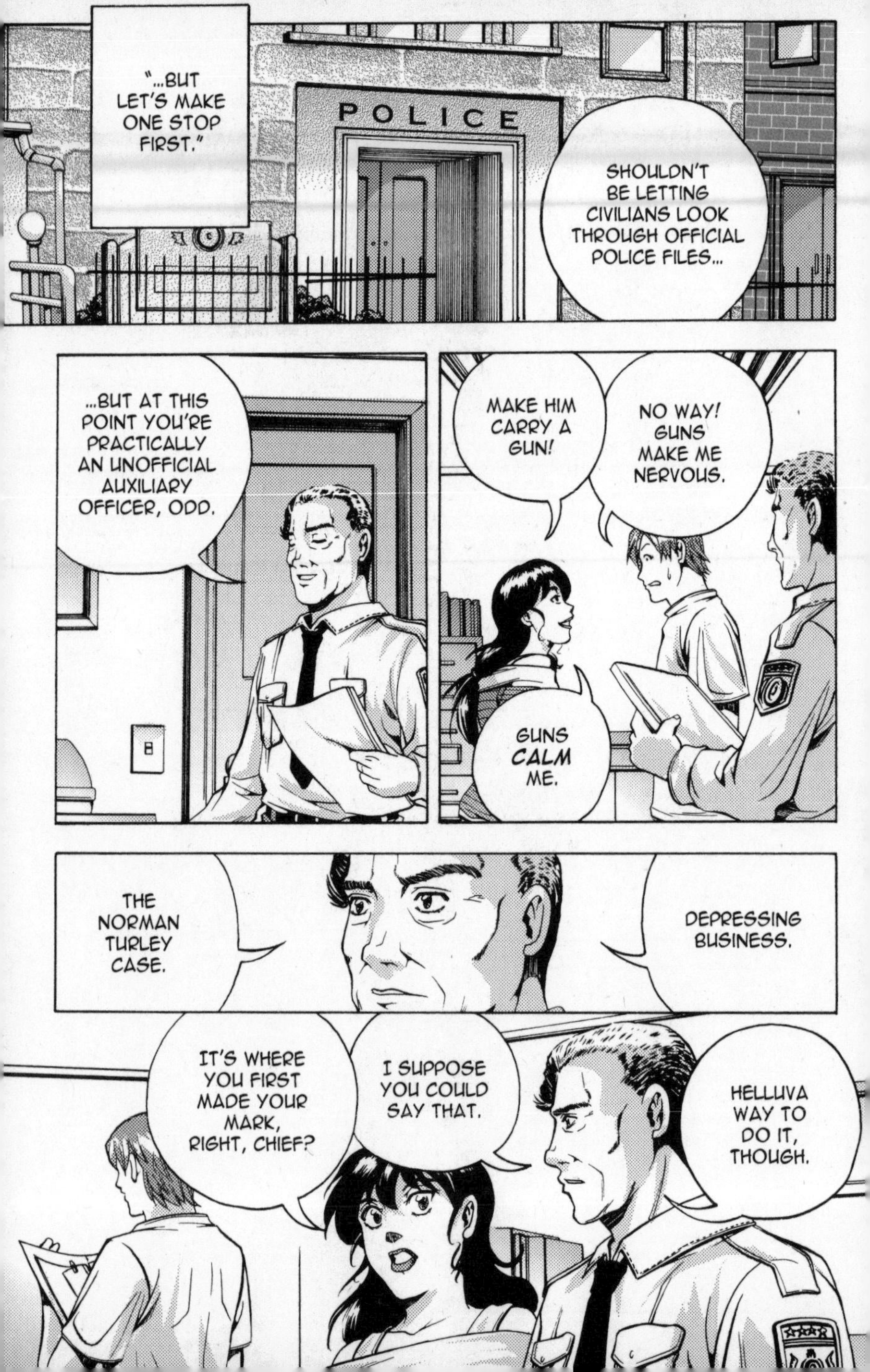
"...BUT LET'S MAKE ONE STOP FIRST."
POLICE
SHOULDN'T BE LETTING CIVILIANS LOOK THROUGH OFFICIAL POLICE FILES...
...BUT AT THIS POINT YOU'RE PRACTICALLY AN UNOFFICIAL AUXILIARY OFFICER, ODD.
MAKE HIM CARRY A GUN!
NO WAY! GUNS MAKE ME NERVOUS.
GUNS *CALM* ME.
THE NORMAN TURLEY CASE.
DEPRESSING BUSINESS.
IT'S WHERE YOU FIRST MADE YOUR MARK, RIGHT, CHIEF?
I SUPPOSE YOU COULD SAY THAT.
HELLUVA WAY TO DO IT, THOUGH.

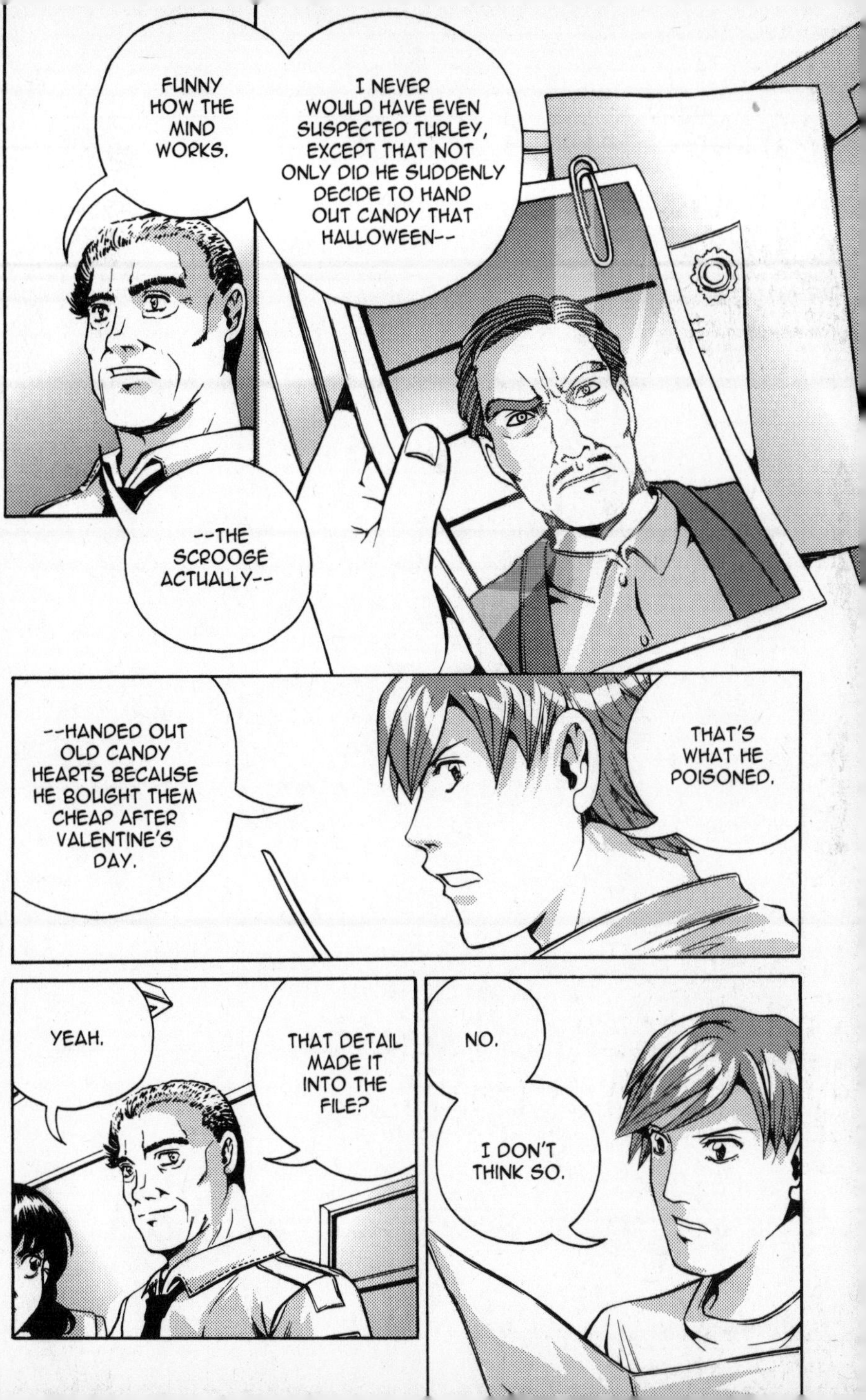
FUNNY HOW THE MIND WORKS.
I NEVER WOULD HAVE EVEN SUSPECTED TURLEY, EXCEPT THAT NOT ONLY DID HE SUDDENLY DECIDE TO HAND OUT CANDY THAT HALLOWEEN--
--THE SCROOGE ACTUALLY--
--HANDED OUT OLD CANDY HEARTS BECAUSE HE BOUGHT THEM CHEAP AFTER VALENTINE'S DAY.
THAT'S WHAT HE POISONED.
YEAH.
THAT DETAIL MADE IT INTO THE FILE?
NO.
I DON'T THINK SO.

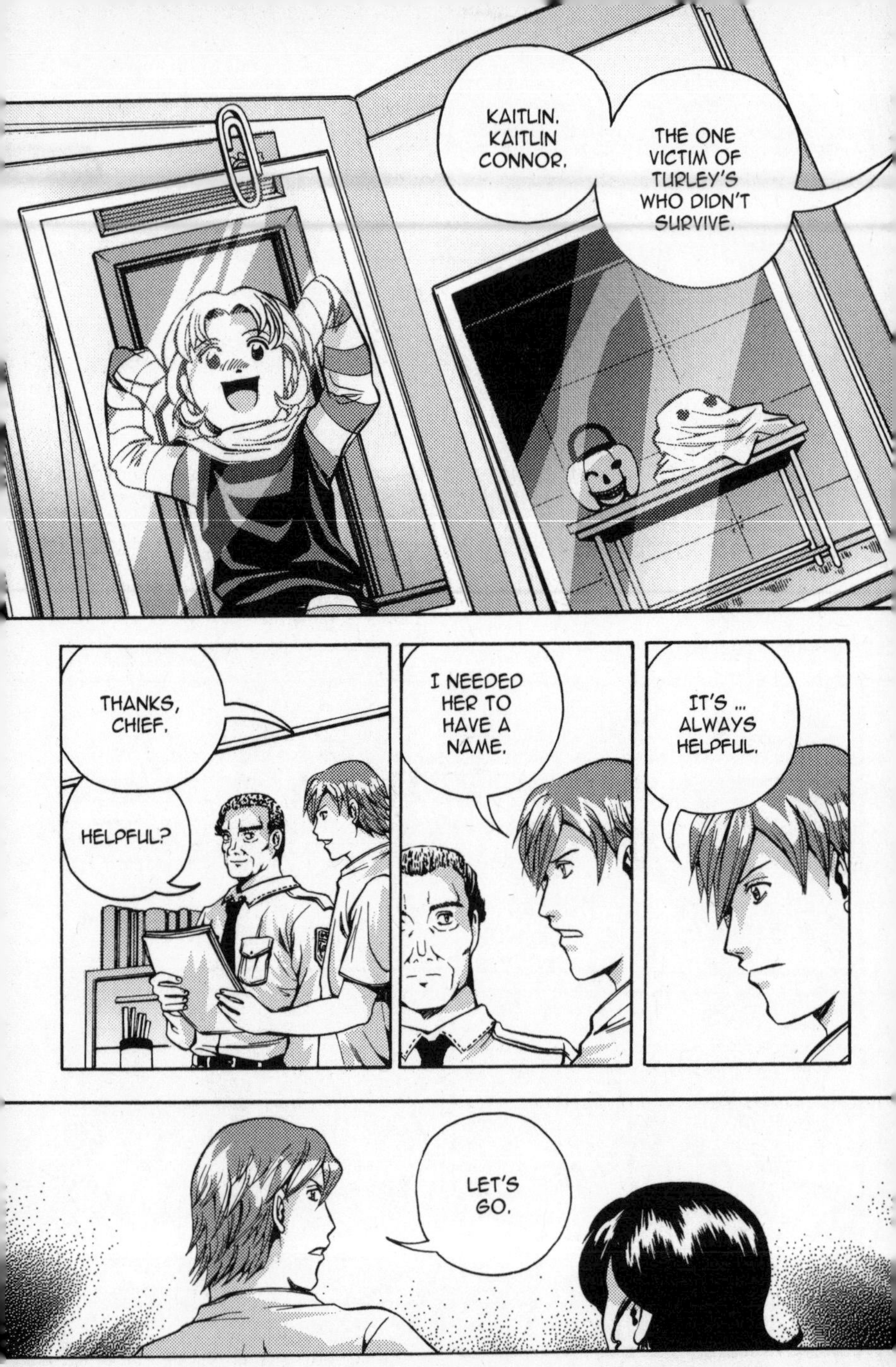
KAITLIN. KAITLIN CONNOR.
THE ONE VICTIM OF TURLEY'S WHO DIDN'T SURVIVE.
THANKS, CHIEF.
HELPFUL?
I NEEDED HER TO HAVE A NAME.
IT'S ... ALWAYS HELPFUL.
LET'S GO.

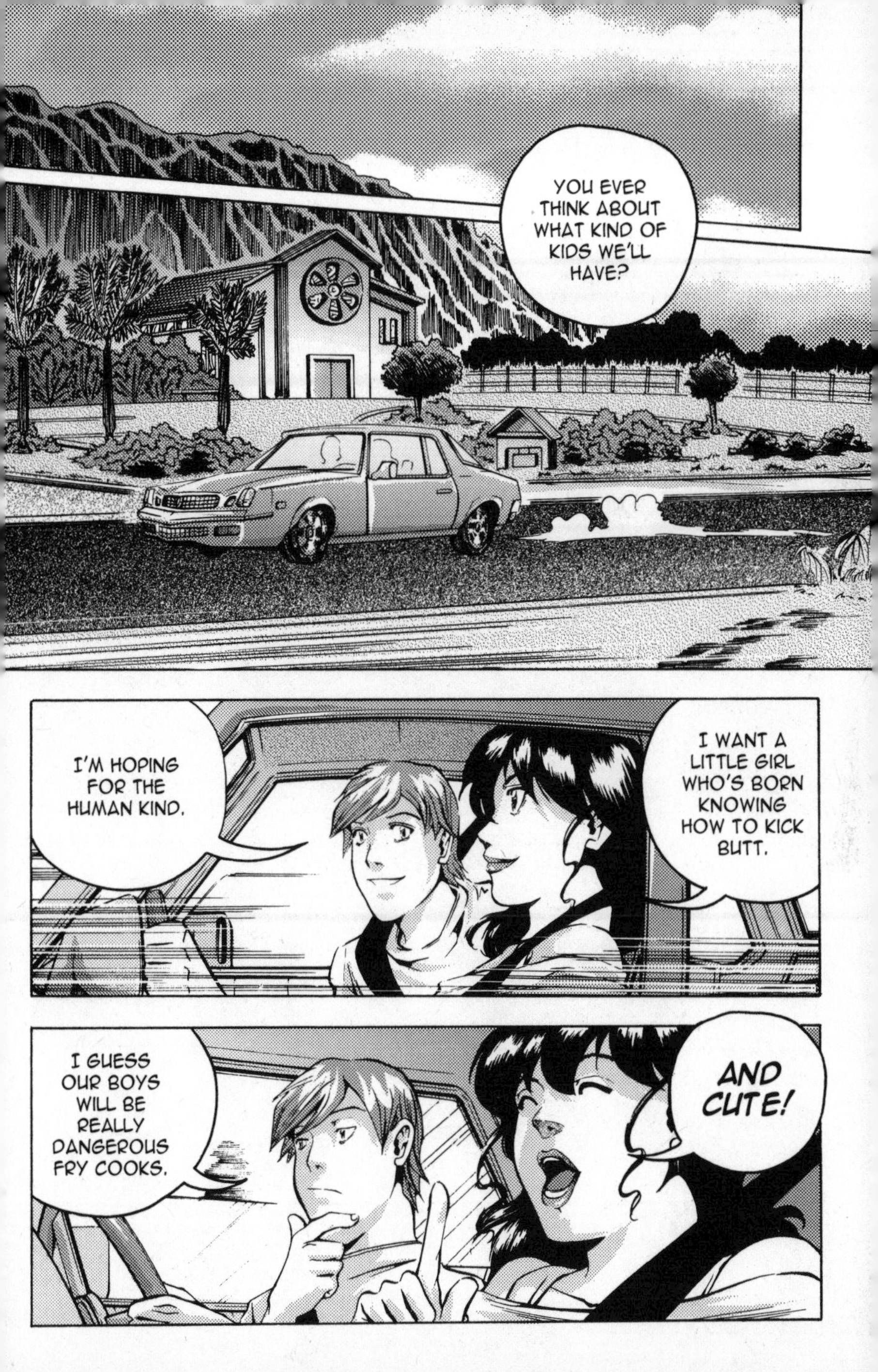
YOU EVER THINK ABOUT WHAT KIND OF KIDS WE'LL HAVE?
I'M HOPING FOR THE HUMAN KIND.
I WANT A LITTLE GIRL WHO'S BORN KNOWING HOW TO KICK BUTT.
I GUESS OUR BOYS WILL BE REALLY DANGEROUS FRY COOKS.
AND CUTE!

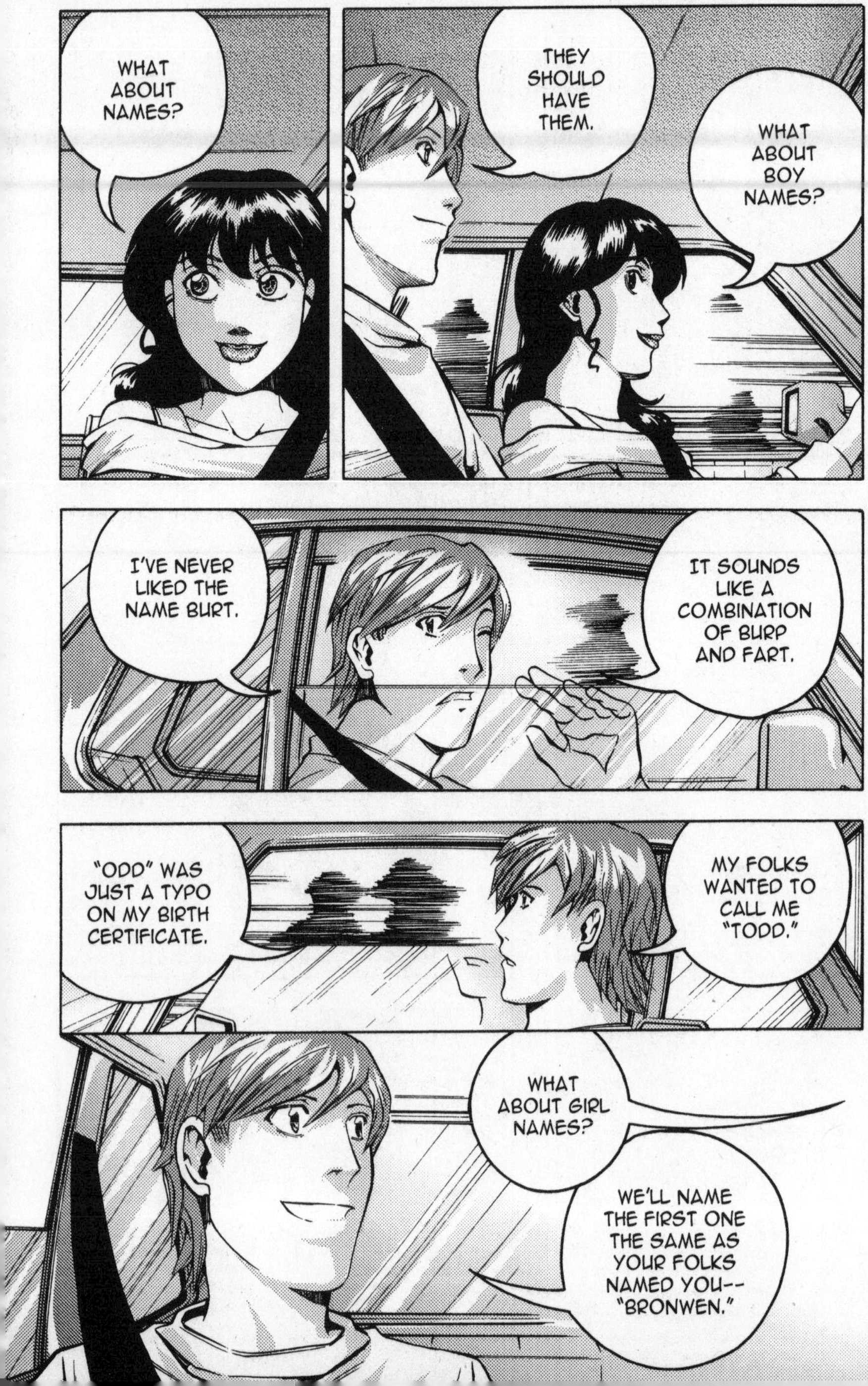
WHAT ABOUT NAMES?
THEY SHOULD HAVE THEM.
WHAT ABOUT BOY NAMES?
I'VE NEVER LIKED THE NAME BURT.
IT SOUNDS LIKE A COMBINATION OF BURP AND FART.
"ODD" WAS JUST A TYPO ON MY BIRTH CERTIFICATE.
MY FOLKS WANTED TO CALL ME "TODD."
WHAT ABOUT GIRL NAMES?
WE'LL NAME THE FIRST ONE THE SAME AS YOUR FOLKS NAMED YOU-- "BRONWEN."

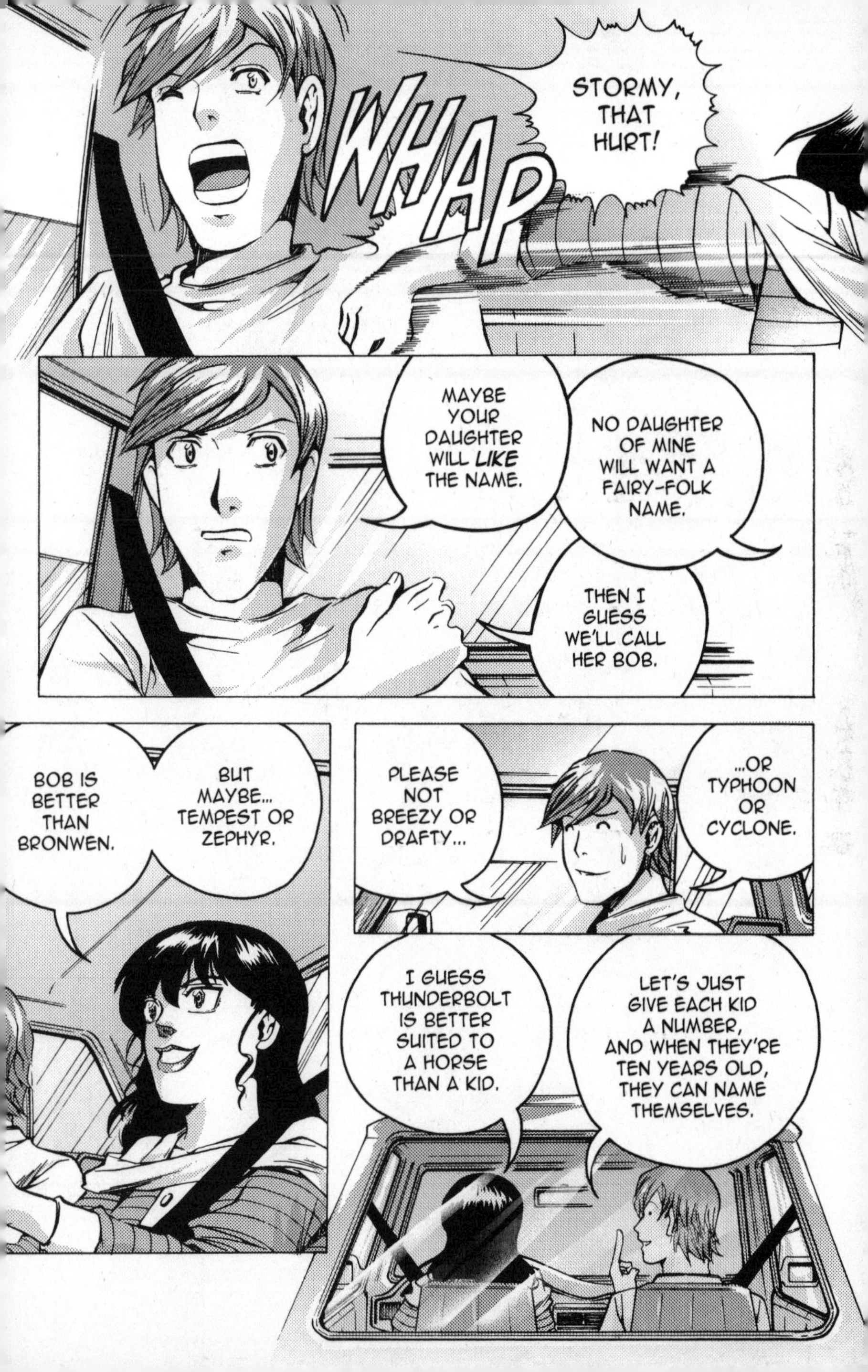
WHAP
STORMY, THAT HURT!
MAYBE YOUR DAUGHTER WILL LIKE THE NAME.
NO DAUGHTER OF MINE WILL WANT A FAIRY-FOLK NAME.
THEN I GUESS WE'LL CALL HER BOB.
BOB IS BETTER THAN BRONWEN.
BUT MAYBE... TEMPEST OR ZEPHYR.
PLEASE NOT BREEZY OR DRAFTY...
...OR TYPHOON OR CYCLONE.
I GUESS THUNDERBOLT IS BETTER SUITED TO A HORSE THAN A KID.
LET'S JUST GIVE EACH KID A NUMBER, AND WHEN THEY'RE TEN YEARS OLD, THEY CAN NAME THEMSELVES.

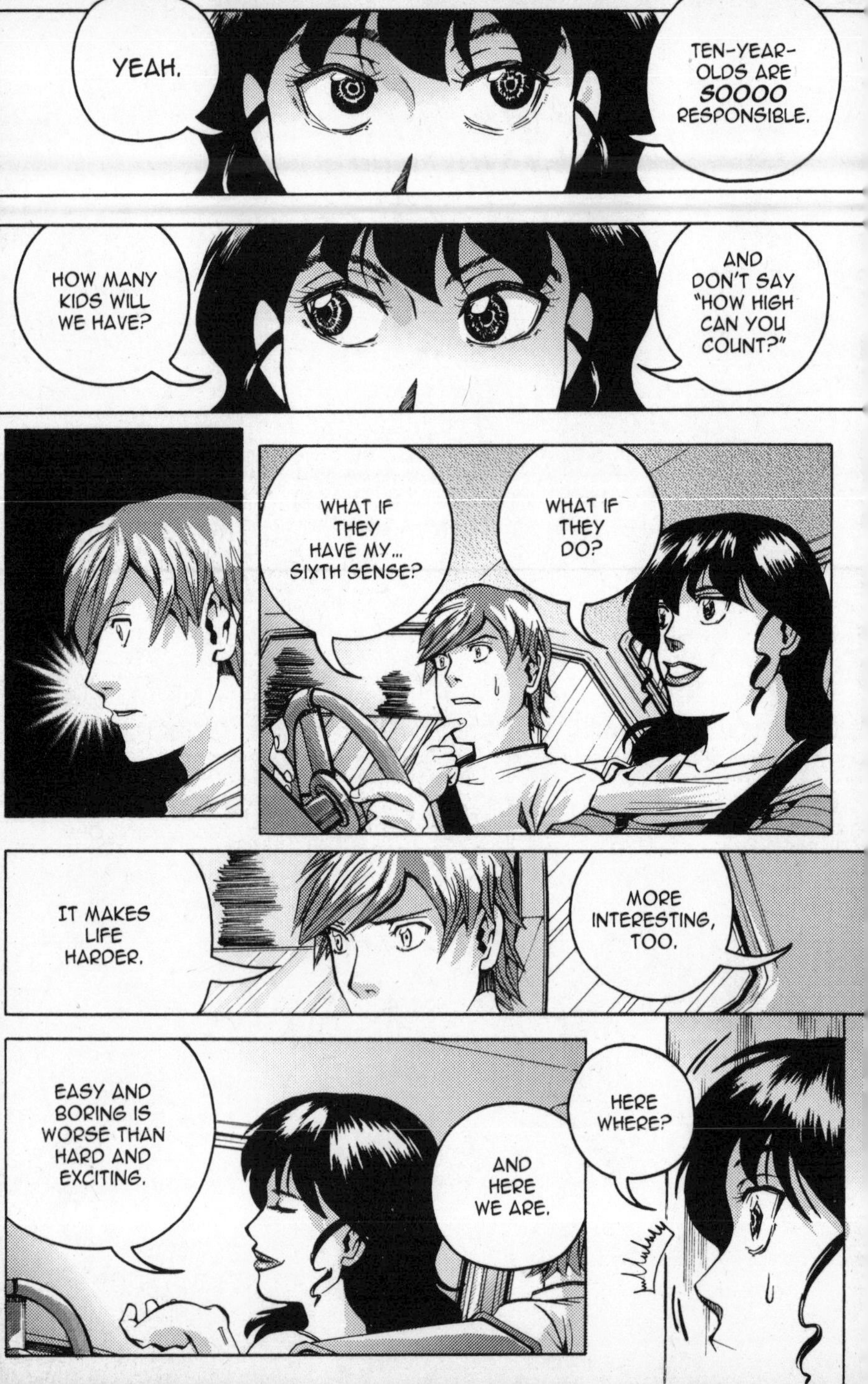
YEAH.
TEN-YEAR-OLDS ARE SOOOO RESPONSIBLE.
HOW MANY KIDS WILL WE HAVE?
AND DON'T SAY "HOW HIGH CAN YOU COUNT?"
WHAT IF THEY HAVE MY... SIXTH SENSE?
WHAT IF THEY DO?
IT MAKES LIFE HARDER.
MORE INTERESTING, TOO.
EASY AND BORING IS WORSE THAN HARD AND EXCITING.
AND HERE WE ARE.
HERE WHERE?

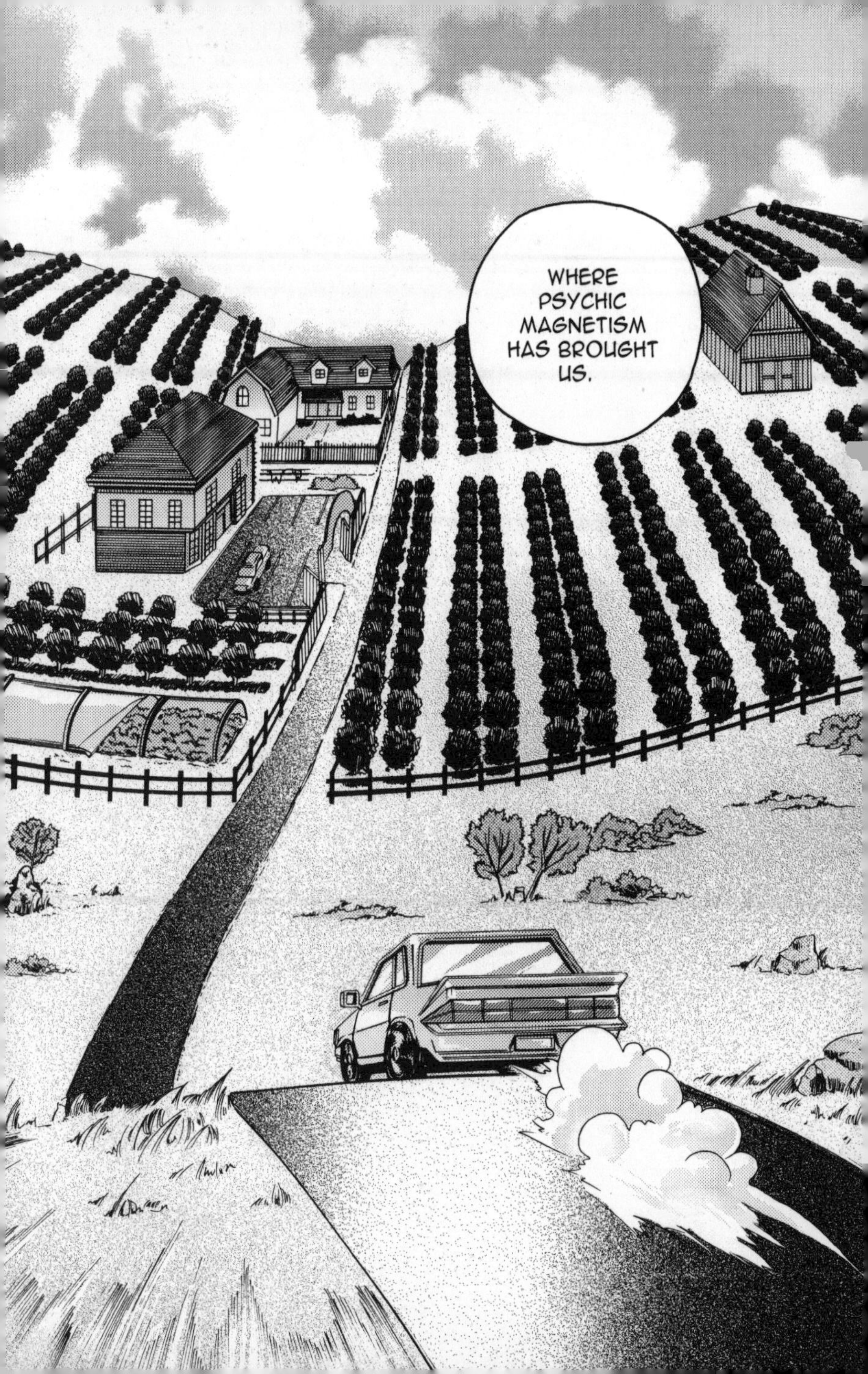
WHERE PSYCHIC MAGNETISM HAS BROUGHT US.

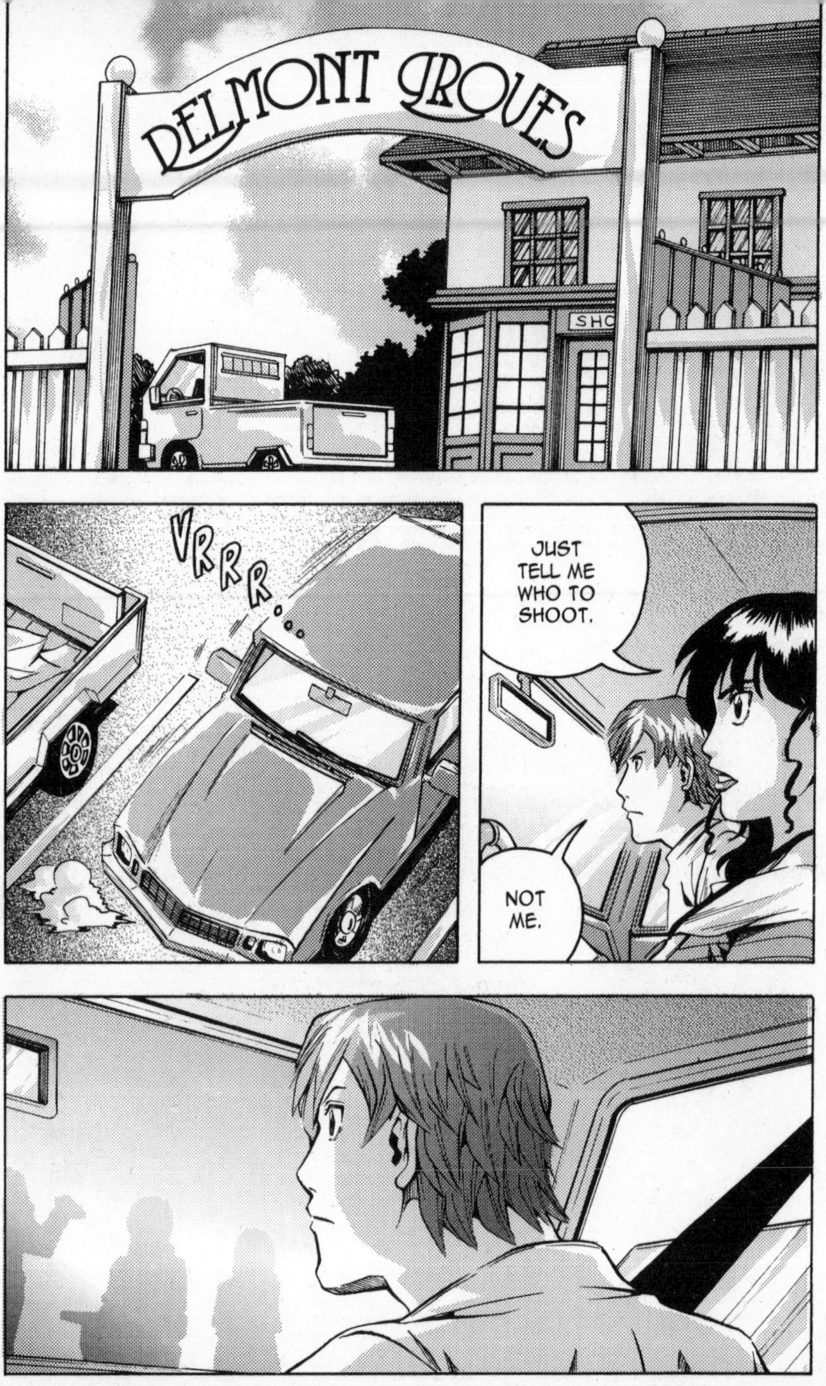
DELMONT GROVES
SHO
VRRR...
JUST TELL ME WHO TO SHOOT.
NOT ME.

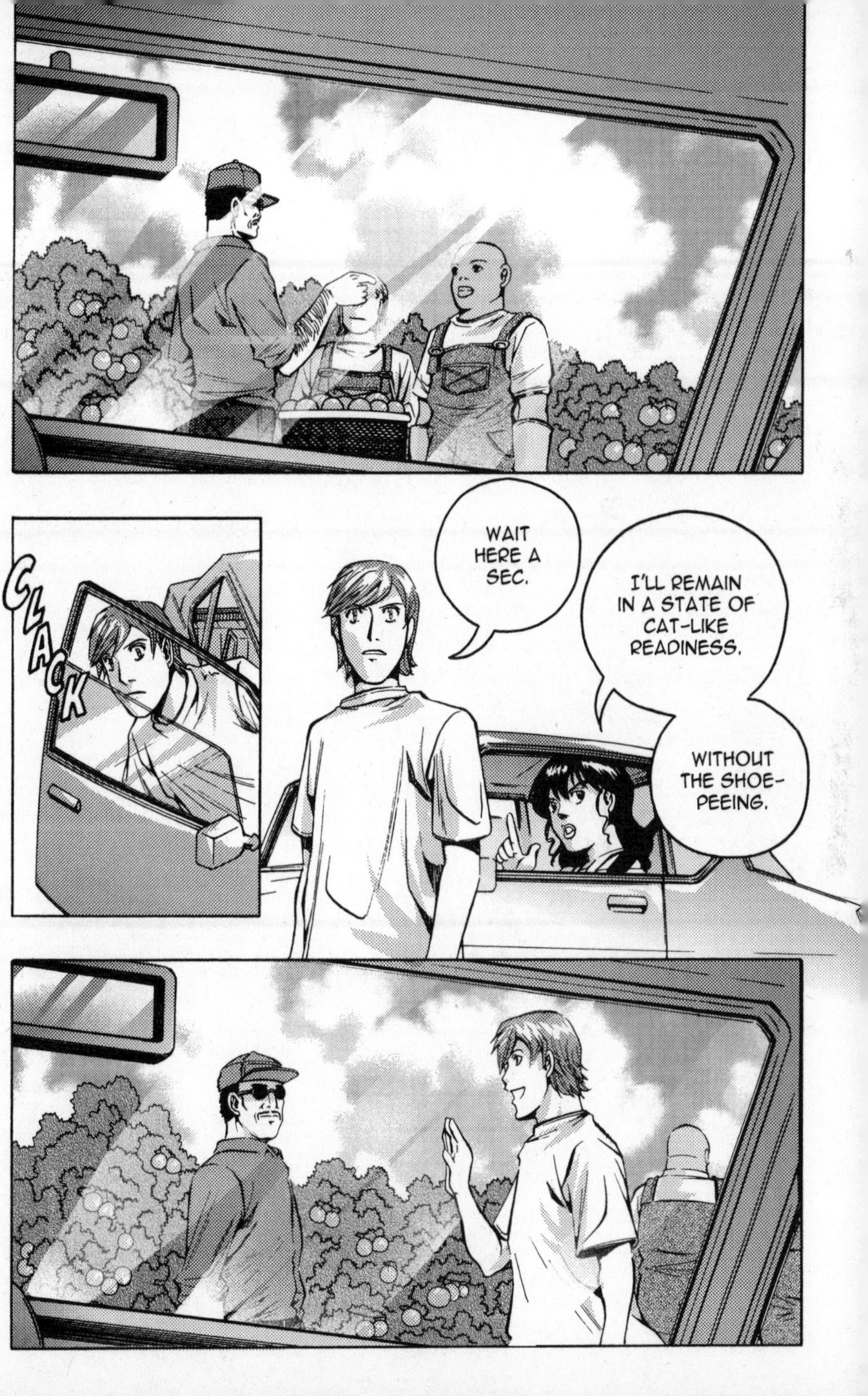
CLACK
WAIT HERE A SEC.
I'LL REMAIN IN A STATE OF CAT-LIKE READINESS.
WITHOUT THE SHOE-PEEING.

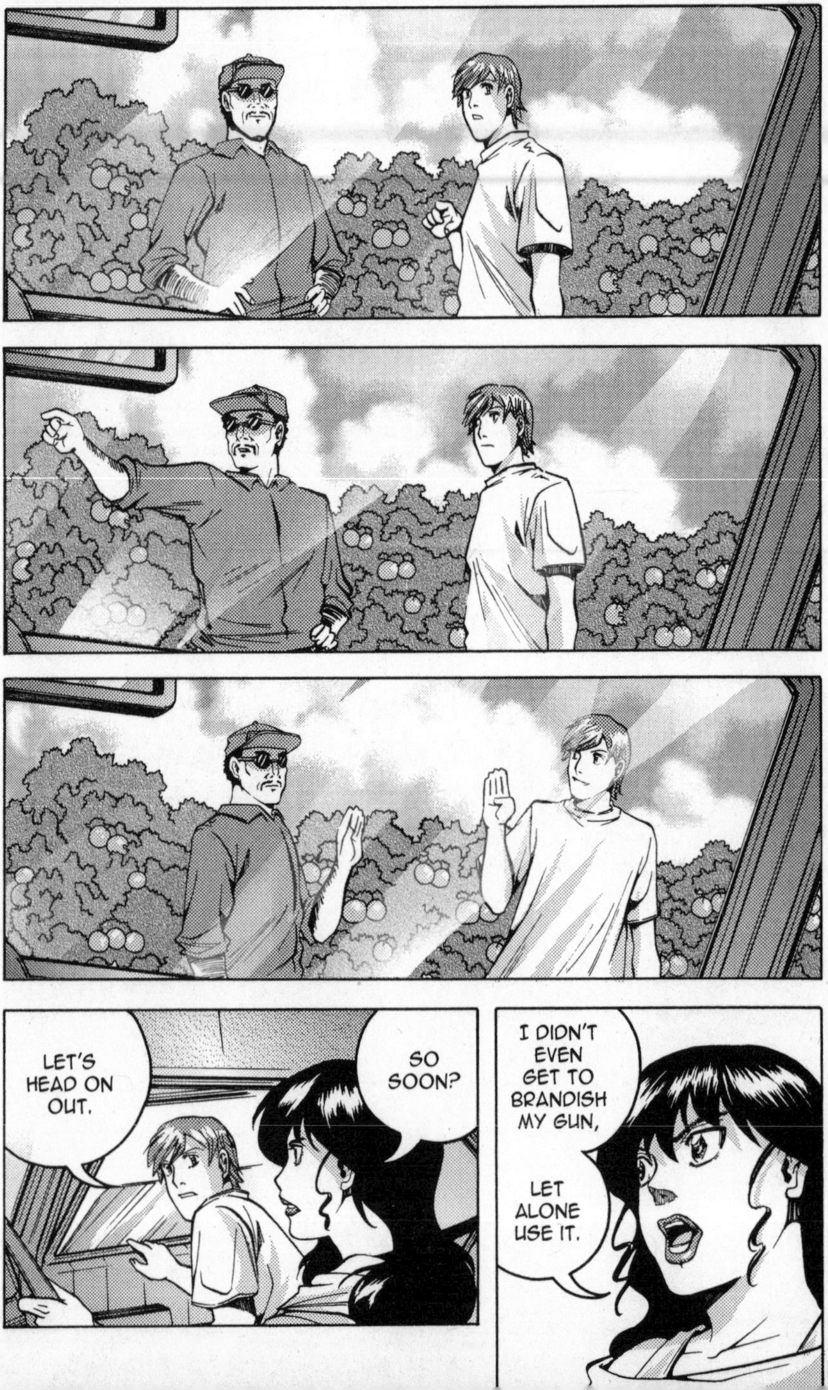
LET'S HEAD ON OUT.
SO SOON?
I DIDN'T EVEN GET TO BRANDISH MY GUN,
LET ALONE USE IT.

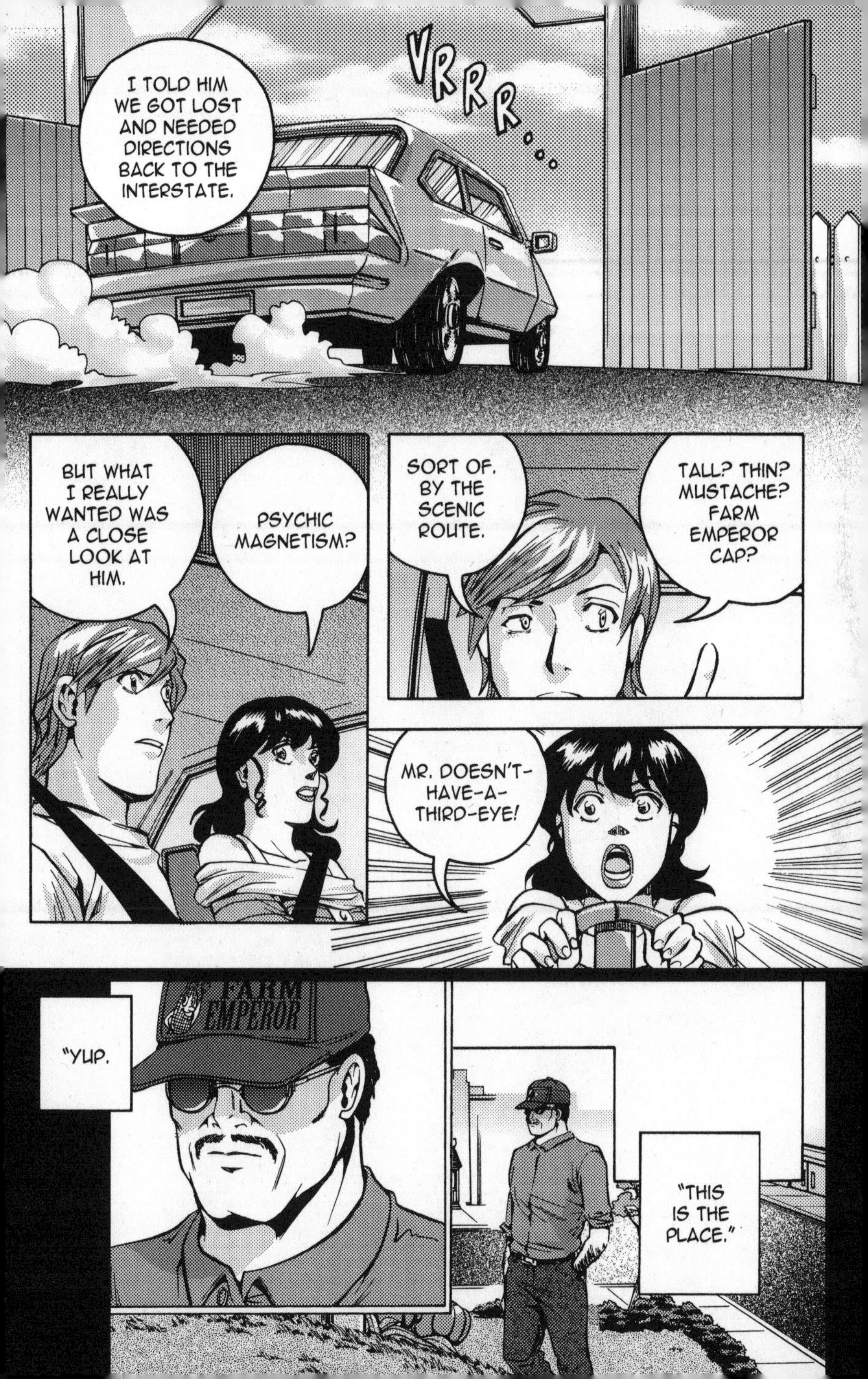
VRRR...
I TOLD HIM WE GOT LOST AND NEEDED DIRECTIONS BACK TO THE INTERSTATE.
BUT WHAT I REALLY WANTED WAS A CLOSE LOOK AT HIM.
PSYCHIC MAGNETISM?
SORT OF. BY THE SCENIC ROUTE.
TALL? THIN? MUSTACHE? FARM EMPEROR CAP?
MR. DOESN'T-HAVE-A-THIRD-EYE!
FARM EMPEROR
"YUP.
"THIS IS THE PLACE."

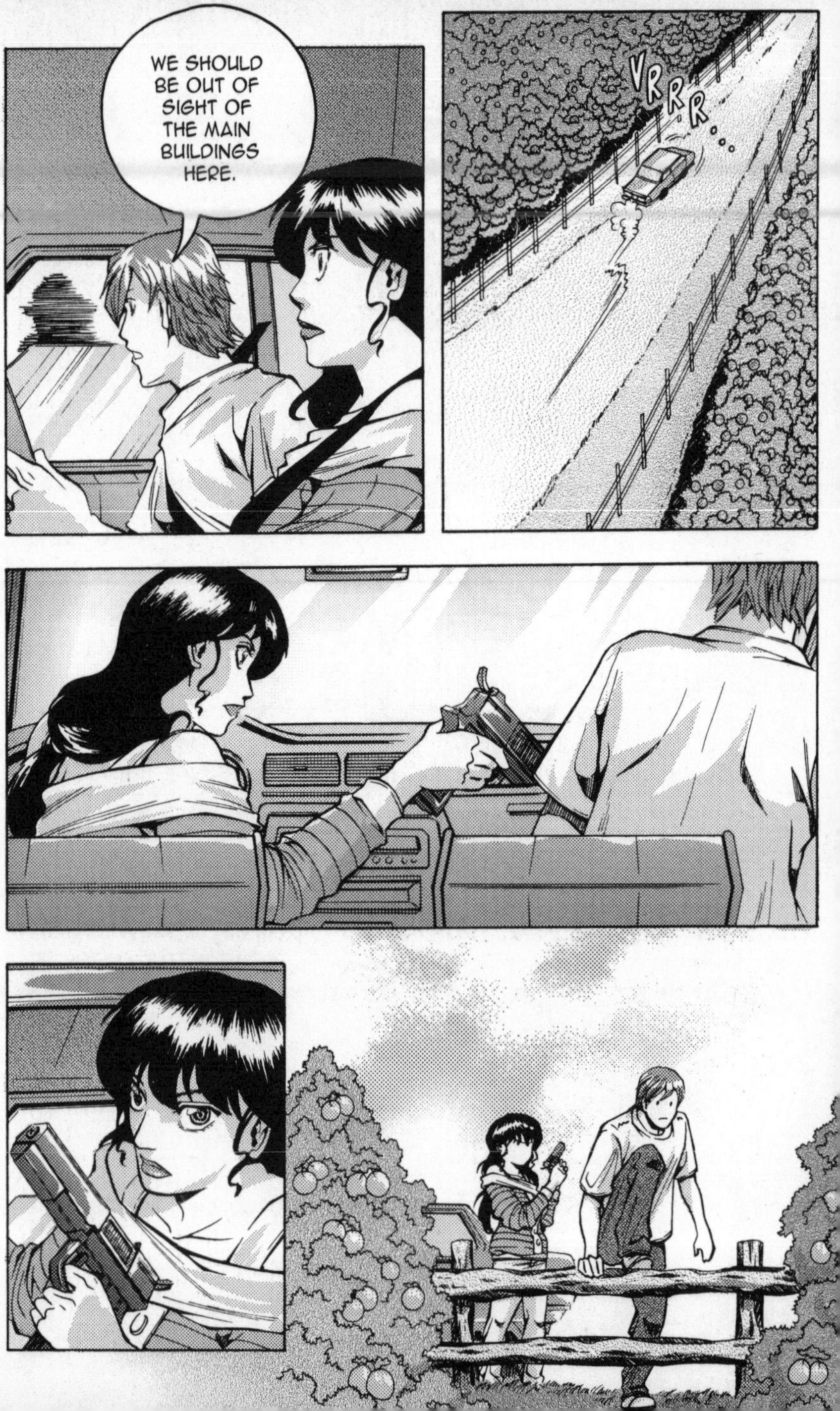
WE SHOULD BE OUT OF SIGHT OF THE MAIN BUILDINGS HERE.
VRRR...

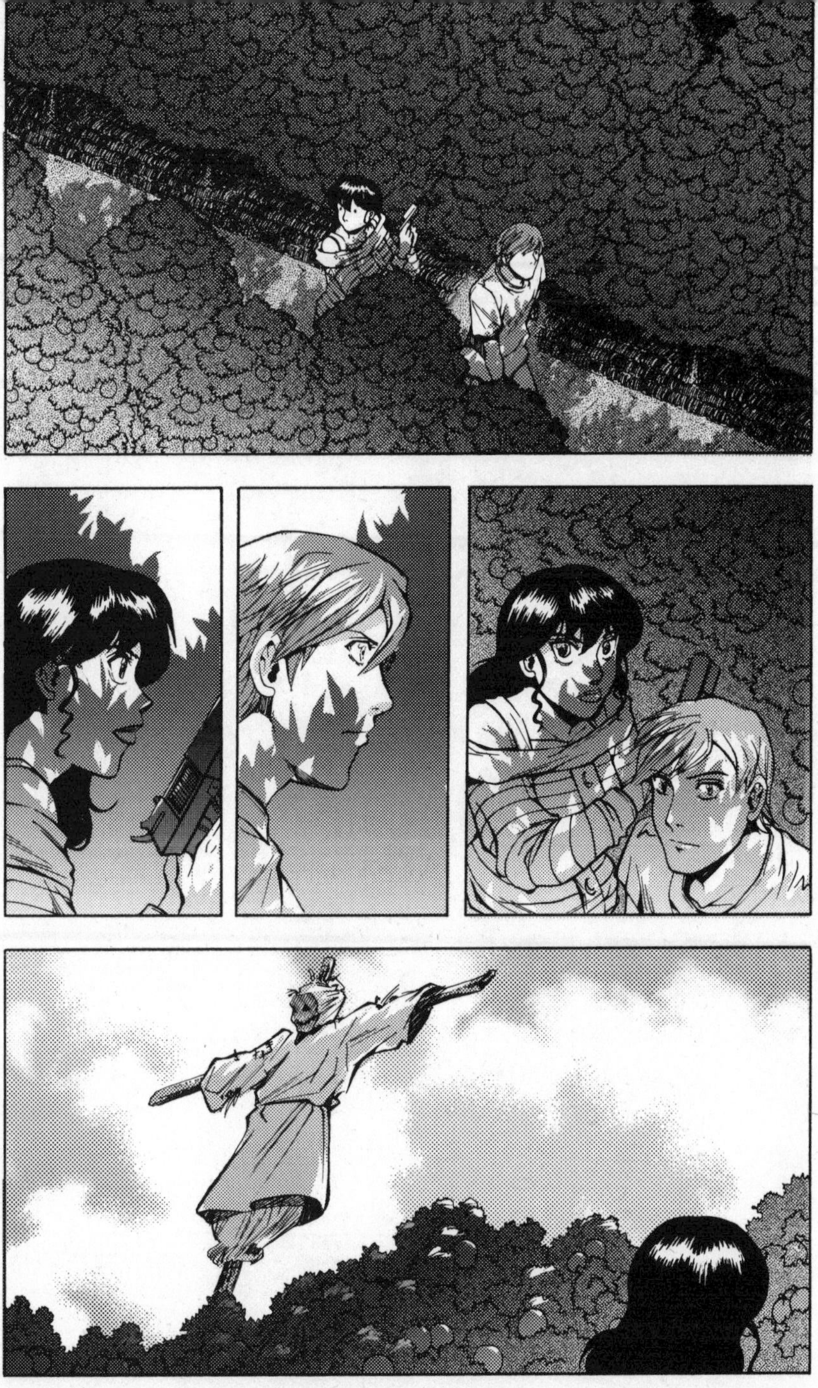

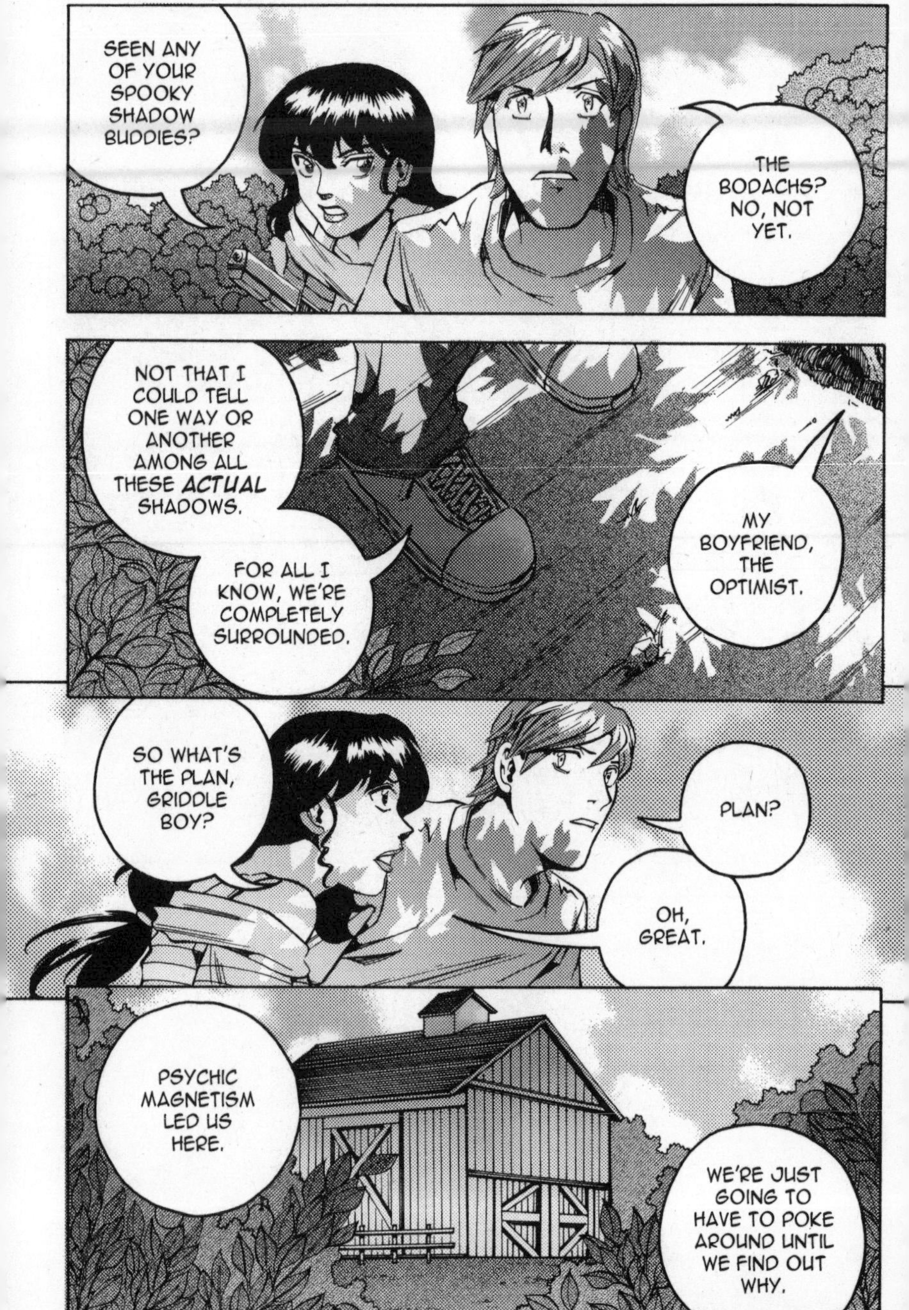
SEEN ANY OF YOUR SPOOKY SHADOW BUDDIES?
THE BODACHS? NO, NOT YET.
NOT THAT I COULD TELL ONE WAY OR ANOTHER AMONG ALL THESE ACTUAL SHADOWS.
FOR ALL I KNOW, WE'RE COMPLETELY SURROUNDED.
MY BOYFRIEND, THE OPTIMIST.
SO WHAT'S THE PLAN, GRIDDLE BOY?
PLAN?
OH, GREAT.
PSYCHIC MAGNETISM LED US HERE.
WE'RE JUST GOING TO HAVE TO POKE AROUND UNTIL WE FIND OUT WHY.

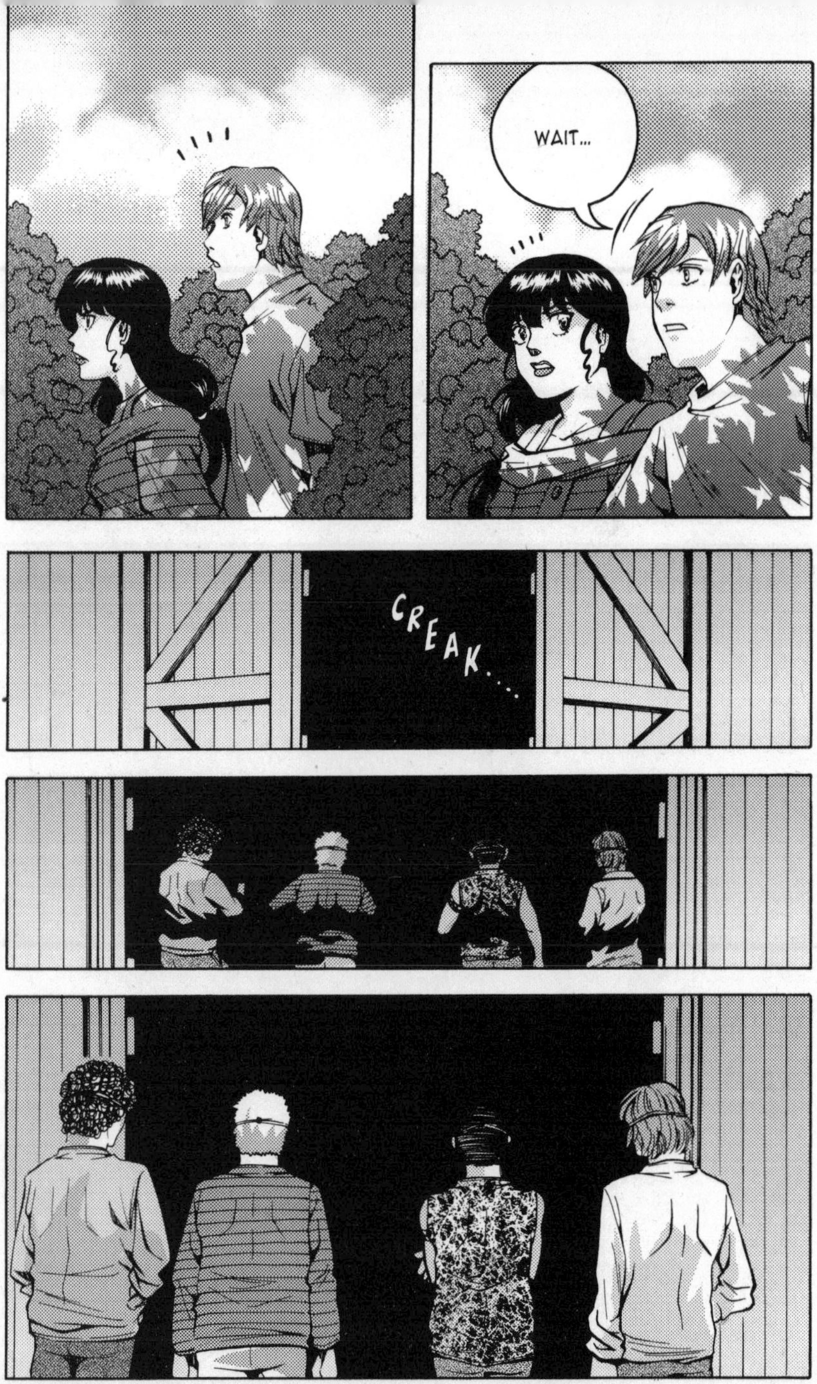
WAIT...
CREAK....

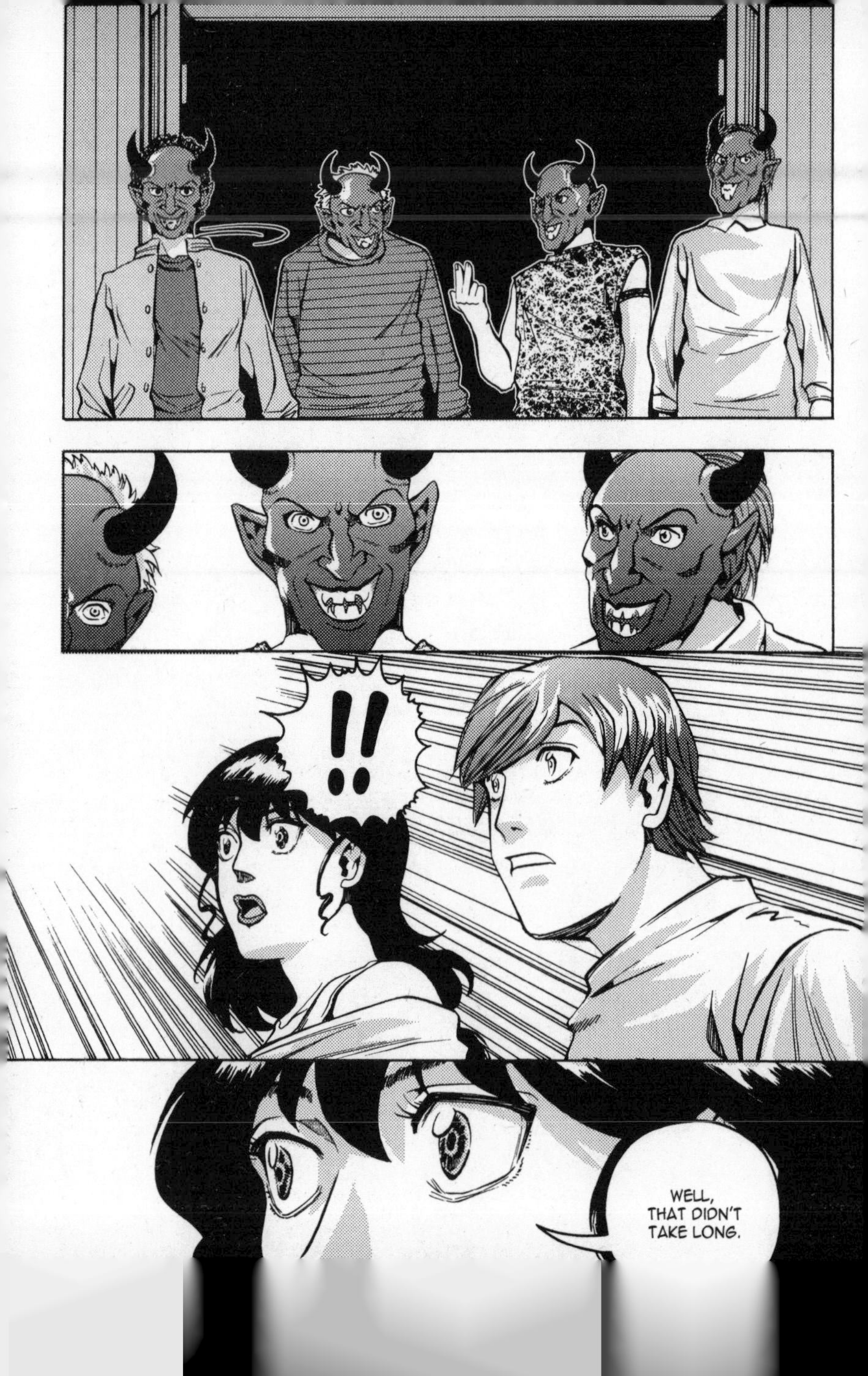
!!
WELL, THAT DIDN'T TAKE LONG.

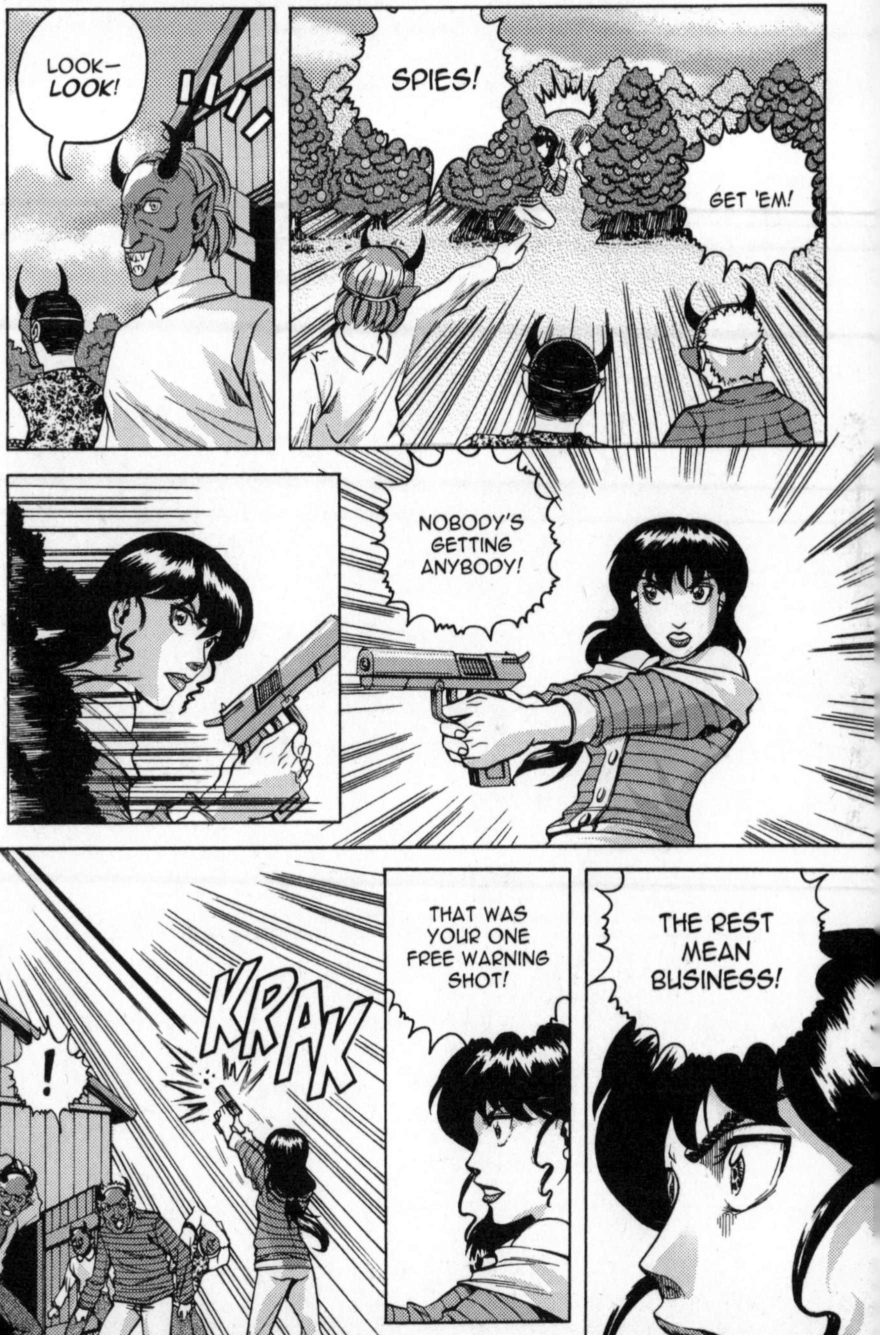
LOOK—
LOOK!
SPIES!
GET 'EM!
NOBODY'S GETTING ANYBODY!
KRAK
!
THAT WAS YOUR ONE FREE WARNING SHOT!
THE REST MEAN BUSINESS!

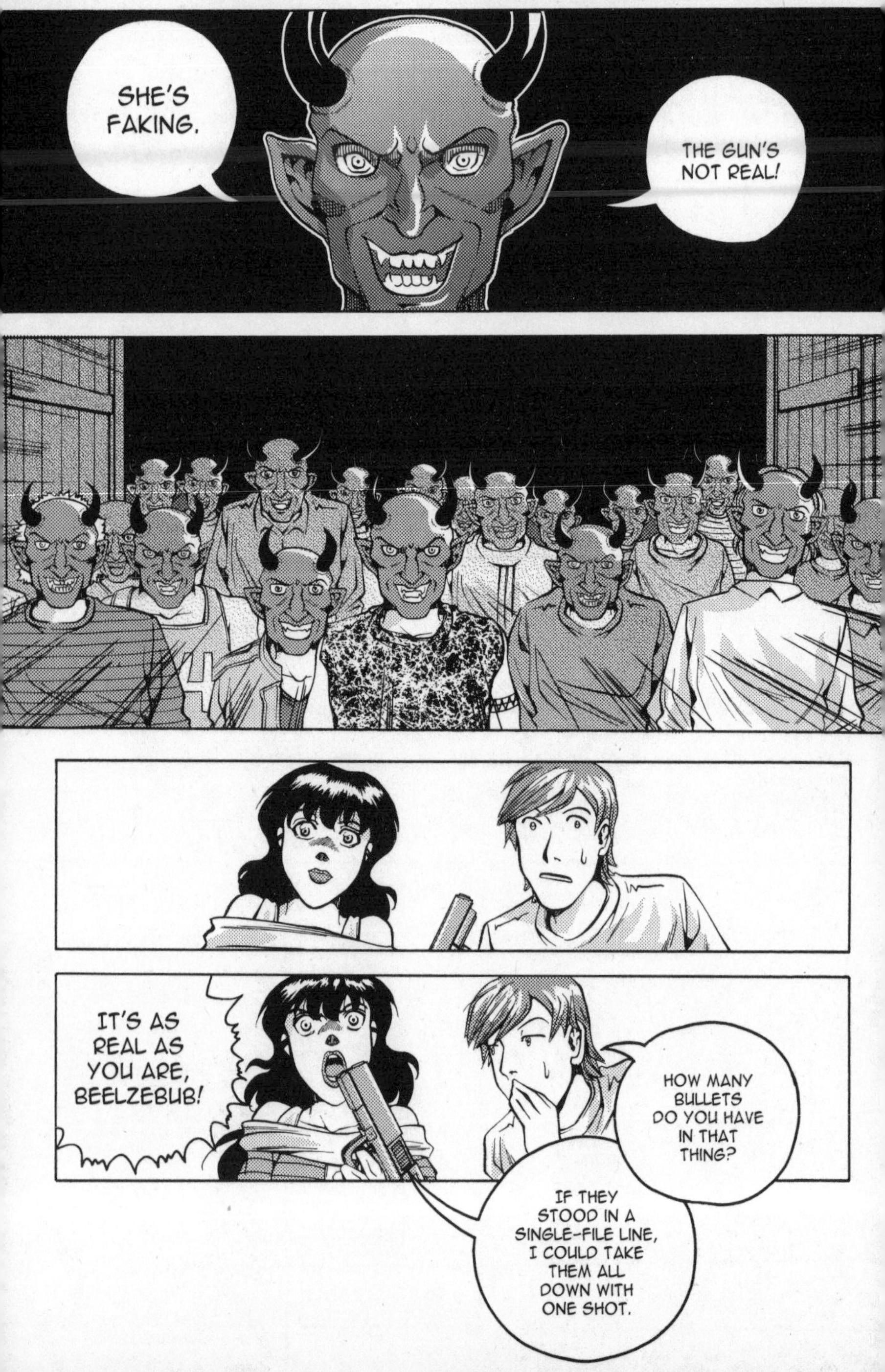
SHE'S FAKING.
THE GUN'S NOT REAL!
IT'S AS REAL AS YOU ARE, BEELZEBUB!
HOW MANY BULLETS DO YOU HAVE IN THAT THING?
IF THEY STOOD IN A SINGLE-FILE LINE, I COULD TAKE THEM ALL DOWN WITH ONE SHOT.

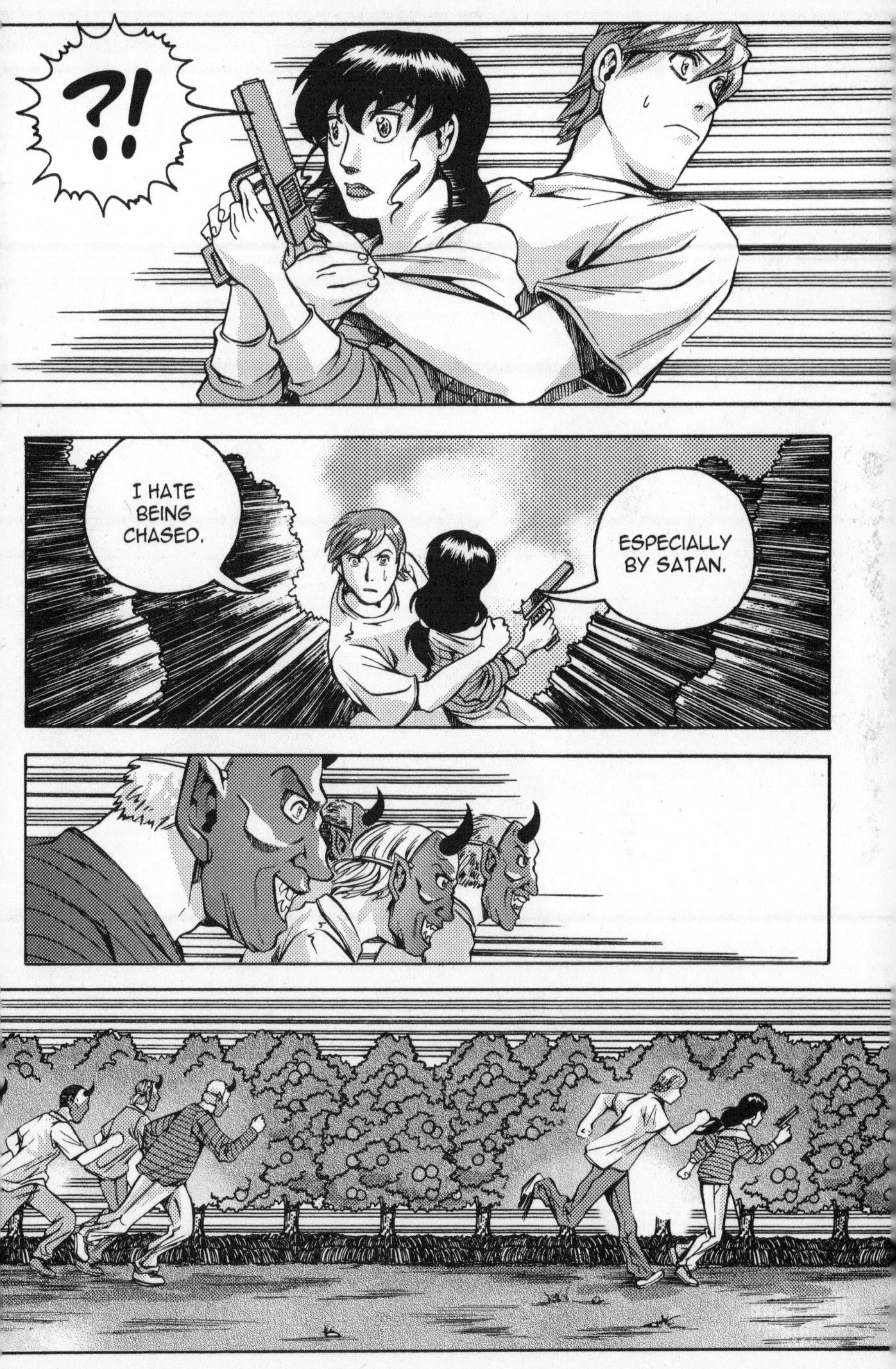
?!
I HATE BEING CHASED.
ESPECIALLY BY SATAN.

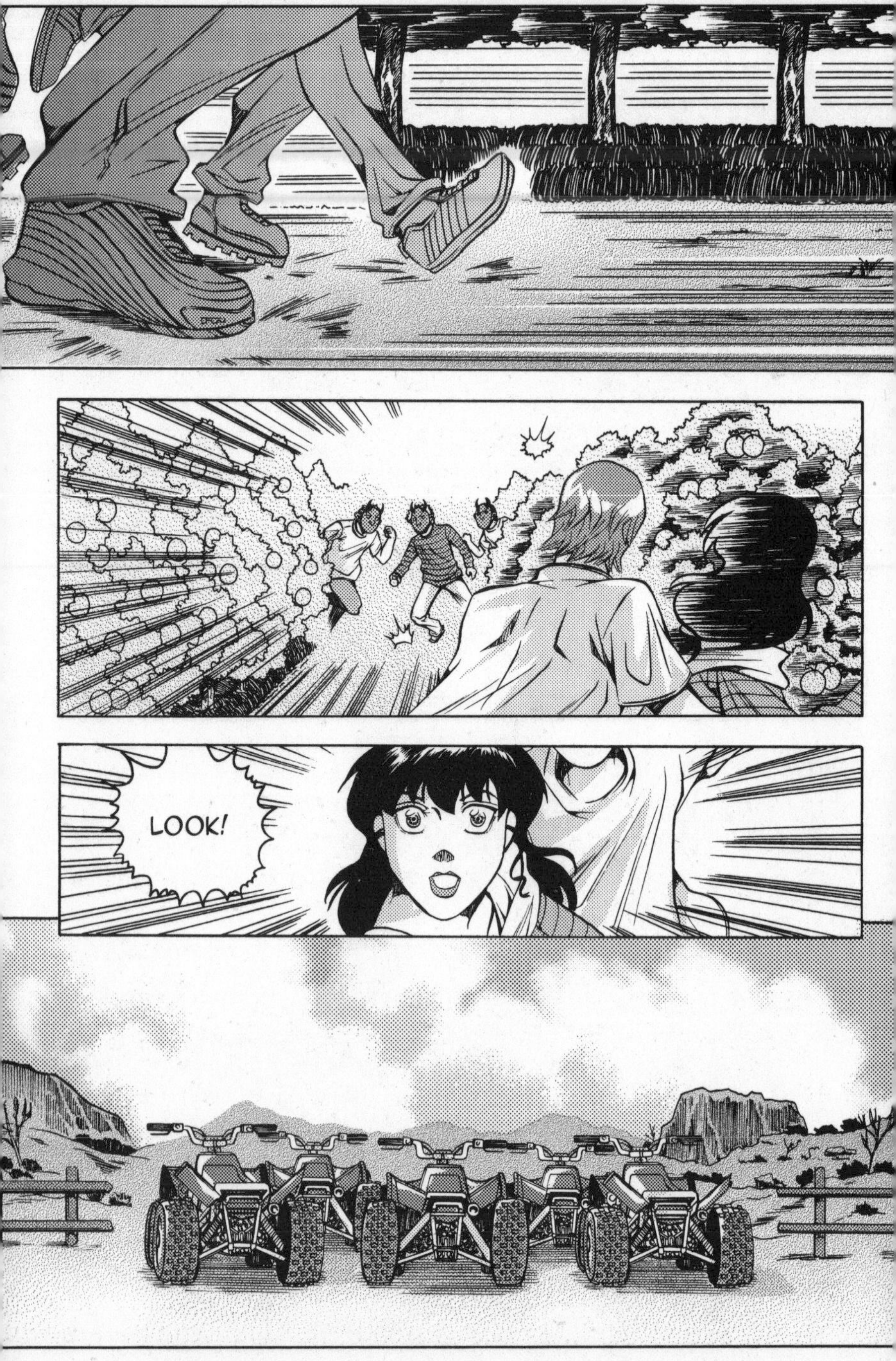
LOOK!

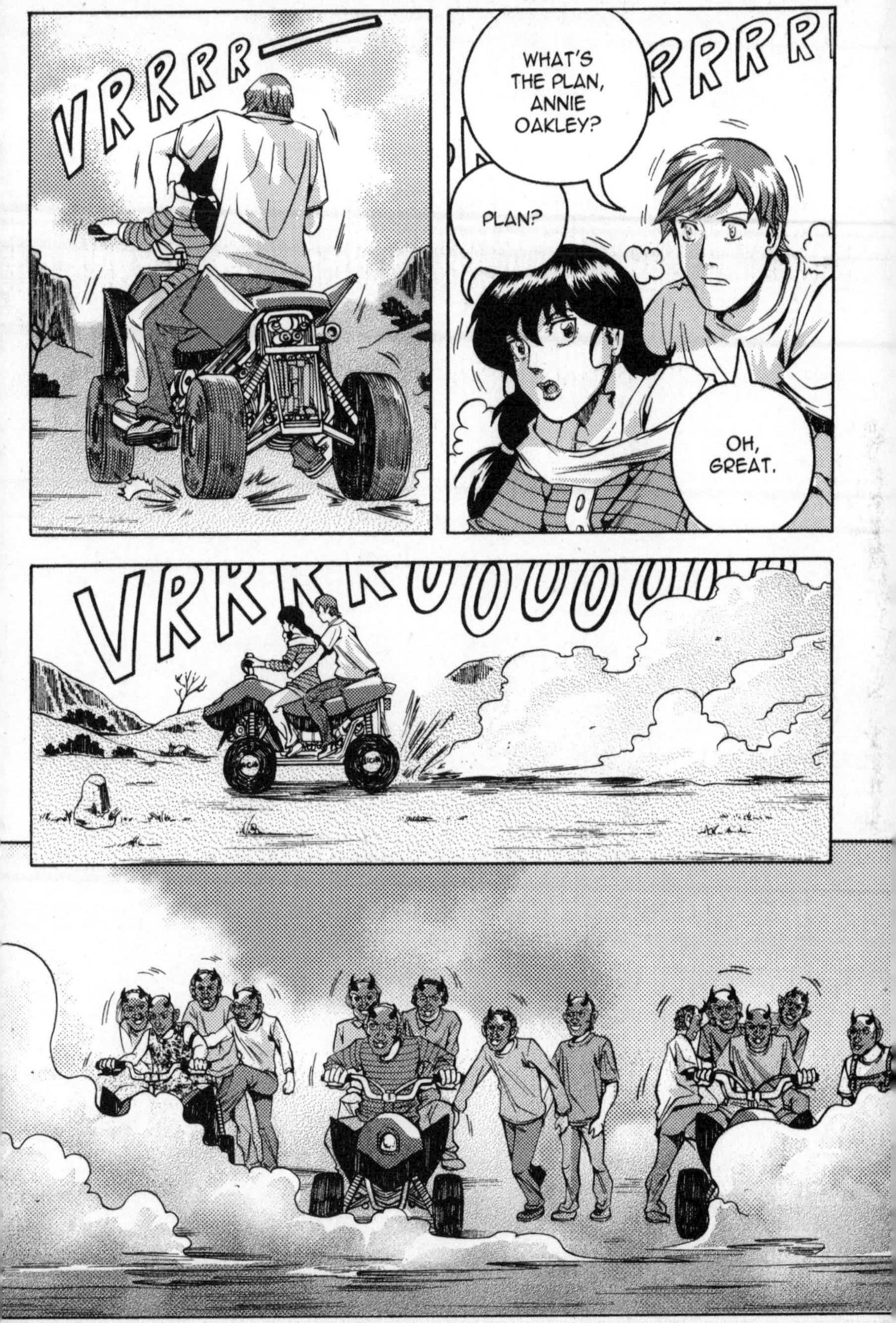
VRRRR—
RRRR
WHAT'S THE PLAN, ANNIE OAKLEY?
PLAN?
OH, GREAT.
VRRRROOOOOO

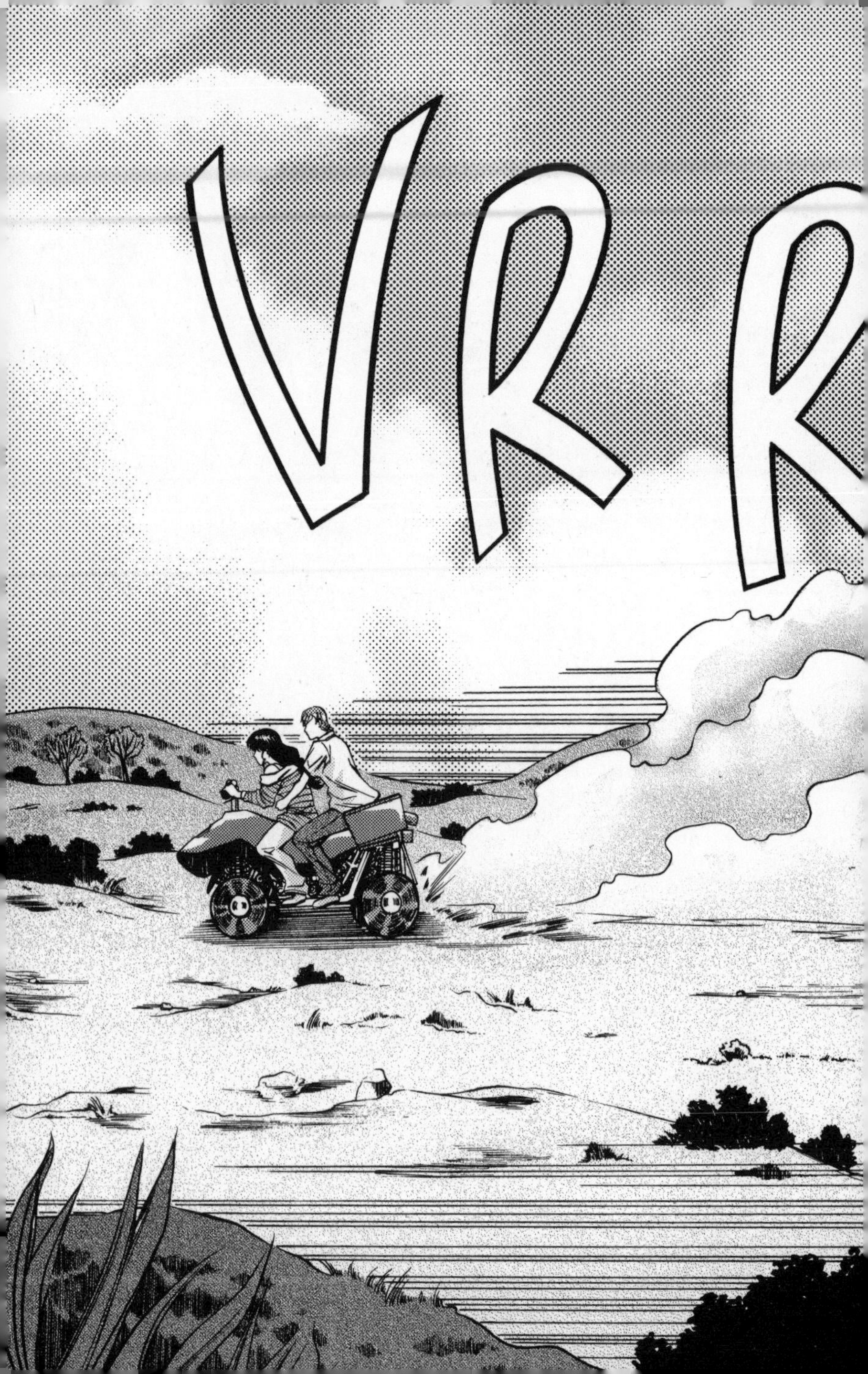
VRR

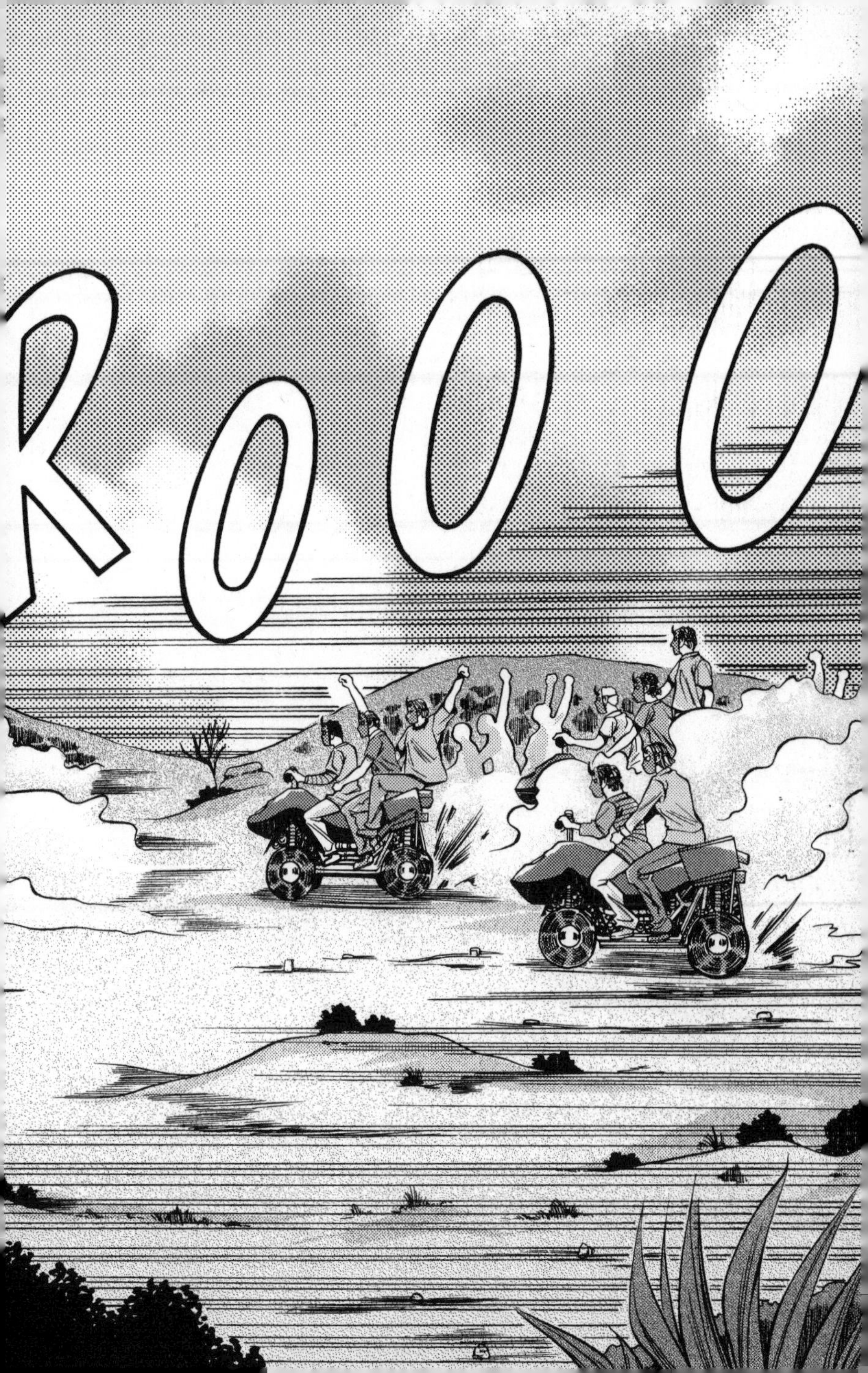
ROOOO

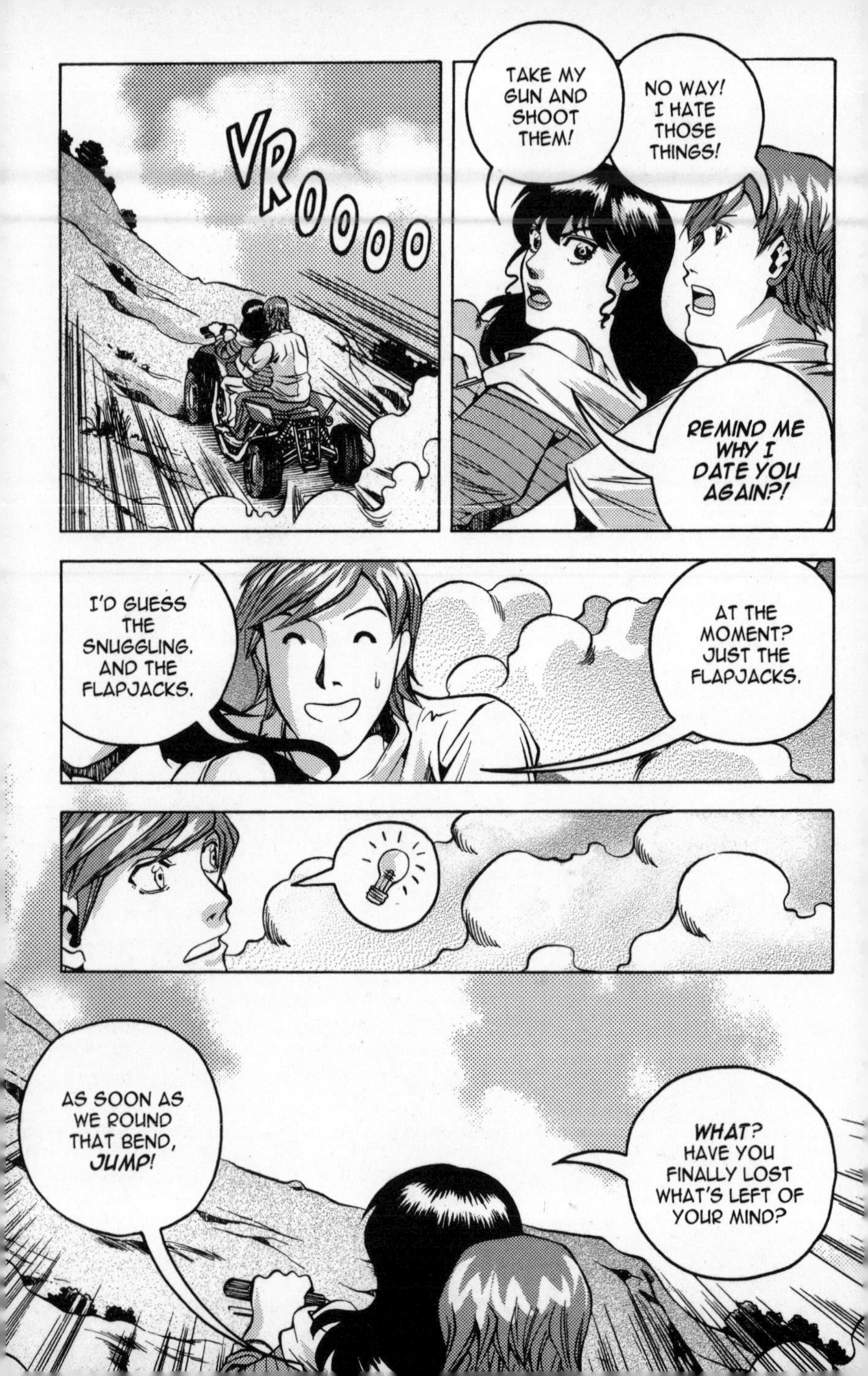
VROOOO
TAKE MY GUN AND SHOOT THEM!
NO WAY! I HATE THOSE THINGS!
REMIND ME WHY I DATE YOU AGAIN?!
I'D GUESS THE SNUGGLING. AND THE FLAPJACKS.
AT THE MOMENT? JUST THE FLAPJACKS.
AS SOON AS WE ROUND THAT BEND, JUMP!
WHAT? HAVE YOU FINALLY LOST WHAT'S LEFT OF YOUR MIND?

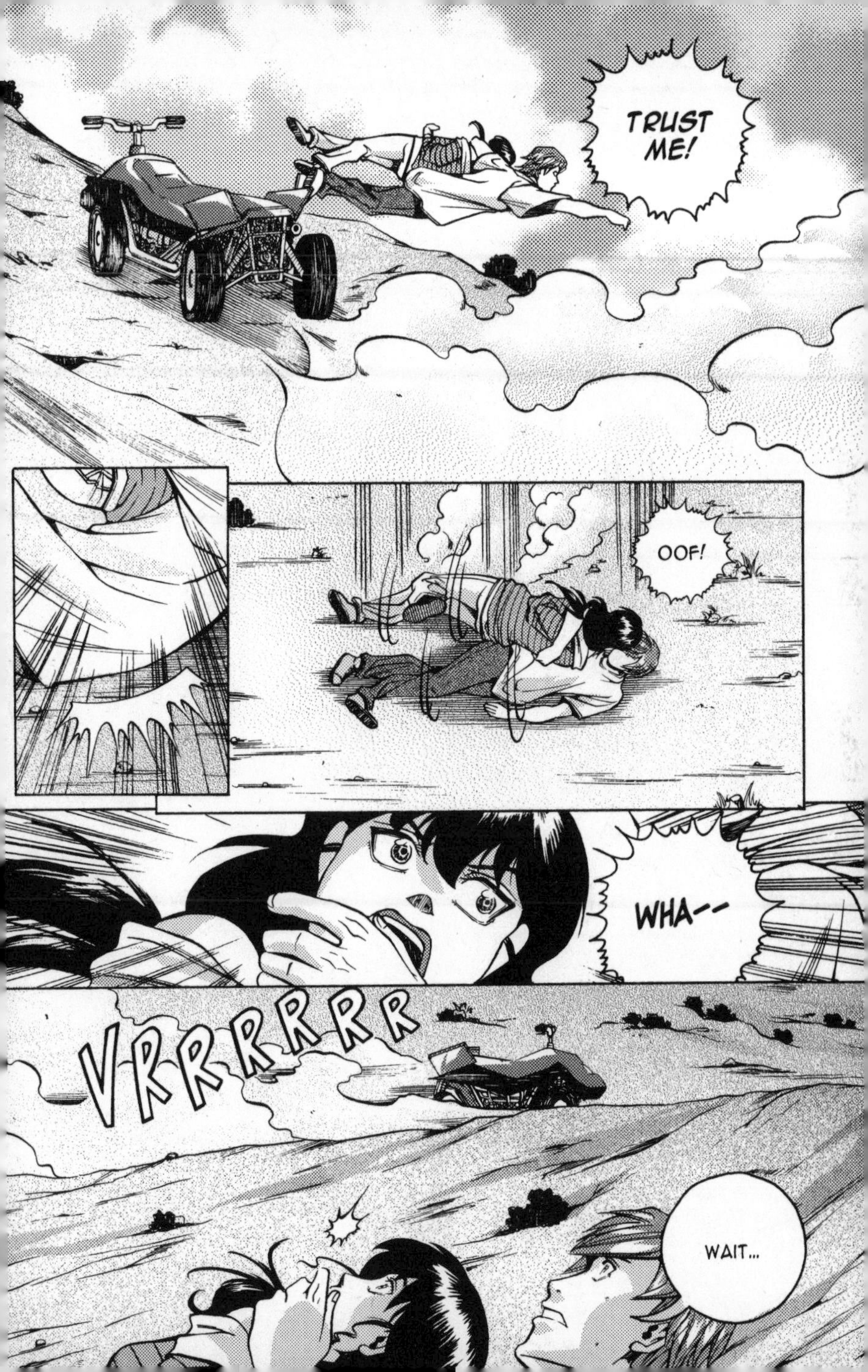
TRUST ME!
OOF!
WHA--
VRRRRRR
WAIT...

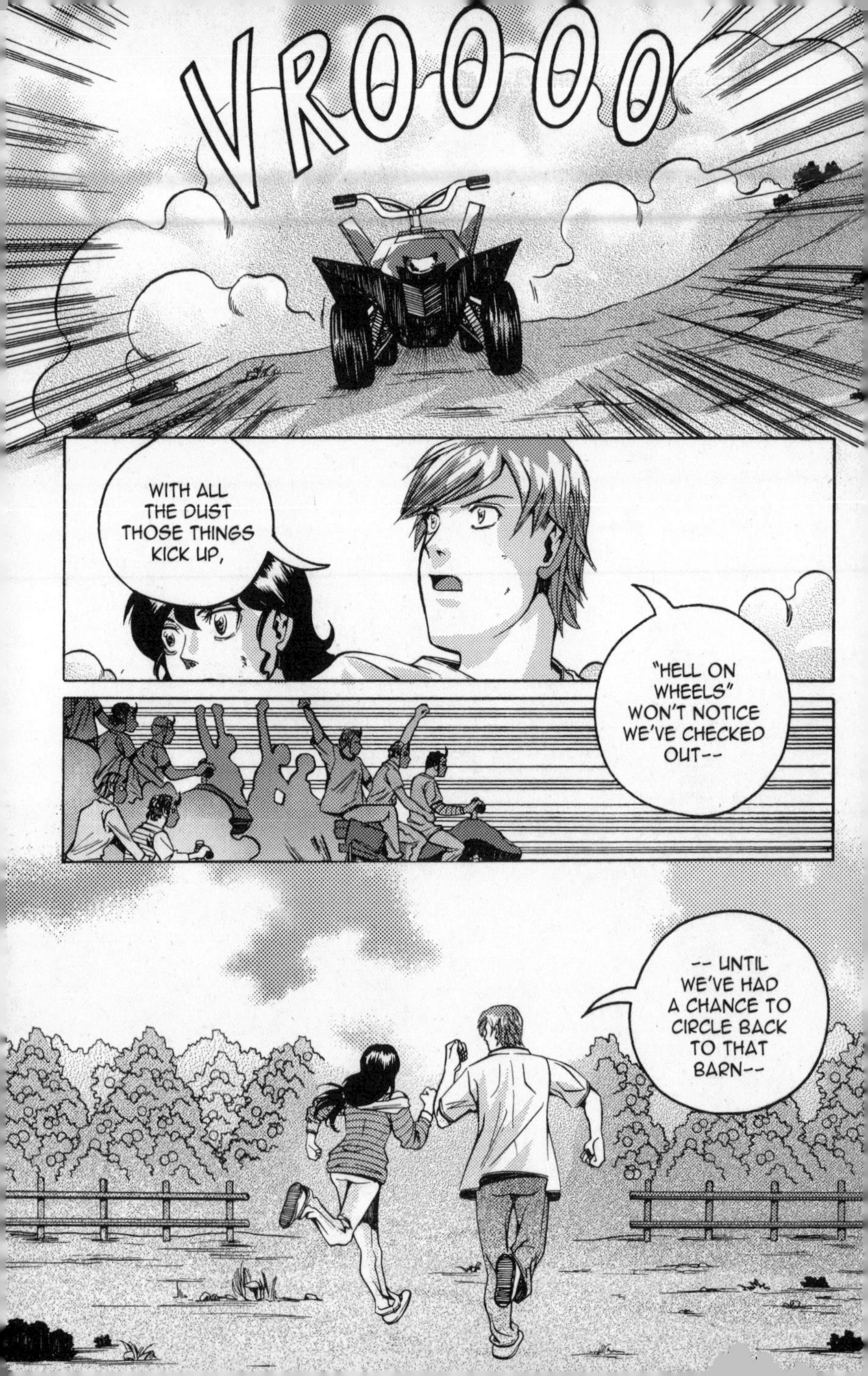
VROOOO
WITH ALL THE DUST THOSE THINGS KICK UP,
"HELL ON WHEELS" WON'T NOTICE WE'VE CHECKED OUT--
-- UNTIL WE'VE HAD A CHANCE TO CIRCLE BACK TO THAT BARN--

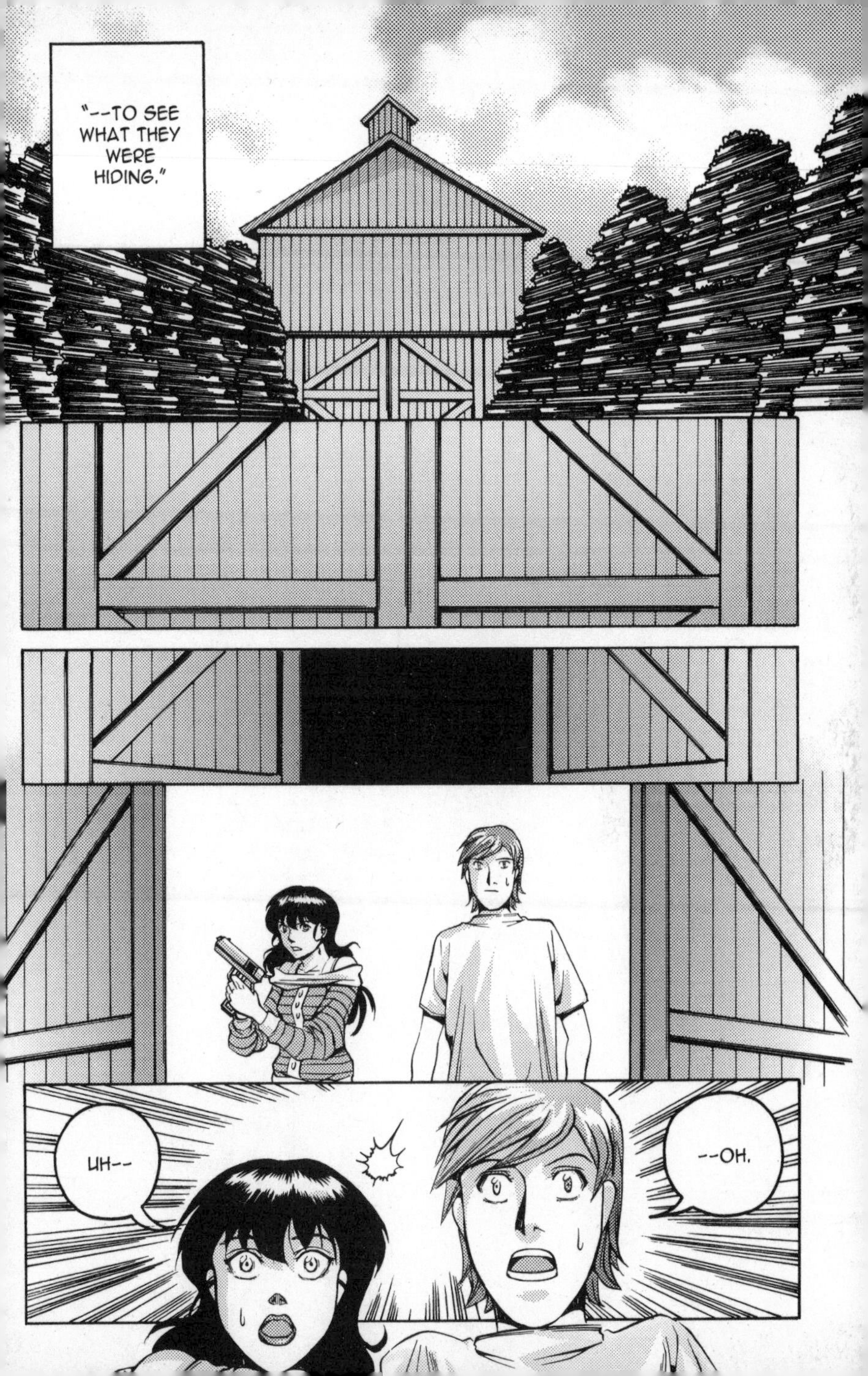
"--TO SEE WHAT THEY WERE HIDING."
UH--
--OH.

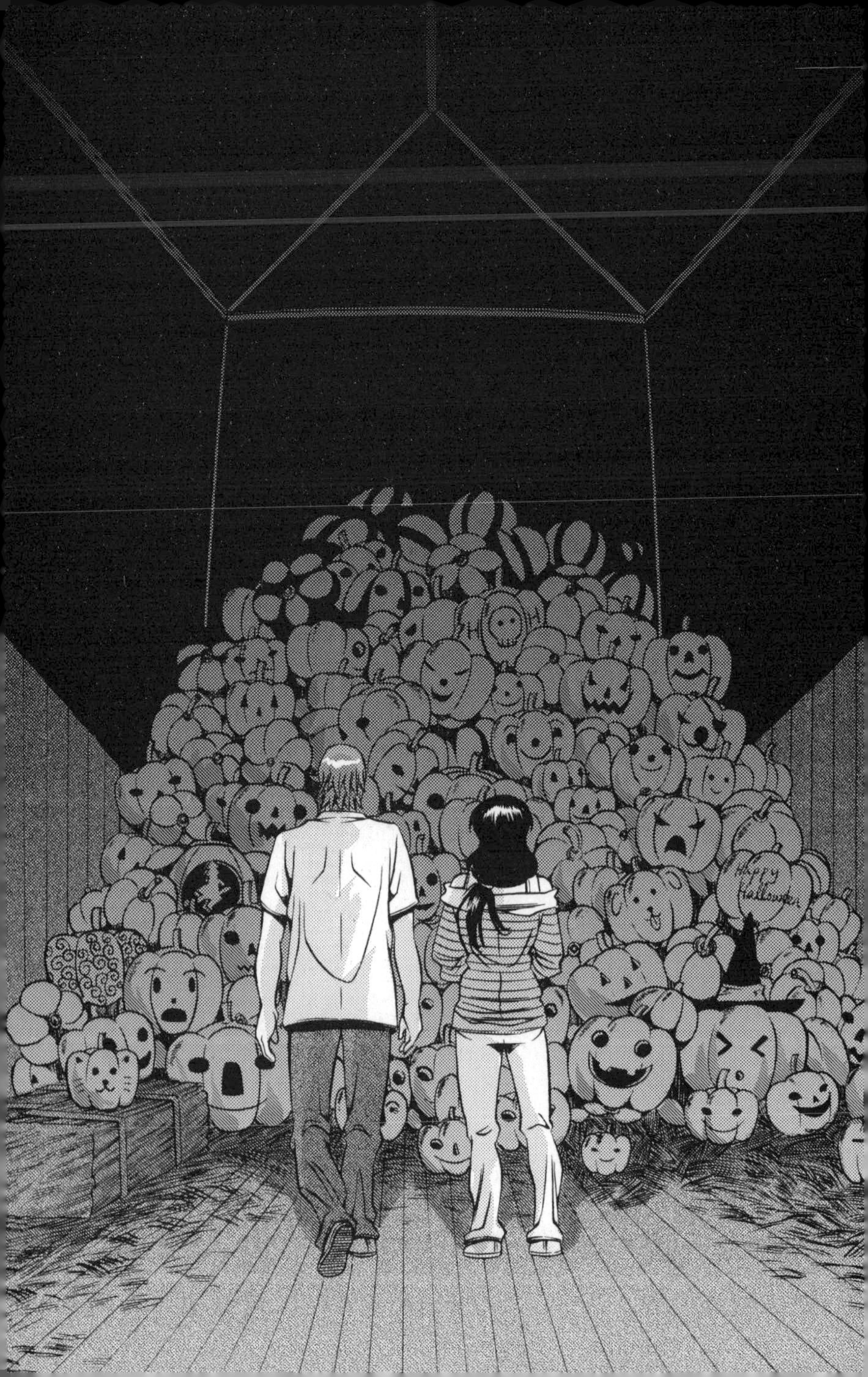
Happy Halloween

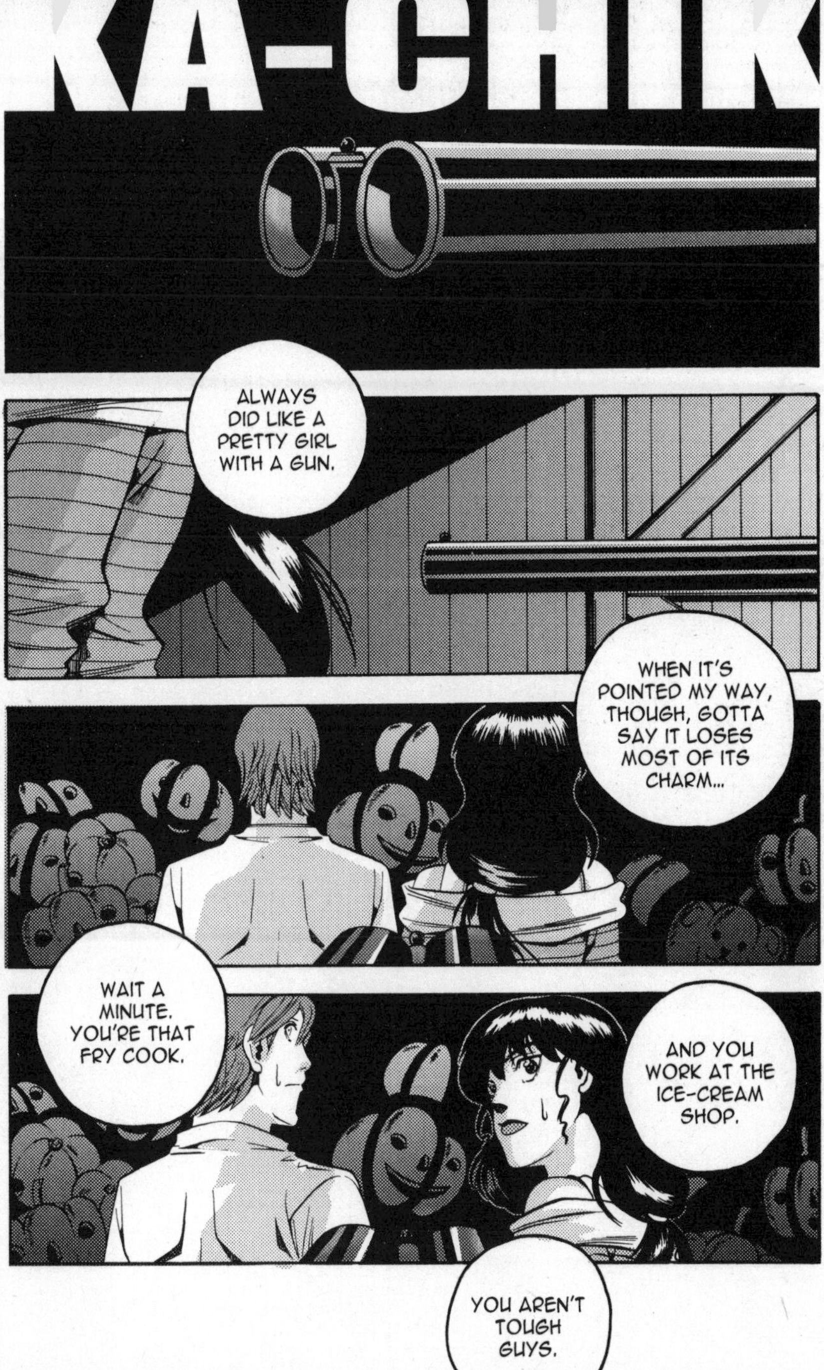
KA-CHIK
ALWAYS DID LIKE A PRETTY GIRL WITH A GUN.
WHEN IT'S POINTED MY WAY, THOUGH, GOTTA SAY IT LOSES MOST OF ITS CHARM...
WAIT A MINUTE. YOU'RE THAT FRY COOK.
AND YOU WORK AT THE ICE-CREAM SHOP.
YOU AREN'T TOUGH GUYS.

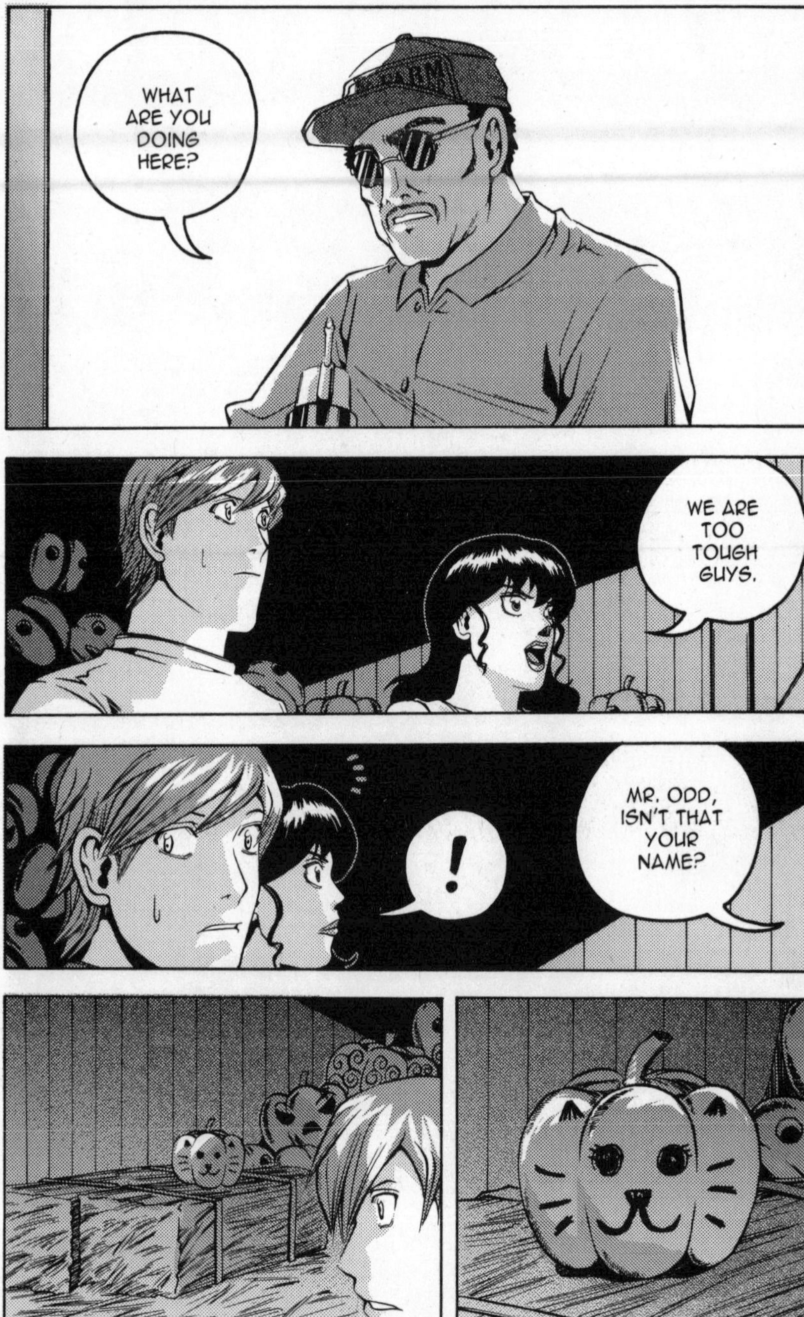
WHAT ARE YOU DOING HERE?
WE ARE TOO TOUGH GUYS.
MR. ODD, ISN'T THAT YOUR NAME?
!

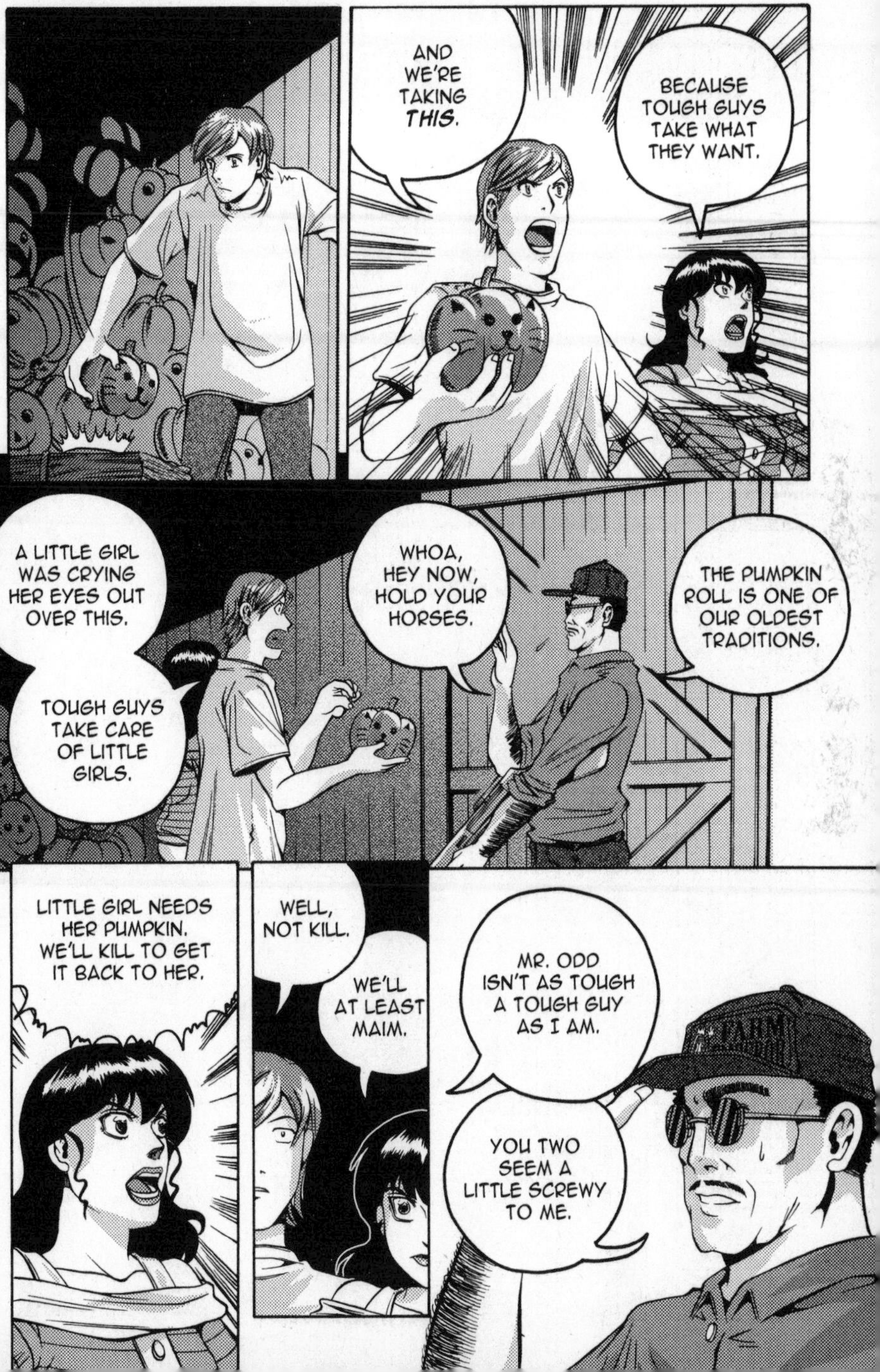
AND WE'RE TAKING *THIS*.
BECAUSE TOUGH GUYS TAKE WHAT THEY WANT.
A LITTLE GIRL WAS CRYING HER EYES OUT OVER THIS.
TOUGH GUYS TAKE CARE OF LITTLE GIRLS.
WHOA, HEY NOW, HOLD YOUR HORSES.
THE PUMPKIN ROLL IS ONE OF OUR OLDEST TRADITIONS.
LITTLE GIRL NEEDS HER PUMPKIN. WE'LL KILL TO GET IT BACK TO HER.
WELL, NOT KILL.
WE'LL AT LEAST MAIM.
MR. ODD ISN'T AS TOUGH A TOUGH GUY AS I AM.
YOU TWO SEEM A LITTLE SCREWY TO ME.

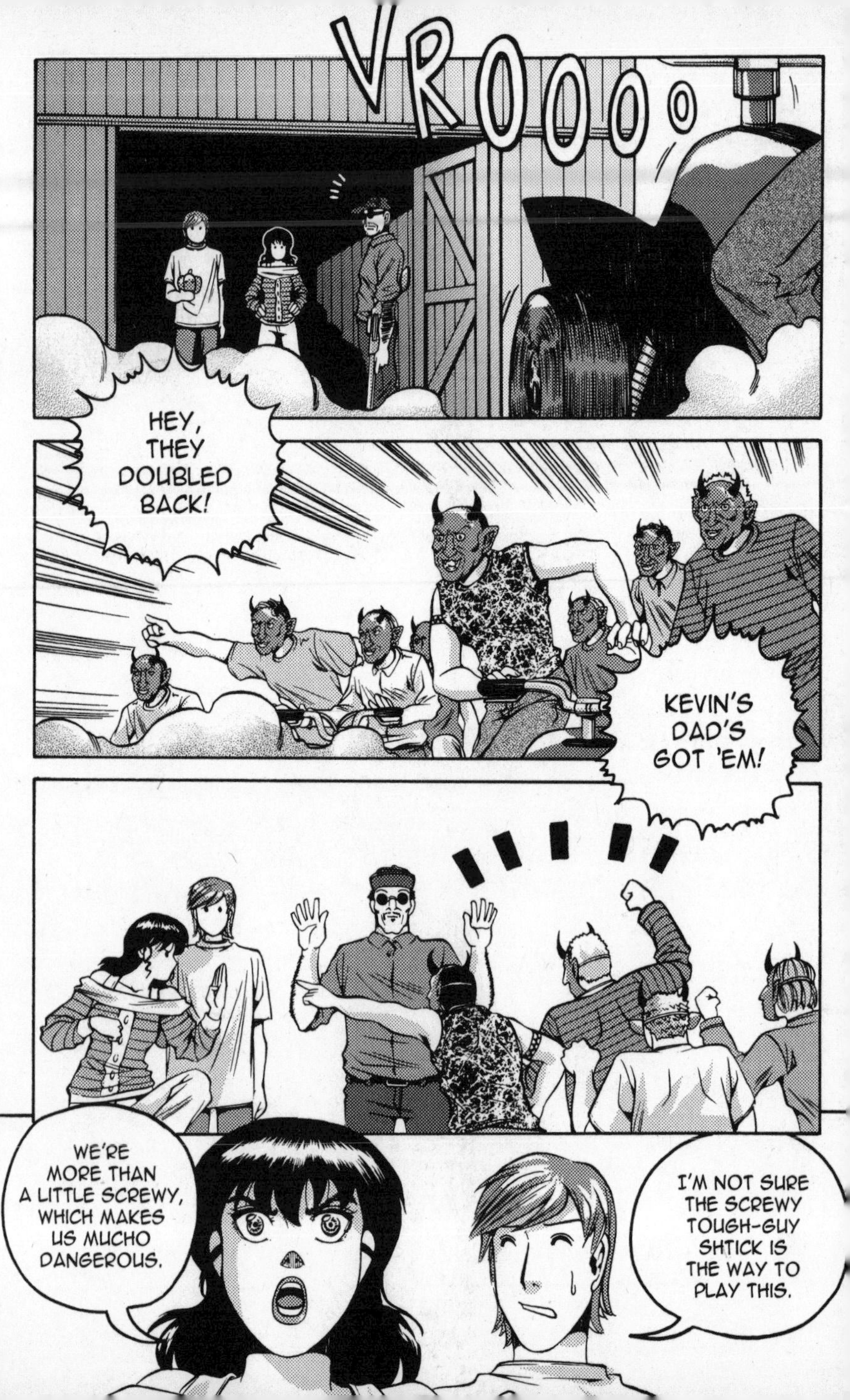
VROOOO
HEY, THEY DOUBLED BACK!
KEVIN'S DAD'S GOT 'EM!
WE'RE MORE THAN A LITTLE SCREWY, WHICH MAKES US MUCHO DANGEROUS.
I'M NOT SURE THE SCREWY TOUGH-GUY SHTICK IS THE WAY TO PLAY THIS.

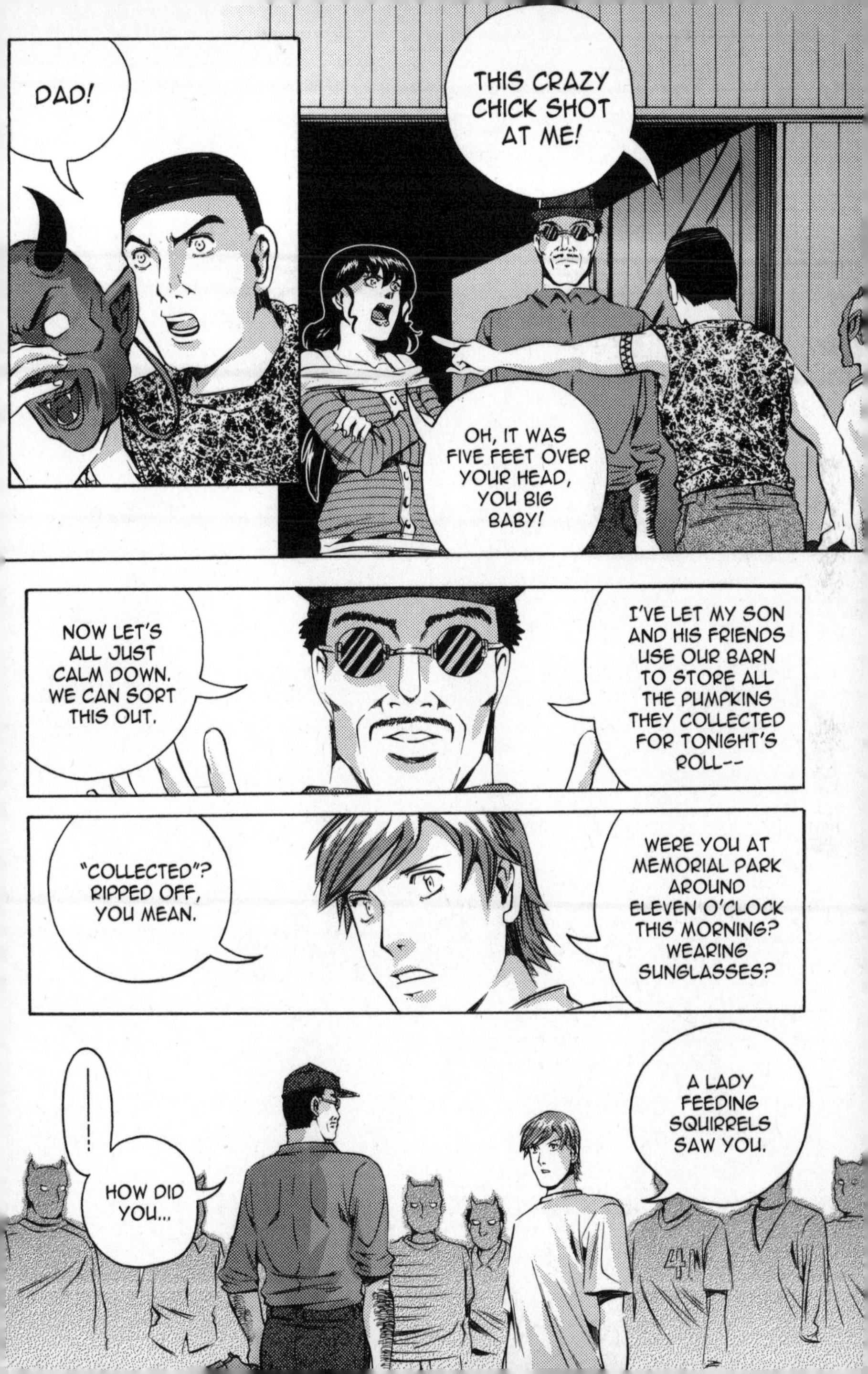
DAD!
THIS CRAZY CHICK SHOT AT ME!
OH, IT WAS FIVE FEET OVER YOUR HEAD, YOU BIG BABY!
NOW LET'S ALL JUST CALM DOWN. WE CAN SORT THIS OUT.
I'VE LET MY SON AND HIS FRIENDS USE OUR BARN TO STORE ALL THE PUMPKINS THEY COLLECTED FOR TONIGHT'S ROLL--
"COLLECTED"? RIPPED OFF, YOU MEAN.
WERE YOU AT MEMORIAL PARK AROUND ELEVEN O'CLOCK THIS MORNING? WEARING SUNGLASSES?
A LADY FEEDING SQUIRRELS SAW YOU.
--!
HOW DID YOU...

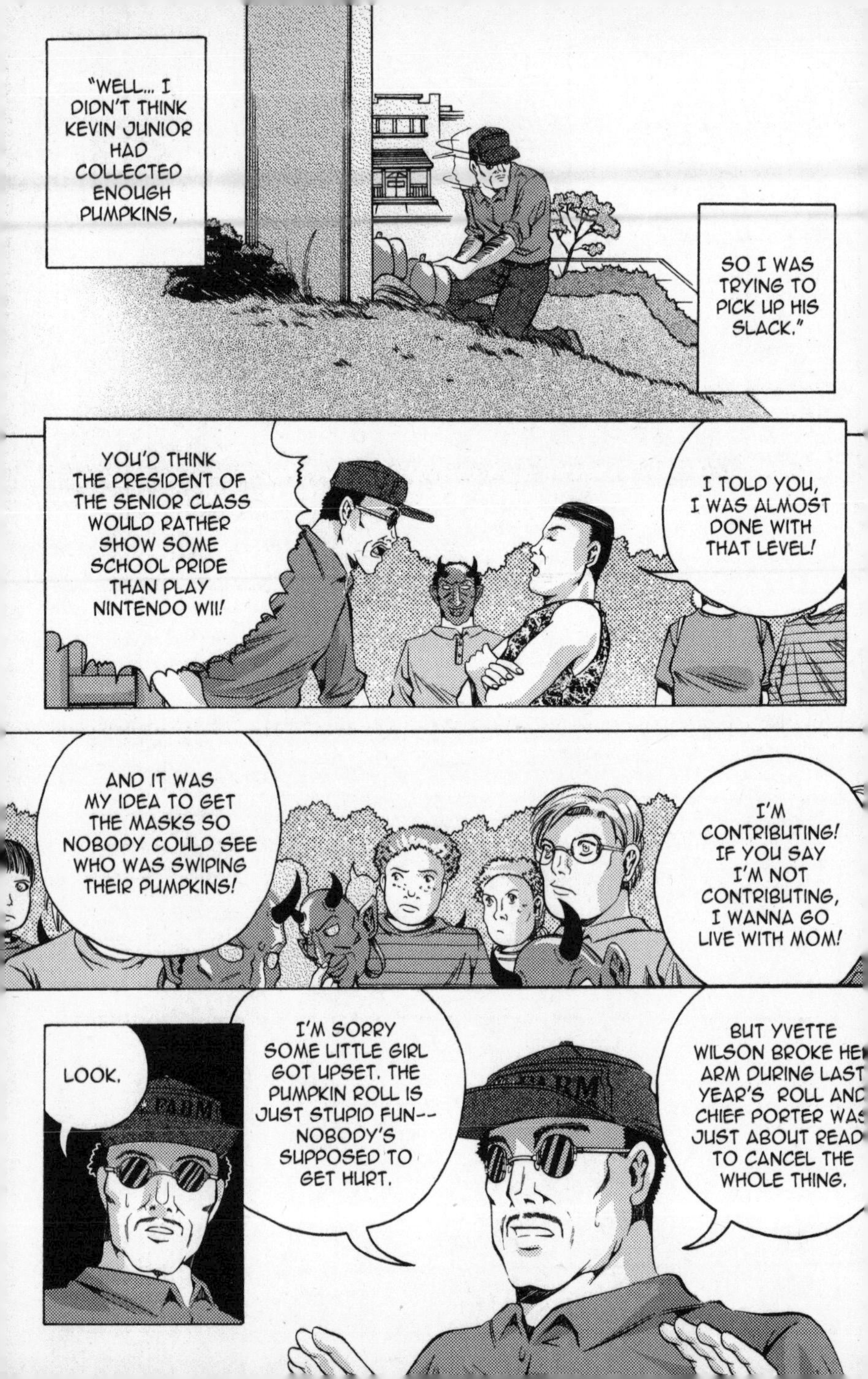
"WELL... I DIDN'T THINK KEVIN JUNIOR HAD COLLECTED ENOUGH PUMPKINS,
SO I WAS TRYING TO PICK UP HIS SLACK."
YOU'D THINK THE PRESIDENT OF THE SENIOR CLASS WOULD RATHER SHOW SOME SCHOOL PRIDE THAN PLAY NINTENDO WII!
I TOLD YOU, I WAS ALMOST DONE WITH THAT LEVEL!
AND IT WAS MY IDEA TO GET THE MASKS SO NOBODY COULD SEE WHO WAS SWIPING THEIR PUMPKINS!
I'M CONTRIBUTING! IF YOU SAY I'M NOT CONTRIBUTING, I WANNA GO LIVE WITH MOM!
LOOK.
I'M SORRY SOME LITTLE GIRL GOT UPSET. THE PUMPKIN ROLL IS JUST STUPID FUN-- NOBODY'S SUPPOSED TO GET HURT.
BUT YVETTE WILSON BROKE HE ARM DURING LAST YEAR'S ROLL AND CHIEF PORTER WAS JUST ABOUT READ TO CANCEL THE WHOLE THING.

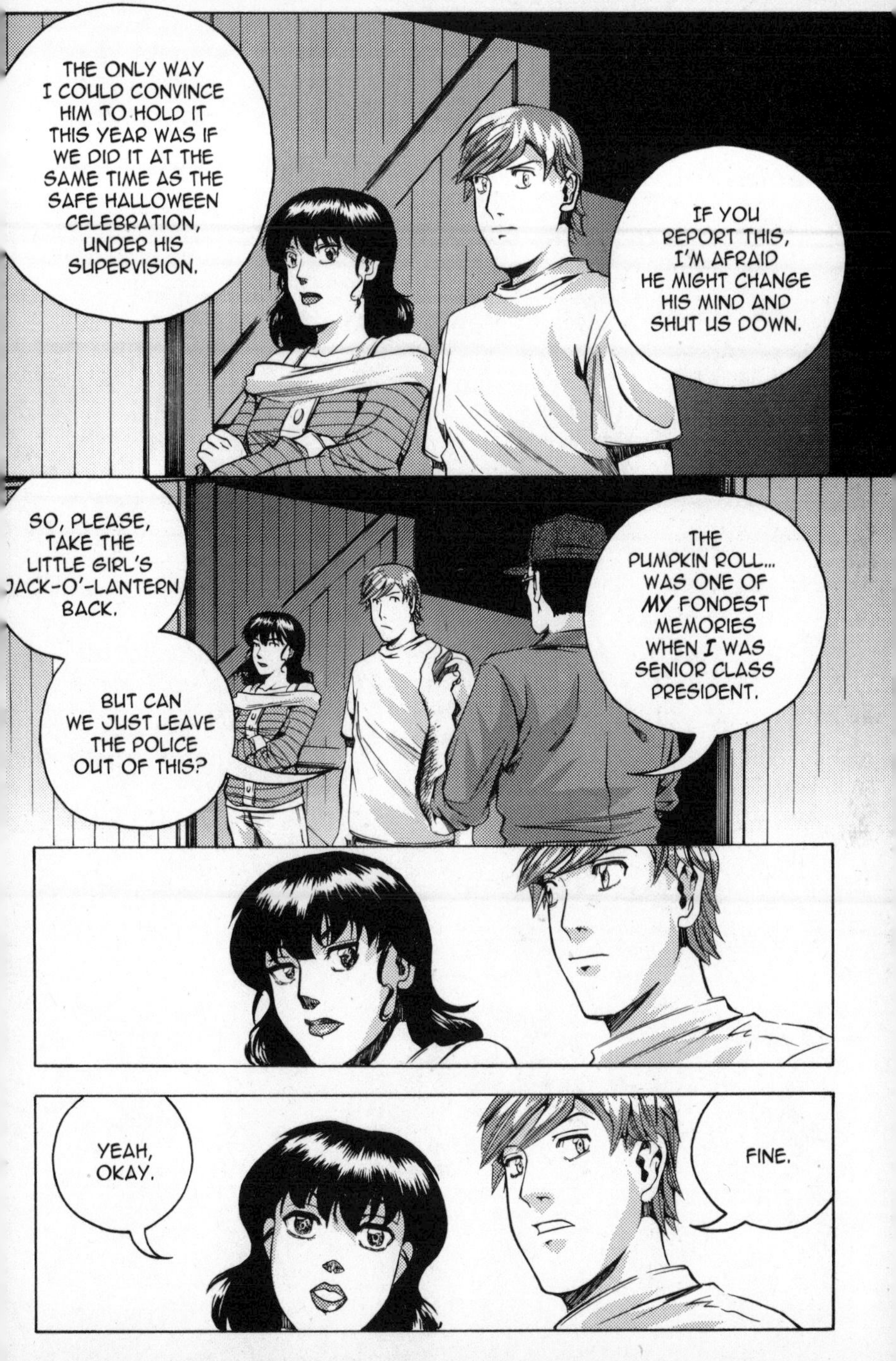
THE ONLY WAY I COULD CONVINCE HIM TO HOLD IT THIS YEAR WAS IF WE DID IT AT THE SAME TIME AS THE SAFE HALLOWEEN CELEBRATION, UNDER HIS SUPERVISION.
IF YOU REPORT THIS, I'M AFRAID HE MIGHT CHANGE HIS MIND AND SHUT US DOWN.
SO, PLEASE, TAKE THE LITTLE GIRL'S JACK-O'-LANTERN BACK.
BUT CAN WE JUST LEAVE THE POLICE OUT OF THIS?
THE PUMPKIN ROLL... WAS ONE OF MY FONDEST MEMORIES WHEN I WAS SENIOR CLASS PRESIDENT.
YEAH, OKAY.
FINE.

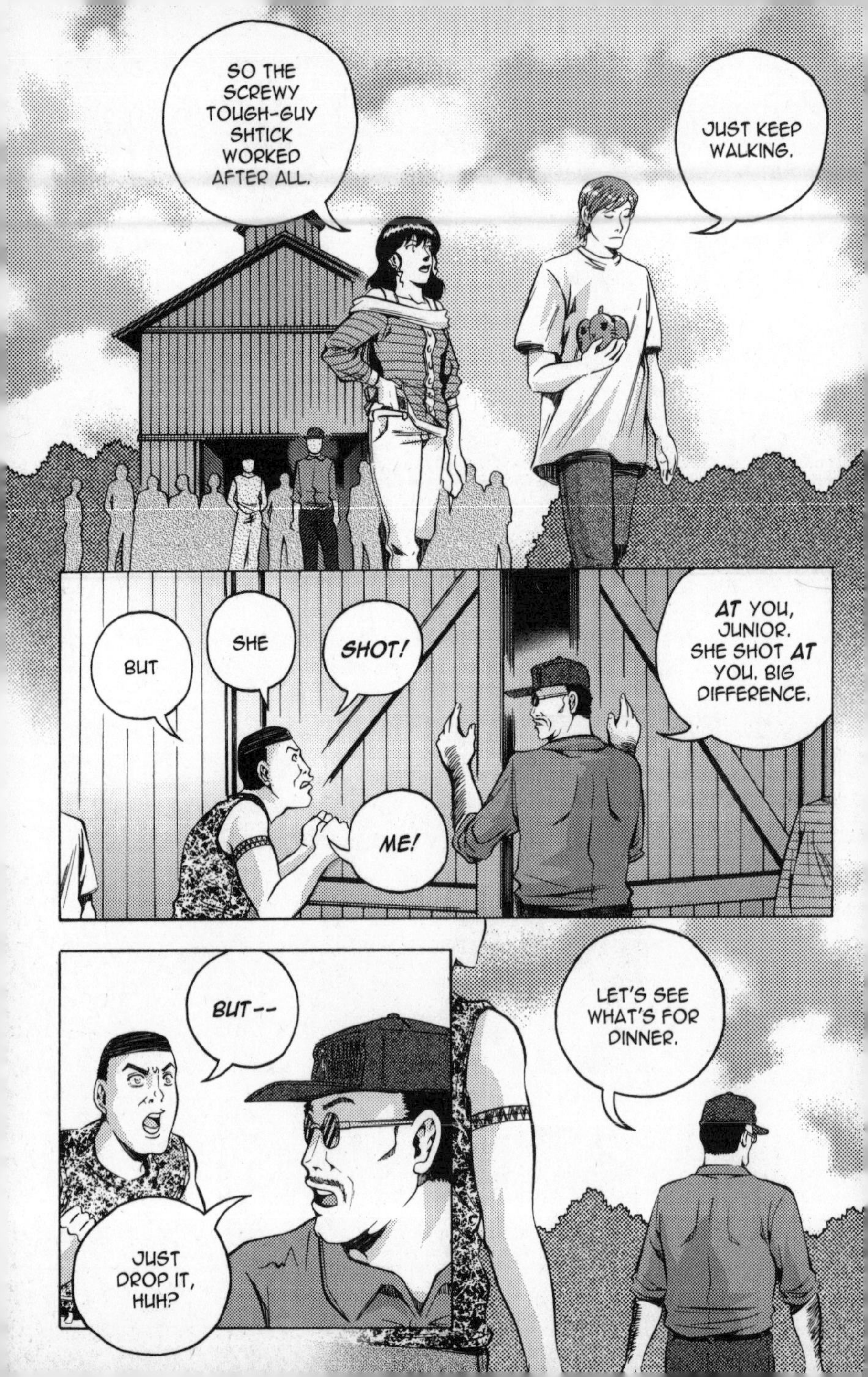
SO THE SCREWY TOUGH-GUY SHTICK WORKED AFTER ALL.
JUST KEEP WALKING.
BUT
SHE
SHOT!
ME!
AT YOU, JUNIOR. SHE SHOT AT YOU. BIG DIFFERENCE.
BUT--
JUST DROP IT, HUH?
LET'S SEE WHAT'S FOR DINNER.

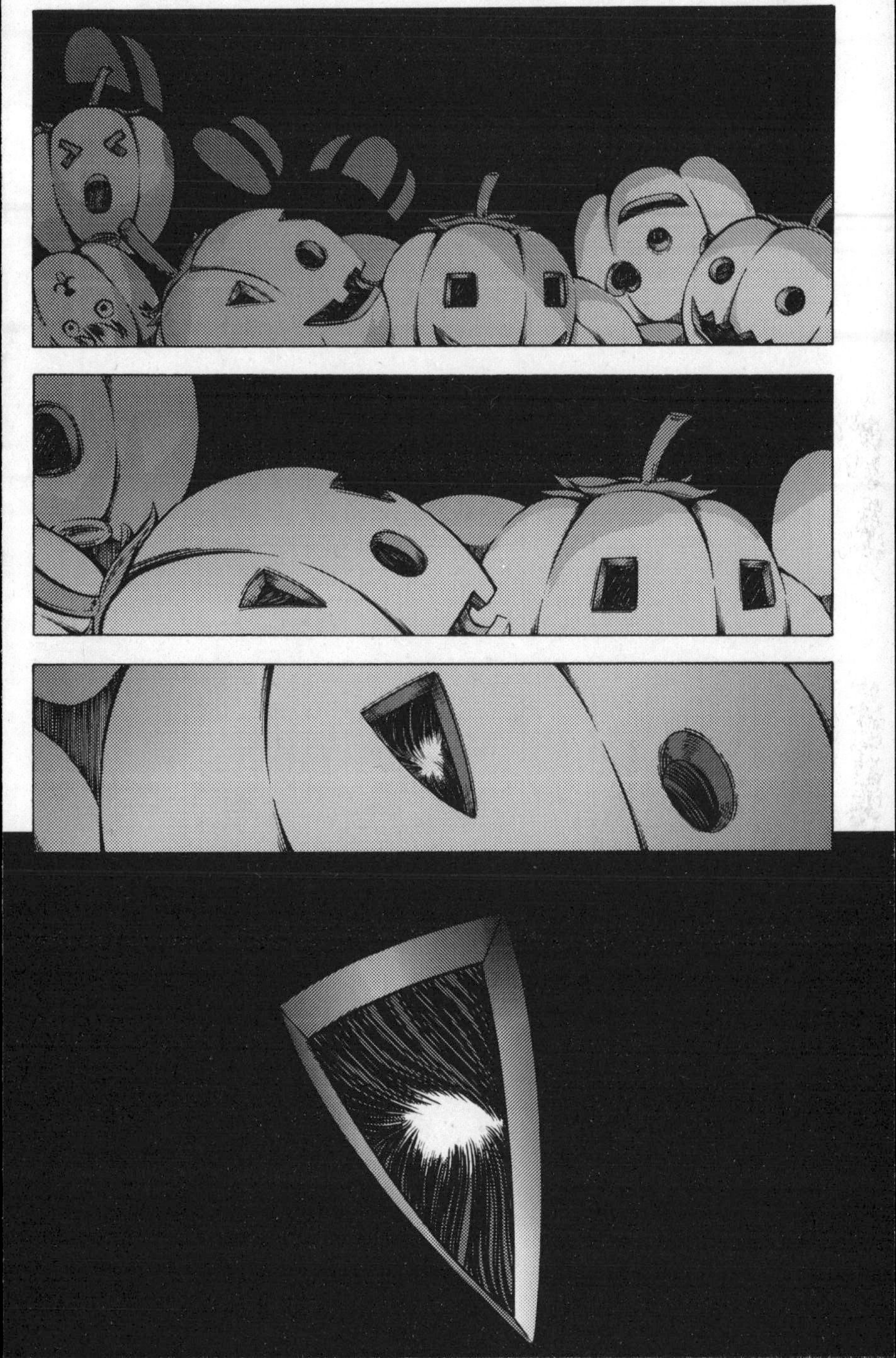

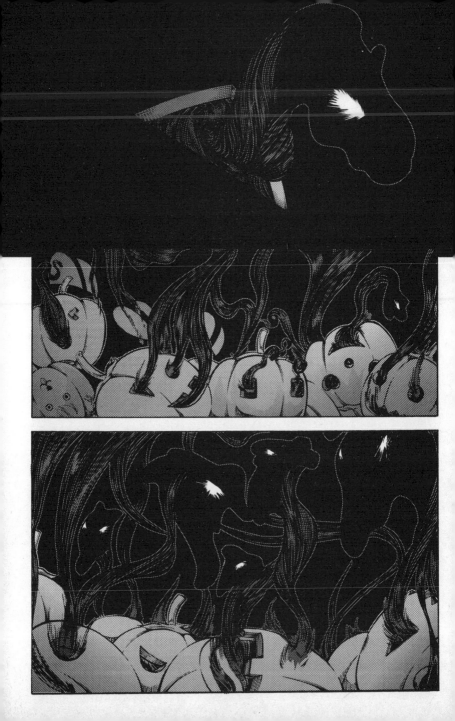

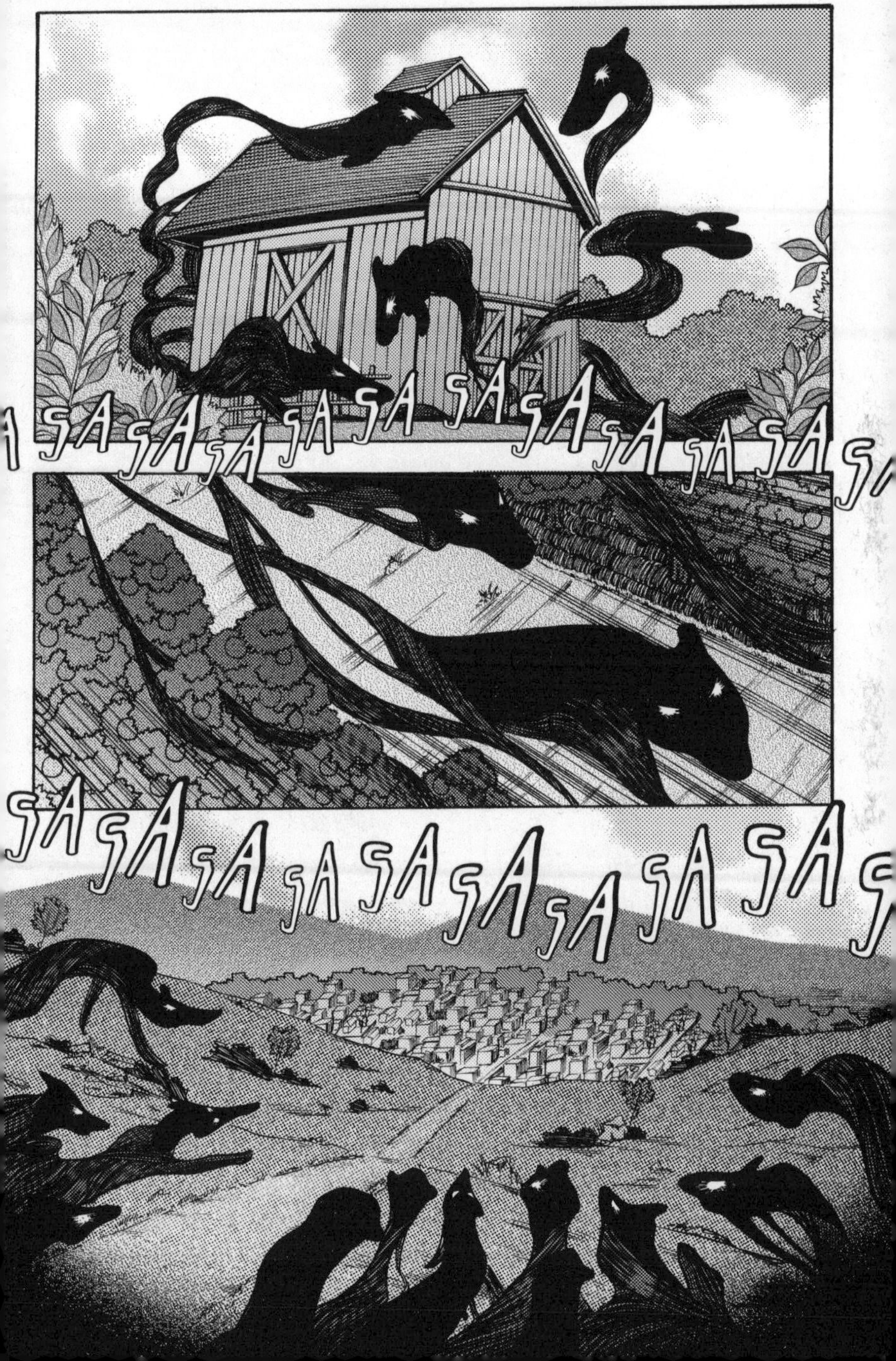
SA SA SA SA SA SA SA SA SA SA
SA SA SA SA SA SA SA SA SA

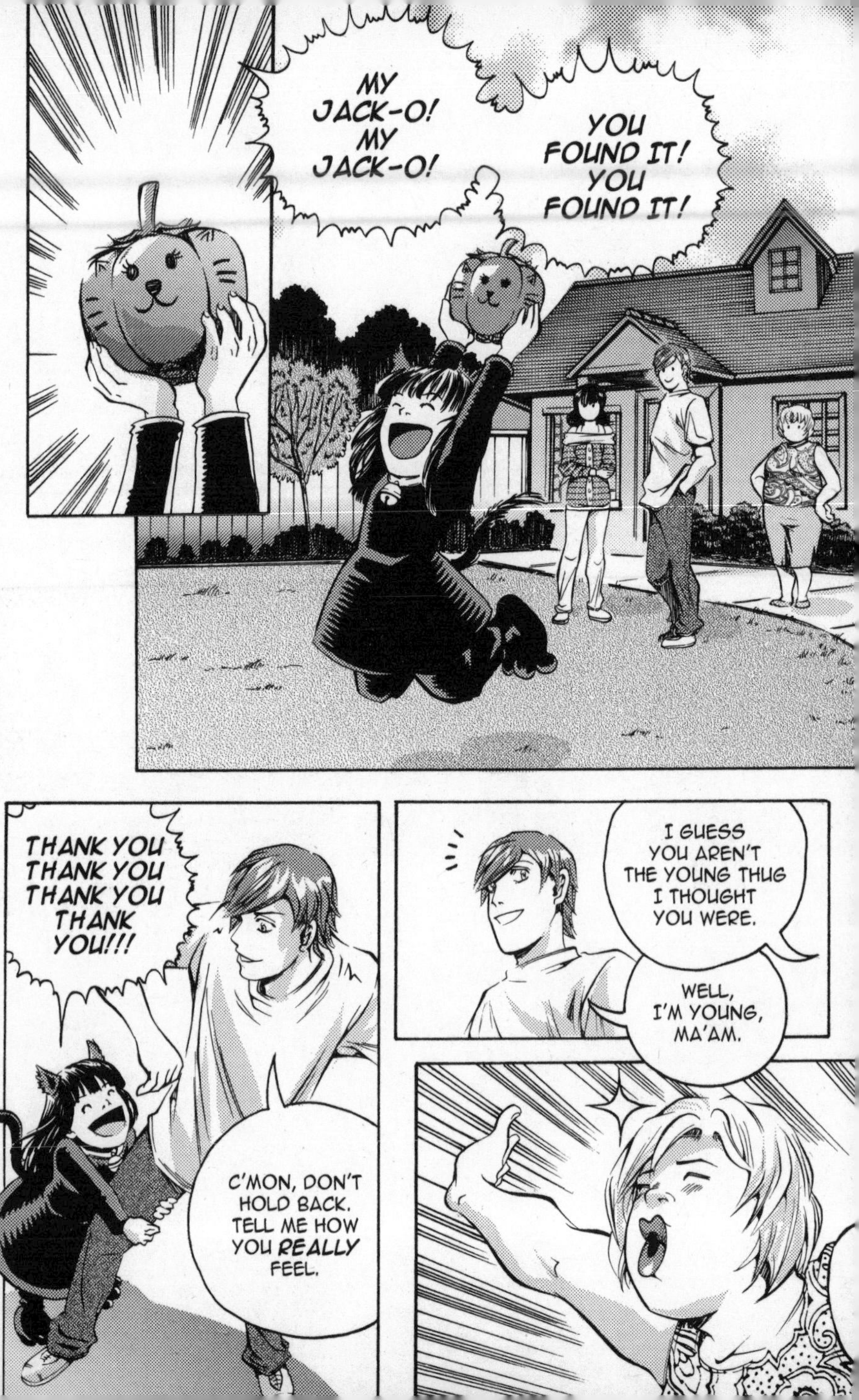

MY JACK-O! MY JACK-O!
YOU FOUND IT! YOU FOUND IT!
THANK YOU THANK YOU THANK YOU THANK YOU!!!
C'MON, DON'T HOLD BACK. TELL ME HOW YOU *REALLY* FEEL.
I GUESS YOU AREN'T THE YOUNG THUG I THOUGHT YOU WERE.
WELL, I'M YOUNG, MA'AM.

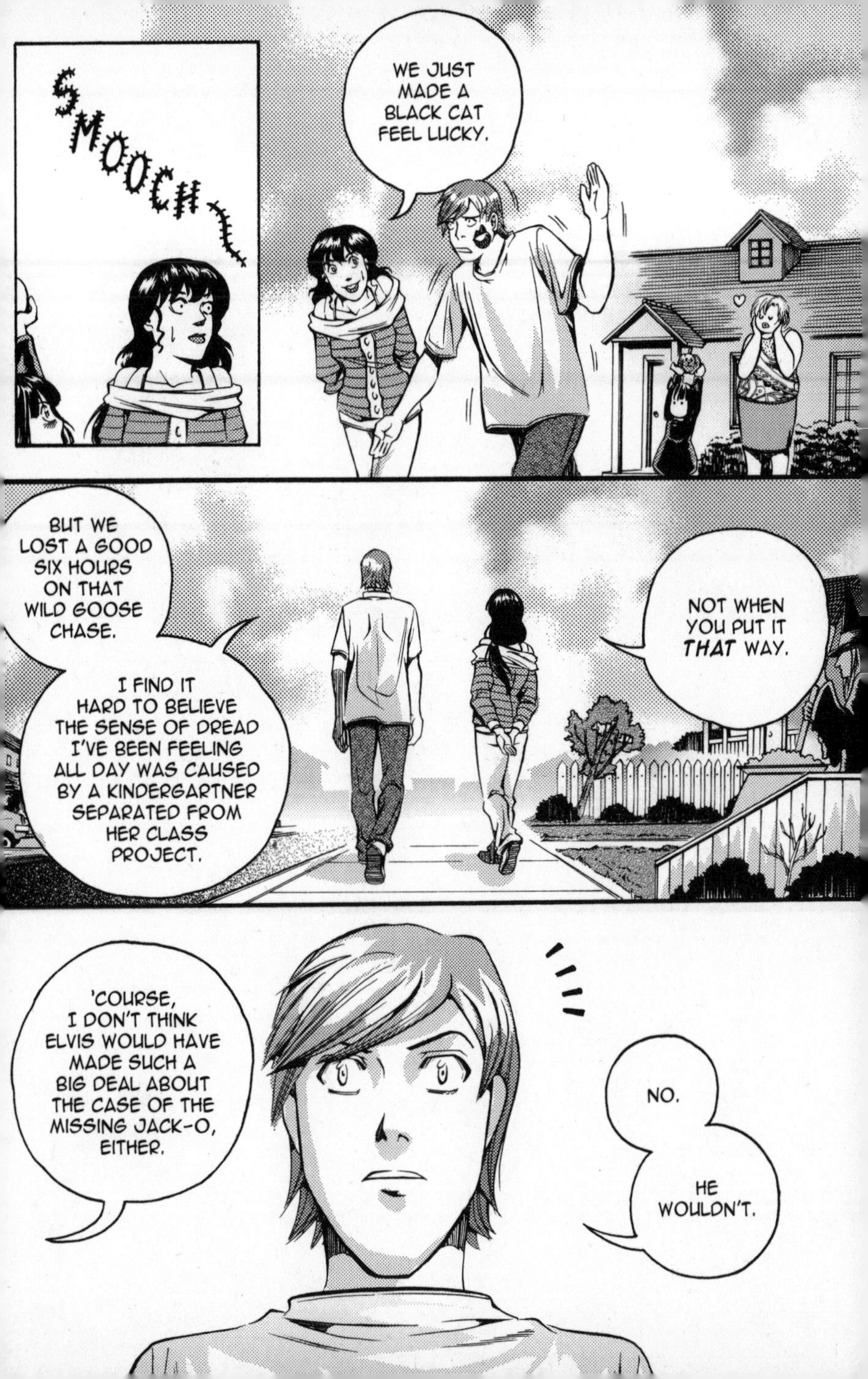
SMOOCH
WE JUST MADE A BLACK CAT FEEL LUCKY.
BUT WE LOST A GOOD SIX HOURS ON THAT WILD GOOSE CHASE.
I FIND IT HARD TO BELIEVE THE SENSE OF DREAD I'VE BEEN FEELING ALL DAY WAS CAUSED BY A KINDERGARTNER SEPARATED FROM HER CLASS PROJECT.
NOT WHEN YOU PUT IT *THAT* WAY.
'COURSE, I DON'T THINK ELVIS WOULD HAVE MADE SUCH A BIG DEAL ABOUT THE CASE OF THE MISSING JACK-O, EITHER.
NO.
HE WOULDN'T.

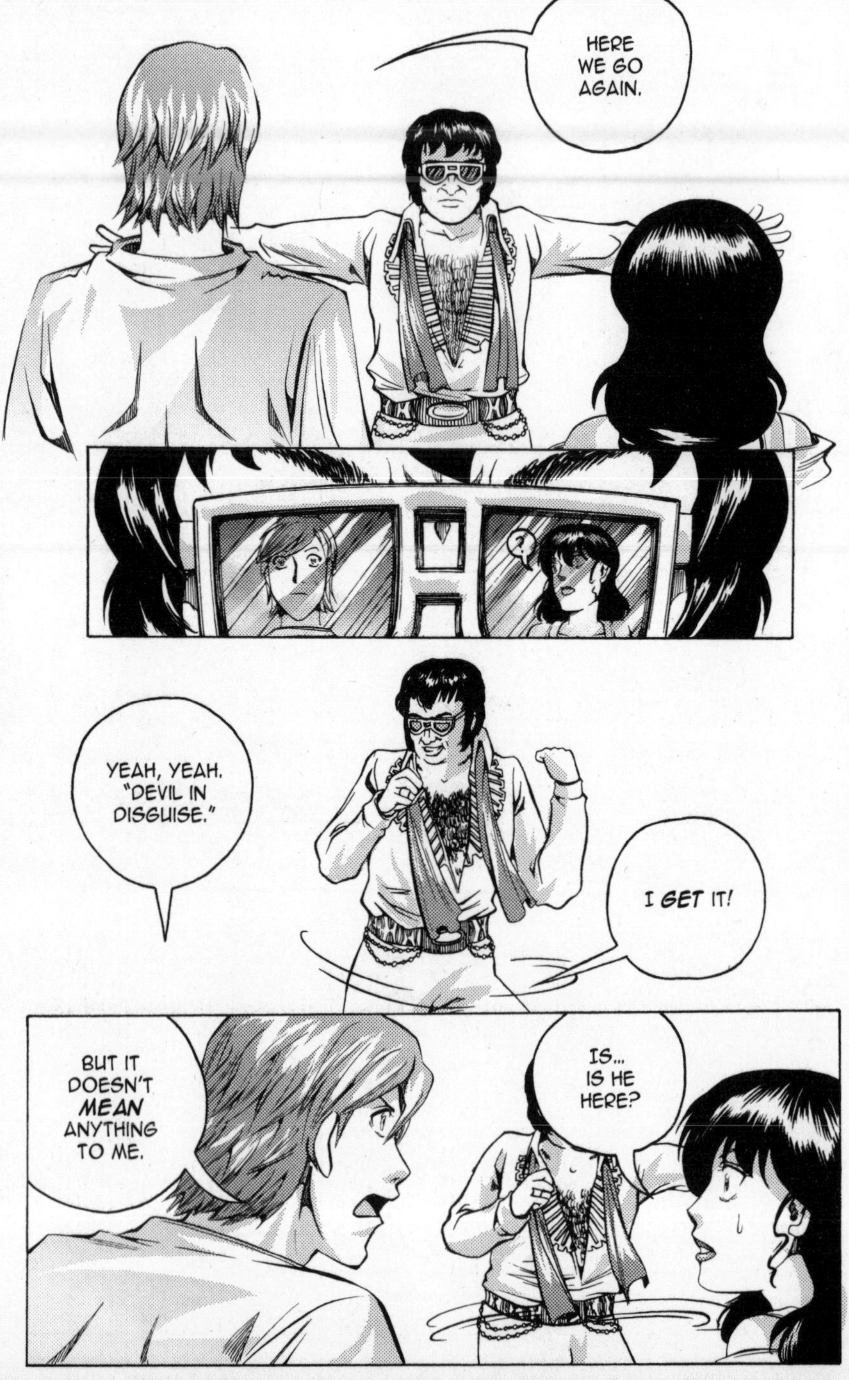
HERE WE GO AGAIN.
YEAH, YEAH. "DEVIL IN DISGUISE."
I GET IT!
BUT IT DOESN'T MEAN ANYTHING TO ME.
IS... IS HE HERE?

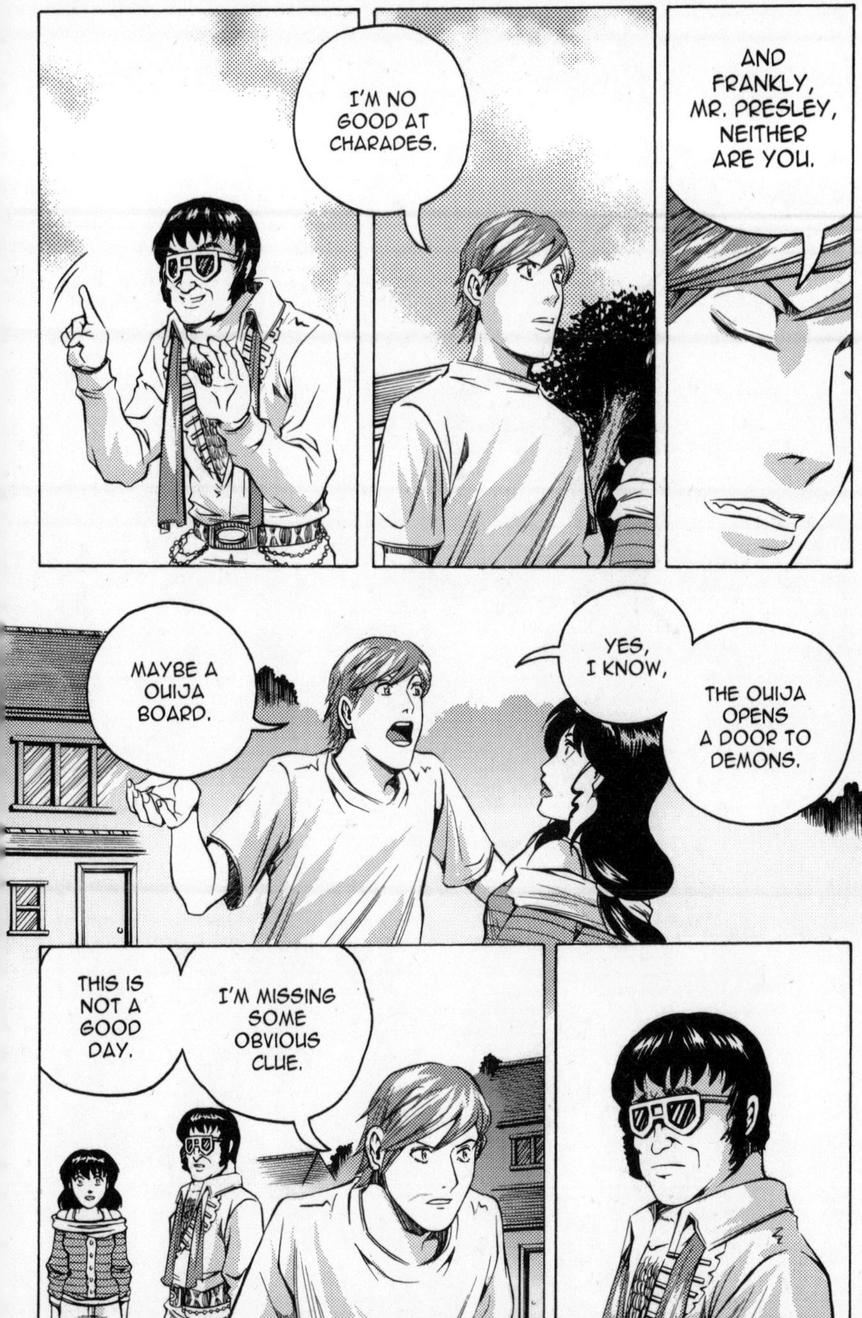
I'M NO GOOD AT CHARADES.
AND FRANKLY, MR. PRESLEY, NEITHER ARE YOU.
MAYBE A OUIJA BOARD.
YES, I KNOW,
THE OUIJA OPENS A DOOR TO DEMONS.
THIS IS NOT A GOOD DAY.
I'M MISSING SOME OBVIOUS CLUE.

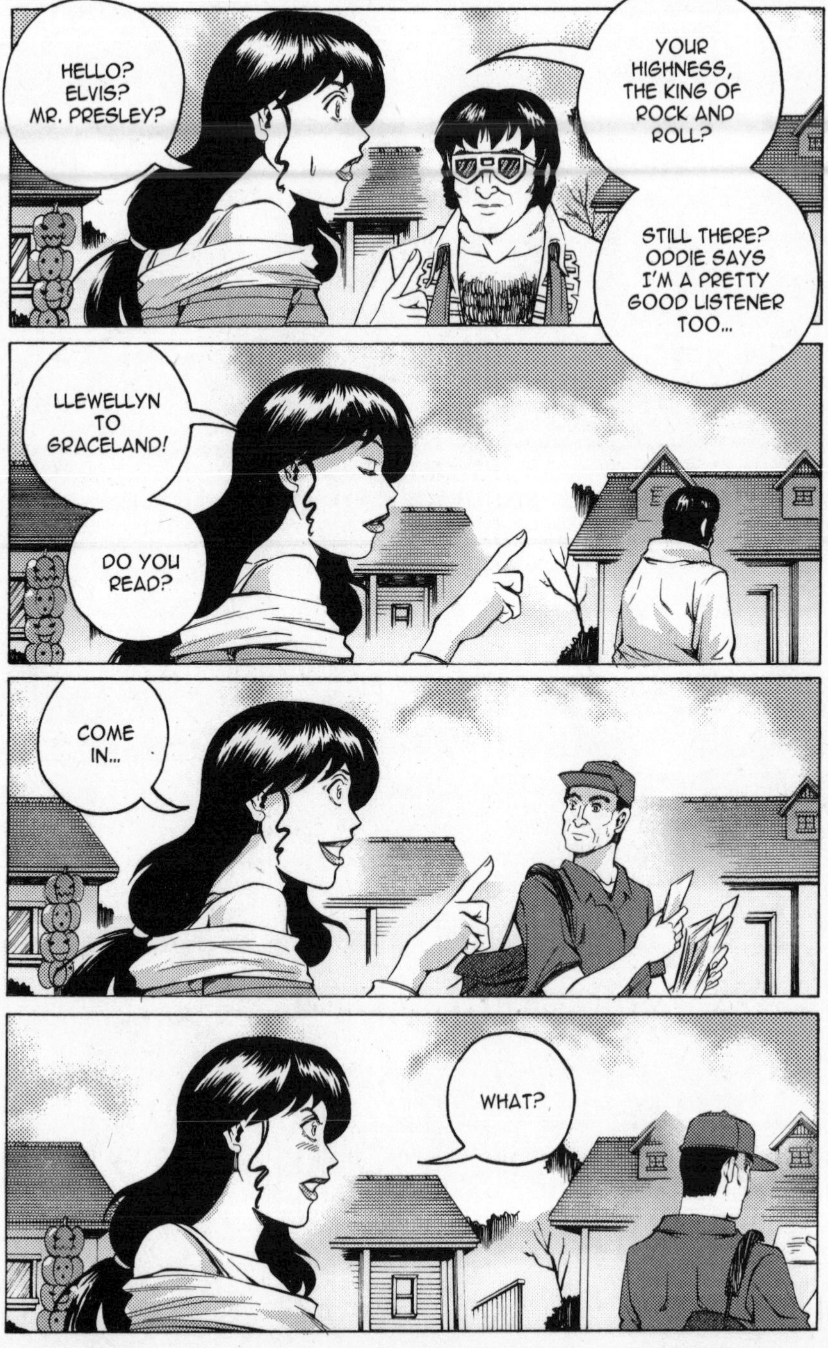
HELLO? ELVIS? MR. PRESLEY?
YOUR HIGHNESS, THE KING OF ROCK AND ROLL?
STILL THERE? ODDIE SAYS I'M A PRETTY GOOD LISTENER TOO...
LLEWELLYN TO GRACELAND!
DO YOU READ?
COME IN...
WHAT?

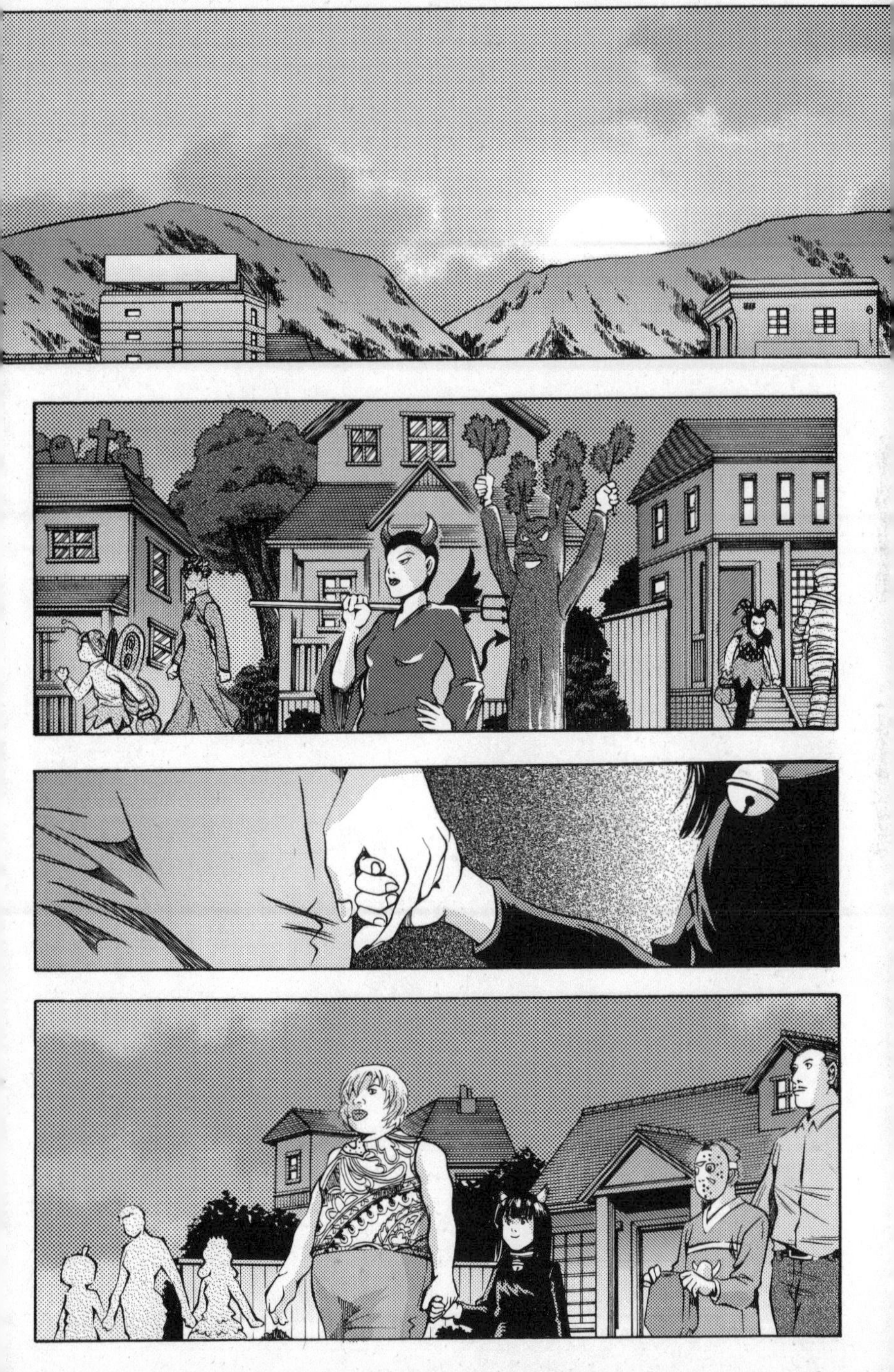

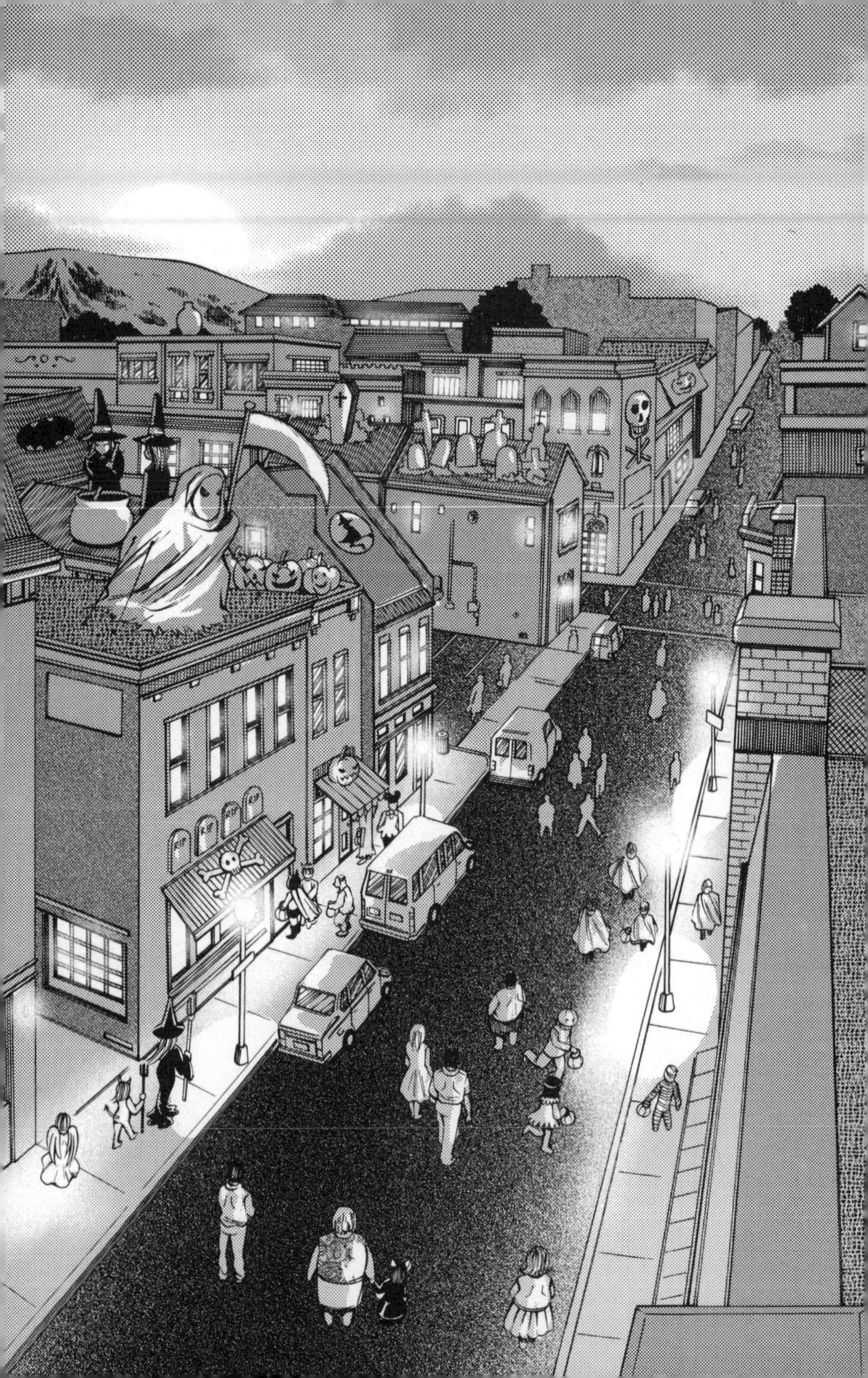

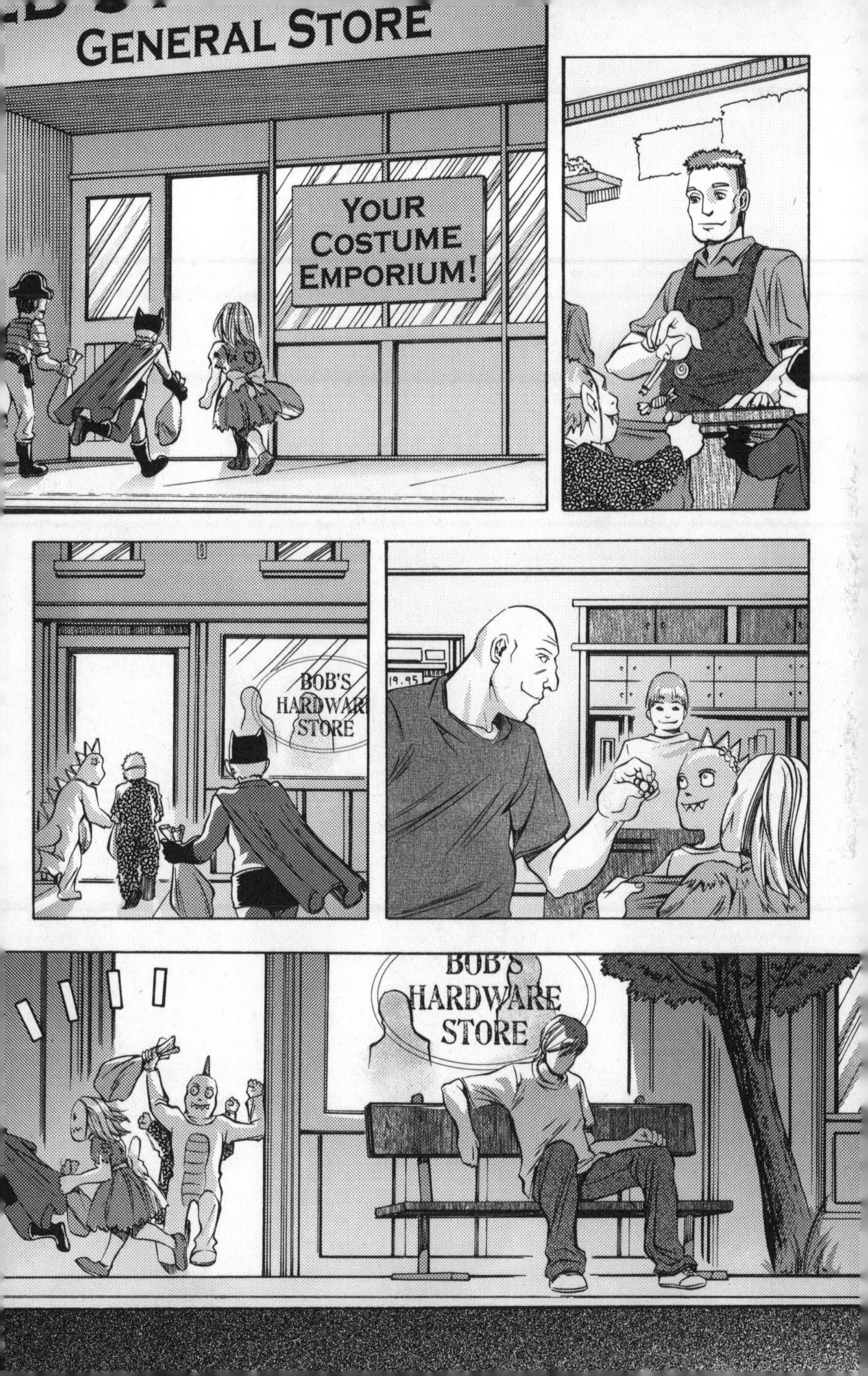
GENERAL STORE
YOUR COSTUME EMPORIUM!
BOB'S HARDWARE STORE
BOB'S HARDWARE STORE

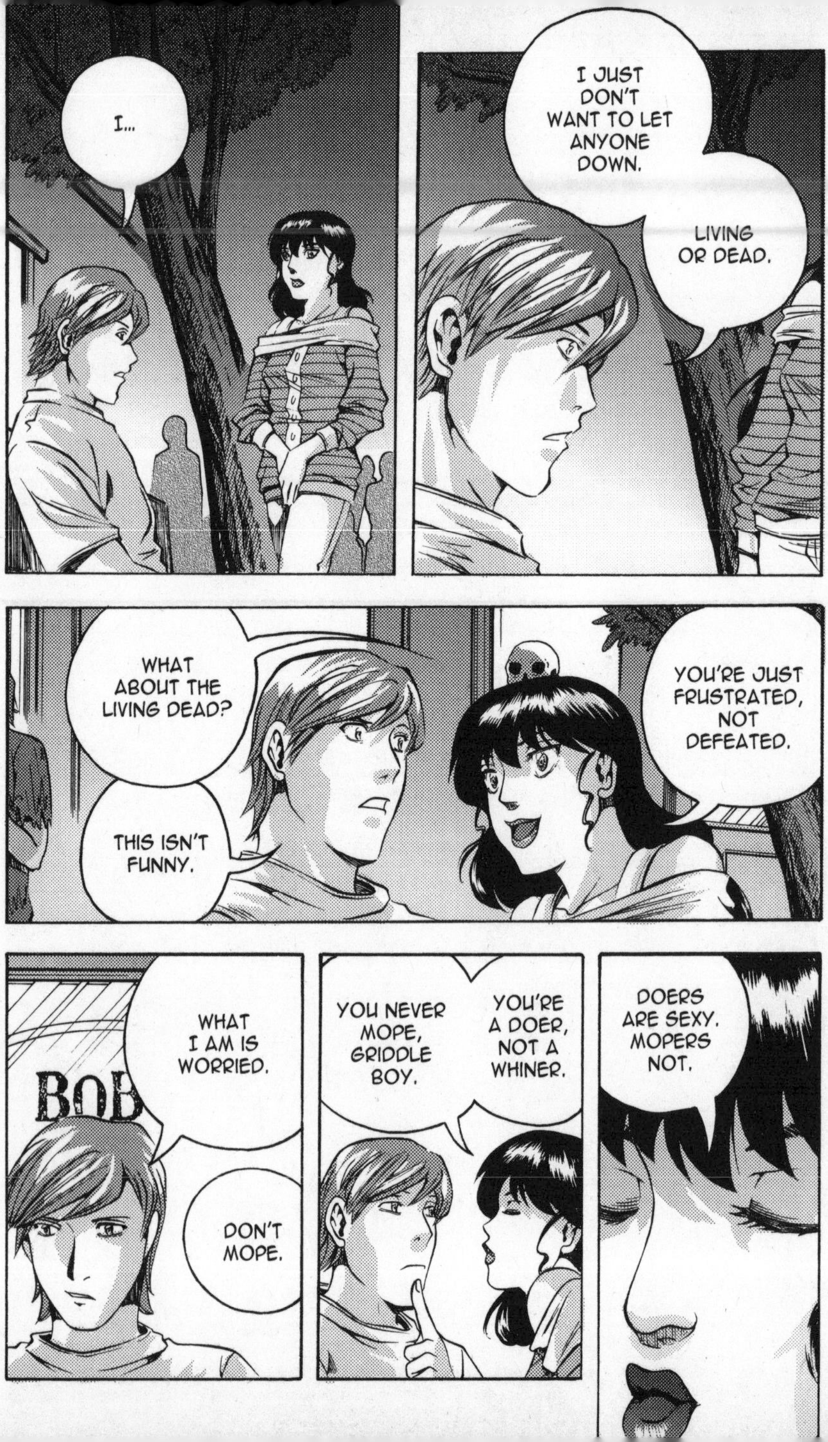
I...
I JUST DON'T WANT TO LET ANYONE DOWN.
LIVING OR DEAD.
WHAT ABOUT THE LIVING DEAD?
THIS ISN'T FUNNY.
YOU'RE JUST FRUSTRATED, NOT DEFEATED.
BOB
WHAT I AM IS WORRIED.
DON'T MOPE.
YOU NEVER MOPE, GRIDDLE BOY.
YOU'RE A DOER, NOT A WHINER.
DOERS ARE SEXY. MOPERS NOT.

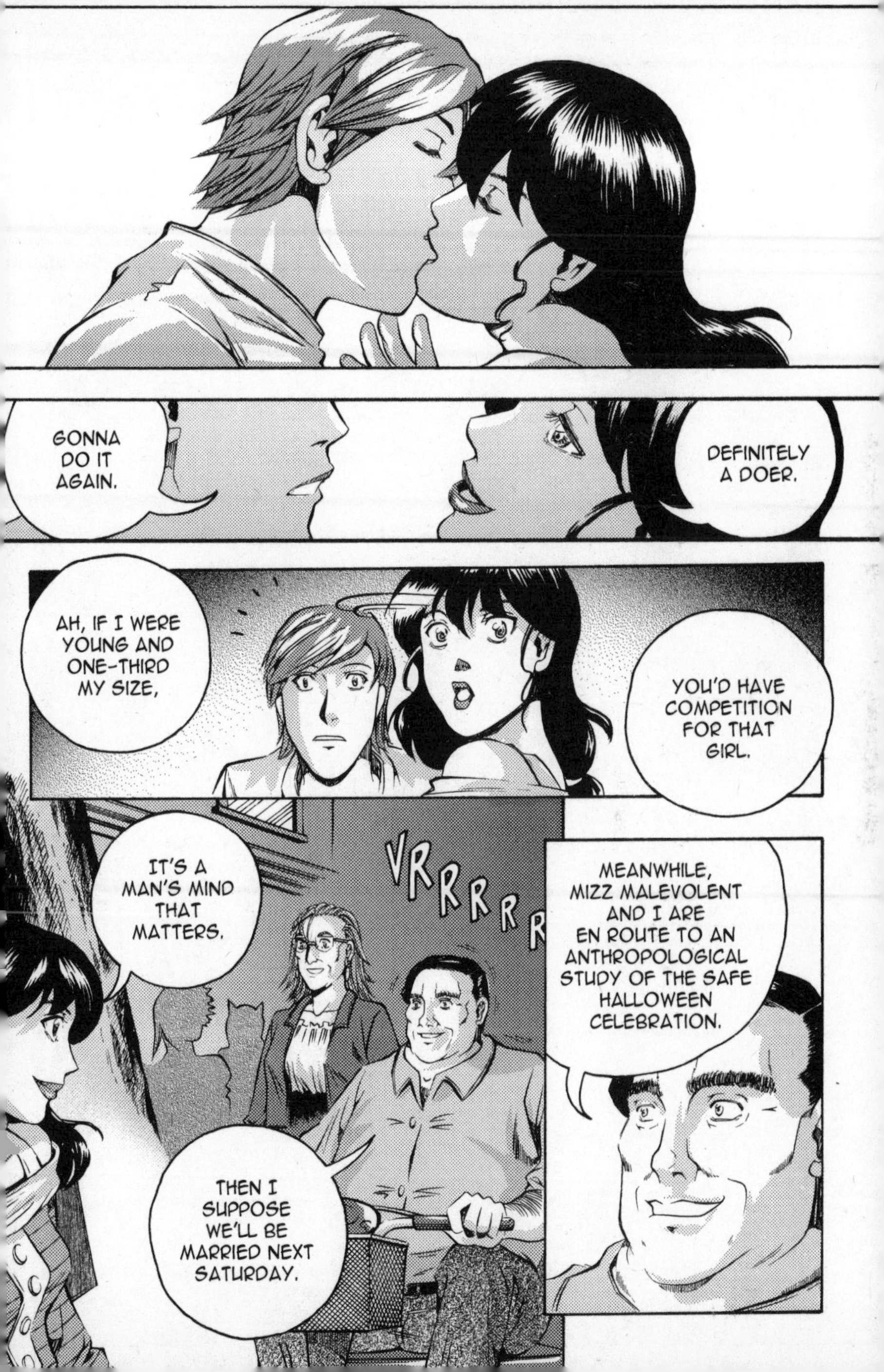
GONNA DO IT AGAIN.
DEFINITELY A DOER.
AH, IF I WERE YOUNG AND ONE-THIRD MY SIZE,
YOU'D HAVE COMPETITION FOR THAT GIRL.
IT'S A MAN'S MIND THAT MATTERS.
VRRRRR
THEN I SUPPOSE WE'LL BE MARRIED NEXT SATURDAY.
MEANWHILE, MIZZ MALEVOLENT AND I ARE EN ROUTE TO AN ANTHROPOLOGICAL STUDY OF THE SAFE HALLOWEEN CELEBRATION.

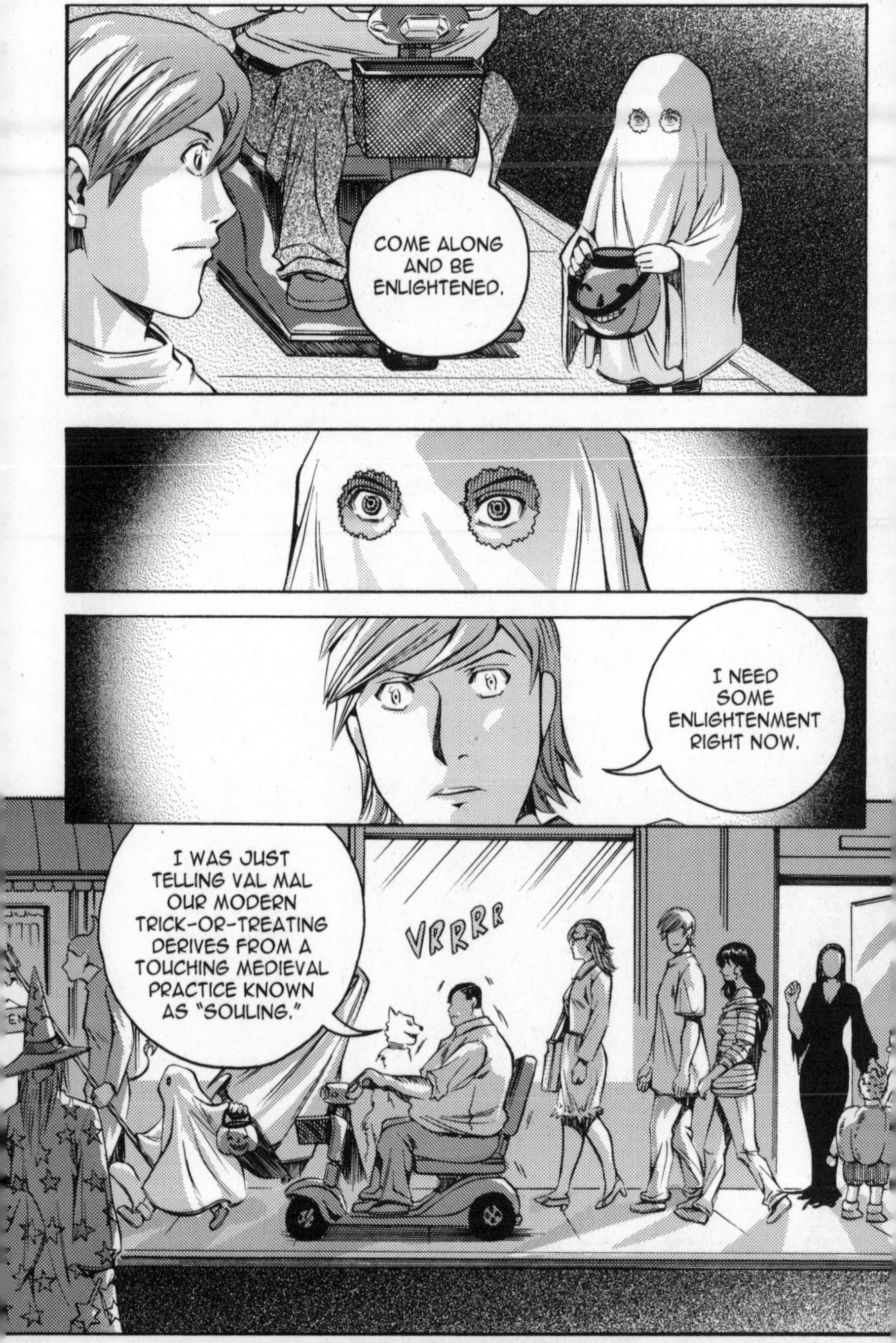
COME ALONG AND BE ENLIGHTENED.
I NEED SOME ENLIGHTENMENT RIGHT NOW.
I WAS JUST TELLING VAL MAL OUR MODERN TRICK-OR-TREATING DERIVES FROM A TOUCHING MEDIEVAL PRACTICE KNOWN AS "SOULING."
VRRRR

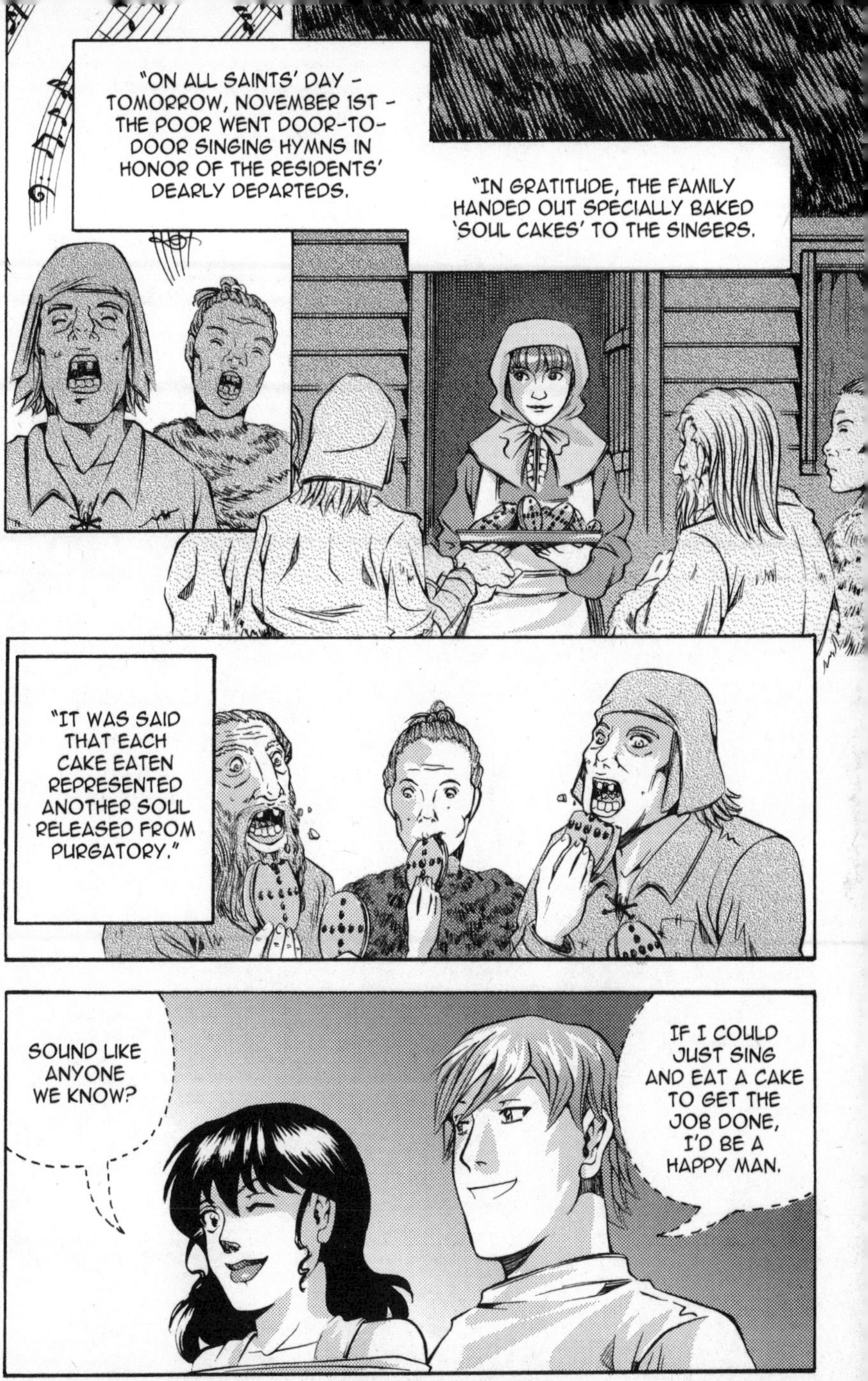
"ON ALL SAINTS' DAY - TOMORROW, NOVEMBER 1ST - THE POOR WENT DOOR-TO-DOOR SINGING HYMNS IN HONOR OF THE RESIDENTS' DEARLY DEPARTEDS.
"IN GRATITUDE, THE FAMILY HANDED OUT SPECIALLY BAKED 'SOUL CAKES' TO THE SINGERS.
"IT WAS SAID THAT EACH CAKE EATEN REPRESENTED ANOTHER SOUL RELEASED FROM PURGATORY."
SOUND LIKE ANYONE WE KNOW?
IF I COULD JUST SING AND EAT A CAKE TO GET THE JOB DONE, I'D BE A HAPPY MAN.

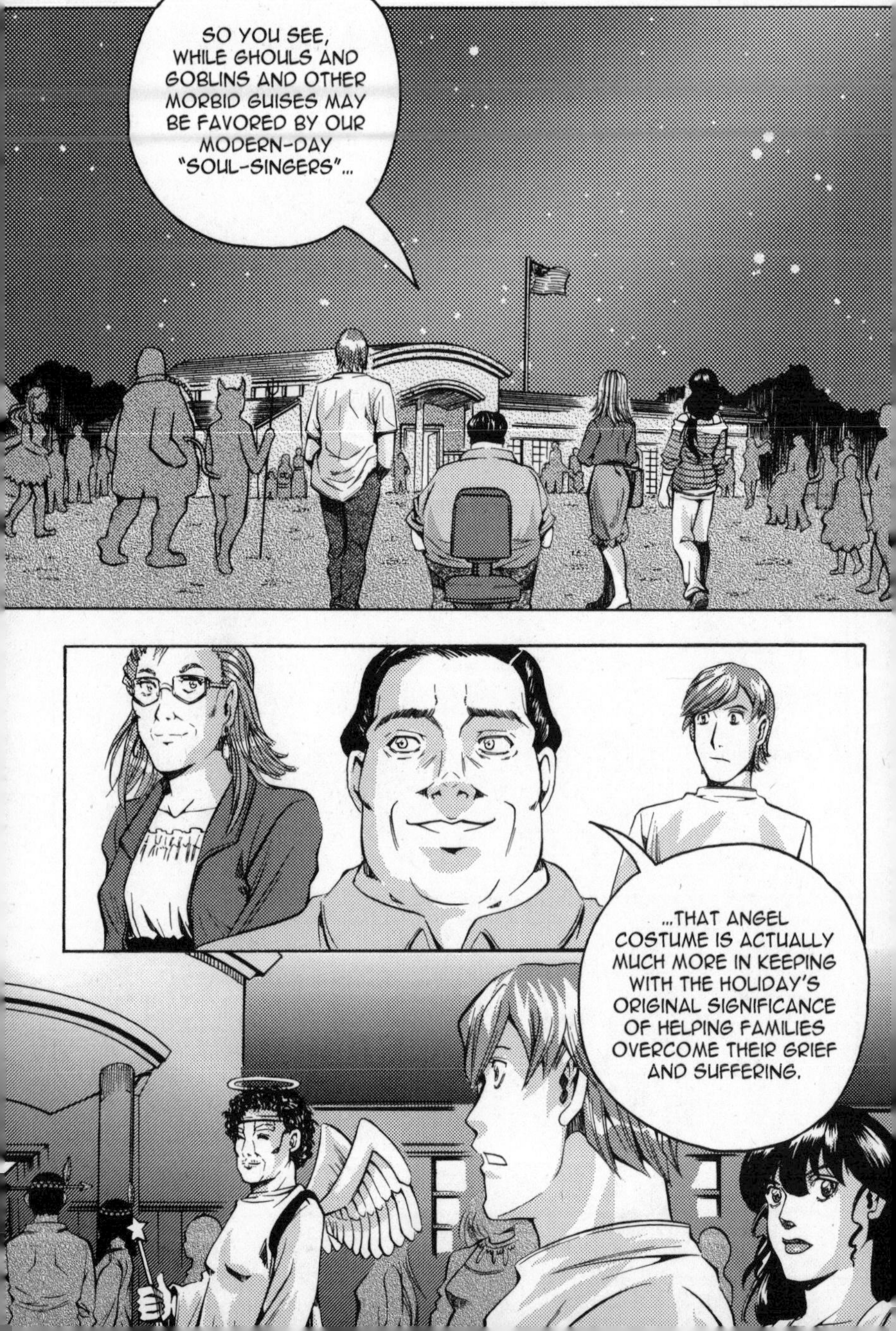
SO YOU SEE, WHILE GHOULS AND GOBLINS AND OTHER MORBID GUISES MAY BE FAVORED BY OUR MODERN-DAY "SOUL-SINGERS"...
...THAT ANGEL COSTUME IS ACTUALLY MUCH MORE IN KEEPING WITH THE HOLIDAY'S ORIGINAL SIGNIFICANCE OF HELPING FAMILIES OVERCOME THEIR GRIEF AND SUFFERING.

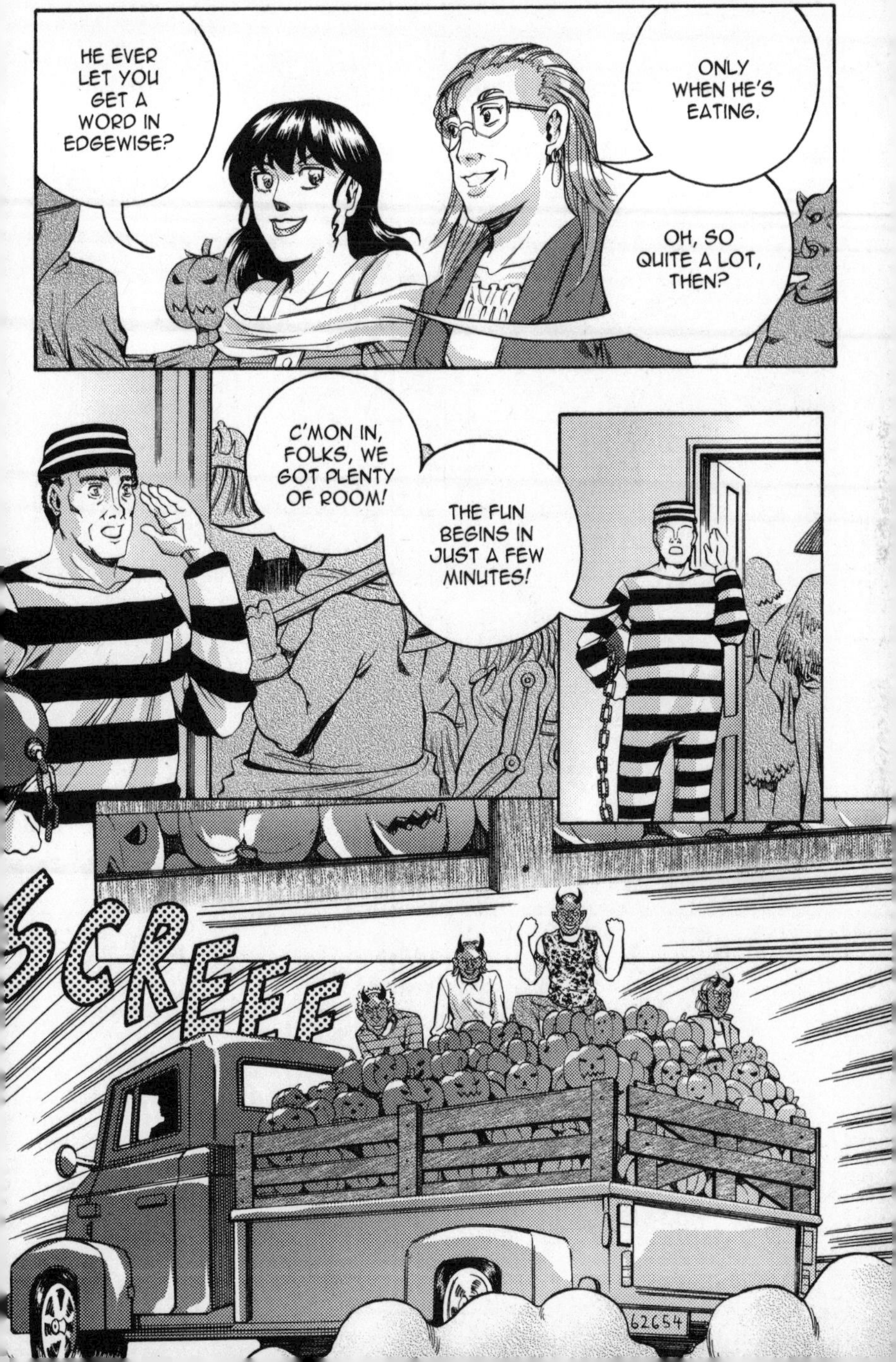
HE EVER LET YOU GET A WORD IN EDGEWISE?
ONLY WHEN HE'S EATING.
OH, SO QUITE A LOT, THEN?
C'MON IN, FOLKS, WE GOT PLENTY OF ROOM!
THE FUN BEGINS IN JUST A FEW MINUTES!
SCREEE
62654

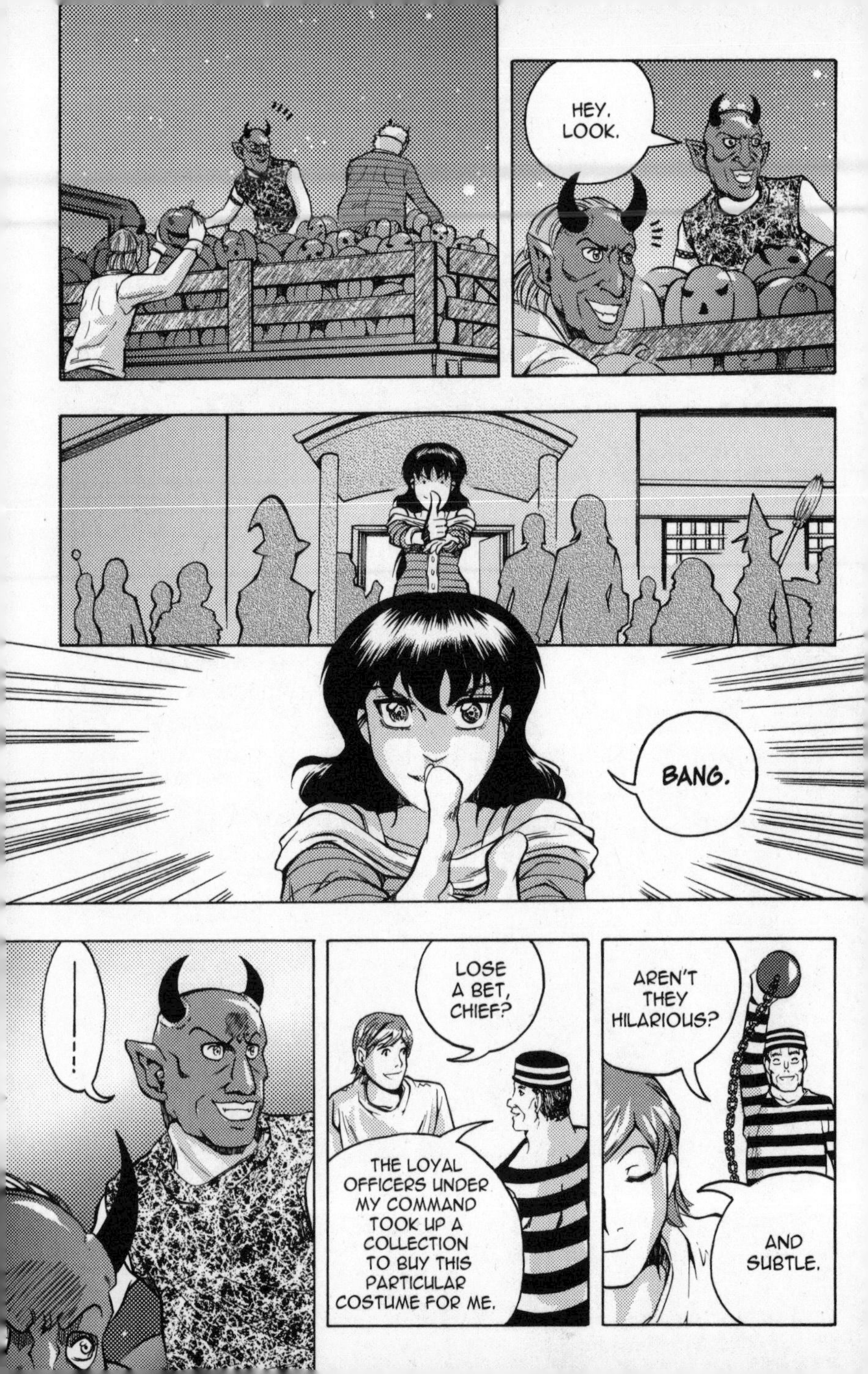
HEY. LOOK.
BANG.
!
LOSE A BET, CHIEF?
THE LOYAL OFFICERS UNDER MY COMMAND TOOK UP A COLLECTION TO BUY THIS PARTICULAR COSTUME FOR ME.
AREN'T THEY HILARIOUS?
AND SUBTLE.

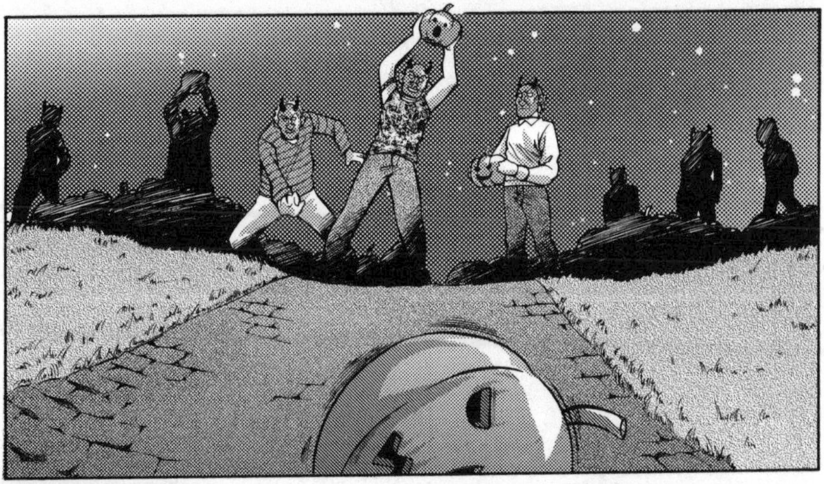

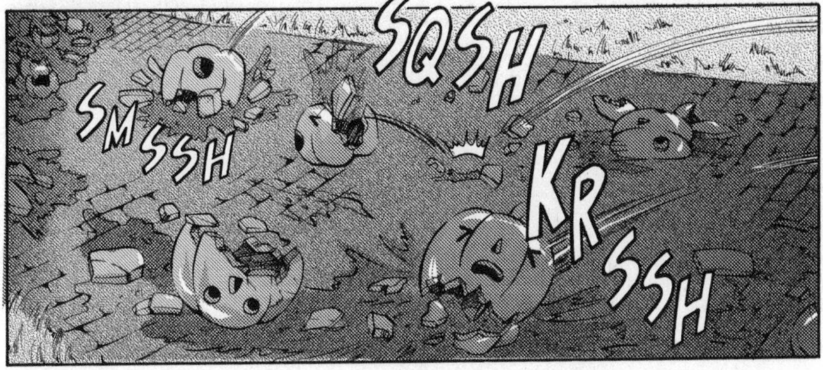
SMSSH
SQSH
KRSSH

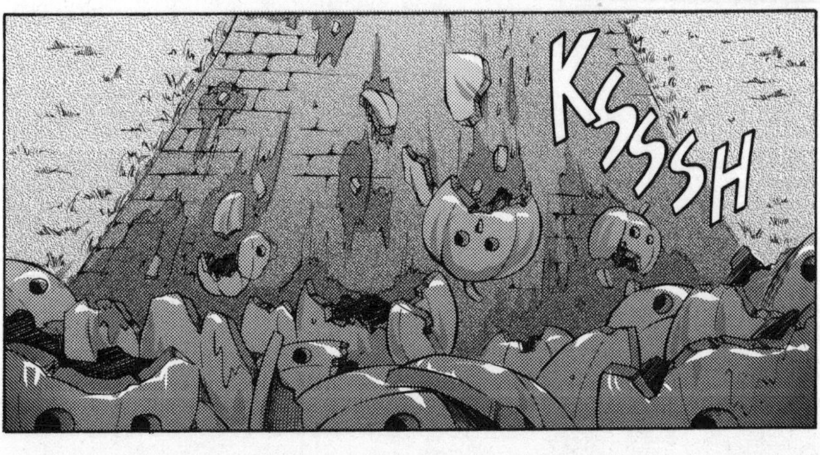
KSSSH

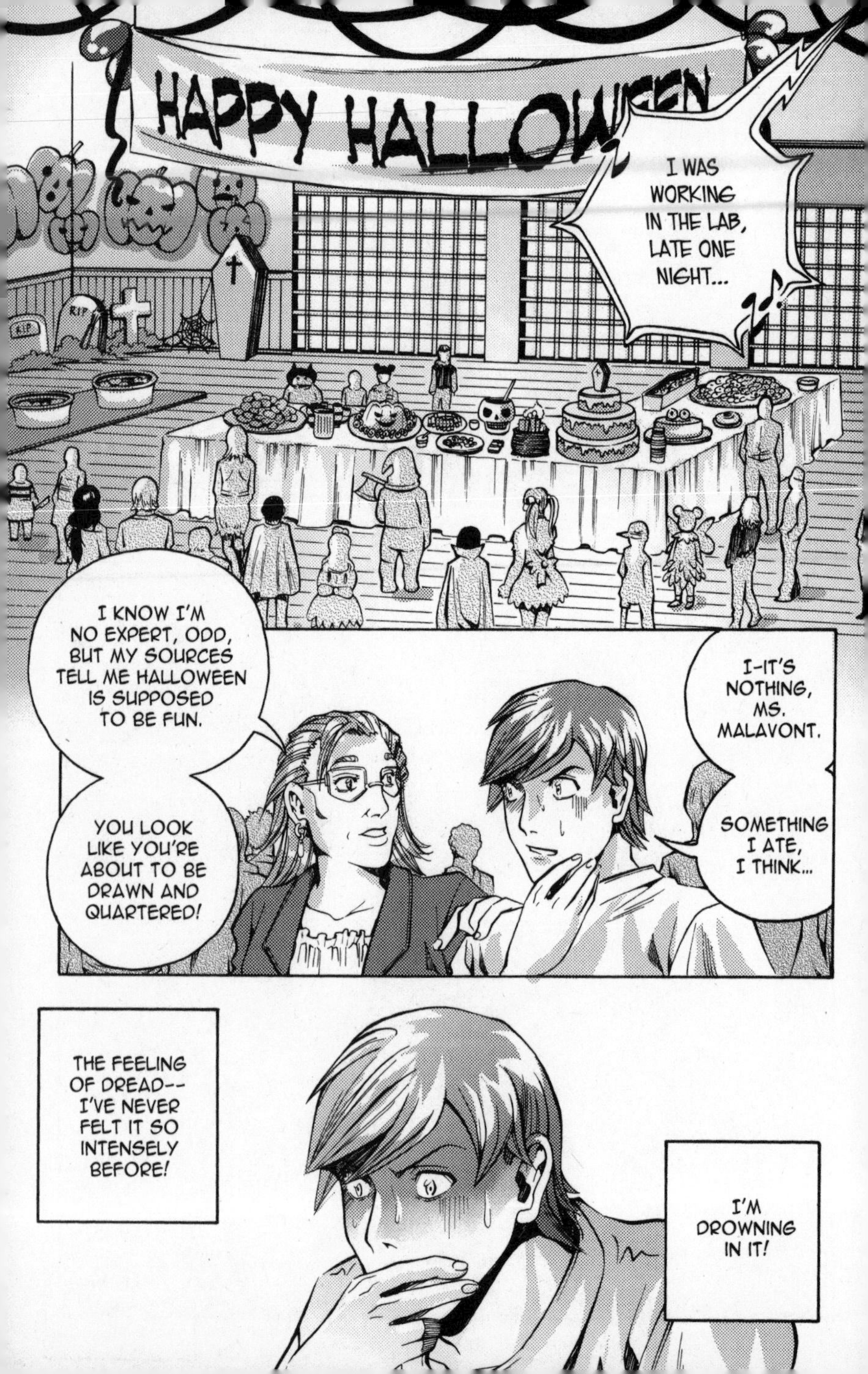
HAPPY HALLOWEEN
I WAS WORKING IN THE LAB, LATE ONE NIGHT...
RIP
RIP
I KNOW I'M NO EXPERT, ODD, BUT MY SOURCES TELL ME HALLOWEEN IS SUPPOSED TO BE FUN.
YOU LOOK LIKE YOU'RE ABOUT TO BE DRAWN AND QUARTERED!
I-IT'S NOTHING, MS. MALAVONT.
SOMETHING I ATE, I THINK...
THE FEELING OF DREAD-- I'VE NEVER FELT IT SO INTENSELY BEFORE!
I'M DROWNING IN IT!

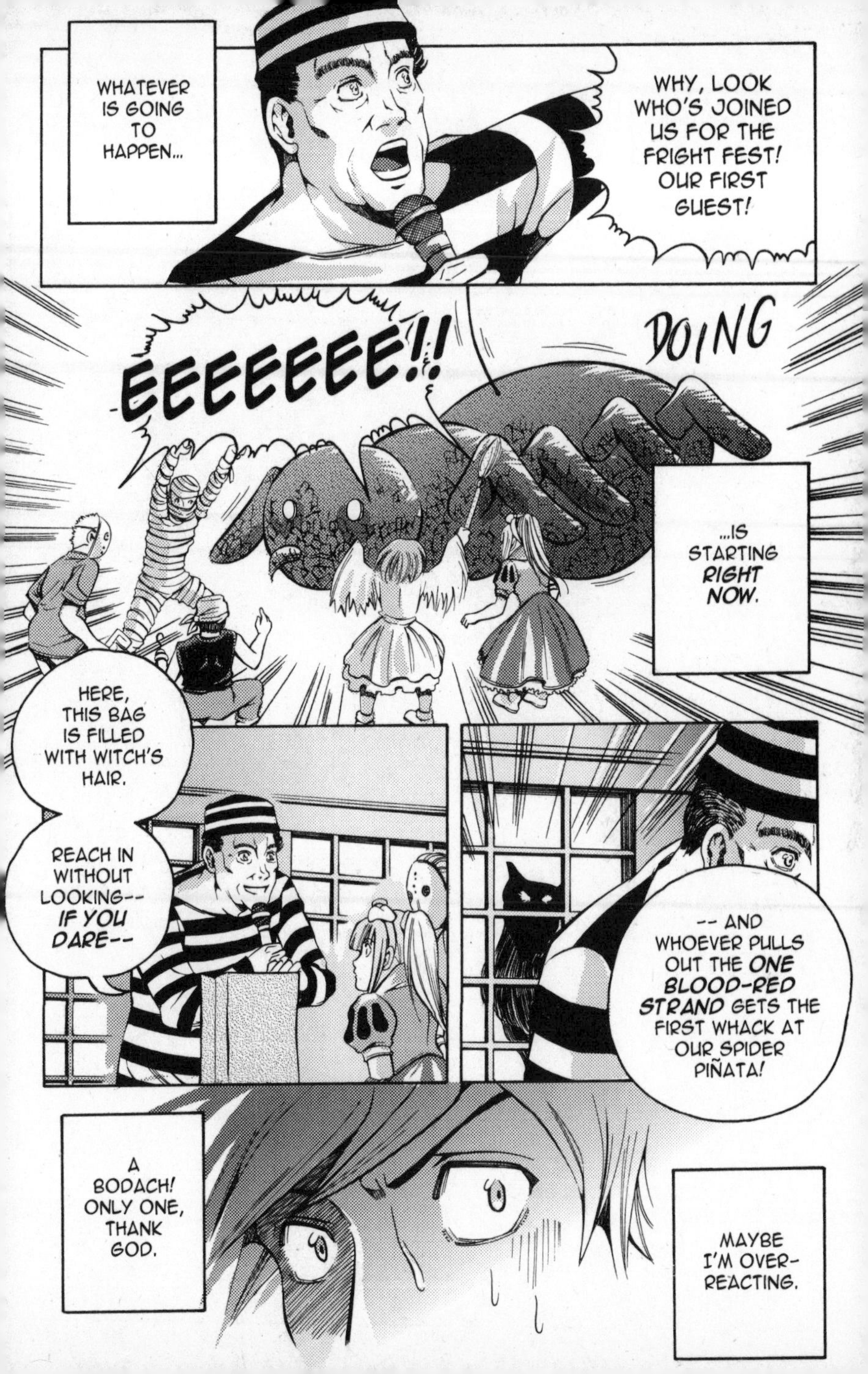

WHATEVER IS GOING TO HAPPEN...
WHY, LOOK WHO'S JOINED US FOR THE FRIGHT FEST! OUR FIRST GUEST!
EEEEEEE!!
DOING
...IS STARTING RIGHT NOW.
HERE, THIS BAG IS FILLED WITH WITCH'S HAIR.
REACH IN WITHOUT LOOKING-- IF YOU DARE--
-- AND WHOEVER PULLS OUT THE ONE BLOOD-RED STRAND GETS THE FIRST WHACK AT OUR SPIDER PIÑATA!
A BODACH! ONLY ONE, THANK GOD.
MAYBE I'M OVER-REACTING.

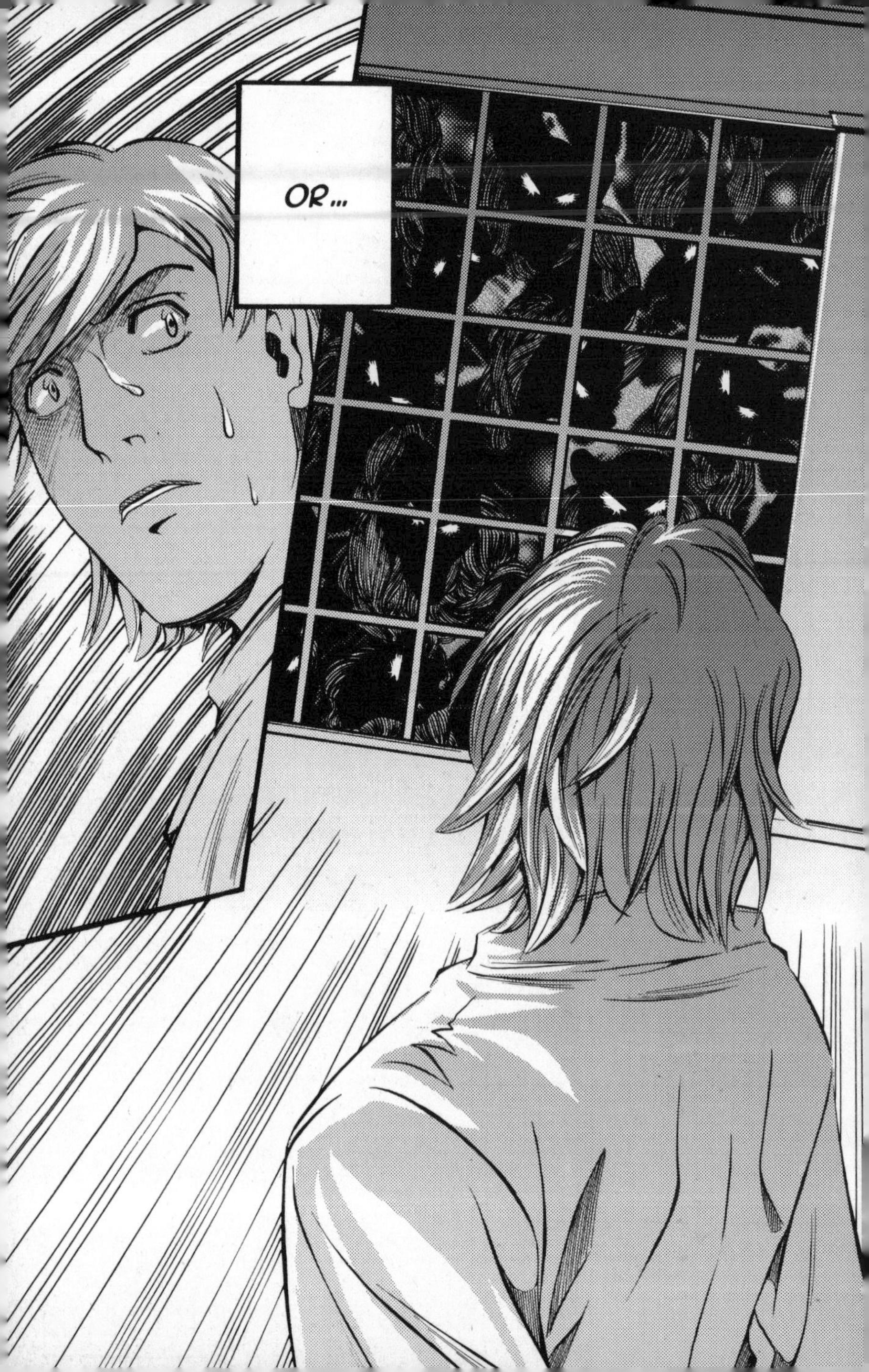
OR...

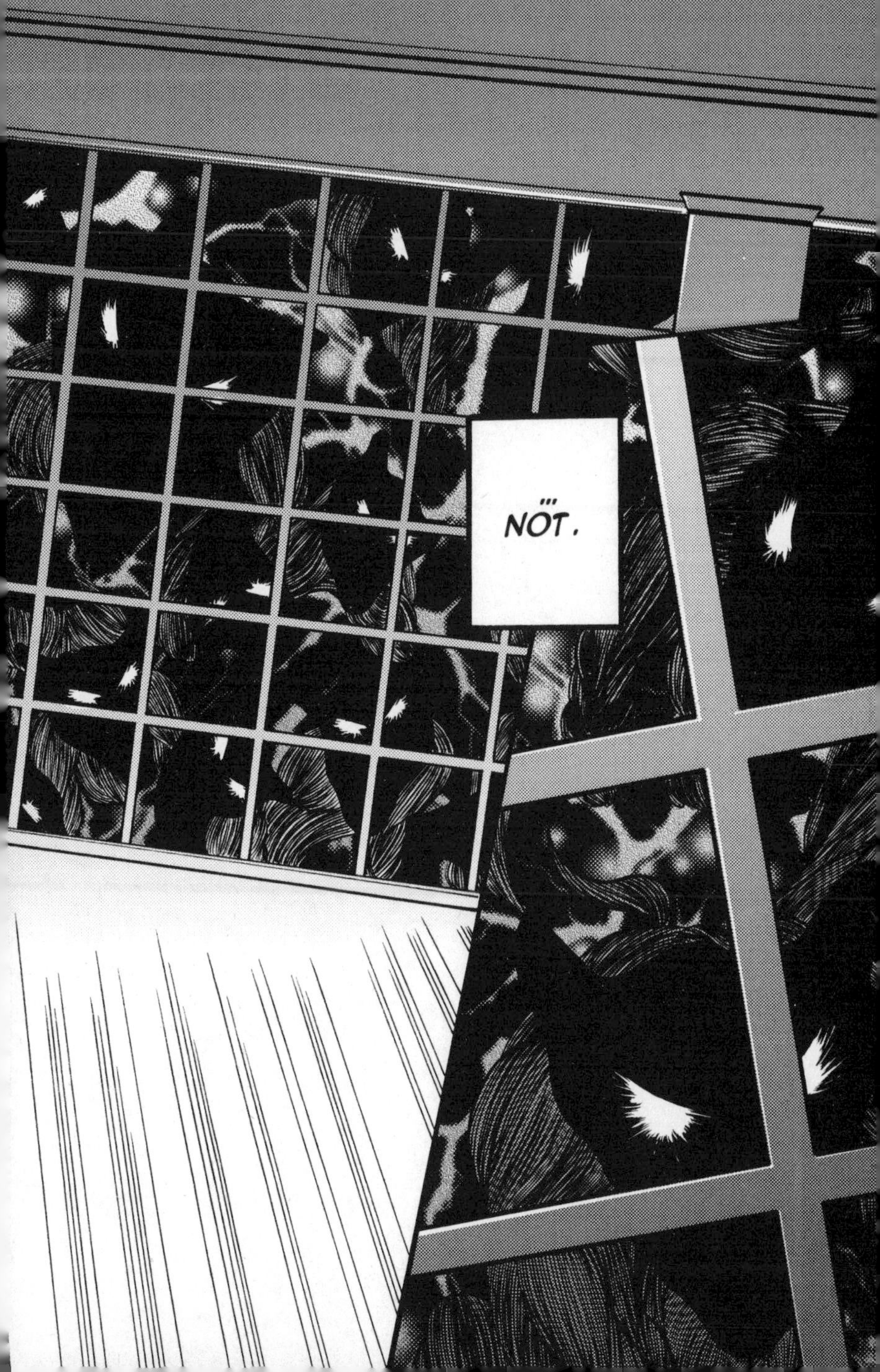
...NOT.

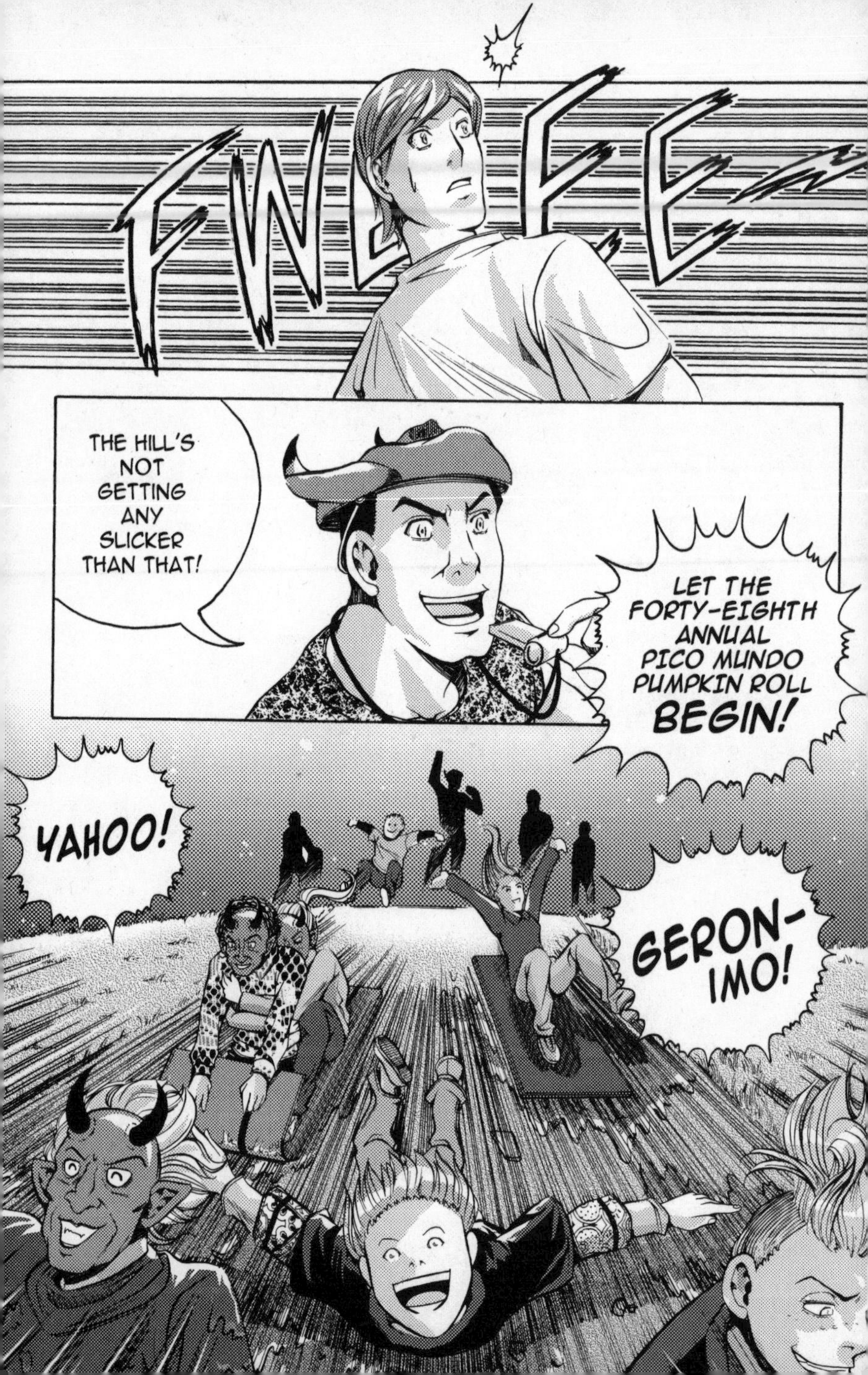
FWEEE
THE HILL'S NOT GETTING ANY SLICKER THAN THAT!
LET THE FORTY-EIGHTH ANNUAL PICO MUNDO PUMPKIN ROLL BEGIN!
YAHOO!
GERON-IMO!

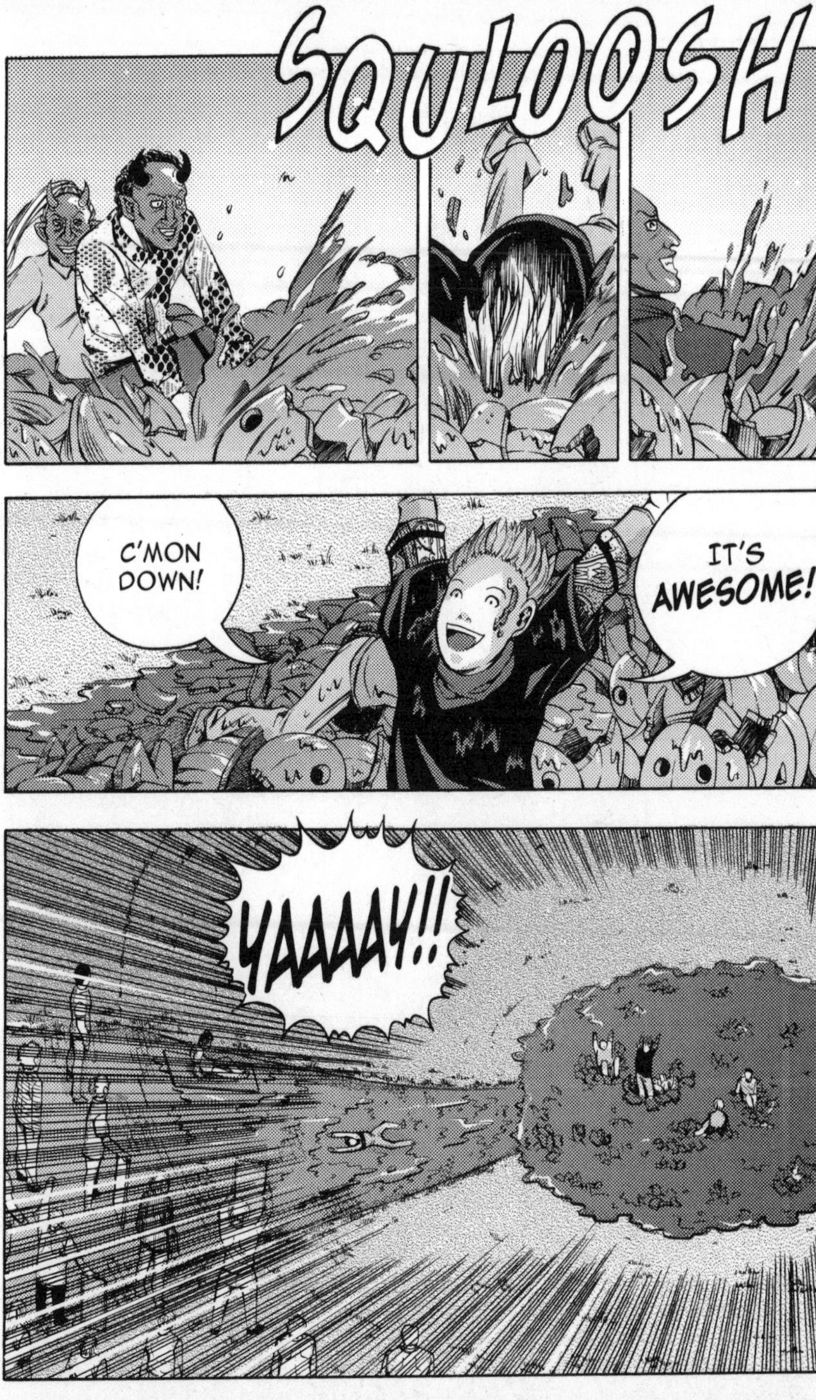
SQULOOSH
C'MON DOWN!
IT'S AWESOME!
YAAAAY!!

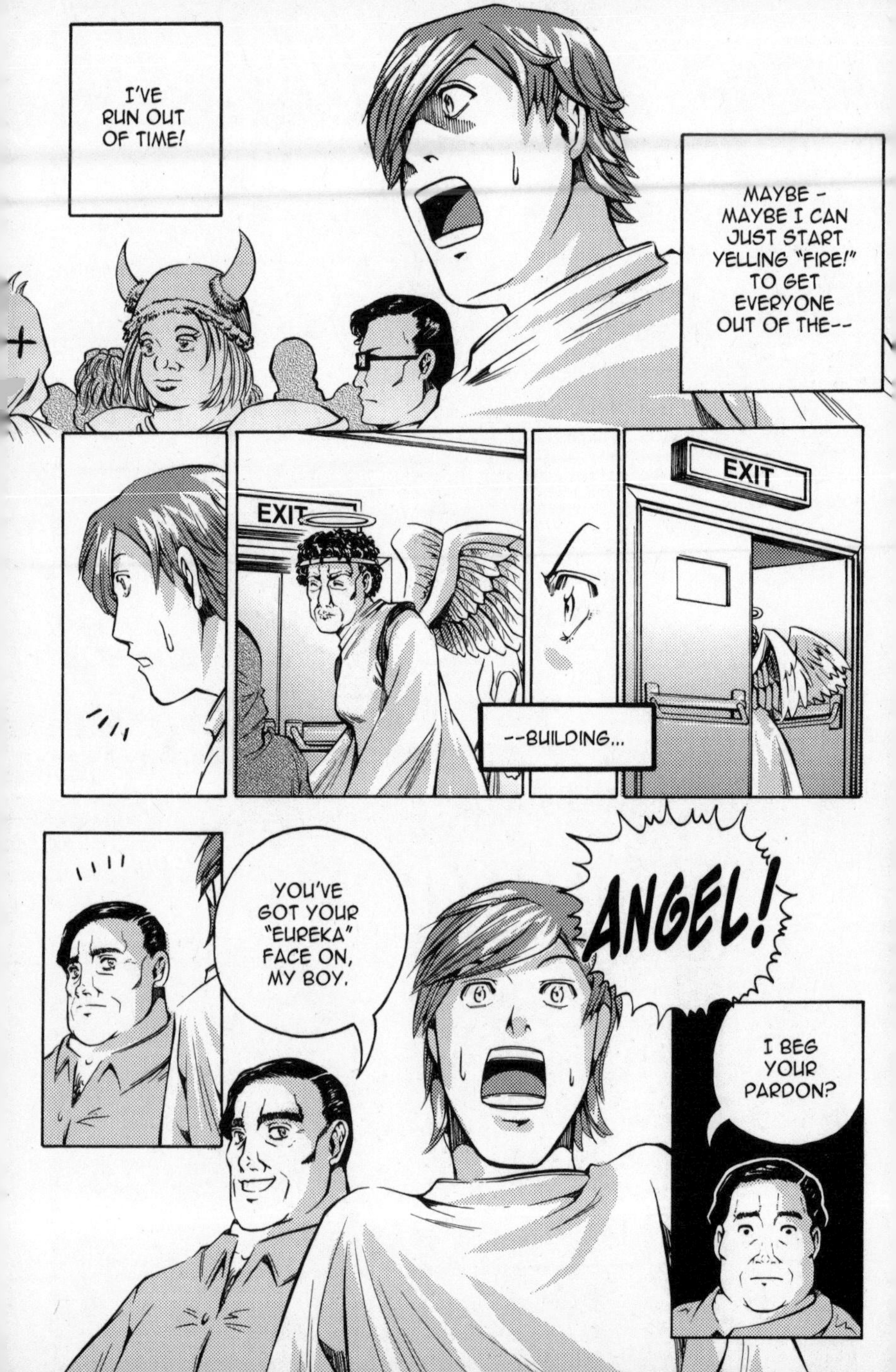
I'VE RUN OUT OF TIME!
MAYBE - MAYBE I CAN JUST START YELLING "FIRE!" TO GET EVERYONE OUT OF THE--
EXIT
EXIT
--BUILDING...
ANGEL!
YOU'VE GOT YOUR "EUREKA" FACE ON, MY BOY.
I BEG YOUR PARDON?

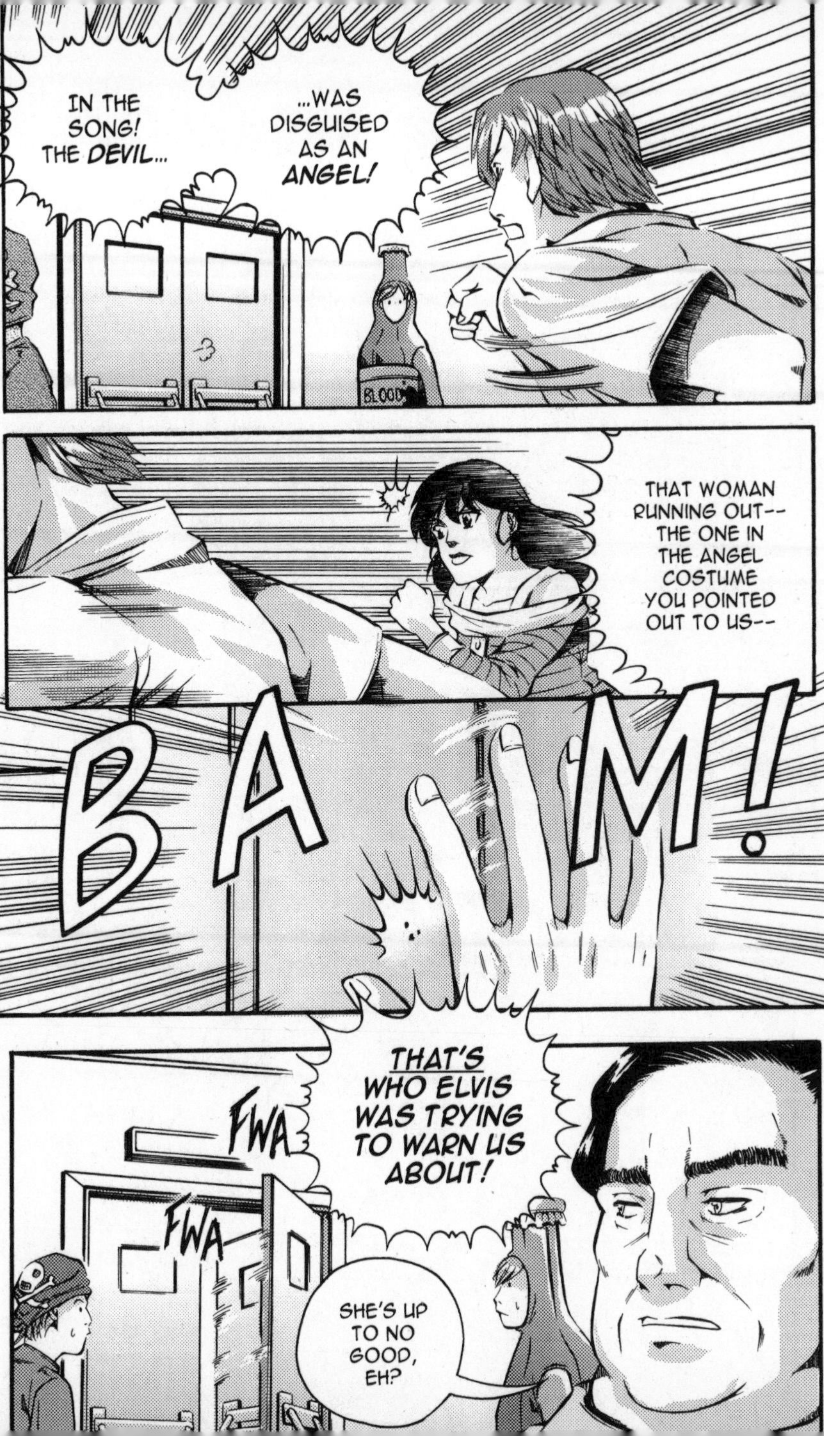
IN THE SONG! THE DEVIL...
...WAS DISGUISED AS AN ANGEL!
BLOOD
THAT WOMAN RUNNING OUT-- THE ONE IN THE ANGEL COSTUME YOU POINTED OUT TO US--
BAM!
THAT'S WHO ELVIS WAS TRYING TO WARN US ABOUT!
FWA
FWA
SHE'S UP TO NO GOOD, EH?

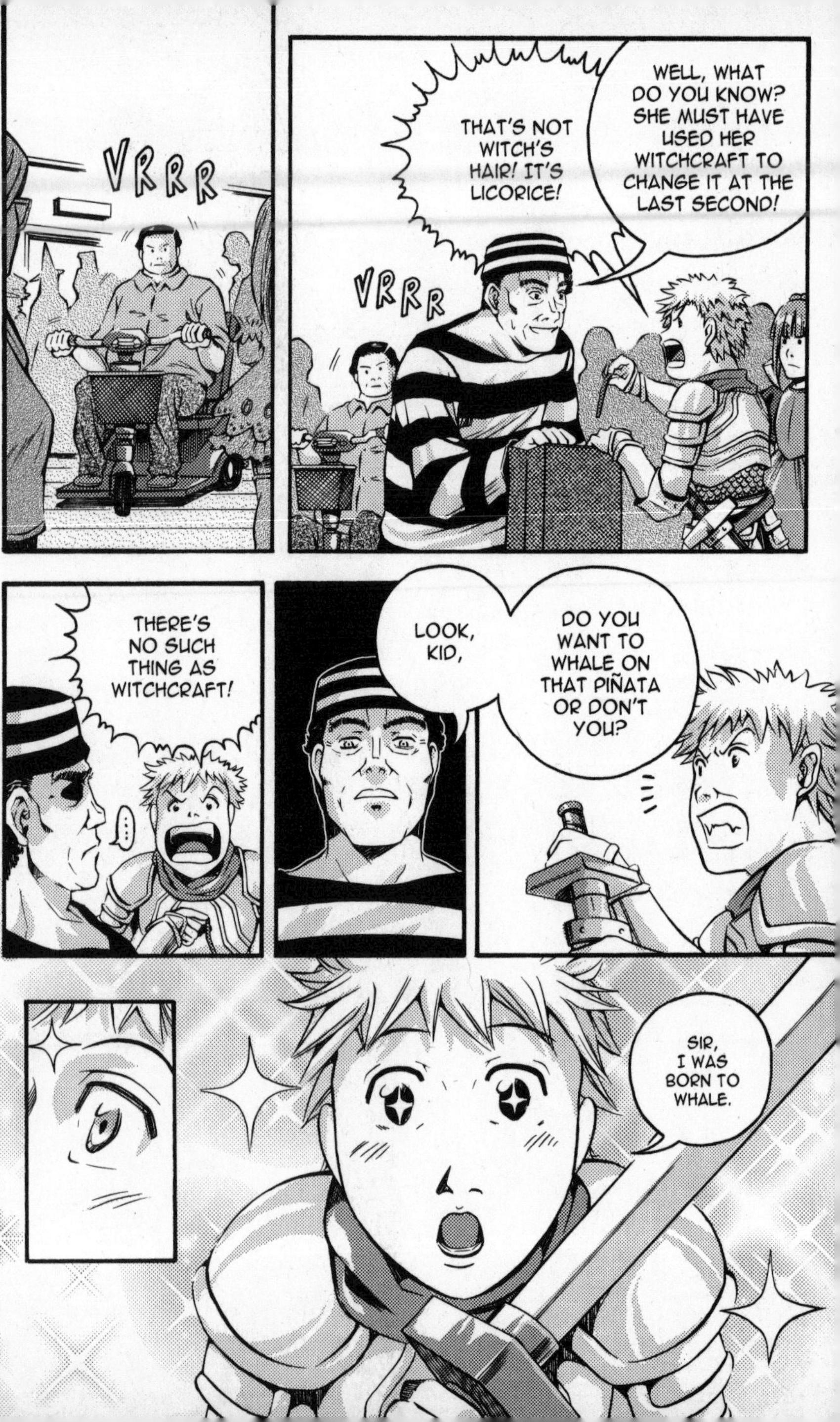
VRRR
VRRR
THAT'S NOT WITCH'S HAIR! IT'S LICORICE!
WELL, WHAT DO YOU KNOW? SHE MUST HAVE USED HER WITCHCRAFT TO CHANGE IT AT THE LAST SECOND!
THERE'S NO SUCH THING AS WITCHCRAFT!
...
LOOK, KID,
DO YOU WANT TO WHALE ON THAT PIÑATA OR DON'T YOU?
SIR, I WAS BORN TO WHALE.

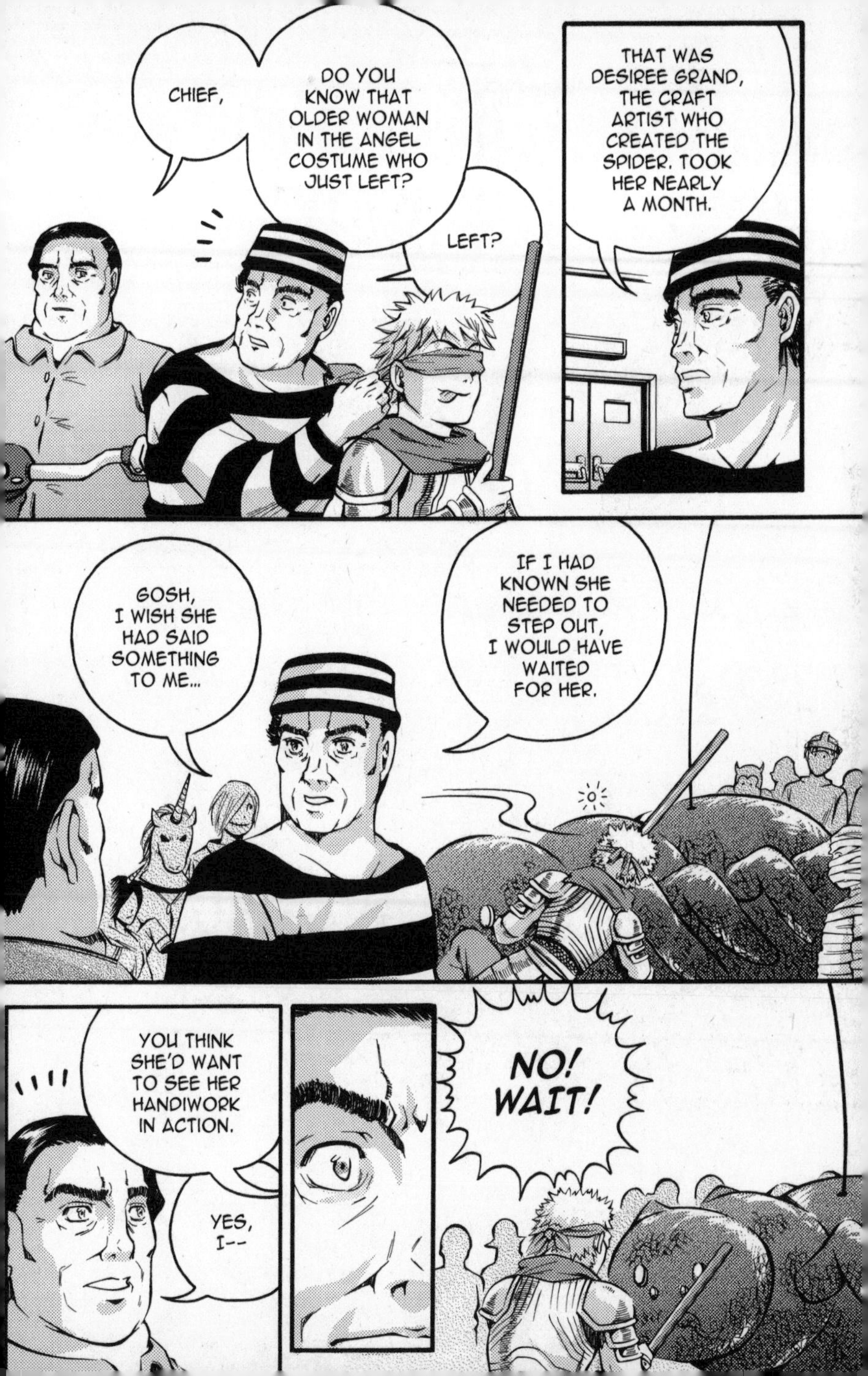
CHIEF,
DO YOU KNOW THAT OLDER WOMAN IN THE ANGEL COSTUME WHO JUST LEFT?
LEFT?
THAT WAS DESIREE GRAND, THE CRAFT ARTIST WHO CREATED THE SPIDER. TOOK HER NEARLY A MONTH.
GOSH, I WISH SHE HAD SAID SOMETHING TO ME...
IF I HAD KNOWN SHE NEEDED TO STEP OUT, I WOULD HAVE WAITED FOR HER.
YOU THINK SHE'D WANT TO SEE HER HANDIWORK IN ACTION.
YES, I--
NO! WAIT!

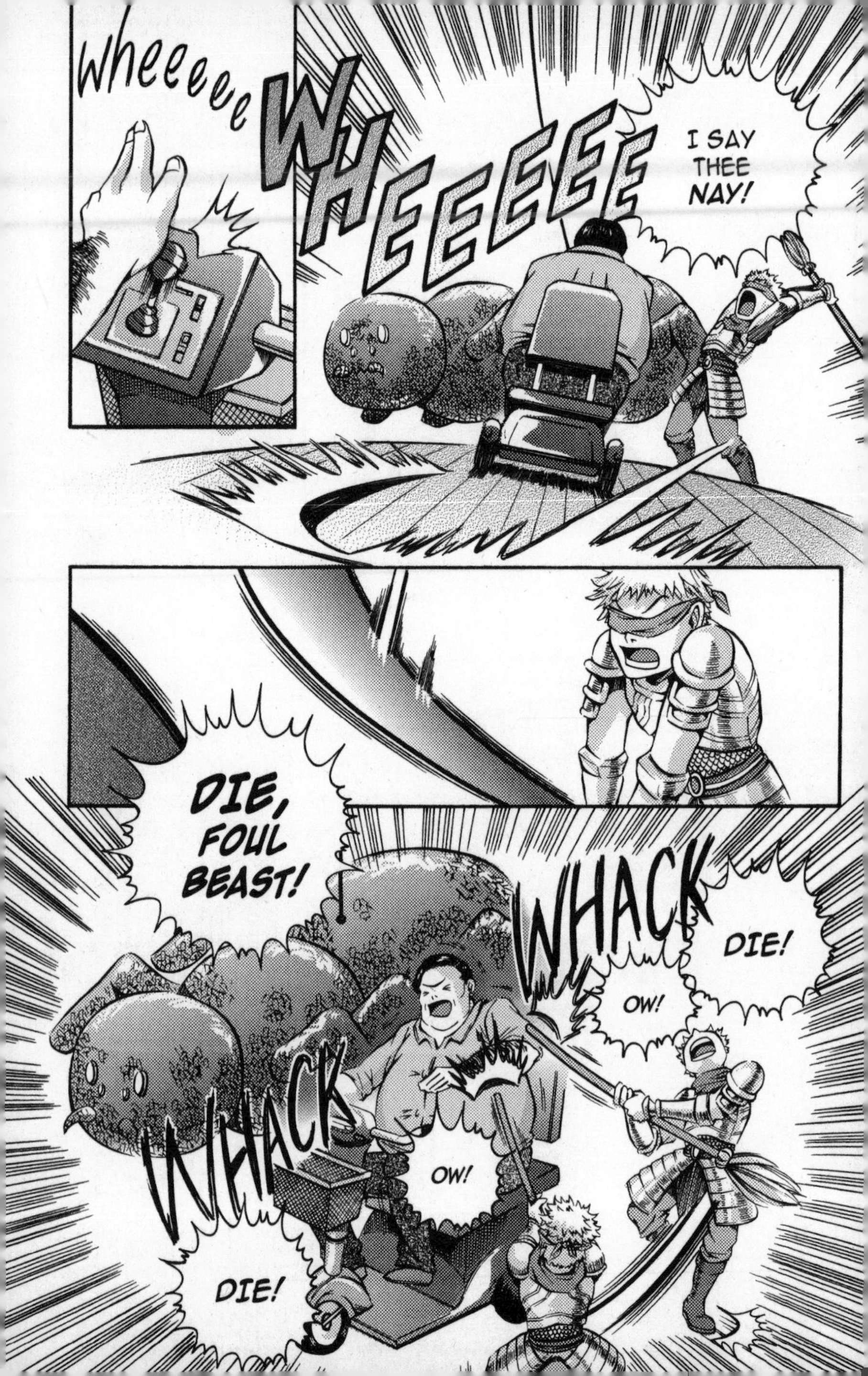
wheeeeee
WHEEEEEE
I SAY THEE NAY!
DIE, FOUL BEAST!
WHACK
DIE!
OW!
WHACK
OW!
DIE!

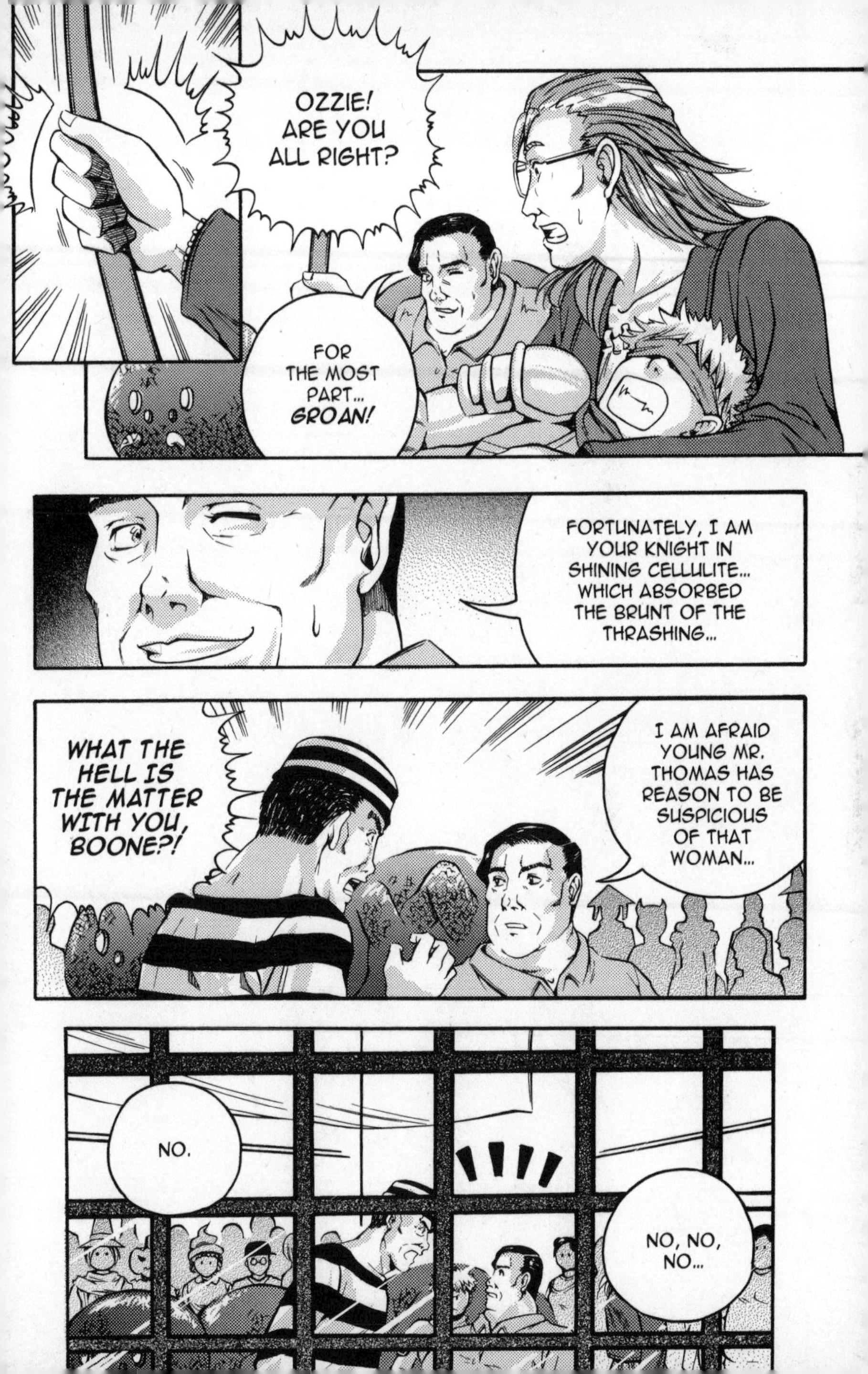
OZZIE! ARE YOU ALL RIGHT?
FOR THE MOST PART... GROAN!
FORTUNATELY, I AM YOUR KNIGHT IN SHINING CELLULITE... WHICH ABSORBED THE BRUNT OF THE THRASHING...
WHAT THE HELL IS THE MATTER WITH YOU, BOONE?!
I AM AFRAID YOUNG MR. THOMAS HAS REASON TO BE SUSPICIOUS OF THAT WOMAN...
NO.
NO, NO, NO...

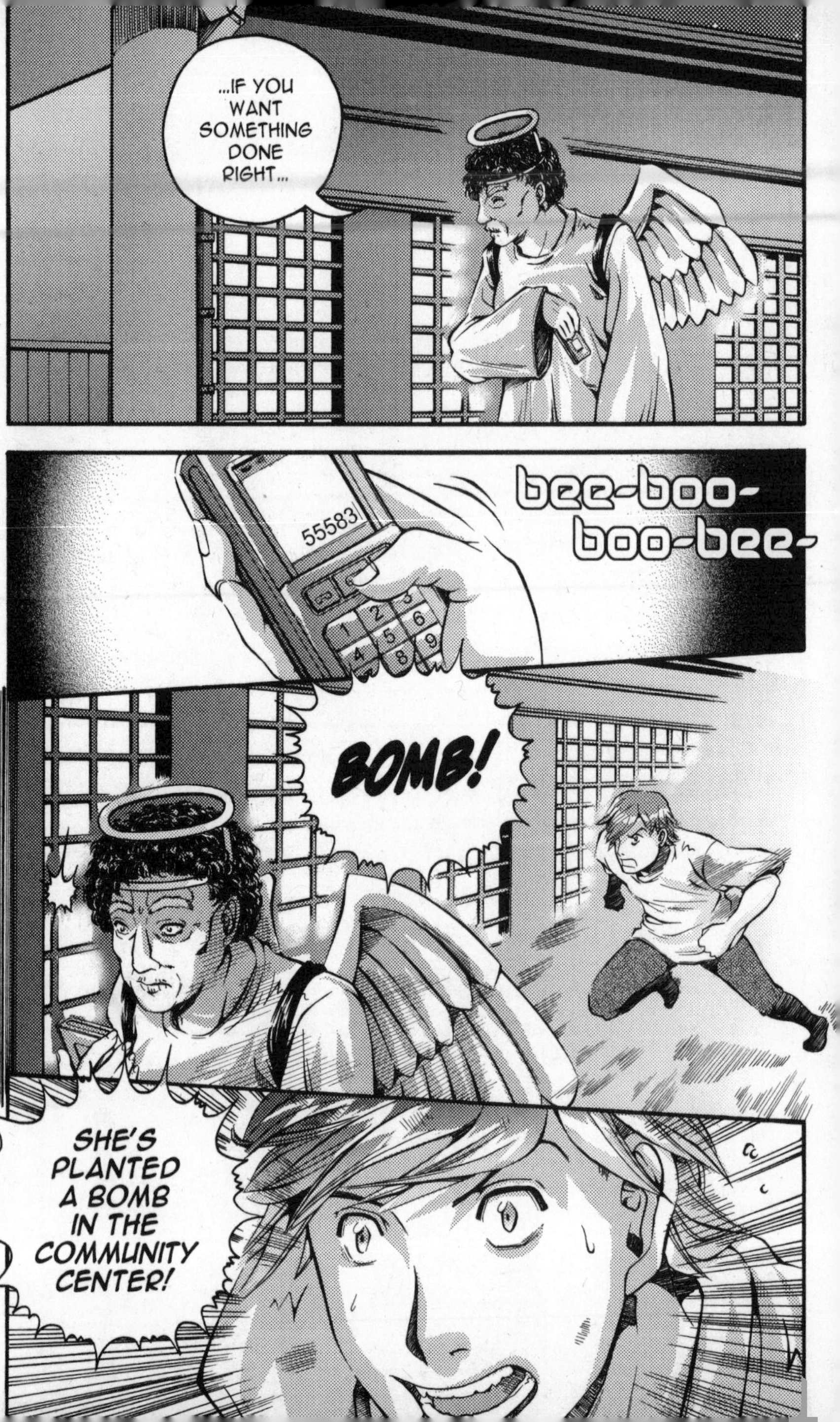

...IF YOU WANT SOMETHING DONE RIGHT...
55583
bee-boo-boo-bee-
BOMB!
SHE'S PLANTED A BOMB IN THE COMMUNITY CENTER!

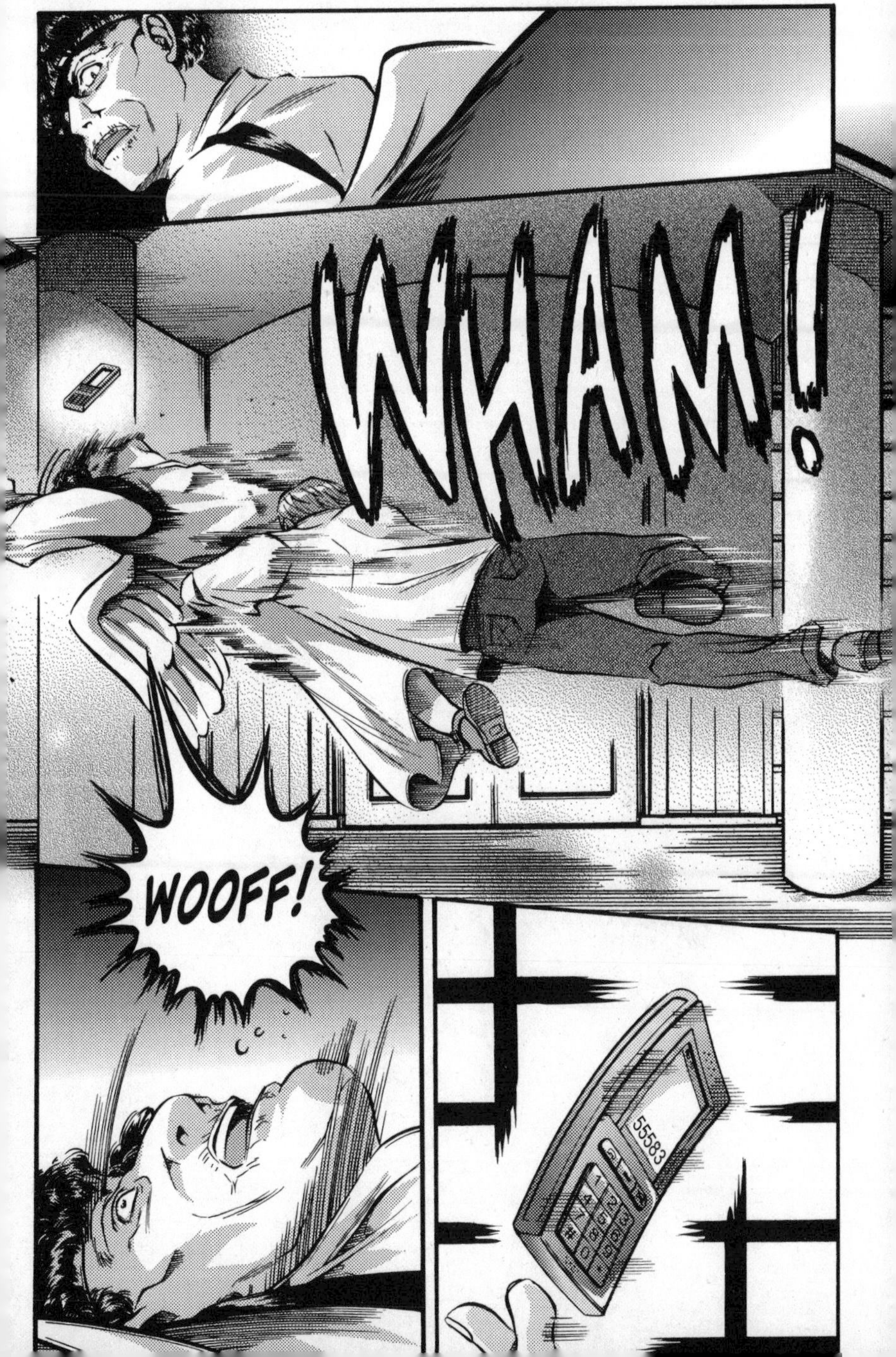
WHAM!
WOOFF!
55583

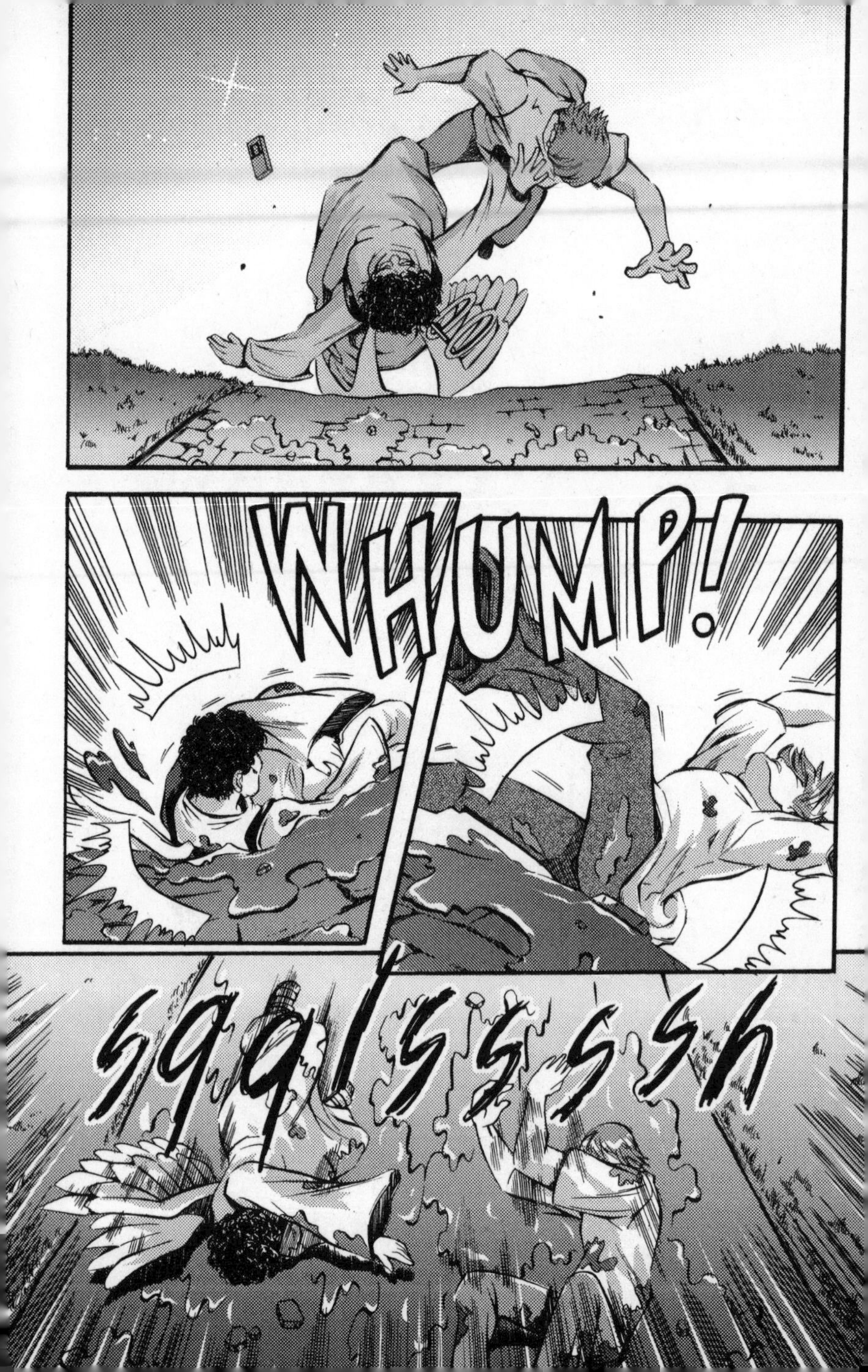
WHUMP!
sqqlsssh

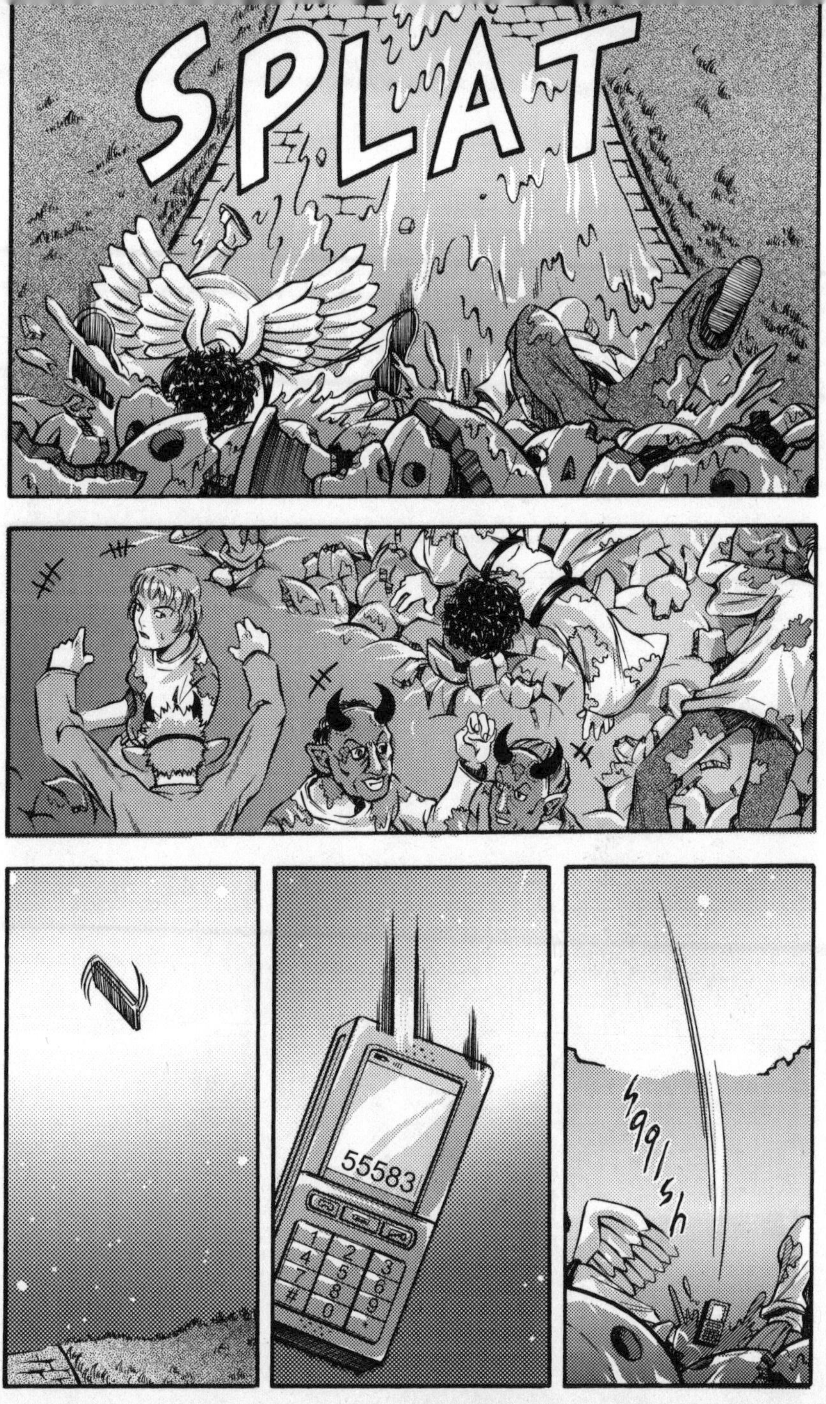
SPLAT
55583
1 2 3
4 5 6
7 8 9
0
sqqlsh

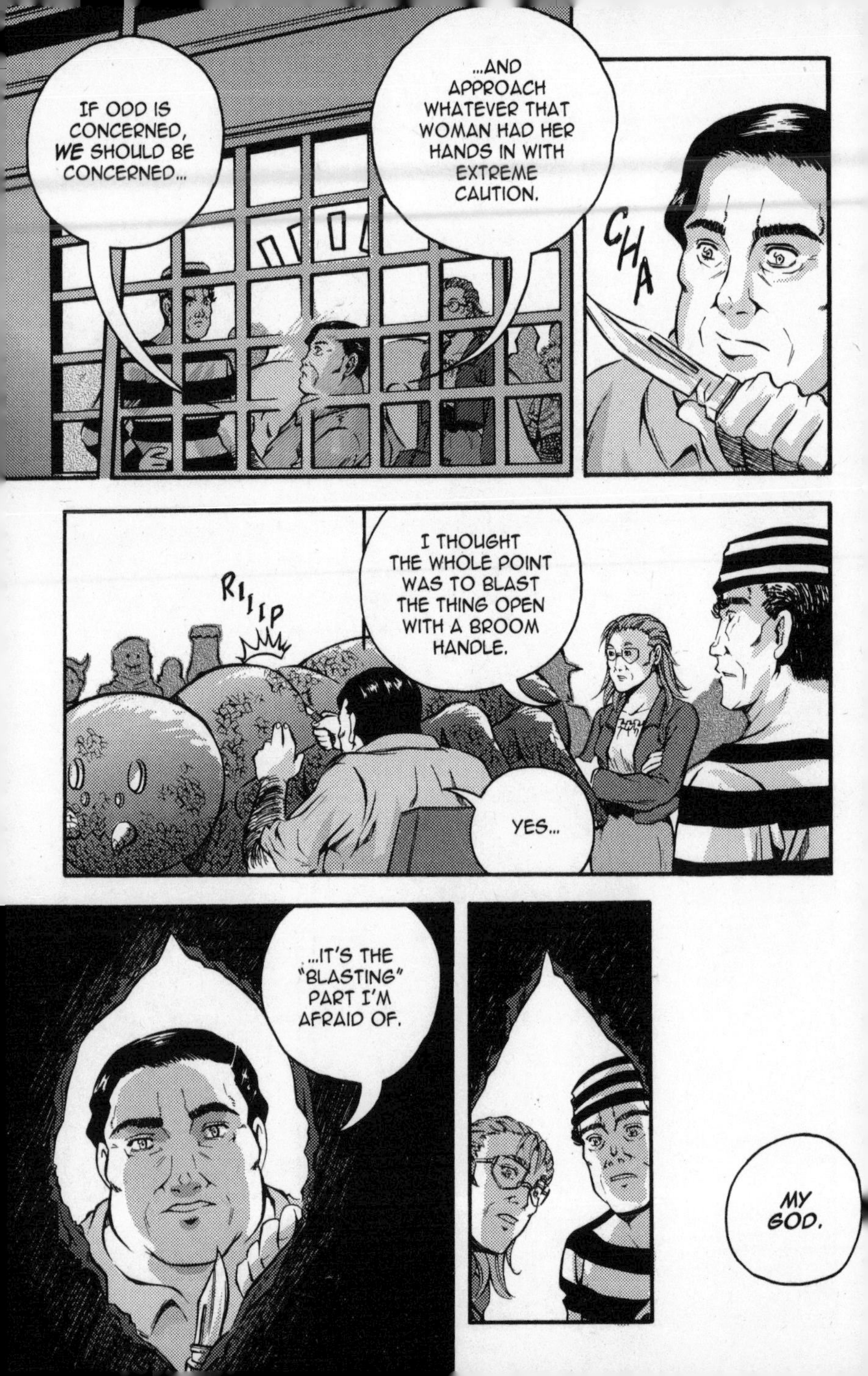
IF ODD IS CONCERNED, WE SHOULD BE CONCERNED...
...AND APPROACH WHATEVER THAT WOMAN HAD HER HANDS IN WITH EXTREME CAUTION.
CHA
RIIIP
I THOUGHT THE WHOLE POINT WAS TO BLAST THE THING OPEN WITH A BROOM HANDLE.
YES...
...IT'S THE "BLASTING" PART I'M AFRAID OF.
MY GOD.

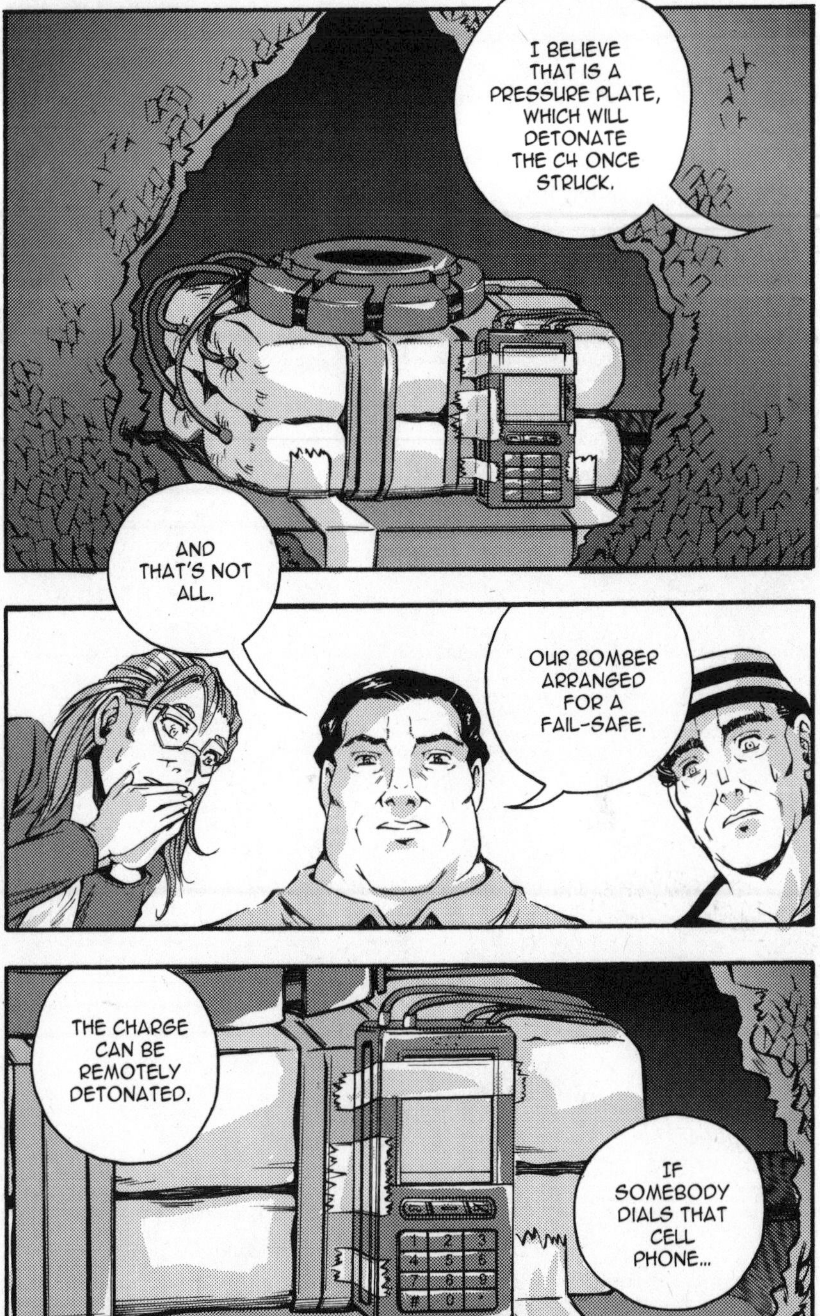
I BELIEVE THAT IS A PRESSURE PLATE, WHICH WILL DETONATE THE C4 ONCE STRUCK.
AND THAT'S NOT ALL.
OUR BOMBER ARRANGED FOR A FAIL-SAFE.
THE CHARGE CAN BE REMOTELY DETONATED.
IF SOMEBODY DIALS THAT CELL PHONE...

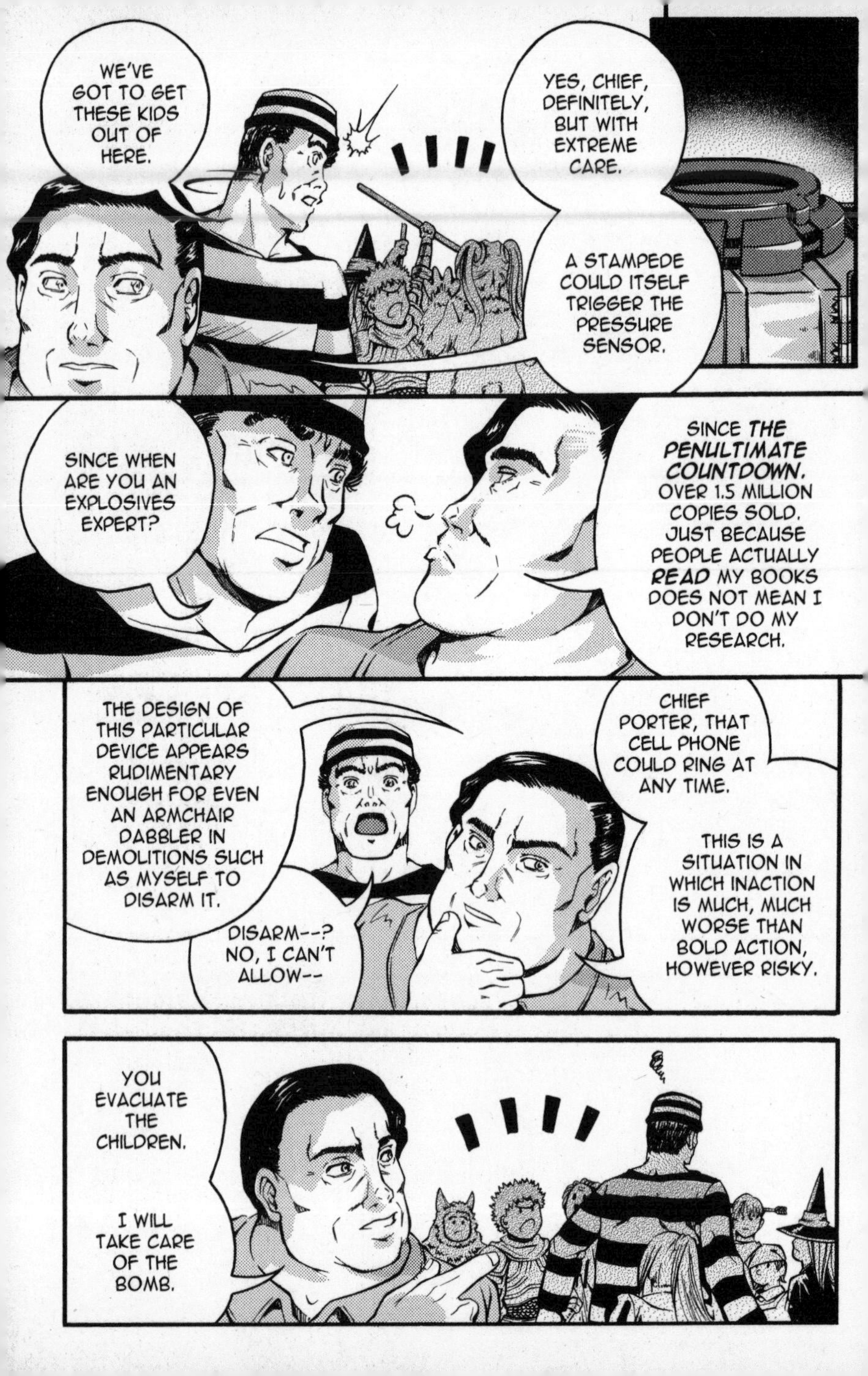
WE'VE GOT TO GET THESE KIDS OUT OF HERE.
YES, CHIEF, DEFINITELY, BUT WITH EXTREME CARE.
A STAMPEDE COULD ITSELF TRIGGER THE PRESSURE SENSOR.
SINCE WHEN ARE YOU AN EXPLOSIVES EXPERT?
SINCE *THE PENULTIMATE COUNTDOWN.* OVER 1.5 MILLION COPIES SOLD. JUST BECAUSE PEOPLE ACTUALLY ***READ*** MY BOOKS DOES NOT MEAN I DON'T DO MY RESEARCH.
THE DESIGN OF THIS PARTICULAR DEVICE APPEARS RUDIMENTARY ENOUGH FOR EVEN AN ARMCHAIR DABBLER IN DEMOLITIONS SUCH AS MYSELF TO DISARM IT.
DISARM--? NO, I CAN'T ALLOW--
CHIEF PORTER, THAT CELL PHONE COULD RING AT ANY TIME.
THIS IS A SITUATION IN WHICH INACTION IS MUCH, MUCH WORSE THAN BOLD ACTION, HOWEVER RISKY.
YOU EVACUATE THE CHILDREN.
I WILL TAKE CARE OF THE BOMB.

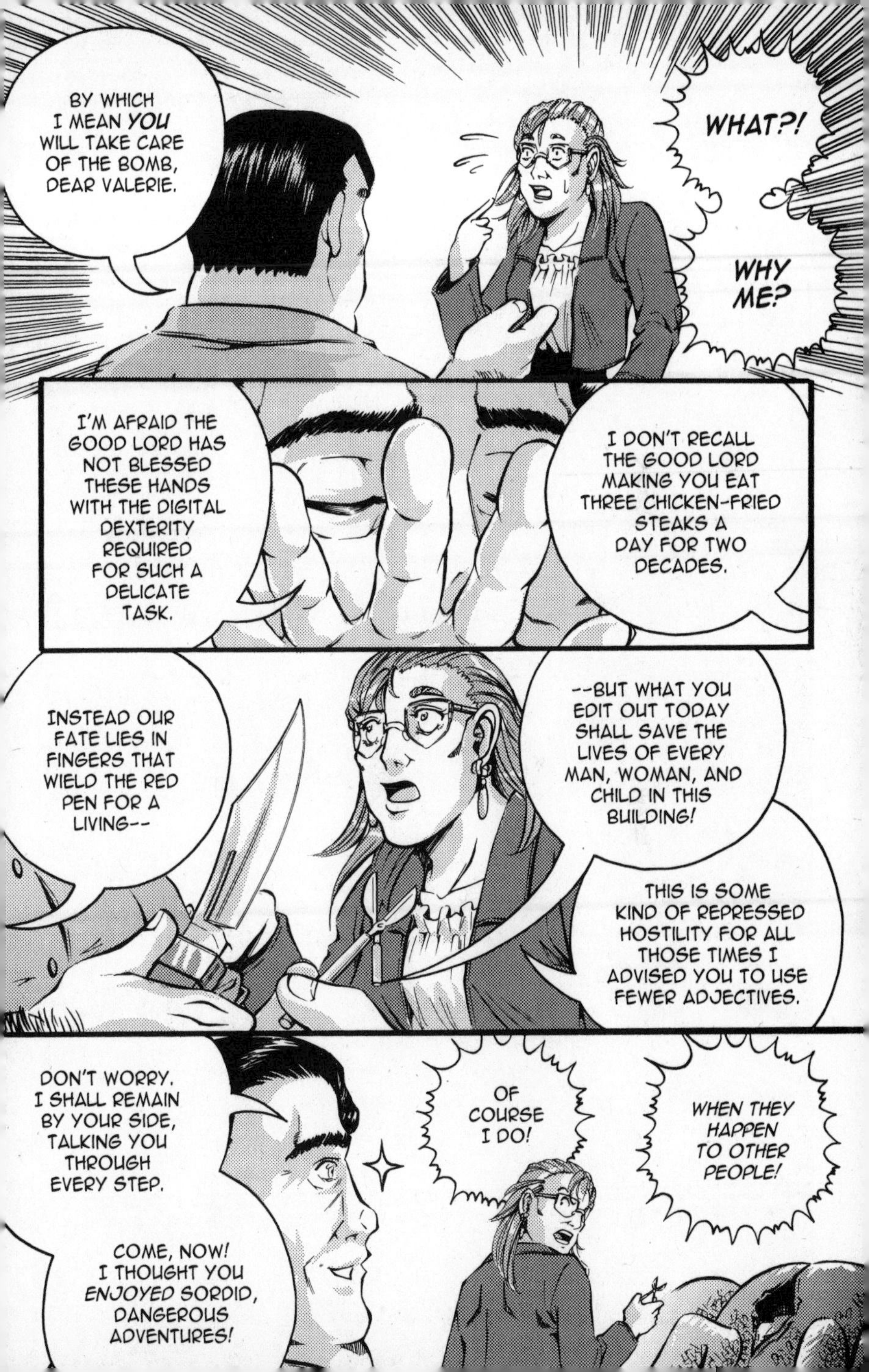
BY WHICH I MEAN YOU WILL TAKE CARE OF THE BOMB, DEAR VALERIE.
WHAT?!
WHY ME?
I'M AFRAID THE GOOD LORD HAS NOT BLESSED THESE HANDS WITH THE DIGITAL DEXTERITY REQUIRED FOR SUCH A DELICATE TASK.
I DON'T RECALL THE GOOD LORD MAKING YOU EAT THREE CHICKEN-FRIED STEAKS A DAY FOR TWO DECADES.
INSTEAD OUR FATE LIES IN FINGERS THAT WIELD THE RED PEN FOR A LIVING--
--BUT WHAT YOU EDIT OUT TODAY SHALL SAVE THE LIVES OF EVERY MAN, WOMAN, AND CHILD IN THIS BUILDING!
THIS IS SOME KIND OF REPRESSED HOSTILITY FOR ALL THOSE TIMES I ADVISED YOU TO USE FEWER ADJECTIVES.
DON'T WORRY. I SHALL REMAIN BY YOUR SIDE, TALKING YOU THROUGH EVERY STEP.
COME, NOW! I THOUGHT YOU ENJOYED SORDID, DANGEROUS ADVENTURES!
OF COURSE I DO!
WHEN THEY HAPPEN TO OTHER PEOPLE!

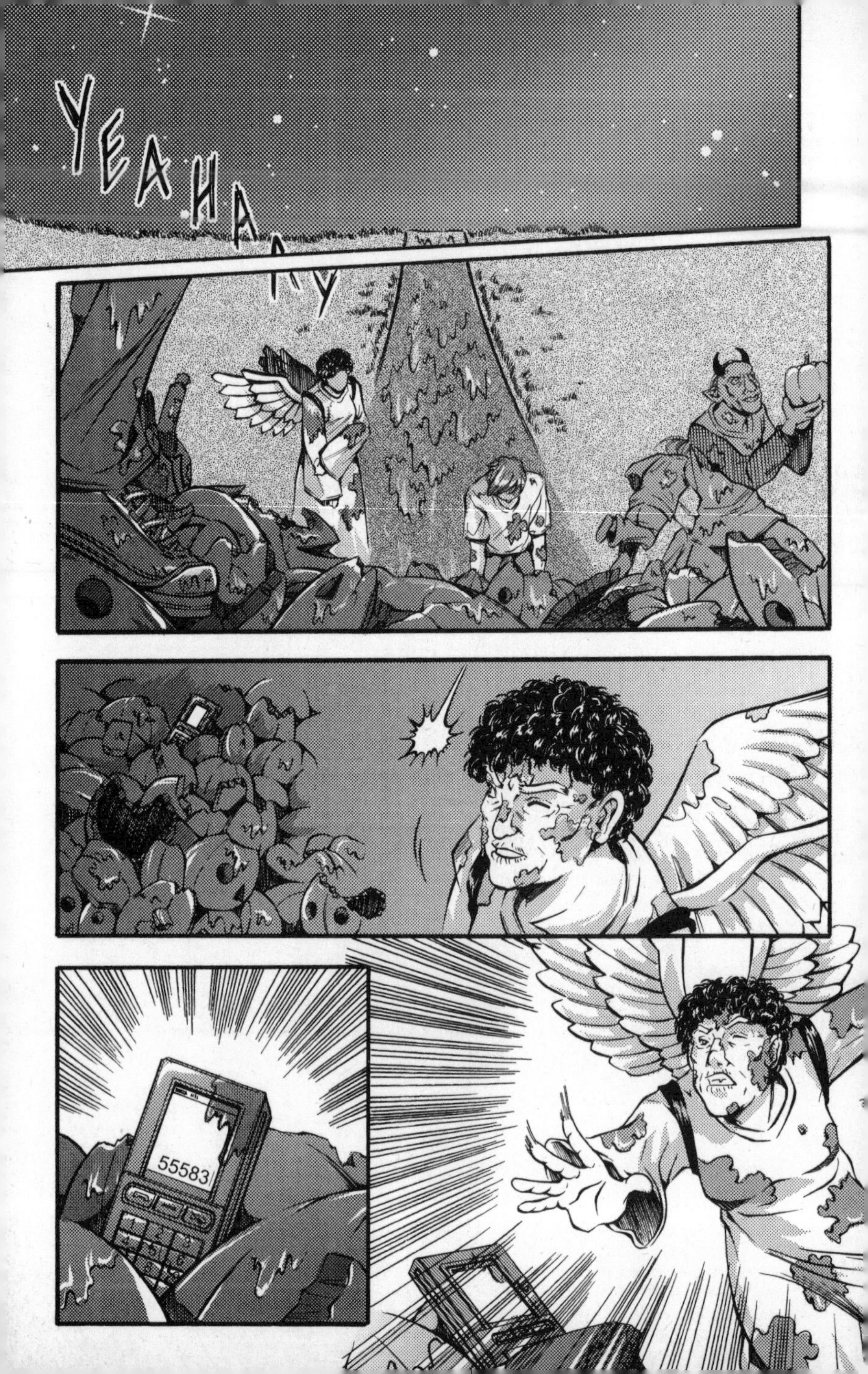
YEAHAAAARGH
55583

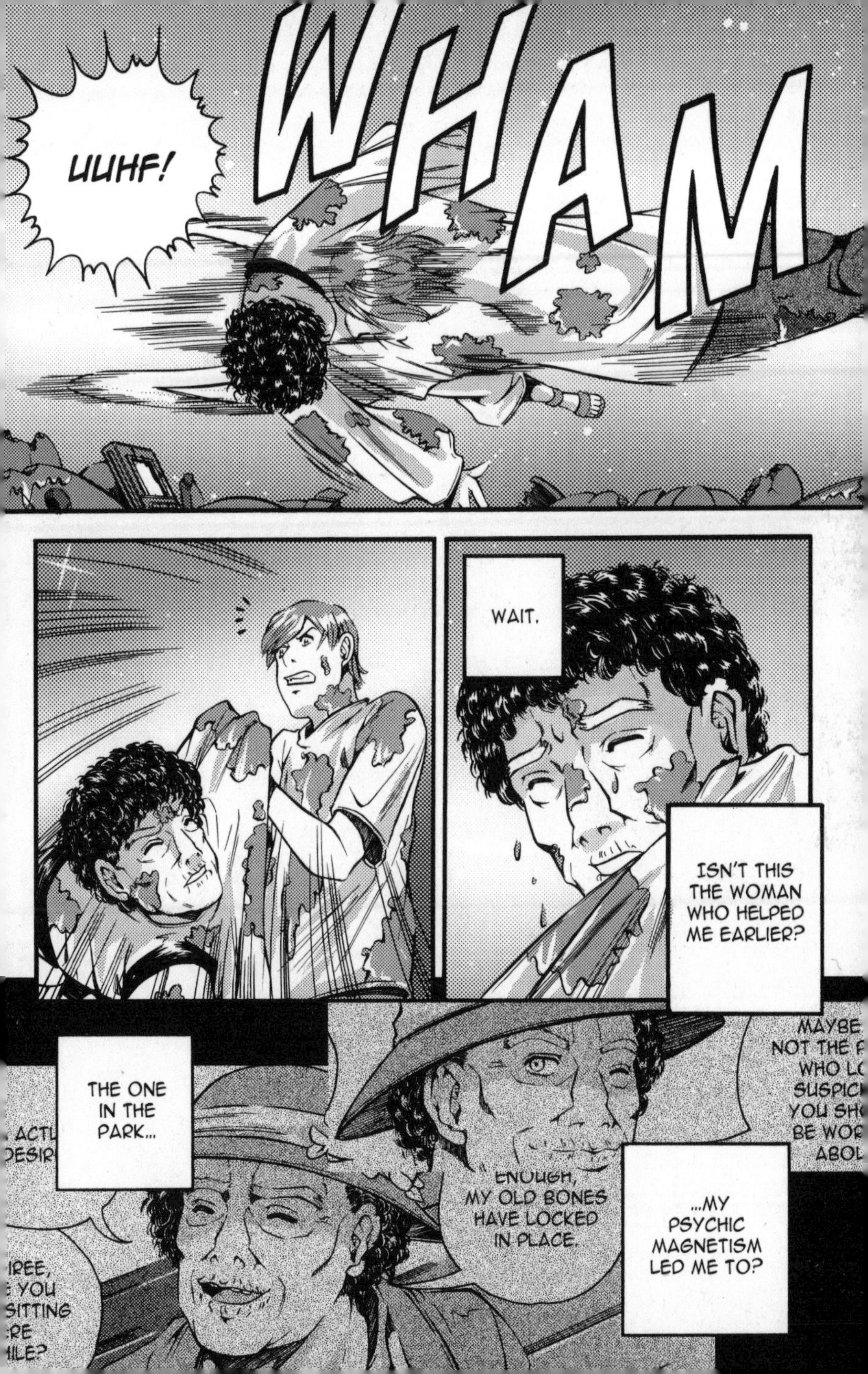
UUHF!
WHAM
WAIT.
ISN'T THIS THE WOMAN WHO HELPED ME EARLIER?
THE ONE IN THE PARK...
ENOUGH, MY OLD BONES HAVE LOCKED IN PLACE.
...MY PSYCHIC MAGNETISM LED ME TO?

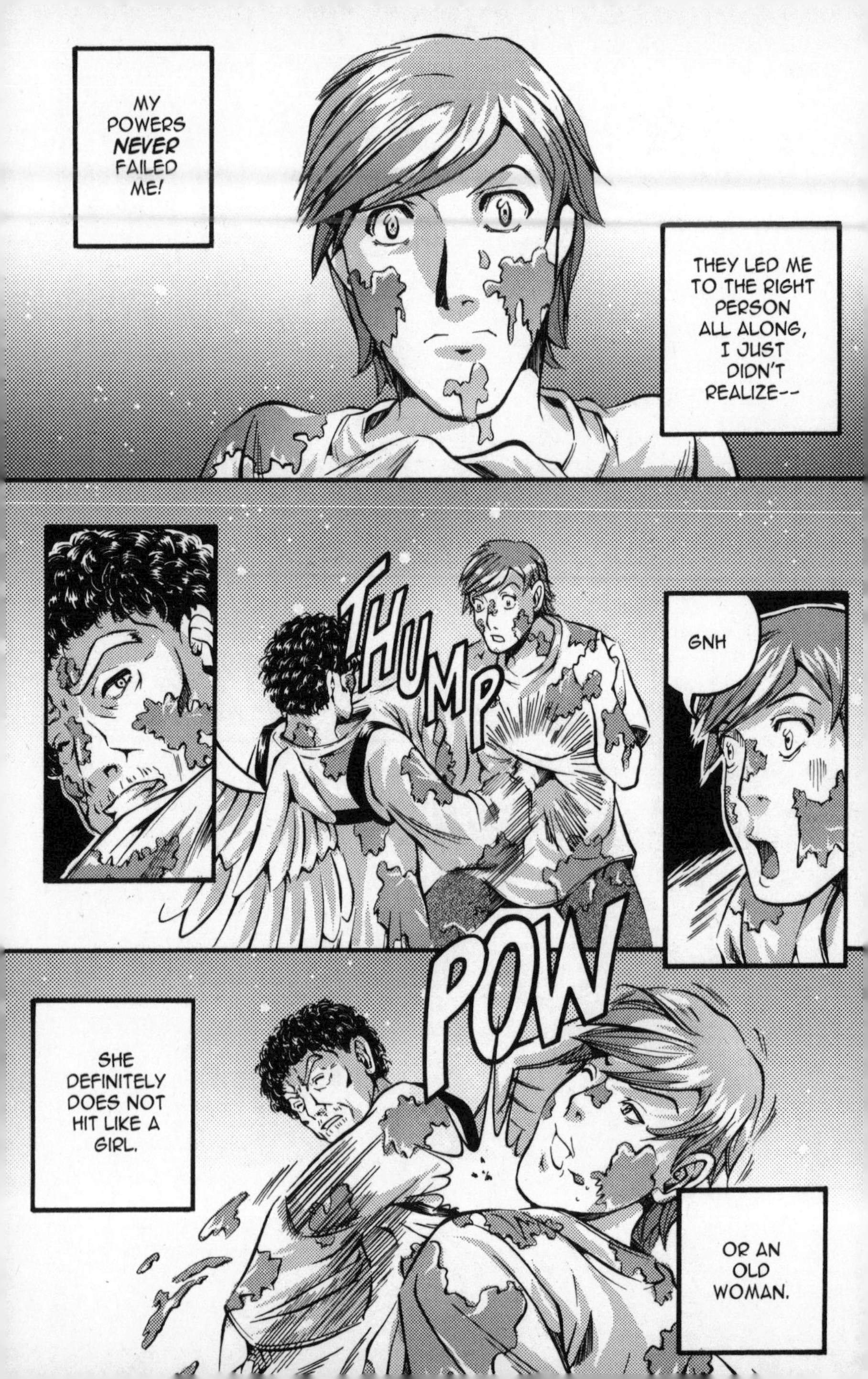
MY POWERS *NEVER* FAILED ME!
THEY LED ME TO THE RIGHT PERSON ALL ALONG, I JUST DIDN'T REALIZE--
THUMP
GNH
POW
SHE DEFINITELY DOES NOT HIT LIKE A GIRL.
OR AN OLD WOMAN.

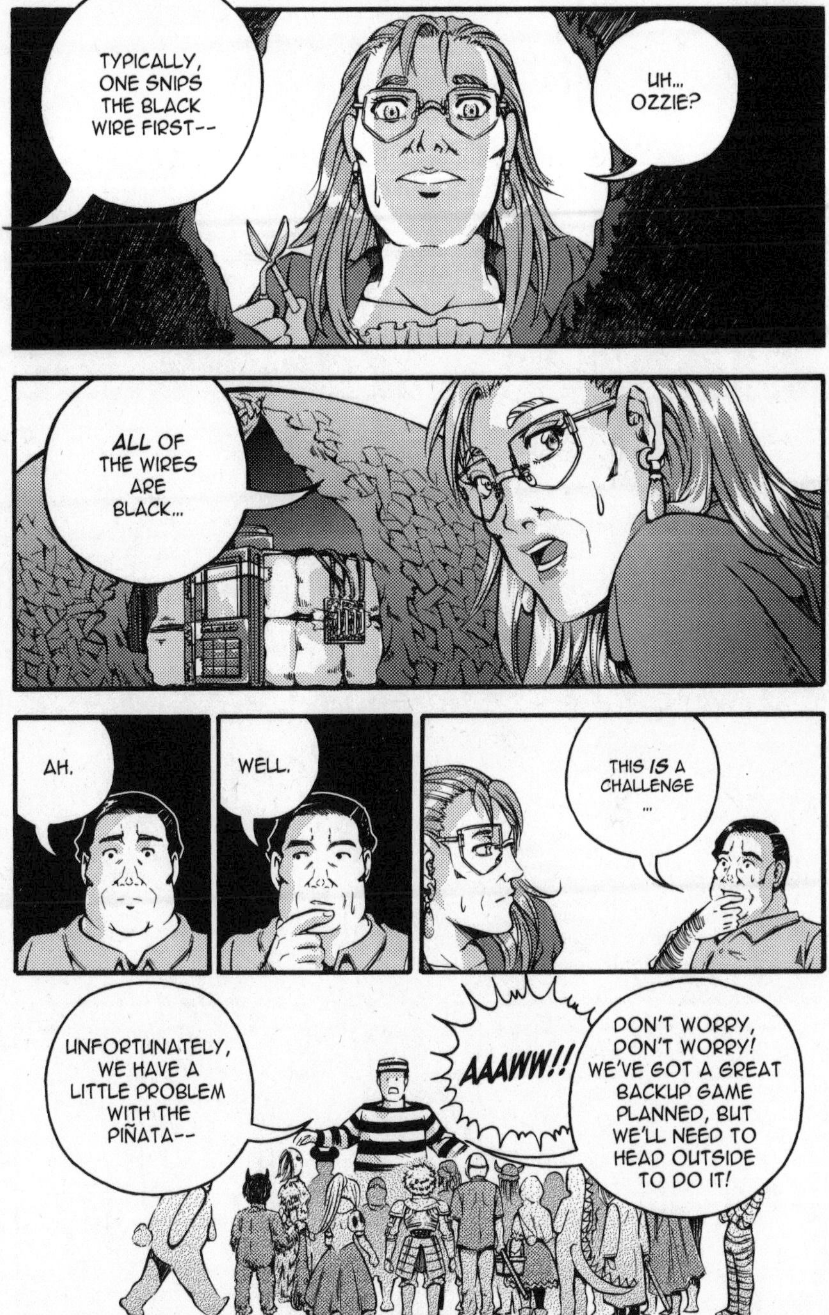
TYPICALLY, ONE SNIPS THE BLACK WIRE FIRST--
UH... OZZIE?
ALL OF THE WIRES ARE BLACK...
AH.
WELL.
THIS *IS* A CHALLENGE ...
UNFORTUNATELY, WE HAVE A LITTLE PROBLEM WITH THE PIÑATA--
AAAWW!!
DON'T WORRY, DON'T WORRY! WE'VE GOT A GREAT BACKUP GAME PLANNED, BUT WE'LL NEED TO HEAD OUTSIDE TO DO IT!

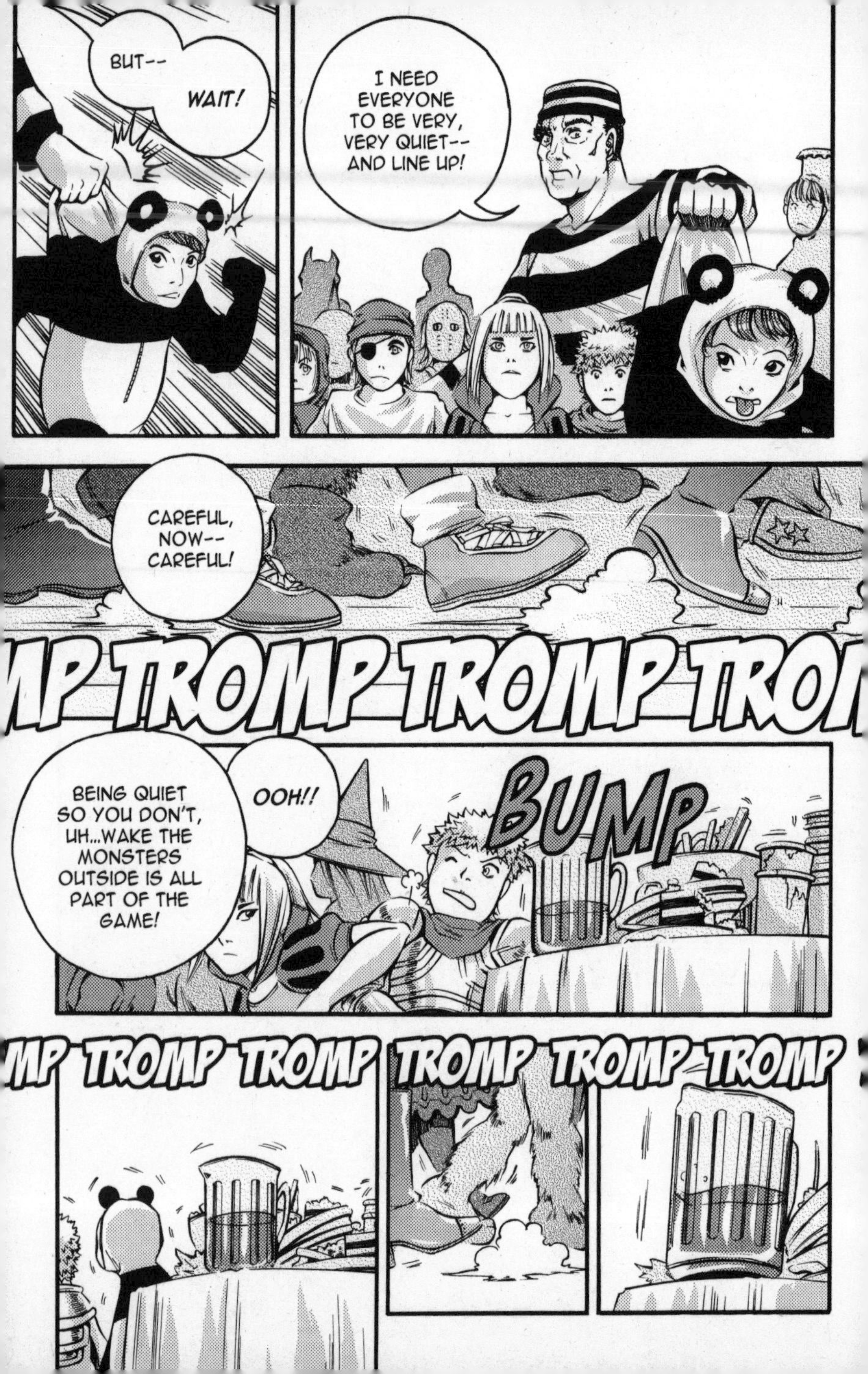
BUT--
WAIT!
I NEED EVERYONE TO BE VERY, VERY QUIET-- AND LINE UP!
CAREFUL, NOW-- CAREFUL!
TROMP TROMP
OOH!!
BEING QUIET SO YOU DON'T, UH...WAKE THE MONSTERS OUTSIDE IS ALL PART OF THE GAME!
BUMP
TROMP TROMP TROMP TROMP TROMP

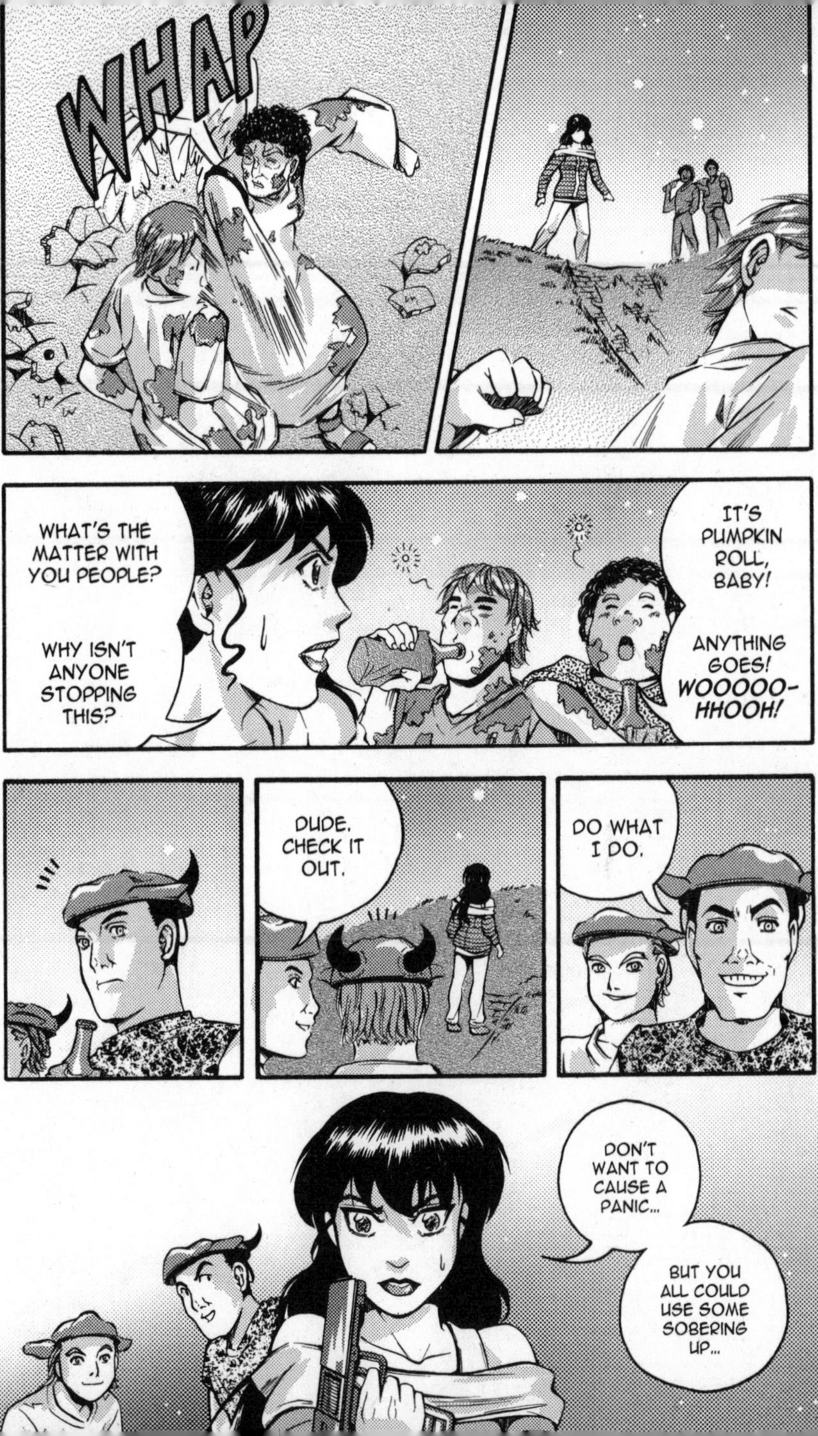
WHAP
WHAT'S THE MATTER WITH YOU PEOPLE?
WHY ISN'T ANYONE STOPPING THIS?
IT'S PUMPKIN ROLL, BABY!
ANYTHING GOES! WOOOOO-HHOOH!
DUDE. CHECK IT OUT.
DO WHAT I DO.
DON'T WANT TO CAUSE A PANIC...
BUT YOU ALL COULD USE SOME SOBERING UP...

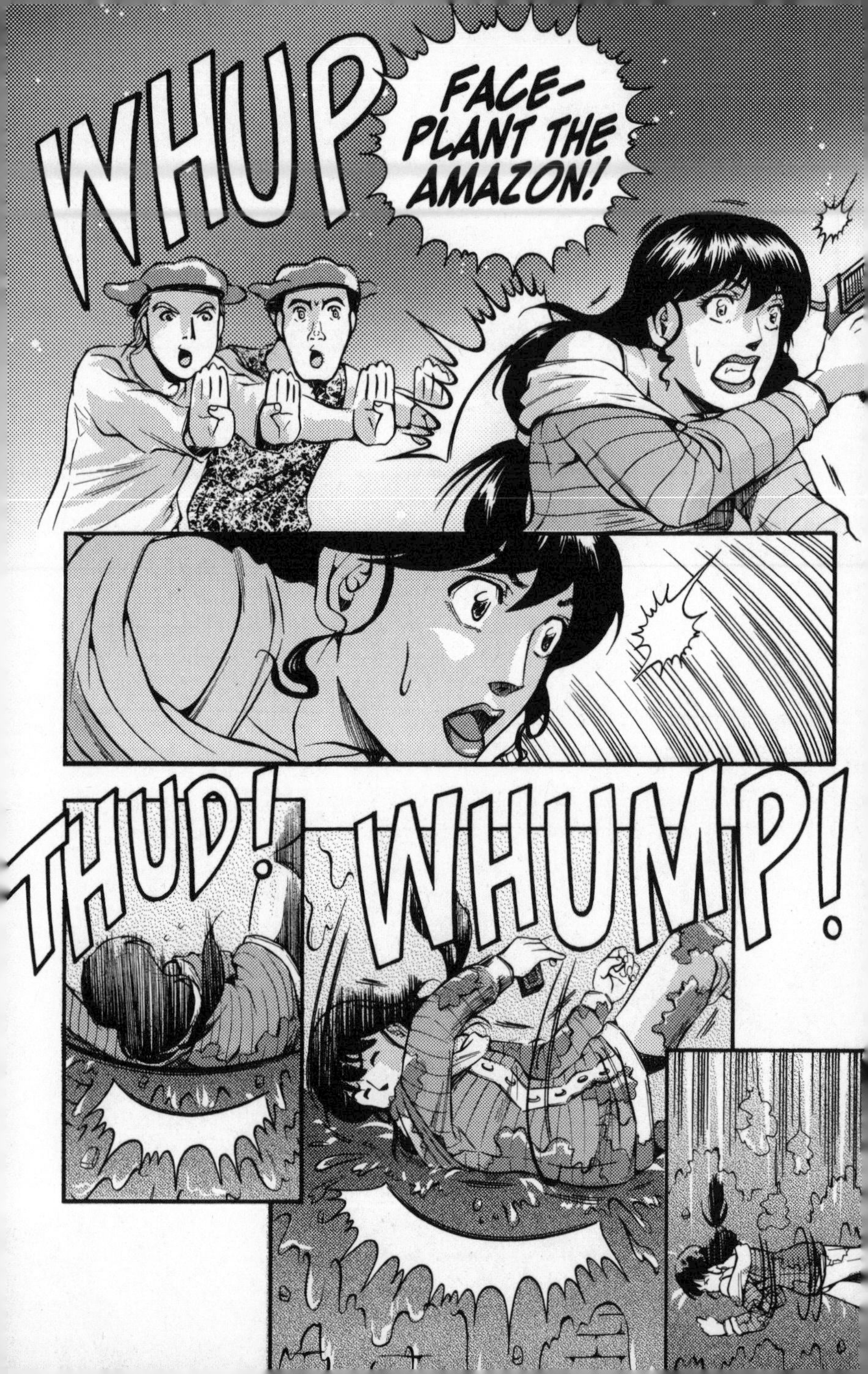
FACE-PLANT THE AMAZON!
WHUP
THUD!
WHUMP!

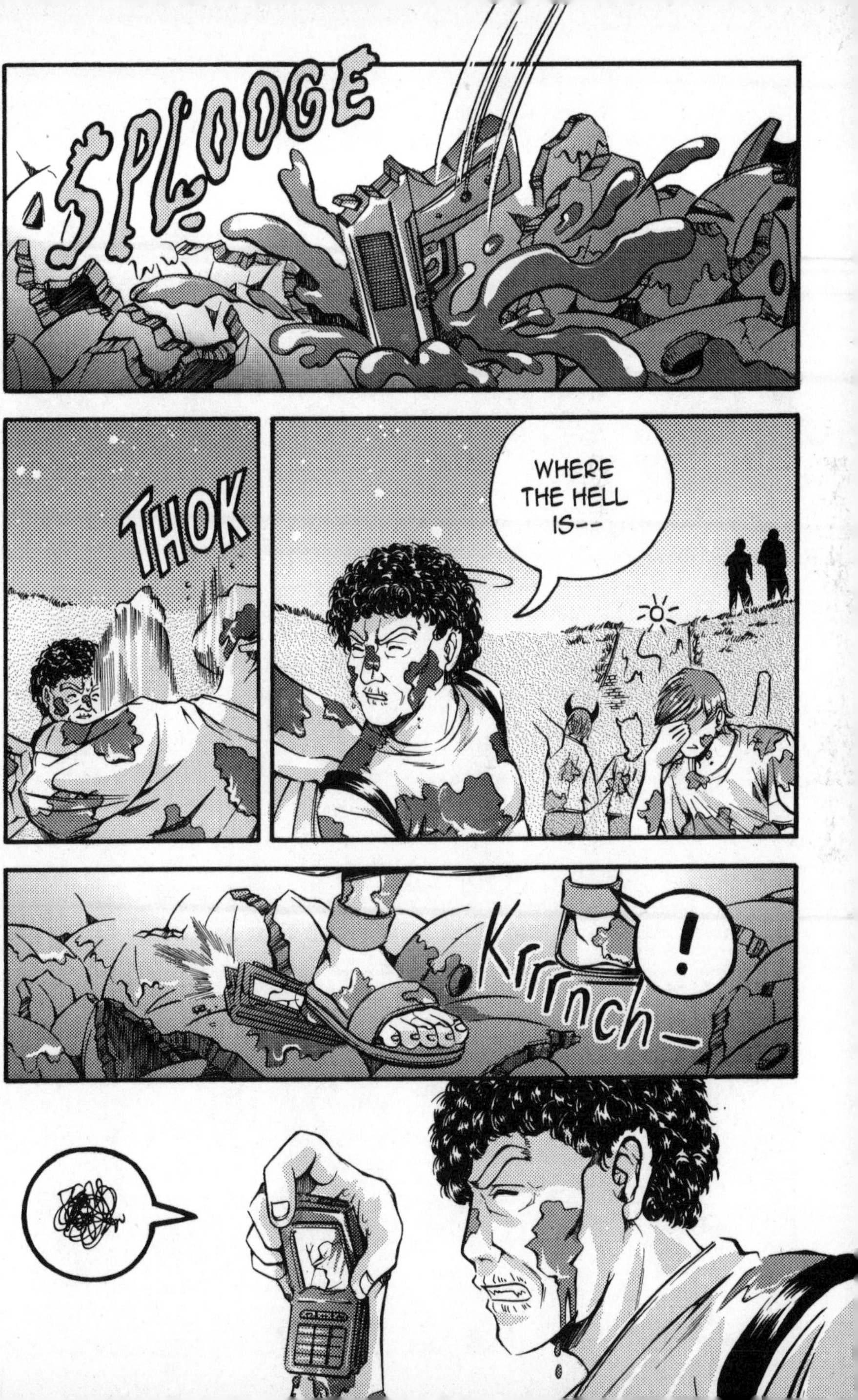
SPLOOGE
THOK
WHERE THE HELL IS--
Krrrnch
!

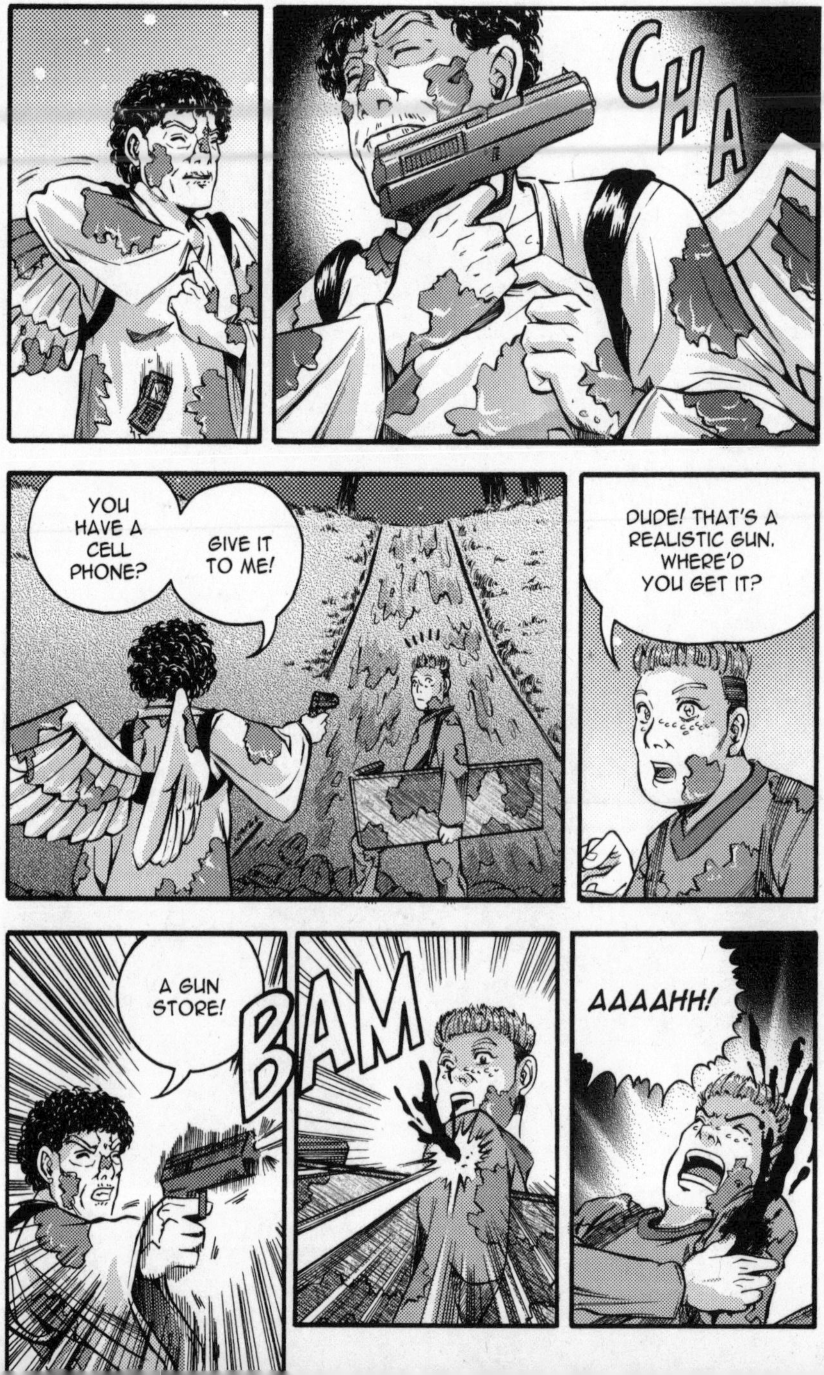
CHA
YOU HAVE A CELL PHONE?
GIVE IT TO ME!
DUDE! THAT'S A REALISTIC GUN. WHERE'D YOU GET IT?
A GUN STORE!
BAM
AAAAHH!

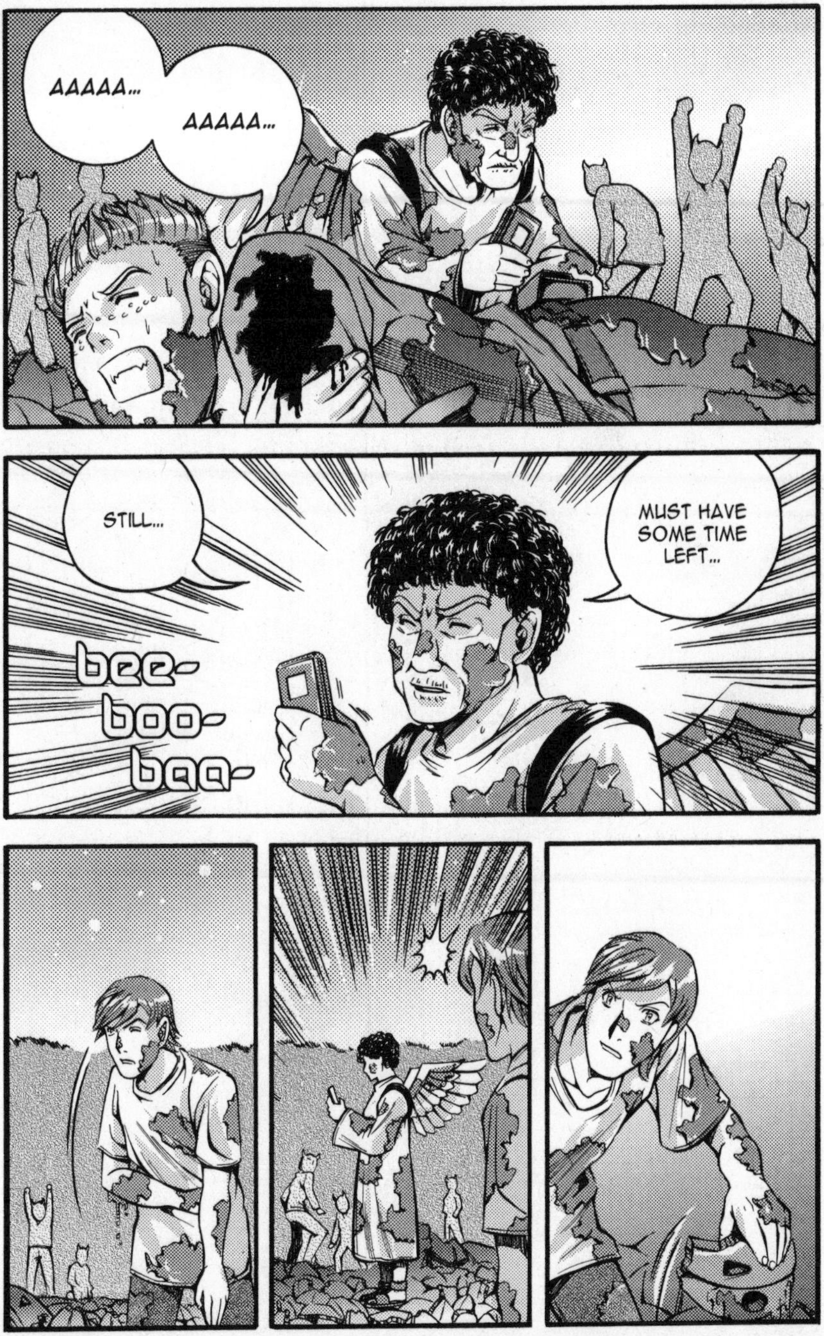
AAAAA...
AAAAA...
STILL...
MUST HAVE SOME TIME LEFT...
bee-boo-baa-

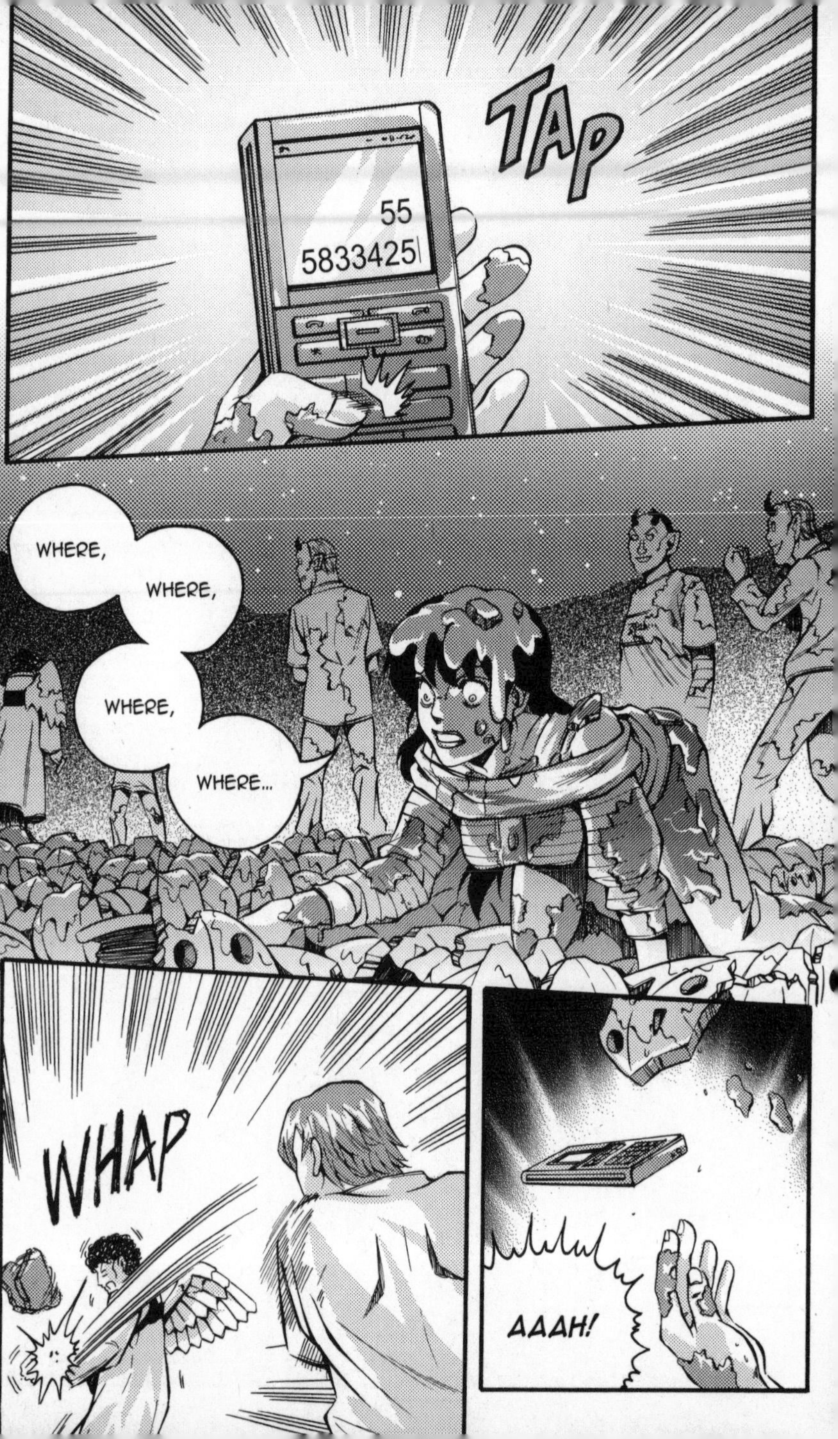
TAP
55
5833425
WHERE,
WHERE,
WHERE,
WHERE...
WHAP
AAAH!

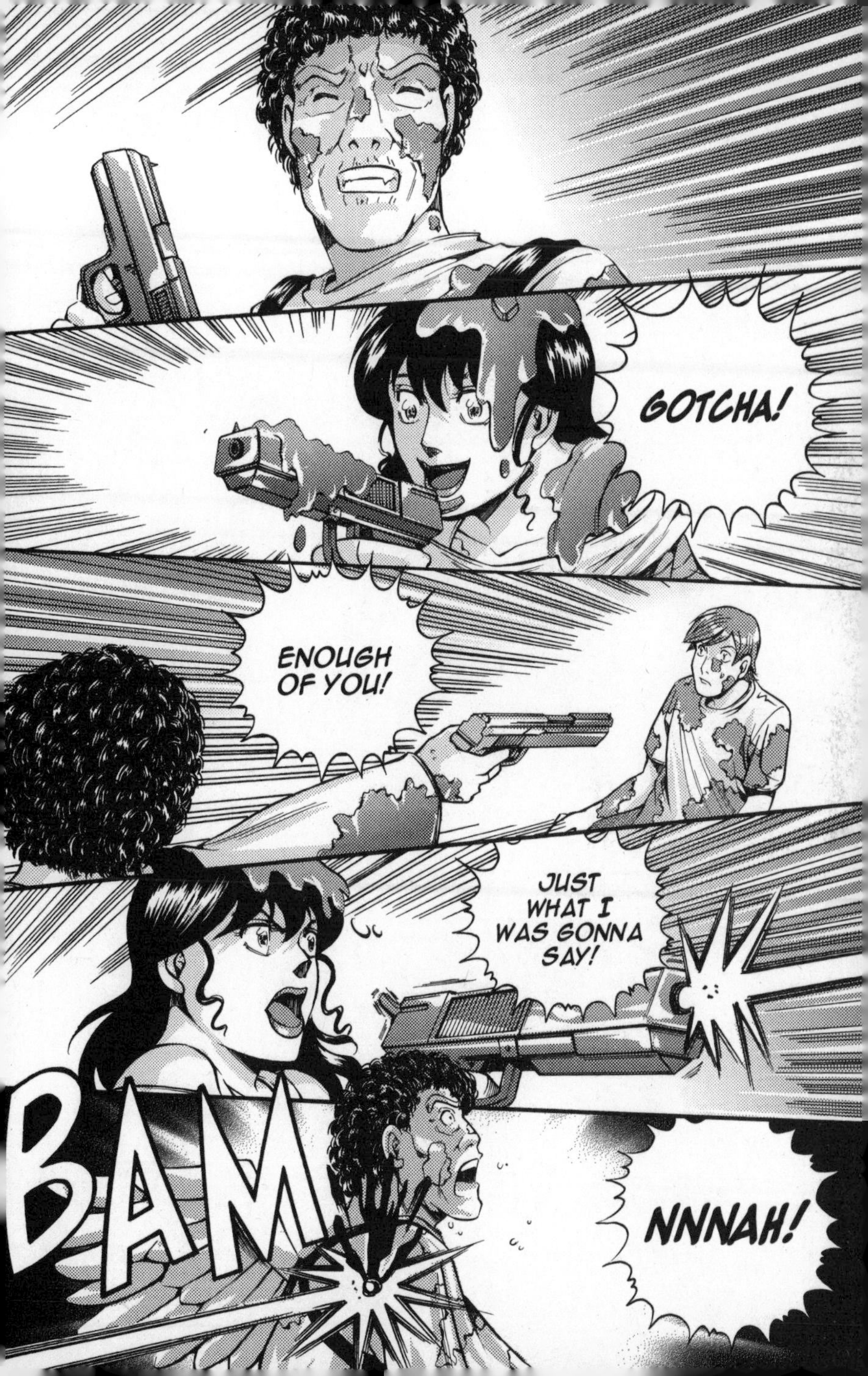
GOTCHA!
ENOUGH OF YOU!
JUST WHAT I WAS GONNA SAY!
BAM
NNNAH!

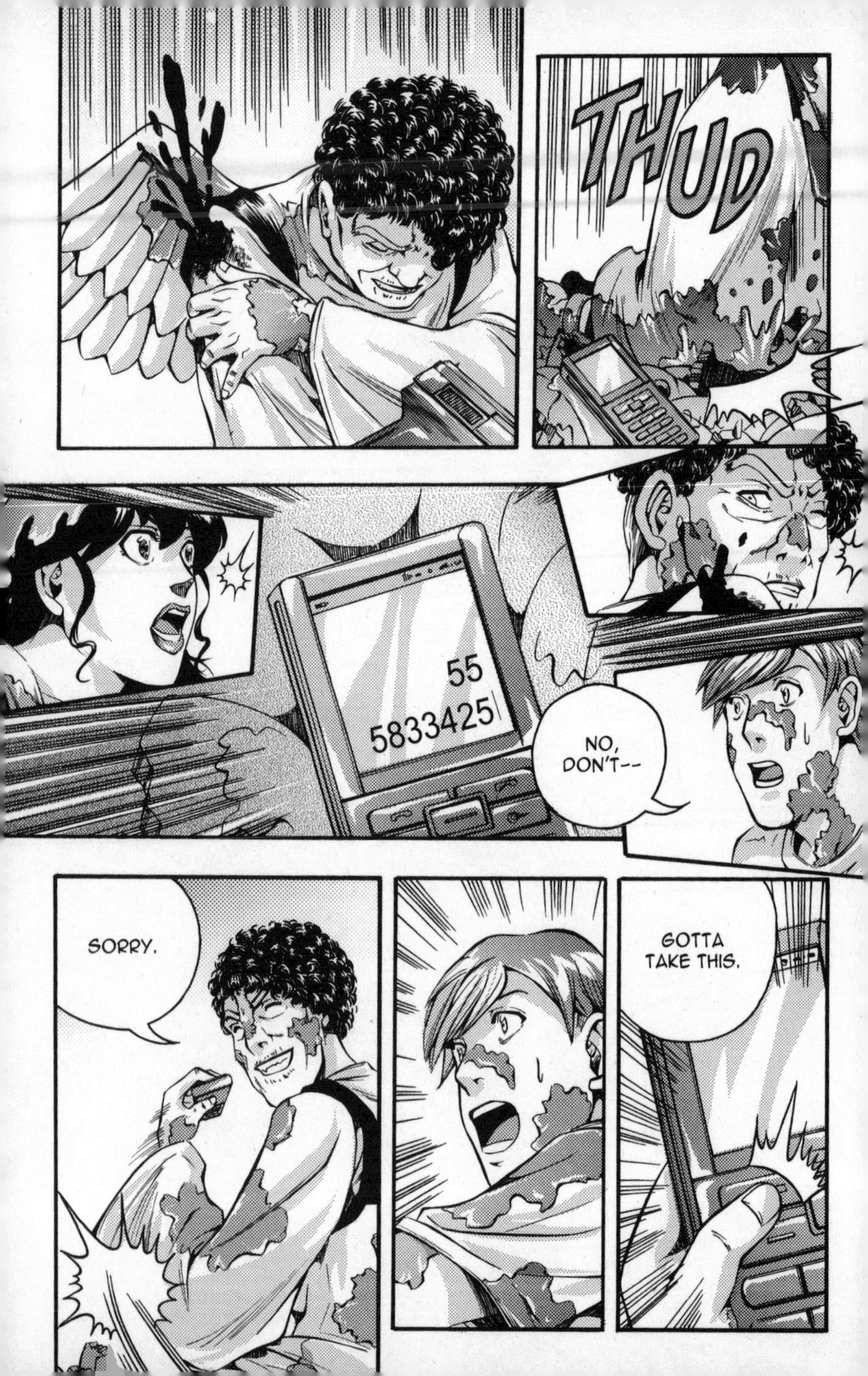
THUD
55
5833425
NO, DON'T--
SORRY.
GOTTA TAKE THIS.

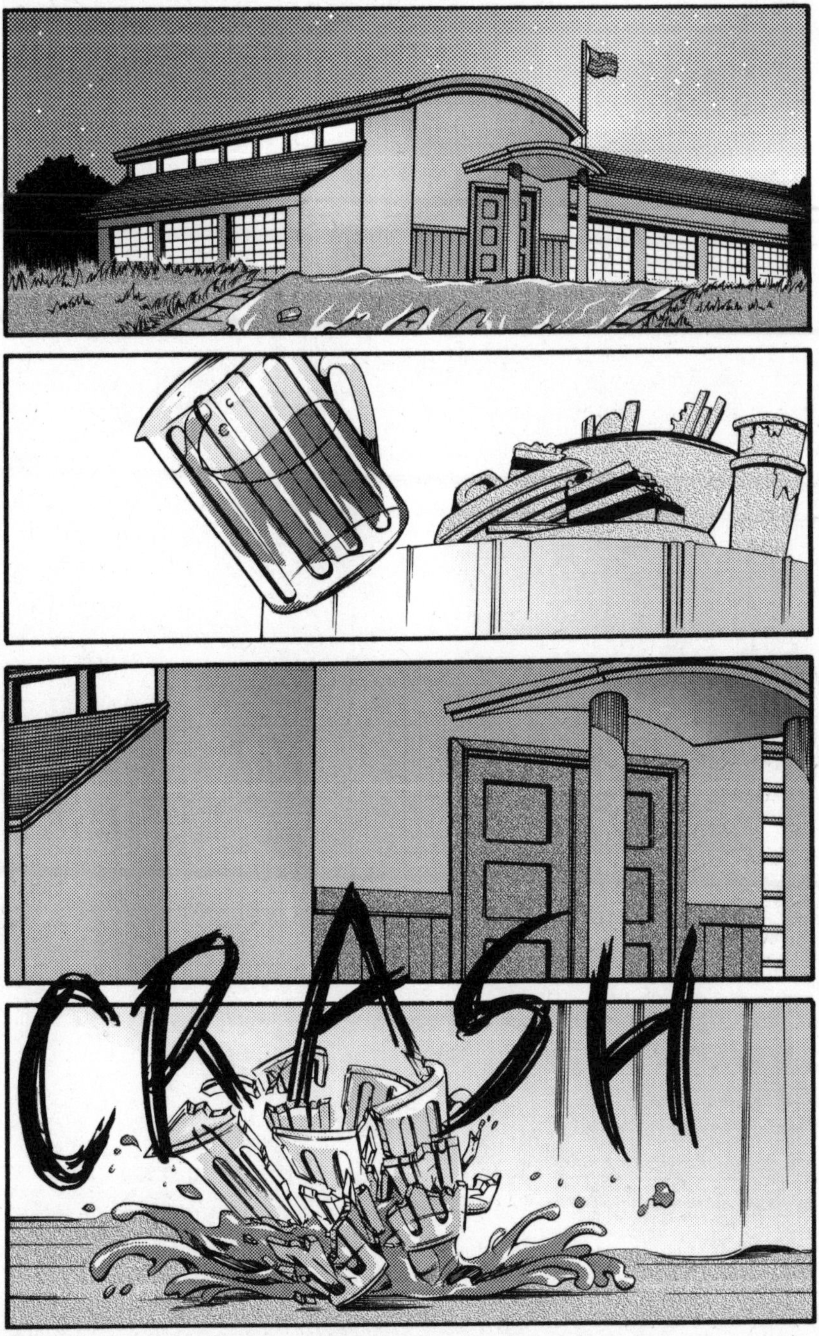
CRASH

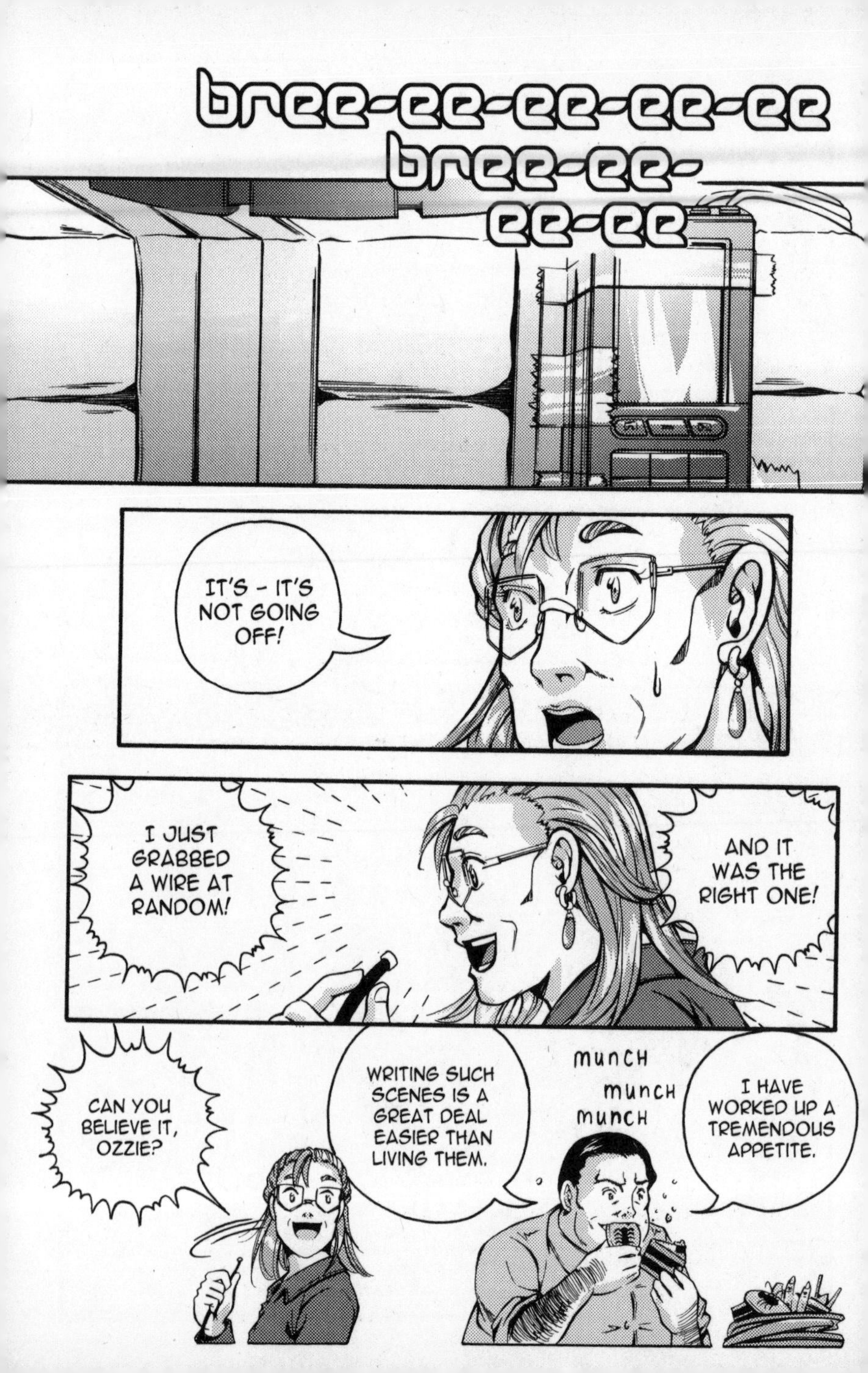
bree-ee-ee-ee-ee
bree-ee-ee-ee
IT'S - IT'S NOT GOING OFF!
I JUST GRABBED A WIRE AT RANDOM!
AND IT WAS THE RIGHT ONE!
CAN YOU BELIEVE IT, OZZIE?
WRITING SUCH SCENES IS A GREAT DEAL EASIER THAN LIVING THEM.
munch munch munch
I HAVE WORKED UP A TREMENDOUS APPETITE.

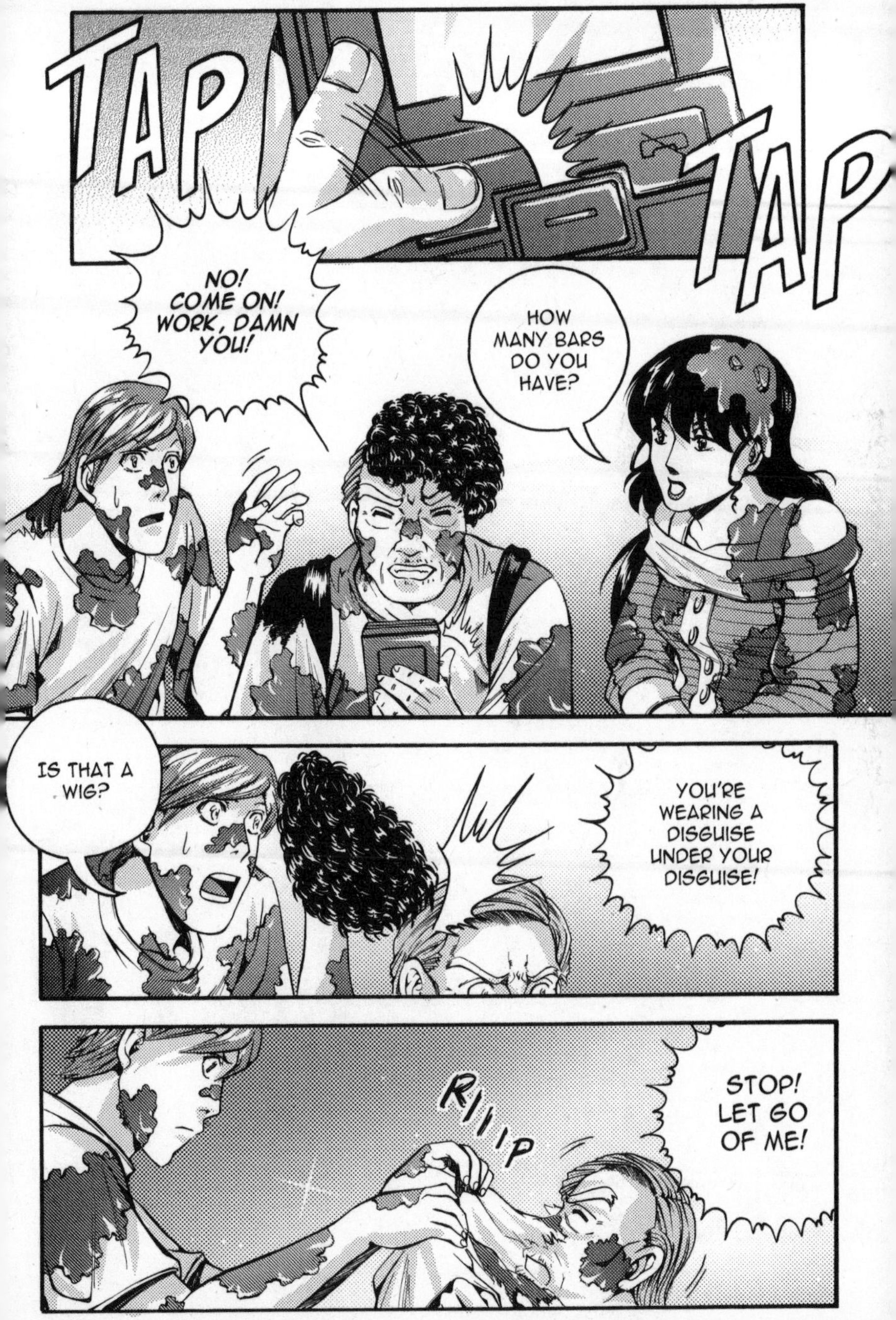
TAP
TAP
NO! COME ON! WORK, DAMN YOU!
HOW MANY BARS DO YOU HAVE?
IS THAT A WIG?
YOU'RE WEARING A DISGUISE UNDER YOUR DISGUISE!
RIIIP
STOP! LET GO OF ME!

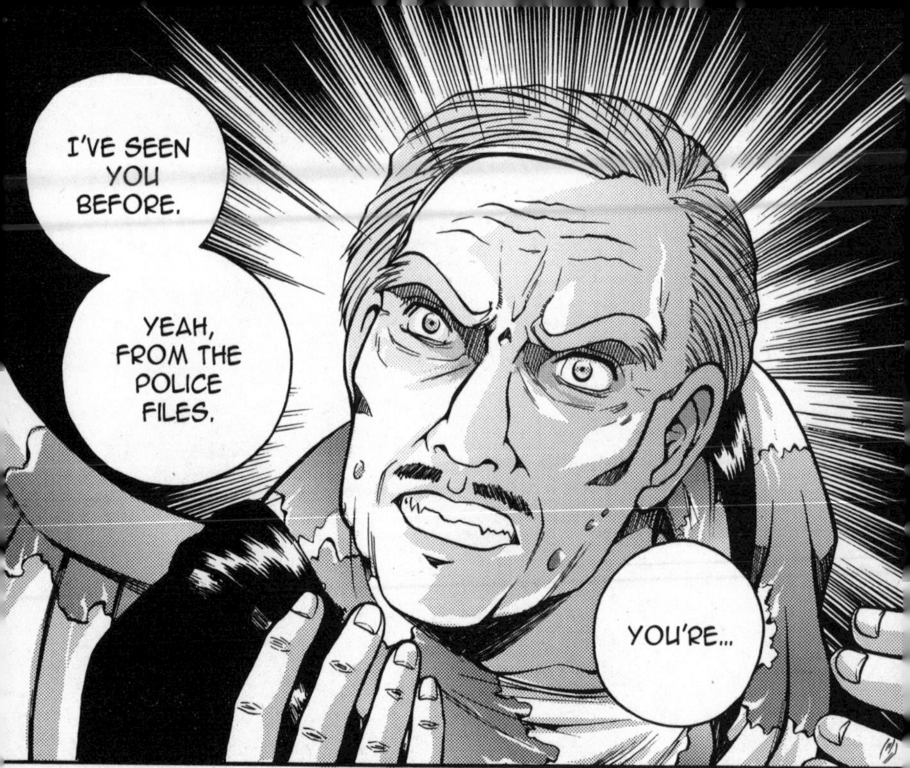
I'VE SEEN YOU BEFORE.
YEAH, FROM THE POLICE FILES.
YOU'RE...

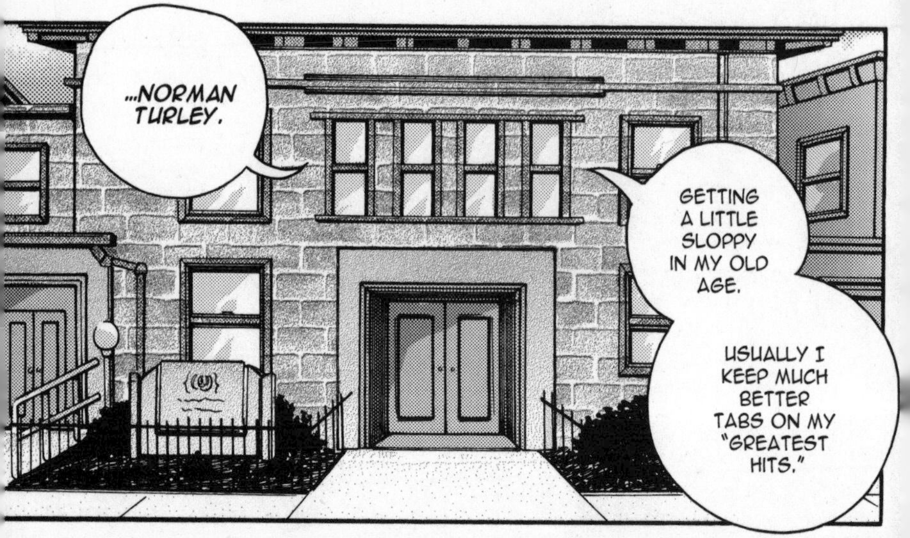
...NORMAN TURLEY.
GETTING A LITTLE SLOPPY IN MY OLD AGE.
USUALLY I KEEP MUCH BETTER TABS ON MY "GREATEST HITS."

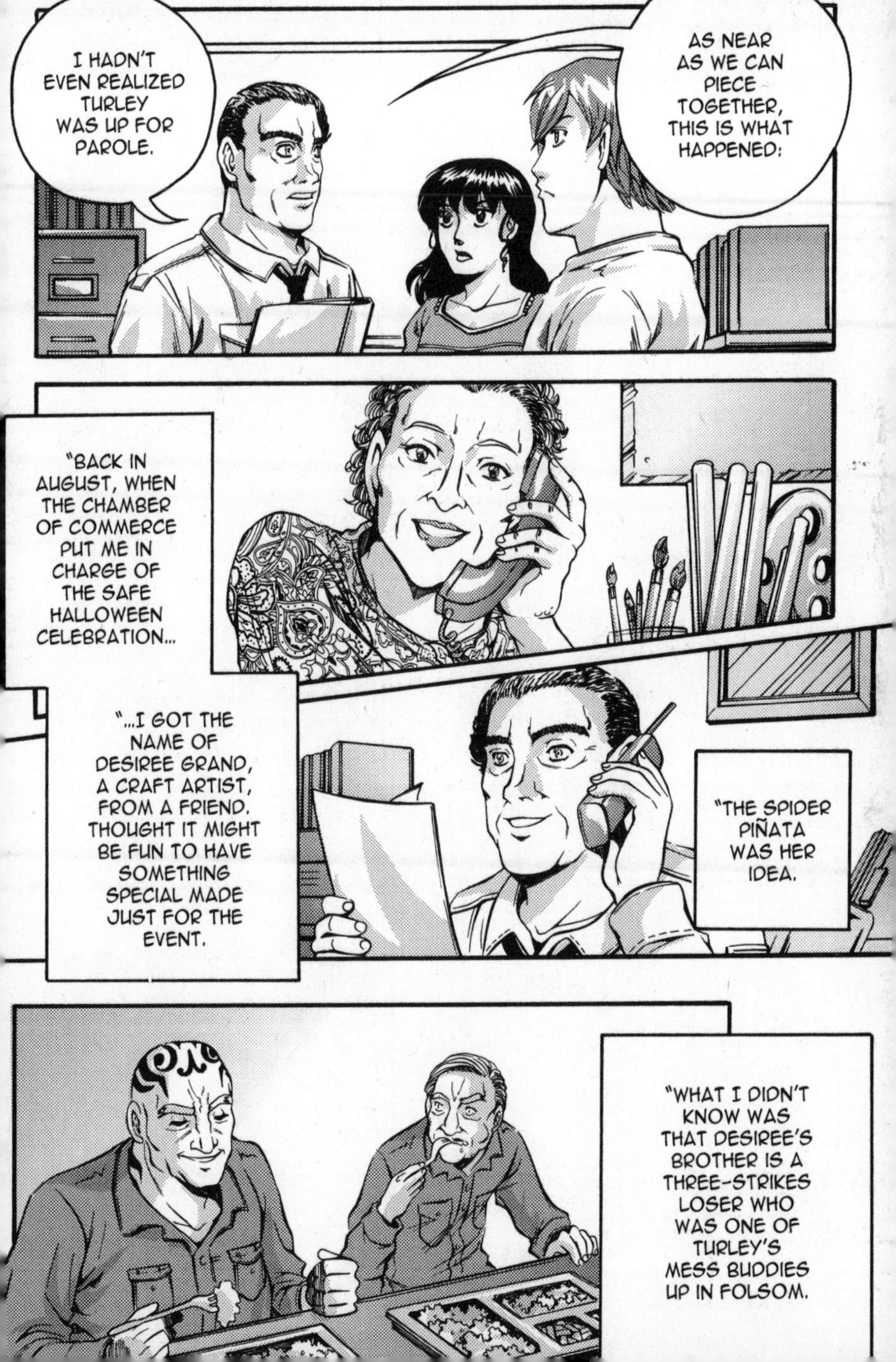
I HADN'T EVEN REALIZED TURLEY WAS UP FOR PAROLE.
AS NEAR AS WE CAN PIECE TOGETHER, THIS IS WHAT HAPPENED:
"BACK IN AUGUST, WHEN THE CHAMBER OF COMMERCE PUT ME IN CHARGE OF THE SAFE HALLOWEEN CELEBRATION...
"...I GOT THE NAME OF DESIREE GRAND, A CRAFT ARTIST, FROM A FRIEND. THOUGHT IT MIGHT BE FUN TO HAVE SOMETHING SPECIAL MADE JUST FOR THE EVENT.
"THE SPIDER PIÑATA WAS HER IDEA.
"WHAT I DIDN'T KNOW WAS THAT DESIREE'S BROTHER IS A THREE-STRIKES LOSER WHO WAS ONE OF TURLEY'S MESS BUDDIES UP IN FOLSOM.

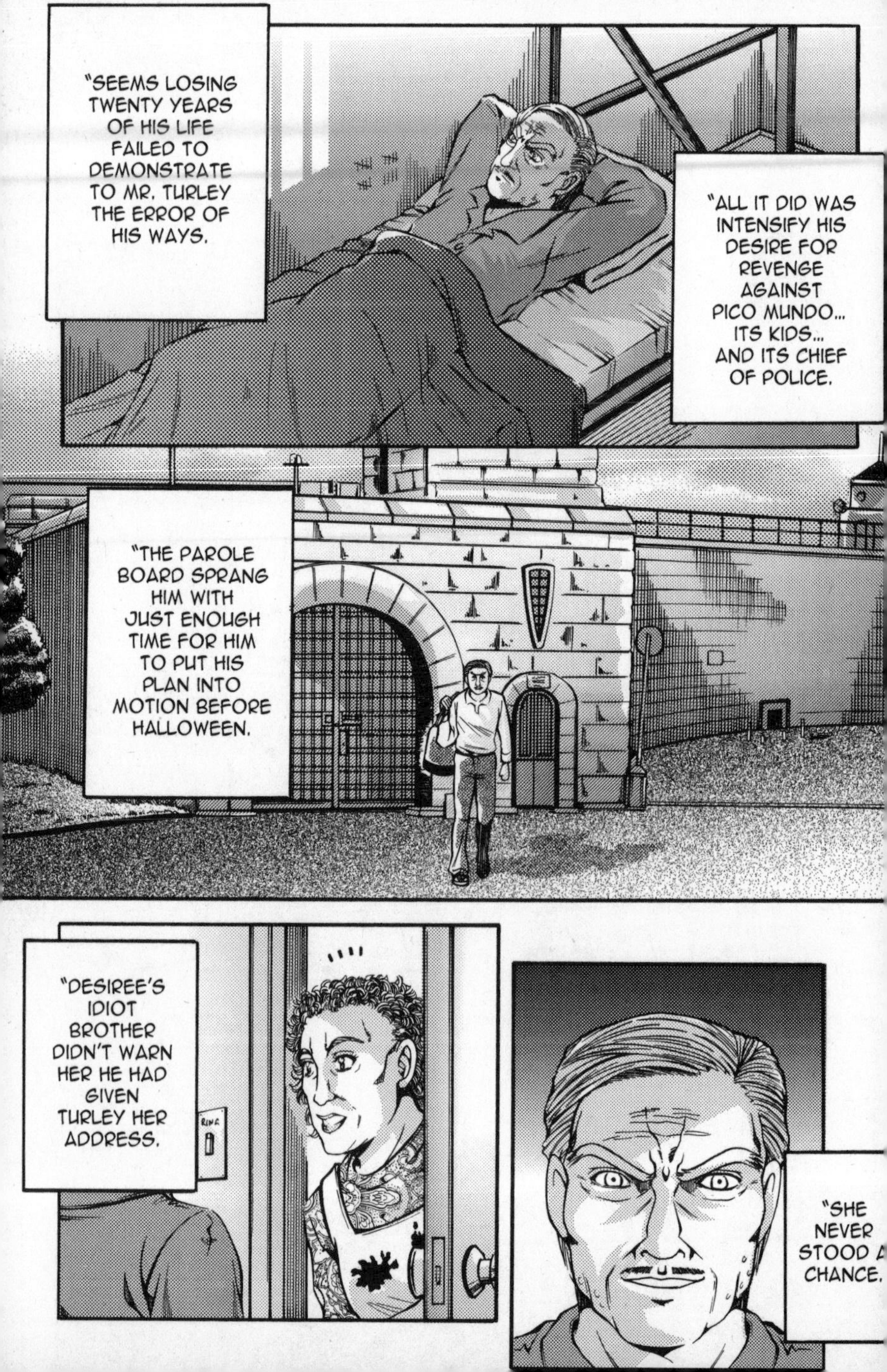
"SEEMS LOSING TWENTY YEARS OF HIS LIFE FAILED TO DEMONSTRATE TO MR. TURLEY THE ERROR OF HIS WAYS.
"ALL IT DID WAS INTENSIFY HIS DESIRE FOR REVENGE AGAINST PICO MUNDO... ITS KIDS... AND ITS CHIEF OF POLICE.
"THE PAROLE BOARD SPRANG HIM WITH JUST ENOUGH TIME FOR HIM TO PUT HIS PLAN INTO MOTION BEFORE HALLOWEEN.
"DESIREE'S IDIOT BROTHER DIDN'T WARN HER HE HAD GIVEN TURLEY HER ADDRESS.
"SHE NEVER STOOD A CHANCE.

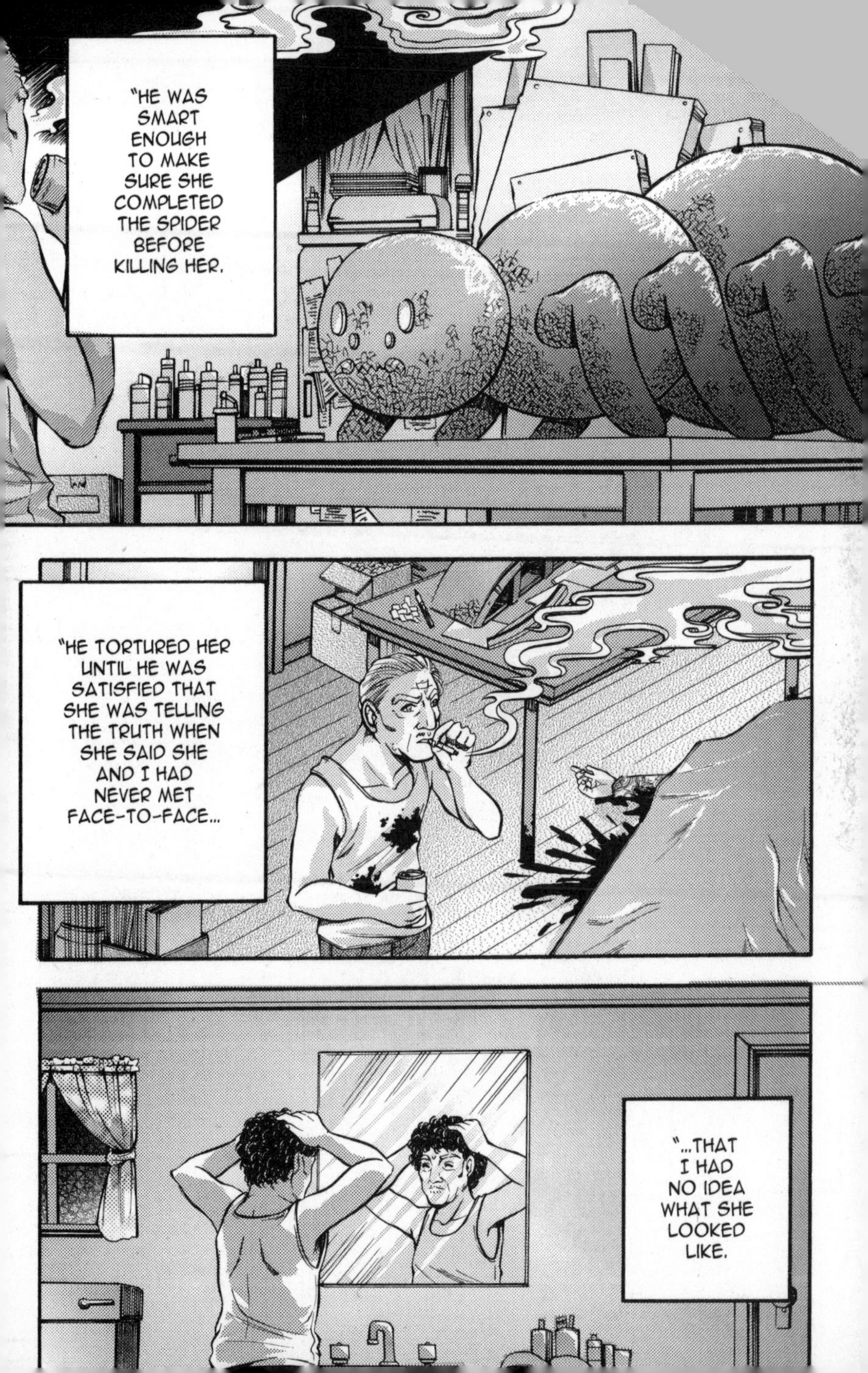
"HE WAS SMART ENOUGH TO MAKE SURE SHE COMPLETED THE SPIDER BEFORE KILLING HER.
"HE TORTURED HER UNTIL HE WAS SATISFIED THAT SHE WAS TELLING THE TRUTH WHEN SHE SAID SHE AND I HAD NEVER MET FACE-TO-FACE...
"...THAT I HAD NO IDEA WHAT SHE LOOKED LIKE.

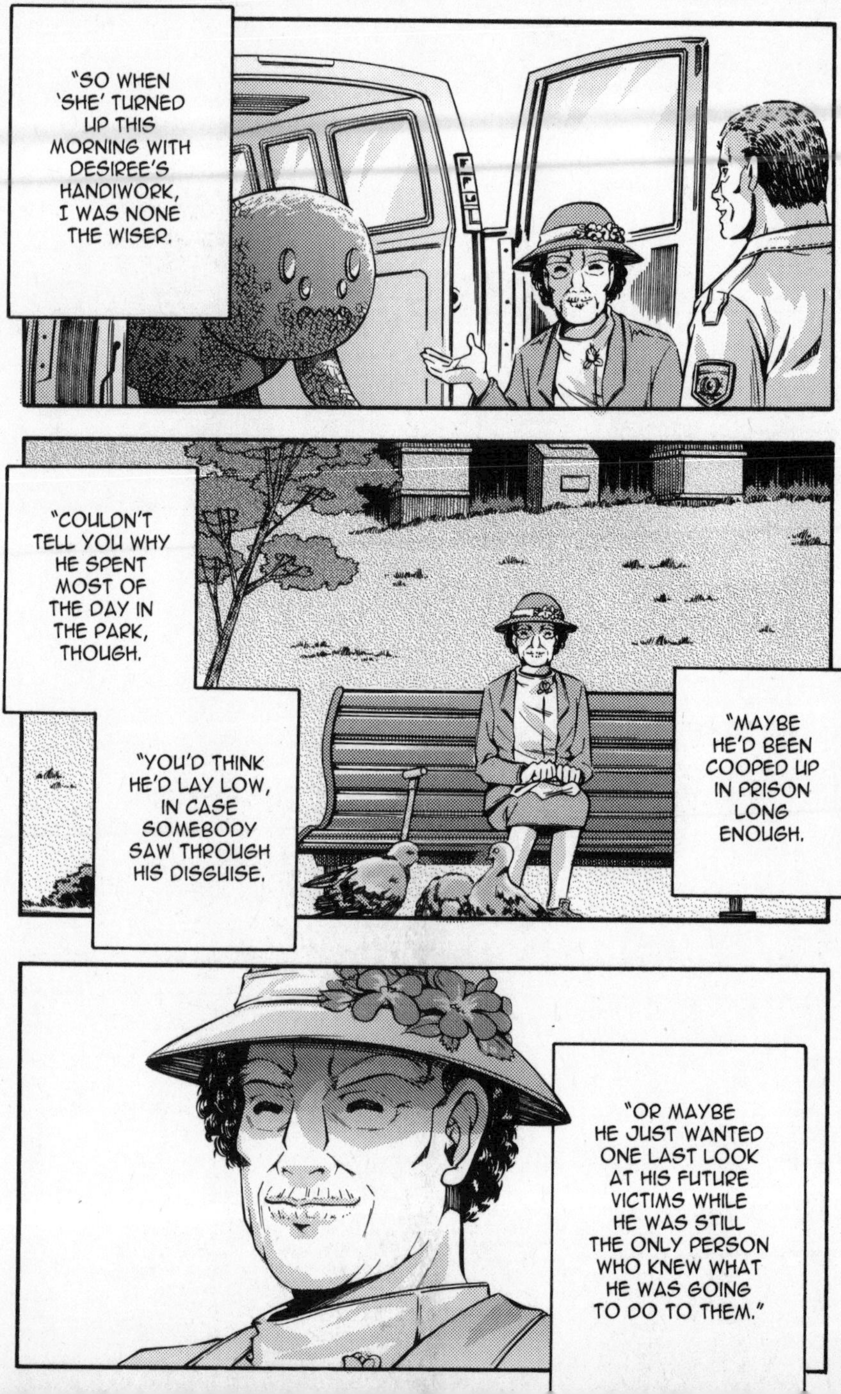
"SO WHEN 'SHE' TURNED UP THIS MORNING WITH DESIREE'S HANDIWORK, I WAS NONE THE WISER.
"COULDN'T TELL YOU WHY HE SPENT MOST OF THE DAY IN THE PARK, THOUGH.
"YOU'D THINK HE'D LAY LOW, IN CASE SOMEBODY SAW THROUGH HIS DISGUISE.
"MAYBE HE'D BEEN COOPED UP IN PRISON LONG ENOUGH.
"OR MAYBE HE JUST WANTED ONE LAST LOOK AT HIS FUTURE VICTIMS WHILE HE WAS STILL THE ONLY PERSON WHO KNEW WHAT HE WAS GOING TO DO TO THEM."

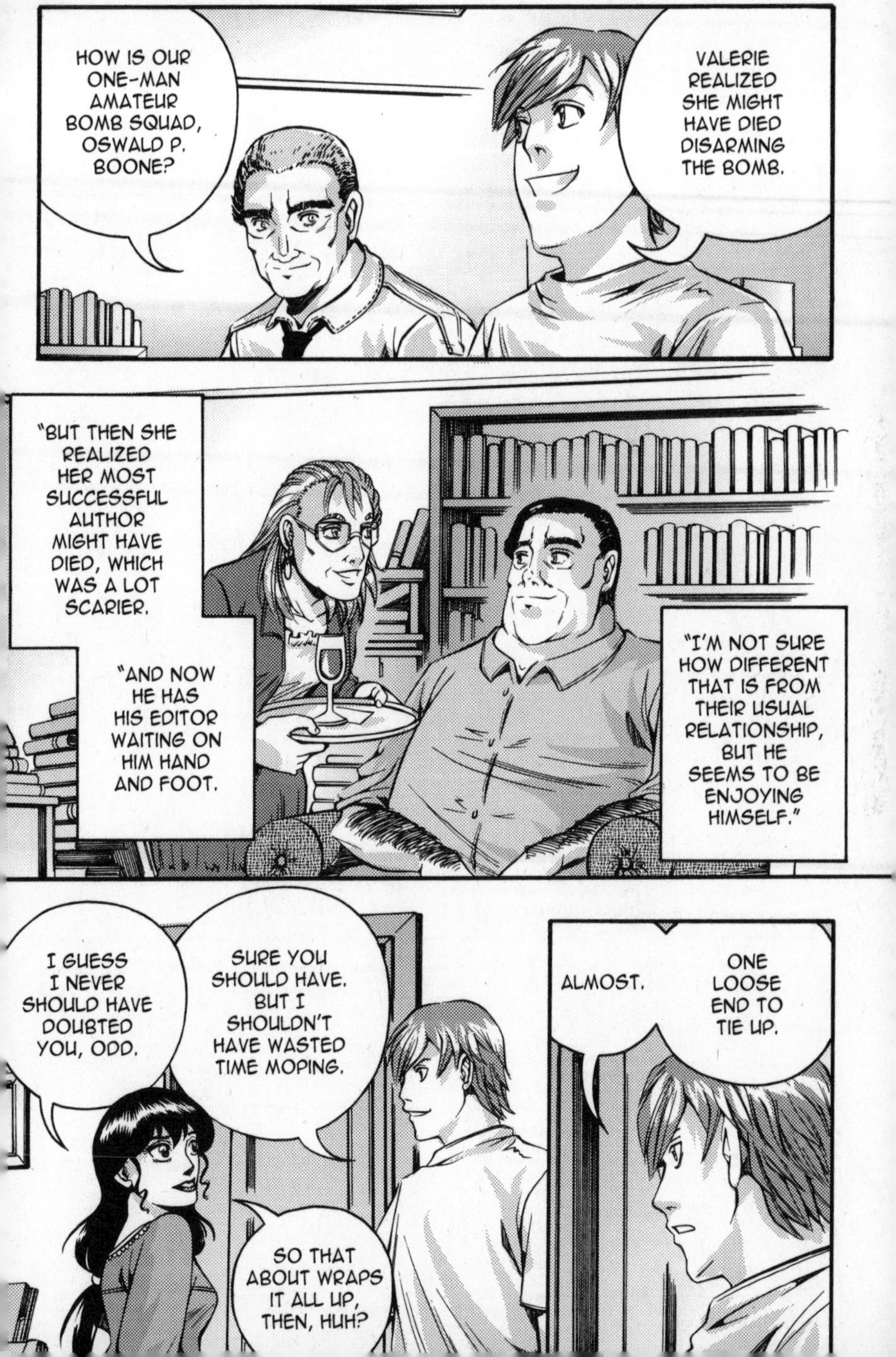
HOW IS OUR ONE-MAN AMATEUR BOMB SQUAD, OSWALD P. BOONE?
VALERIE REALIZED SHE MIGHT HAVE DIED DISARMING THE BOMB.
"BUT THEN SHE REALIZED HER MOST SUCCESSFUL AUTHOR MIGHT HAVE DIED, WHICH WAS A LOT SCARIER.
"AND NOW HE HAS HIS EDITOR WAITING ON HIM HAND AND FOOT.
"I'M NOT SURE HOW DIFFERENT THAT IS FROM THEIR USUAL RELATIONSHIP, BUT HE SEEMS TO BE ENJOYING HIMSELF."
I GUESS I NEVER SHOULD HAVE DOUBTED YOU, ODD.
SURE YOU SHOULD HAVE. BUT I SHOULDN'T HAVE WASTED TIME MOPING.
SO THAT ABOUT WRAPS IT ALL UP, THEN, HUH?
ALMOST.
ONE LOOSE END TO TIE UP.

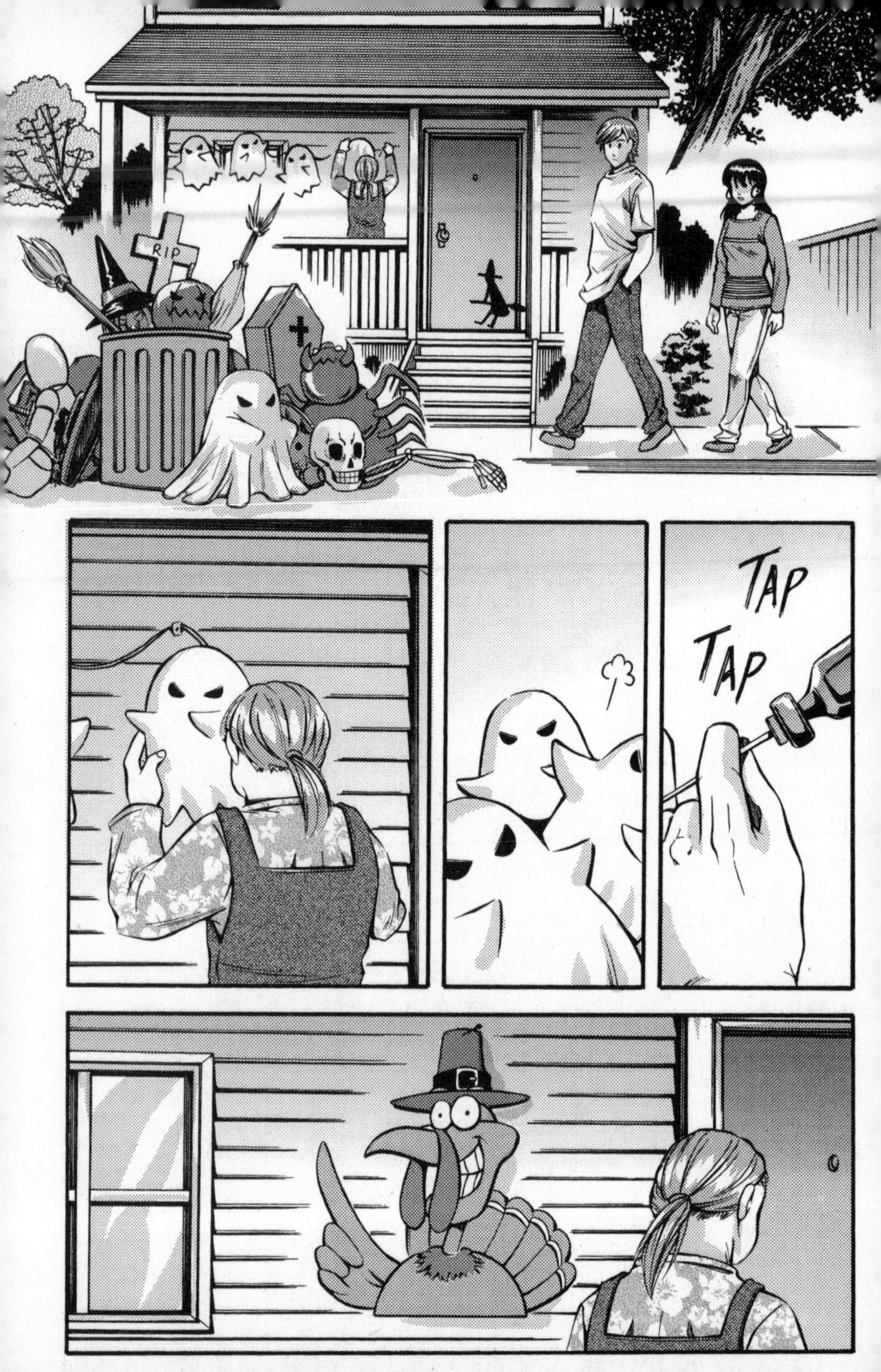
RIP
TAP
TAP

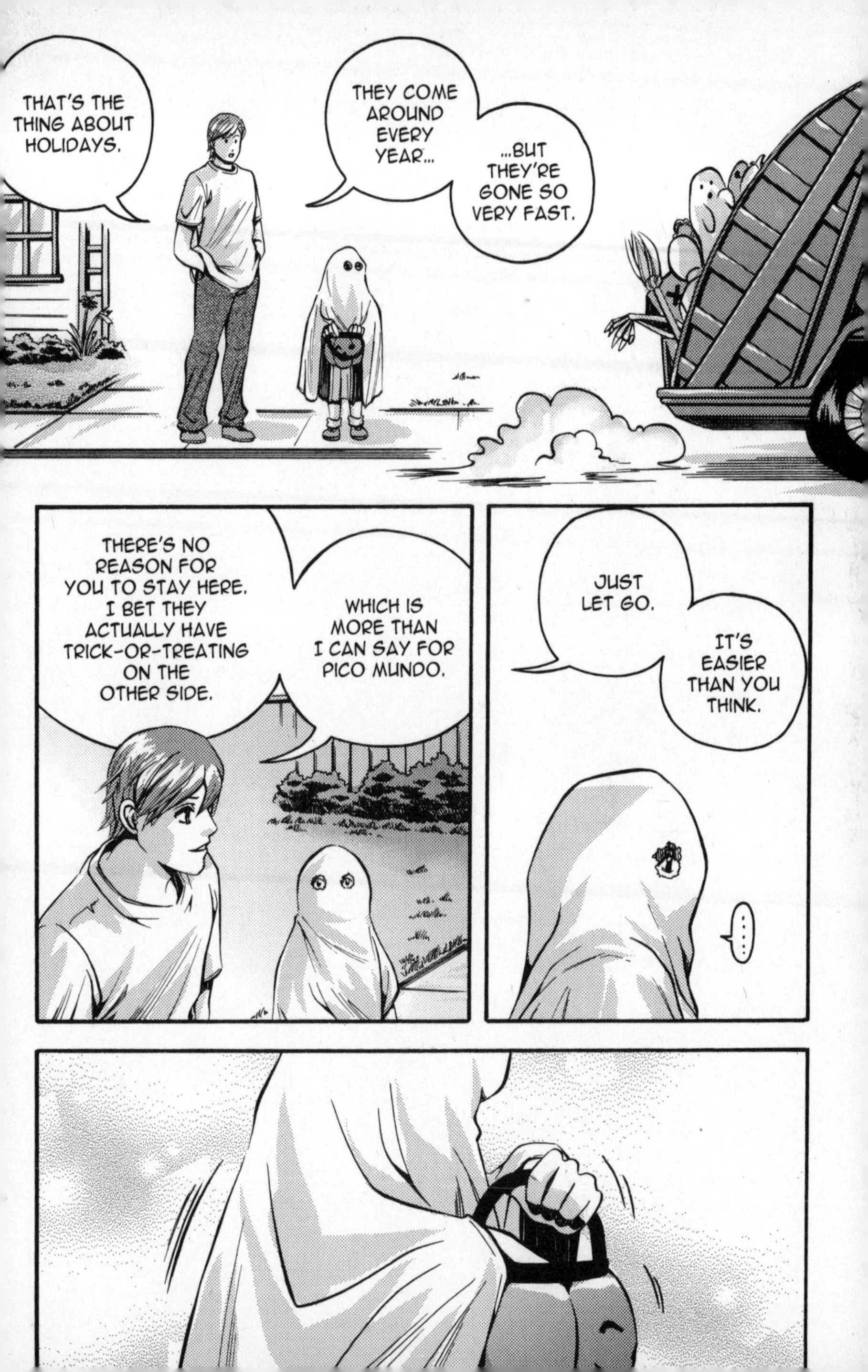

THAT'S THE THING ABOUT HOLIDAYS.
THEY COME AROUND EVERY YEAR...
...BUT THEY'RE GONE SO VERY FAST.
THERE'S NO REASON FOR YOU TO STAY HERE. I BET THEY ACTUALLY HAVE TRICK-OR-TREATING ON THE OTHER SIDE.
WHICH IS MORE THAN I CAN SAY FOR PICO MUNDO.
JUST LET GO.
IT'S EASIER THAN YOU THINK.
......

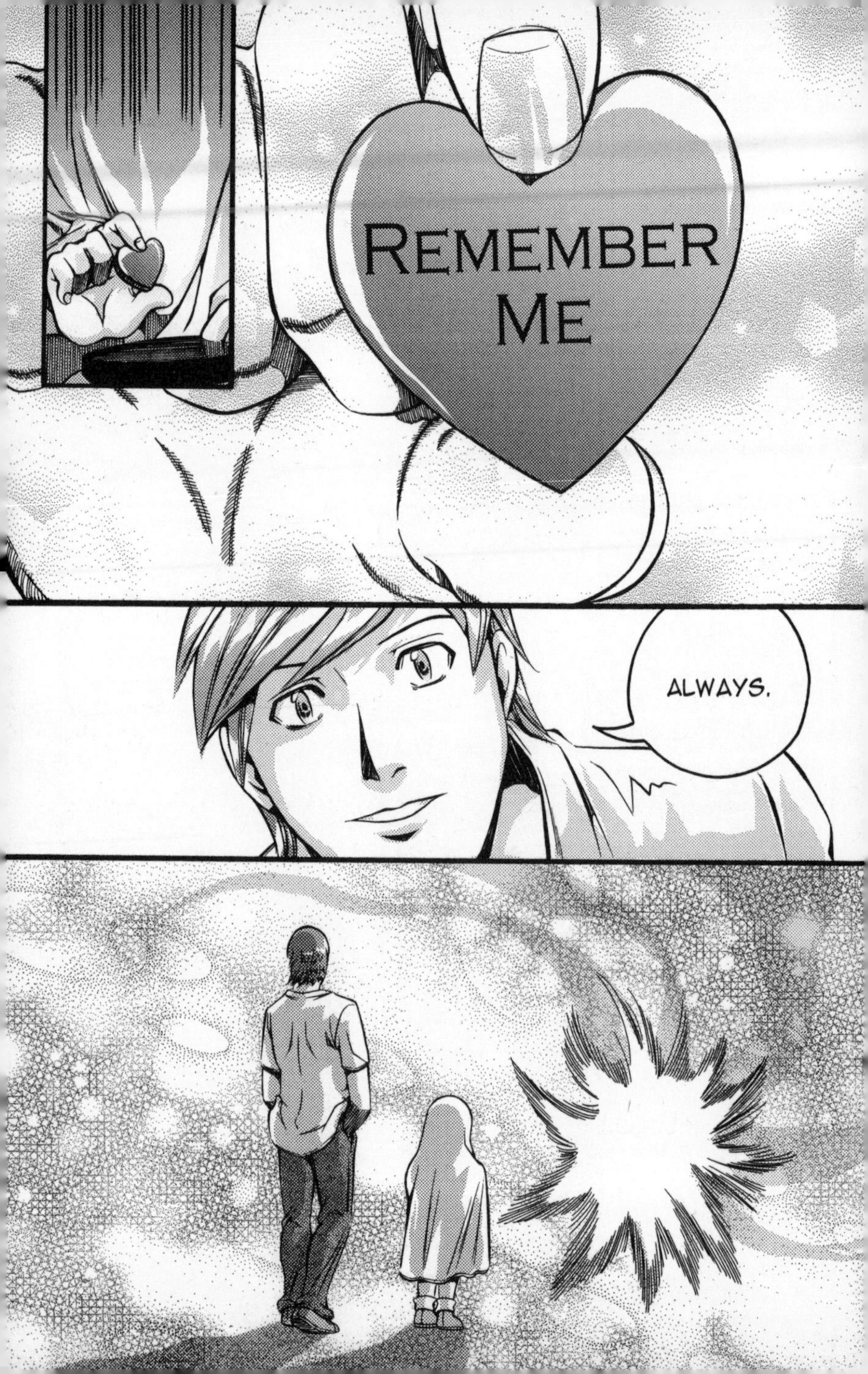
REMEMBER
ME
ALWAYS.

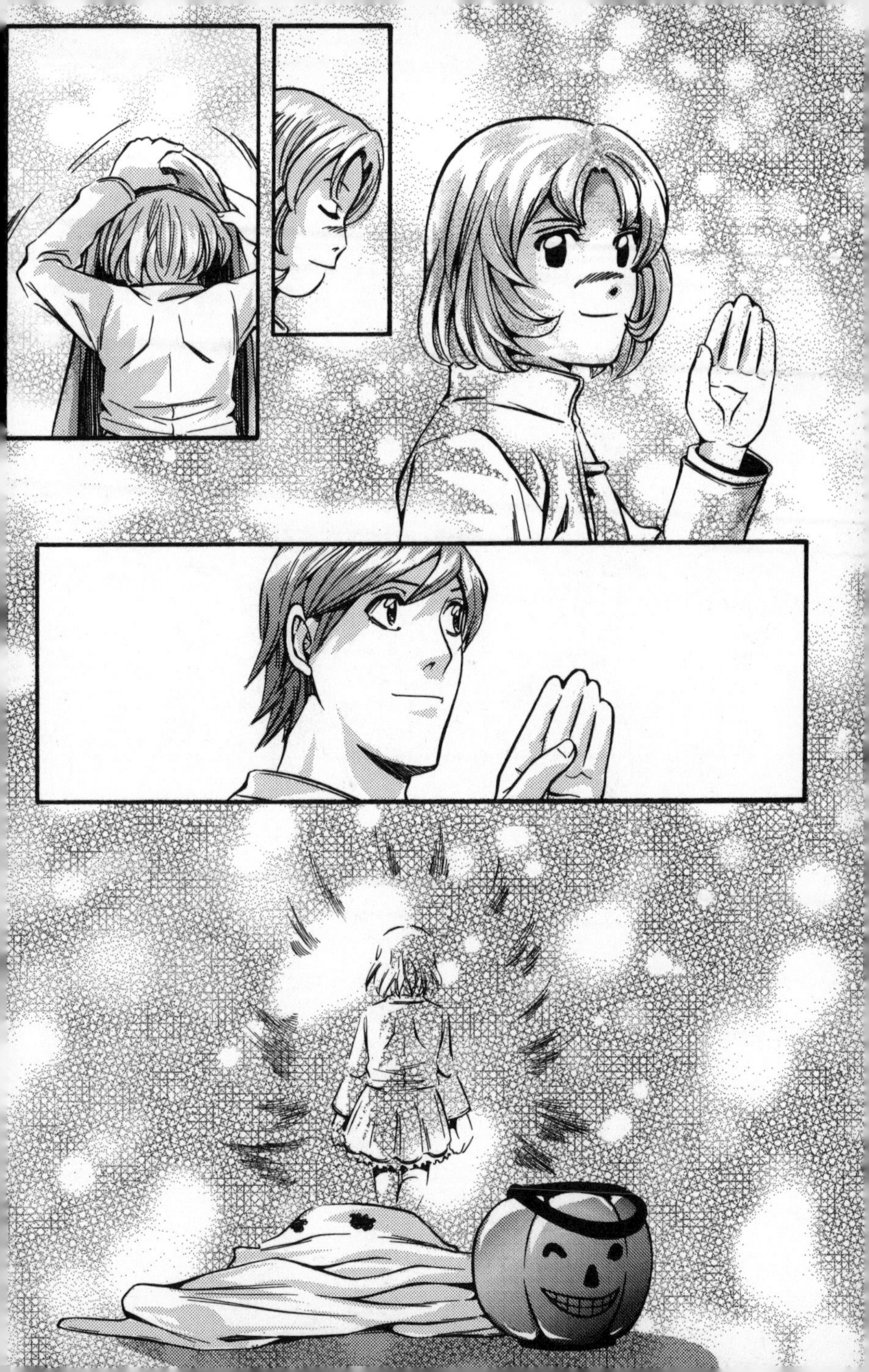

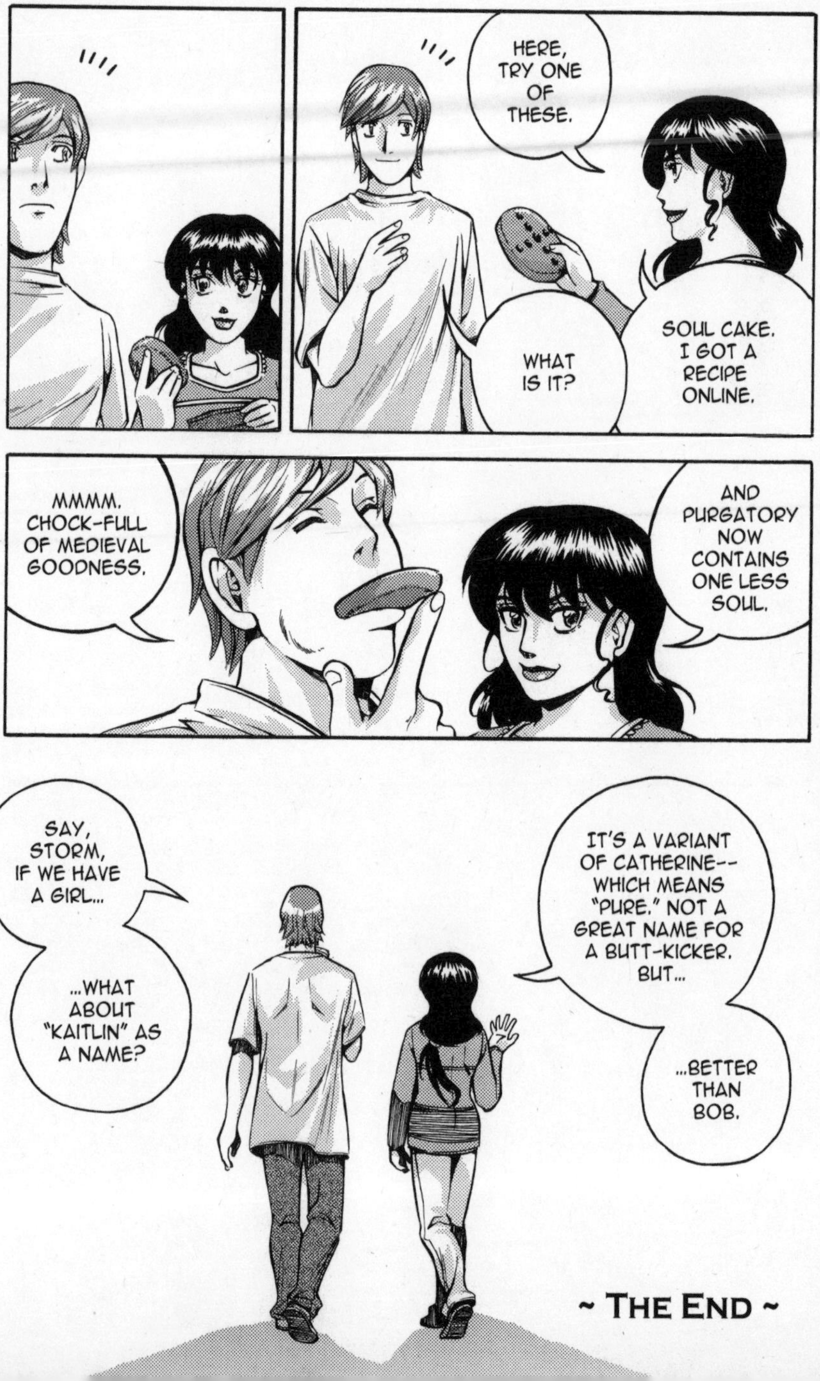
HERE, TRY ONE OF THESE.
WHAT IS IT?
SOUL CAKE. I GOT A RECIPE ONLINE.
MMMM. CHOCK-FULL OF MEDIEVAL GOODNESS.
AND PURGATORY NOW CONTAINS ONE LESS SOUL.
SAY, STORM, IF WE HAVE A GIRL...
...WHAT ABOUT "KAITLIN" AS A NAME?
IT'S A VARIANT OF CATHERINE--WHICH MEANS "PURE." NOT A GREAT NAME FOR A BUTT-KICKER. BUT...
...BETTER THAN BOB.
~ THE END ~

ABOUT THE CREATORS

DEAN KOONTZ is the author of many #1 *New York Times* bestsellers. He lives with his wife, Gerda, in Southern California.

QUEENIE CHAN was born in Hong Kong and emigrated to Australia when she was six years old. She is the creator of the mystery-horror graphic novel series *The Dreaming* and illustrated two graphic novels based on Dean Koontz's character Odd Thomas. She provided art for the *Boy's Book of Positive Quotations* by Steve Deger and draws a number of online comic strips on her personal website: www.queeniechan.com

FRED VAN LENTE is the *New York Times* bestselling author of *Incredible Hercules* (with Greg Pak) and three entries in the *Marvel Zombies* series, as well as the American Library Association award-winning *Action Philosophers*. His original graphic novel *Cowboys & Aliens* (co-written with Andrew Foley) is being adapted into motion picture form by Dreamworks and Universal. Visit his website at www.fredvanlente.com

Odd's adventures continue in a series of full-length novels by Dean Koontz. The first novel is *Odd Thomas*, which was excerpted in the graphic novel *In Odd We Trust*. Here you can read a sample chapter of *Forever Odd*, second in the series. When a childhood friend disappears, Odd discovers something worse than a dead body . . . and embarks on a heart-stopping battle of will and wits with an enemy of exceptional cunning.

ONE

WAKING, I HEARD A WARM WIND STRUMMING the loose screen at the open window, and I thought *Stormy,* but it was not.

The desert air smelled faintly of roses, which were not in bloom, and of dust, which in the Mojave flourishes twelve months of the year.

Precipitation falls on the town of Pico Mundo only during our brief winter. This mild February night was not, however, sweetened by the scent of rain.

I hoped to hear the fading rumble of thunder. If a peal had awakened me, it must have been thunder in a dream.

Holding my breath, I lay listening to the silence, and felt the silence listening to me.

The nightstand clock painted glowing numbers on the gloom—2:41 A.M,

For a moment I considered remaining in bed. But these days I do not sleep as well as I did when I was young. I am twenty-one and much older than when I was twenty.

Certain that I had company, expecting to find two

Elvises watching over me, one with a cocky smile and one with sad concern, I sat up and switched on the lamp.

A single Elvis stood in a corner: a life-size cardboard figure that had been part of a theater-lobby display for *Blue Hawaii*. In a Hawaiian shirt and a lei, he looked self-confident and happy.

Back in 1961, he'd had much to be happy about. *Blue Hawaii* was a hit film, and the album went to number one. He had six gold records that year, including "Can't Help Falling in Love," and he was falling in love with Priscilla Beaulieu.

Less happily, at the insistence of his manager, Tom Parker, he had turned down the lead in *West Side Story* in favor of mediocre movie fare like *Follow That Dream*. Gladys Presley, his beloved mother, had been dead three years, and still he felt the loss of her, acutely. Only twenty-six, he'd begun to have weight problems.

Cardboard Elvis smiles eternally, forever young, incapable of error or regret, untouched by grief, a stranger to despair.

I envy him. There is no cardboard replica of me as I once was and as I can never be again.

The lamplight revealed another presence, as patient as he was desperate. Evidently he had been watching me sleep, waiting for me to wake.

I said, "Hello, Dr. Jessup."

Dr. Wilbur Jessup was incapable of a response. Anguish flooded his face. His eyes were desolate pools; all hope had drowned in those lonely depths.

"I'm sorry to see you here," I said.

He made fists of his hands, not with the intention of

striking anything, but as an expression of frustration. He pressed his fists to his chest.

Dr. Jessup had never previously visited my apartment; and I knew in my heart that he no longer belonged in Pico Mundo. But I clung to denial, and I spoke to him again as I got out of bed.

"Did I leave the door unlocked?"

He shook his head. Tears blurred his eyes, but he did not wail or even whimper.

Fetching a pair of jeans from the closet, slipping into them, I said, "I've been forgetful lately."

He opened his fists and stared at his palms. His hands trembled. He buried his face in them.

"There's so much I'd like to forget," I continued as I pulled on socks and shoes, "but only the small stuff slips my mind—like where I left the keys, whether I locked the door, that I'm out of milk. . . ."

Dr. Jessup, a radiologist at County General Hospital, was a gentle man, and quiet, although he had never before been *this* quiet.

Because I had not worn a T-shirt to bed, I plucked a white one from a drawer.

I have a few black T-shirts, but mostly white. In addition to a selection of blue jeans, I have two pair of white chinos.

This apartment provides only a small closet. Half of it is empty. So are the bottom drawers of my dresser.

I do not own a suit. Or a tie. Or shoes that need to be shined.

For cool weather, I own two crew-neck sweaters.

Once I bought a sweater vest. Temporary insanity. Realizing that I had introduced an unthinkable level of complexity to my wardrobe, I returned it to the store the next day.

My four-hundred-pound friend and mentor, P. Oswald Boone, has warned me that my sartorial style represents a serious threat to the apparel industry.

I've noted more than once that the articles in Ozzie's wardrobe are of such enormous dimensions that he keeps in business those fabric mills I might otherwise put in jeopardy.

Barefoot, Dr. Jessup wore cotton pajamas. They were wrinkled from the rigors of restless sleep.

"Sir, I wish you'd say something," I told him. "I really wish you would."

Instead of obliging me, the radiologist lowered his hands from his face, turned, and walked out of the bedroom.

I glanced at the wall above the bed. Framed behind glass is a card from a carnival fortune-telling machine. It promises YOU ARE DESTINED TO BE TOGETHER FOREVER.

Each morning, I begin my day by reading those seven words. Each night, I read them again, sometimes more than once, before sleep, if sleep will come to me.

I am sustained by the certainty that life has meaning. As does death.

From a nightstand, I retrieved my cell phone. The first number on speed dial is the office of Wyatt Porter, chief of the Pico Mundo Police Department. The second is his home number. The third is his cell phone.

More likely than not, I would be calling Chief Porter, one place or another, before dawn.

In the living room, I turned on a light and discovered that Dr. Jessup had been standing in the dark, among the thrift-shop treasures with which the place is furnished.

When I went to the front door and opened it, he did not follow. Although he had sought my assistance, he couldn't find the courage for what lay ahead.

In the rubescent light from an old bronze lamp with a beaded shade, the eclectic decor—Stickley-style armchairs, plump Victorian footstools, Maxfield Parrish prints, carnival-glass vases—evidently appealed to him.

"No offense," I said, "but you don't belong here, sir."

Dr. Jessup silently regarded me with what might have been supplication.

"This place is filled to the brim with the past. There's room for Elvis and me, and memories, but not for anyone new."

I stepped into the public hall and pulled the door shut.

My apartment is one of two on the first floor of a converted Victorian house. Once a rambling single-family home, the place still offers considerable charm.

For years I lived in one rented room above a garage. My bed had been just a few steps from my refrigerator. Life was simpler then, and the future clear.

I traded that place for this not because I needed more space, but because my heart is here now, and forever.

The front door of the house featured an oval of leaded glass. The night beyond looked sharply beveled and organized into a pattern that anyone could understand.

When I stepped onto the porch, this night proved to

be like all others: deep, mysterious, trembling with the potential for chaos.

From porch steps to flagstone path, to public sidewalk, I looked around for Dr. Jessup but didn't see him.

In the high desert, which rises far east beyond Pico Mundo, winter can be chilly, while our low-desert nights remain mild even in February. The curbside Indian laurels sighed and whispered in the balmy wind, and moths soared to street lamps.

The surrounding houses were as quiet as their windows were dark. No dogs barked. No owls hooted.

No pedestrians were out, no traffic on the streets. The town looked as if the Rapture had occurred, as if only I had been left behind to endure the reign of Hell on Earth.

By the time I reached the corner, Dr. Jessup rejoined me. His pajamas and the lateness of the hour suggested that he had come to my apartment from his home on Jacaranda Way, five blocks north in a better neighborhood than mine. Now he led me in that direction.

He could fly, but he plodded. I ran, drawing ahead of him.

Although I dreaded what I would find no less than he might have dreaded revealing it to me, I wanted to get to it quickly. As far as I knew, a life might still be in jeopardy.

Halfway there, I realized that I could have taken the Chevy. For most of my driving life, having no car of my own, I borrowed from friends as needed. The previous autumn, I had inherited a 1980 Chevrolet Camaro Berlinetta Coupe.

Often I still act as though I have no wheels. Owning a

few thousand pounds of vehicle oppresses me when I think about it too much. Because I try not to think about it, I sometimes forget I have it.

Under the cratered face of the blind moon, I ran.

On Jacaranda Way, the Jessup residence is a white-brick Georgian with elegant ornamentation. It is flanked by a delightful American Victorian with so many decorative moldings that it resembles a wedding cake, and by a house that is baroque in all the wrong ways.

None of these architectural styles seems right for the desert, shaded by palm trees, brightened by climbing bougainvillea. Our town was founded in 1900 by newcomers from the East Coast, who fled the harsh winters but brought with them cold-climate architecture and attitude.

Terri Stambaugh, my friend and employer, owner of the Pico Mundo Grille, tells me that this displaced architecture is better than the dreary acres of stucco and graveled roofs in many California desert towns.

I assume that she is right. I have seldom crossed the city line of Pico Mundo and have never been beyond the boundaries of Maravilla County.

My life is too full to allow either a jaunt or a journey. I don't even watch the Travel Channel.

The joys of life can be found anywhere. Far places only offer exotic ways to suffer.

Besides, the world beyond Pico Mundo is haunted by strangers, and I find it difficult enough to cope with the dead who, in life, were known to me.

Upstairs and down, soft lamplight shone at some windows of the Jessup residence. Most panes were dark.

By the time I reached the foot of the front-porch steps, Dr. Wilbur Jessup waited there.

The wind stirred his hair and ruffled his pajamas, although why he should be subject to the wind, I do not know. The moonlight found him, too, and shadow.

The grieving radiologist needed comforting before he could summon sufficient strength to lead me into his house, where he himself no doubt lay dead, and perhaps another.

I embraced him. Only a spirit, he was invisible to everyone but me, yet he felt warm and solid.

Perhaps I see the dead affected by the weather of this world, and see them touched by light and shadow, and find them as warm as the living, not because this is the way they are but because this is the way I want them to be. Perhaps by this device, I mean to deny the power of death.

My supernatural gift might reside not in my mind but instead in my heart. The heart is an artist that paints over what profoundly disturbs it, leaving on the canvas a less dark, less sharp version of the truth.

Dr. Jessup had no substance, but he leaned heavily upon me, a weight. He shook with the sobs that he could not voice.

The dead don't talk. Perhaps they know things about death that the living are not permitted to learn from them.

In this moment, my ability to speak gave me no advantage. Words would not soothe him.

Nothing but justice could relieve his anguish. Perhaps not even justice.

When he'd been alive, he had known me as Odd Thomas, a local character. I am regarded by some people—wrongly—as a hero, as an eccentric by nearly everyone.

Odd is not a nickname; it's my legal handle.

The story of my name is interesting, I suppose, but I've told it before. What it boils down to is that my parents are dysfunctional. Big-time.

I believe that in life Dr. Jessup had found me intriguing, amusing, puzzling. I think he had liked me.

Only in death did he know me for what I am: a companion to the lingering dead.

I see them and wish I did not. I cherish life too much to turn the dead away, however, for they deserve my compassion by virtue of having suffered this world.

When Dr. Jessup stepped back from me, he had changed. His wounds were now manifest.

He had been hit in the face with a blunt object, maybe a length of pipe or a hammer. Repeatedly. His skull was broken, his features distorted.

Torn, cracked, splintered, his hands suggested that he had desperately tried to defend himself—or that he had come to the aid of someone. The only person living with him was his son, Danny.

My pity was quickly exceeded by a kind of righteous rage, which is a dangerous emotion, clouding judgment, precluding caution.

In this condition, which I do not seek, which frightens

me, which comes over me as though I have been possessed, I can't turn away from what must be done. I plunge.

My friends, those few who know my secrets, think my compulsion has a divine inspiration. Maybe it's just temporary insanity.

Step to step, ascending, then crossing the porch, I considered phoning Chief Wyatt Porter. I worried, however, that Danny might perish while I placed the call and waited for the authorities.

The front door stood ajar.

I glanced back and saw that Dr. Jessup preferred to haunt the yard instead of the house. He lingered in the grass.

His wounds had vanished. He appeared as he had appeared before Death had found him—and he looked scared.

Until they move on from this world, even the dead can know fear. You would think they have nothing to lose, but sometimes they are wretched with anxiety, not about what might lie Beyond, but about those whom they have left behind.

I pushed the door inward. It moved as smoothly, as silently as the mechanism of a well-crafted, spring-loaded trap.

ARTIST'S SKETCHBOOK

This is the second graphic novel to star Odd Thomas, following *In Odd We Trust*. In that first book, artist Queenie Chan established the visual appearance of Odd, Stormy, and Chief Porter. In *Odd Is On Our Side*, her challenge was to come up with the look of another major character, bestselling mystery novelist Ozzie Boone, as well as his New York editor, Valerie Malavont.

MERYL STREEP LOOKALIKE. NEW YORK LITERARY TYPE.

Ms. Malavont was approved right away, but Ozzie proved to pose a challenge!

FOR SOME STRANGE REASON, I THOUGHT OZZIE WAS BLACK.
AFTER IT WAS CONFIRMED THAT HE WASN'T, I REREAD THE
BOOKS—AND WHILE THERE WAS NOTHING THERE THAT SAID
OZZIE WAS BLACK, I DIDN'T SPOT ANYTHING THAT SAID HE
WAS WHITE, EITHER. SINCE OZZIE WAS KNOWN FOR BEING
SAGACIOUS, I PROBABLY SUBCONSCIOUSLY THOUGHT OF
HIM AS MORPHEUS FROM THE *MATRIX* MOVIES (HENCE WHY
HE WAS BLACK IN MY MIND).

Dean's immediate comment was that Ozzie is not black. Queenie
wrote back,

"For some reason I've always imagined him as dark-skinned. I
guess I've had this image of Ozzie in my mind from the start of reading *Odd Thomas*, and couldn't separate myself from it. I'm perfectly
happy to do a redesign."

The second sketch wasn't right either.

WHEN IT TURNED OUT THAT OZZIE LOOKED MORE LIKE
ORSON WELLES, I IMMEDIATELY ASSUMED HE LOOKED LIKE
THE OLDER, MORE INTENSE ORSON (RATHER THAN THE
YOUNGER VERSION). HOWEVER, I PERSONALLY DIDN'T FEEL
THIS IMAGE SUITED THE CHARACTER OF OZZIE (AND INDEED,
IT DIDN'T REALLY).

"All we know about Ozzie's appearance is that he's HUGE, and not much more," Queenie wrote after this sketch was rejected. "Perhaps Dean can suggest another celebrity who looks like Ozzie, like he did with Valerie and Chief Porter. That makes it *infinitely* easier."

Dean replied: "Ozzie Boone is in his late forties, weighs 400-plus pounds, and has a sweet but not babyish face. Herewith several photos of the comedian Lou Costello. He was not as heavy as Ozzie, but his face is a good place to begin. He had a sweet pudgy face but in his way he was handsome, too. His hair would work well for Ozzie, also."

THIS FINAL OZZIE SKETCH, BASED ON LOU COSTELLO, WAS
DEFINITELY THE ONE I LIKED THE MOST.

Queenie put pen to paper once again, and the final result was approved.

* * *

THE GREAT BODACH STRUGGLE

The other artistic challenge in *Odd Is On Our Side* was that of the bodachs, the supernatural heralds of death and disaster. The bodachs
feature heavily in the Odd Thomas books, and yet they proved difficult to render in a way that communicates the menace and evil they
embody in the novels. Here is Queenie's first attempt:

This proved to have too much of a specific form. Dean described the
bodachs as slinky, wolfish shadows that flow from place to place. He
asked Queenie to try again.

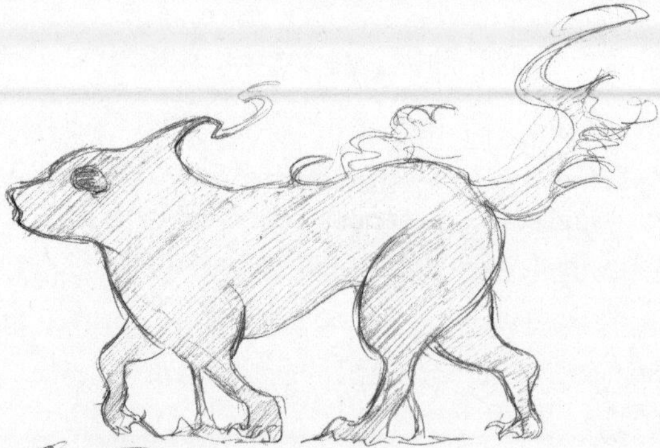

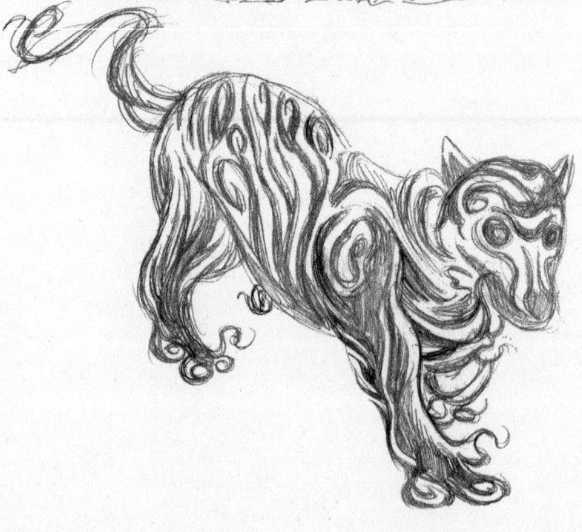

Still not quite right. This guidance came back:

"Delete all the curlicues. This design element makes the creature seem too cute and almost friendly. It takes away from the menace they are supposed to convey. Imagine what it would look like if you drop black ink in a pan of water. There would be no pattern to how the ink moves in the water from time to time. Rather, it's an amorphous blob shifting."

BECAUSE THE FIRST SKETCH WAS TOO "PRECISE," I DECIDED
TO DRAW THE NEXT TWO SKETCHES AS LOOSELY AS I COULD.

BUT AS IT TURNED OUT, BODACHS HAD NO DEFINITE SHAPE
SINCE THEY LOOKED MORE LIKE BLOTCHES OF INK FLOATING
IN WATER, SO I JUST DECIDED TO DRAW THEM DIRECTLY
ONTO THE PAGES.

This final version was approved. Said Queenie: "It's hard to make a
shape-shifting blob look menacing . . . so I gave them glowing eyes."

* * *

SCRIPT DEVELOPMENT

Adaptor Fred Van Lente had the task of turning Dean's story for *Odd Is On Our Side* into a panel-by-panel script. Questions came up as he did so, not all of which could be answered by reference to the novels. Odd fans will be interested to learn these details.

Fred: Does Odd automatically know the identity of every ghost he comes into contact with?

Dean: When Odd looks at the lingering spirit of someone he didn't know in life, he has to figure out who they are by the context of their apparition (as, for example, the various ghosts in the burnt-out casino in *Forever Odd*). He does *not* automatically intuit the spirit's identity.

Fred: Can Odd tell at first glance whether someone is a ghost?

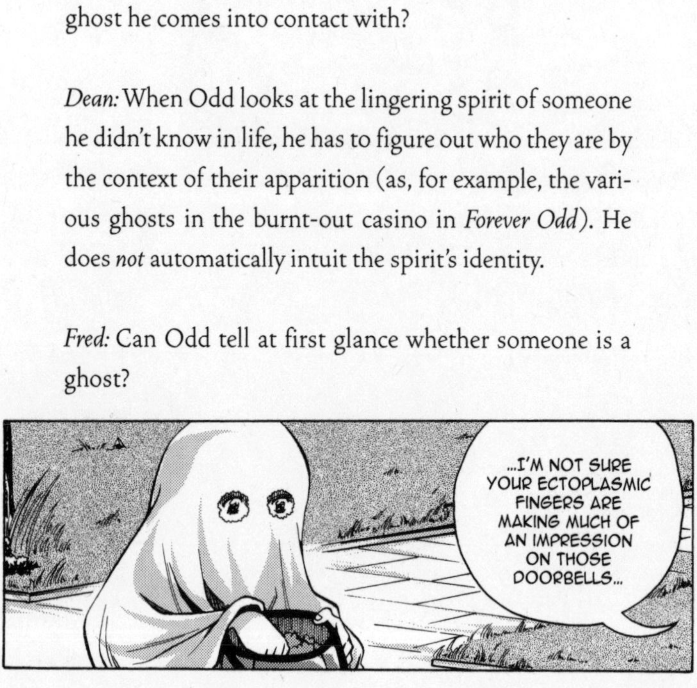
...I'M NOT SURE YOUR ECTOPLASMIC FINGERS ARE MAKING MUCH OF AN IMPRESSION ON THOSE DOORBELLS...

Dean: Odd knows a ghost is a ghost only if he knew the dead person or if the apparition displays its mortal wounds. As in the first book in the series—with "Fungus Man," alias Bob Roberts—Odd sometimes can mistake a lingering spirit for a living person, until the entity is either unable to speak (the dead don't talk) or does something ghostlike, such as walk through a wall, whereupon Odd knows with what he's dealing.

The ghost has no aura or identifying essence. Of course, if Odd sees someone but Stormy or another living person *doesn't* see them, Odd knows at once that he's seeing a ghost.

* * *

OZZIE BOONE

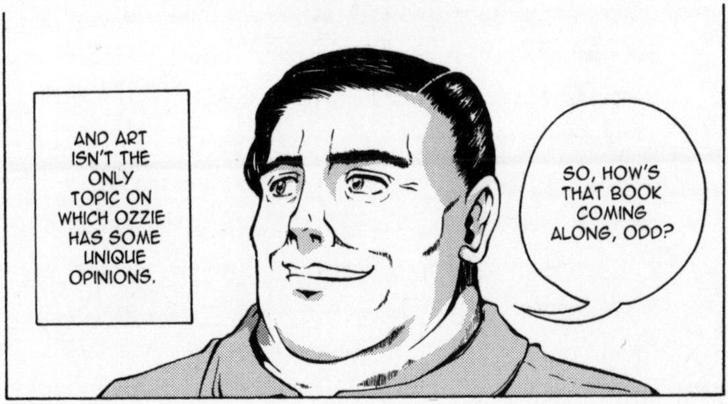
AND ART ISN'T THE ONLY TOPIC ON WHICH OZZIE HAS SOME UNIQUE OPINIONS.
SO, HOW'S THAT BOOK COMING ALONG, ODD?

The script introduced Dean's character Ozzie Boone, bestselling novelist, to graphic novel readers for the first time, and Dean wanted to make sure that the Ozzie readers meet in this book is the same in all details as the Ozzie we get to know and love in the novels. In the first-draft script, Fred included a few lines indicating that Ozzie knew how to defuse the bomb inside the spider piñata because of research he'd undertaken to write a book series about a police bomb squad expert named Paddy McSorely. Dean wrote back:

Dear Fred,

Ozzie's famous detective series are described in *Odd Thomas*, in chapter sixteen: The first is about a very "fat detective of incomparable brilliance who solves crimes while tossing off hilarious bon mots. He relies on his beautiful and highly athletic wife (who utterly adores him) to undertake all the investigative footwork and to perform all the derring-do." The second series involves "a likable heroine in spite of numerous neuroses and bulimia." Ozzie proudly—and slyly—proclaims that no novels in the history of literature have featured so much vomiting to the delight of so many readers. I want to avoid adding character facts that contradict those in the books, so I'd like to avoid this series about Boston Bomb Squad inspector Paddy McSorely. Being a mystery writer and a demon for detail, Ozzie will know something about bombs when he needs to act late in the story; he should just mention, at the time, having written a story about a mad bomber.

* * *

THE VILLAIN

Early in the process, Fred proposed a religion-based motive for Norman Turley, the villain of *Odd Is On Our Side*, to have poisoned a number of trick-or-treaters. Dean responded with this:

> The Odd Thomas stories try to avoid both politically correct villains and needlessly negative characterizations of whole groups. Consequently, I would like to see Norman Turley *not* be a crazy Christian trying to warn people about a "pagan" holiday. Maybe make him the owner of a flower shop and a neighborhood greenhouse who got tired of having his windows soaped by trick-or-treaters. Then he might use a plant poison to contaminate the candy he gave out.

Dean provided helpful details about what type of poison would work best for such a plan:

"THE SYMPTOMS SUGGESTED THEY HAD INGESTED THE SEEDS OF THE CORN COCKLE, A CLASS 4 TOXIN.

"TURLEY GREW CORN COCKLE AS ORNAMENTAL PLANTS IN HIS GARDEN.

Strychnine is almost too powerful a poison for this. It's a Class 6 toxin, with a victim-reaction time of ten to twenty minutes, and faster in children. It wouldn't be logical to assume that most—or in fact *any*—of the kids who ate that candy survived. Better to go with something like the seeds of corn cockle—a Class 4 toxin—which would give authorities time to recognize the symptoms as those of poisoning and time for physicians to successfully treat the victims. Corn cockle is sometimes grown as an ornamental plant. If Norman Turley *was* a florist/greenhouse operator, he might use corn cockle as filler in some flower arrangements and would know the power of the seeds. It might be fun if he was caught because the symptoms of poisoned children— nausea, acute gastroenteritis, fever, giddiness, delirium, weakness, depressed breathing, sharp pains in the spine—were reminiscent of those Turley's wife suffered before *she* died three years before the little girl who was costumed as a ghost. Mrs. Turley was thought to have died of anaphylactic shock caused by an unspecified allergic reaction. But when Turley replayed the trick on the kids, Wyatt Porter made the connection.

* * *